D0875301

James I in Parliament
Renold Elstrack, 1604
Reproduced with the permission of the trustees
of the British Museum.

THE HOUSE OF LORDS

1603–1649

STRUCTURE, PROCEDURE, AND

THE NATURE OF ITS BUSINESS

ELIZABETH READ FOSTER

The University of North Carolina Press

Chapel Hill and London

The publication of this work was made possible
in part through a grant from the
National Endowment for the Humanities,
a federal agency whose mission is to award grants
to support education, scholarship, media programming,
libraries, and museums, in order to bring
the results of cultural activities to a
broad, general public.

© 1983 The University of North Carolina Press

All rights reserved

Manufactured in the United States of America

Library of Congress Cataloging in Publication Data

Foster, Elizabeth Read.
The House of Lords, 1603–1649.

Includes index.
1. Great Britain. Parliament. House of Lords—
History. 2. Great Britain—Politics and government—
1603–1649. I. Title.
JN623 1603   328.41′071′09   82-6909
ISBN 0-8078-1533-0   AACR2

328.41
F 75

84-3515

CONTENTS

ACKNOWLEDGMENTS

It is pleasant to look back over the years to many friendships made as research progressed. My chief professional obligation is to Maurice F. Bond, formerly clerk of the records, House of Lords. He has enthusiastically encouraged my work, answered my questions, and set me straight on a variety of points. He has read the whole of the typescript of this book and sent me important commentaries upon it. The present clerk of the records, H. S. Cobb, and the deputy clerk of the records, David J. Johnson, have helped in many ways, bringing documents to my attention, enabling me to make good use of my time at the House of Lords Record Office, and patiently answering queries after I had left. John C. Sainty, reading clerk and clerk of the journals, House of Lords, has been generous in sharing the results of his own research. He has read most of the typescript and I have relied heavily on his knowledge of the House and its history. Conrad Russell has sent many references and valuable bits of parliamentary information. He too has read the whole typescript and forwarded useful suggestions. Colin Tite, W. J. Jones, Allen Horstman, and the late Joel Hurstfield have read parts of the book at various stages in its development and have given me valuable criticism. Clyve Jones has been helpful. Paul Gay helped me find my way in the Biddle Law Library of the University of Pennsylvania. My thanks go to them all. Errors that have escaped their scrutiny are, of course, mine.

At a late stage in the preparation of this book, Michael Graves's book on the House of Lords under Edward VI and Mary I was announced. Through the courtesy of Mr. Graves and of the Cambridge University Press, I have been able to read it in page proof and to incorporate some of its findings in my own work. I am grateful to the duke of Buccleuch and Queensberry, the duke of Northumberland, the trustees of the Bedford Estates, the treasurer and masters of the Bench of the Inner Temple, the benchers of Lincoln's Inn, and the Society of Antiquaries of London for permission to use material in their collections. I am grateful also to the British Library, the Bodleian Library, the trustees of the Henry E. Huntington Library, the Folger Shakespeare Library, and the James Marshall and Marie-Louise Osborn Collection, Yale University Library. In referring to the Braye manuscripts in the Osborn Collection, I have used the numbers assigned to the photocopies at the House of Lords Record Office. Maurice Bond's *Guide to the Records of Parliament* makes a bibliography unnecessary.

Finally, but most important of all, my thanks go to my husband, who has helped with this book in so many ways.

Elizabeth Read Foster
Wayne, Pennsylvania
1 November 1981

Orders of the House in a roll to be read at the opening of each session. A succession of able clerks, equally concerned for the record, performed these duties and also prepared a series of committee books and similar collections for their own use.

The other characteristic of the House was its marked interest in parliamentary procedure. Sir Simonds D'Ewes, in his compilation of the journals of all the parliaments of Elizabeth, noted that the Lords were indifferent to procedure at that time.[2] This was not true of the years 1603–49. In 1621 the House appointed its first Committee for Privileges, which investigated matters of procedure. It began to register Standing Orders. The clerks, particularly Robert Bowyer and Henry Elsyng, observed and recorded points of procedure in the "scribbled books" of notes that they took in the chamber. Bowyer collected precedents and Elsyng composed several short treatises on procedure and a long essay on judicature. The earl of Huntingdon and Lord Montagu noted procedure in their private accounts of the parliaments in which they sat. It was a subject of as much concern to men of the seventeenth century as to us.

This study is based primarily on the Main Papers that the House so carefully preserved, on the accounts of proceedings kept by the clerks and their assistants, and on the various books of committees, books of petitions, books of orders, and other records that they compiled. It also draws on the private diaries and notes of members of the House and on parliamentary material in the state papers and elsewhere. The papers of the House, formerly in the Jewel Tower, but now ably calendared and preserved in the Victoria Tower, provide an invaluable archive. Some of the clerk's papers that fell into private hands have been retrieved for the House of Lords Record Office, and many others, in the library of the Inner Temple, the Bodleian Library, the British Library, or the Osborn Collection at Yale University, are available in photocopy there. Patiently endorsed and docketed by the clerks, the Main Papers of the House show what business came in day by day and how the House proceeded upon it. They provide a picture of the House as a living organism. The same living picture emerges from the clerk's notes for the journal and his drafts of it, the lords' private accounts of proceedings, and even from the clerk's essays on procedure, because they reflect his experience on the floor of the House. Used in connection with this other material, the journal, though laconic, is a valuable source. It represents the Lords' idea of a proper record. It usually registers attendance. It is accurate about bills and the stages of bills, although it omits the actual vote on them and on other questions. The printed index is often unsatisfactory; but when it failed me, I have occasionally found the old calendar to be helpful. The precedents collected by later clerks are extremely useful. If checked back against the journal, they serve as specialized subject indexes.[3]

PART ONE

THE STRUCTURE OF THE HOUSE

I

THE MEMBERS OF THE HOUSE

AND THEIR CHAMBER

A splendid royal procession, "trumpetts soundinge," marked the opening of parliament.[1] Heralds set the order of precedence and, gorgeous in their embroidered coats, guided and punctuated the procession as it moved from Whitehall to the Abbey and from the Abbey to the parliament chamber. Trumpeters on horseback led the pageant in 1614, followed by heralds in full dress. Then on horseback[2] and on foot came the gentlemen of the law: the masters in Chancery, the king's legal counselors, the masters of Requests "2 and 2," the barons of the Exchequer, the justices of the Courts of Common Pleas and King's Bench. The two lord chief justices followed, pursuivants at arms, privy councillors, and two heralds. Next came the barons of parliament in their scarlet parliament robes and the bishops in the order of their consecration; after them, two more heralds and then the viscounts, also in parliament robes. Two heralds preceded the earls, the great officers of state, and the two archbishops. Two gentlemen ushers, one of them Black Rod, walked before the prince. Young Charles wore a great crimson velvet cape lined with ermine, wide breeches, a pleated jacket of white satin with a lace collar, and a hat in lieu of a coronet since he had not yet been invested as Prince of Wales. The earl of Shrewsbury with the cap of maintenance and the duke of Lennox with the sceptre followed the prince; after them came the earl of Derby with the sword, the lord high admiral serving as lord high steward, and the earl of Suffolk, lord chamberlain. Their horses were most richly caparisoned. The king, on a superb horse, was brilliantly dressed in a crimson velvet cape, lavishly trimmed and lined with ermine. He wore a lace ruff; his jacket and breeches were white. On his head was a jeweled crown and he carried an unsheathed sword in his right hand, point upward. Gentlemen pensioners with halberds surrounded him.

On this occasion, bad weather rather spoiled the show. Many lords, our observer noted, rode badly. At the start, an old bishop fell off his horse and injured himself, to the delight of a Puritan noble who remarked that already a bishopric had been pulled down. Shortly thereafter, when his horse reared, he too was dashed to the ground. The bishops then offered their own interpretation of God's intent and a Catholic witness saw a sign that He was displeased with Protestants of every shade of opinion. But despite these homely catastrophes, the opening procession was impressive, and parliament after parliament drew people to Westminster.[3] In 1621 Sir Simonds D'Ewes, pressing through the crowds, observed that Prince Charles wore a "rich coronet" upon his head, and James his crown. The king, "most royally caparisoned," spoke often and lovingly to those lined three deep along the streets to see him pass. "God bless ye!" he cried, "God bless ye!" but he expressed dismay on seeing a window full of men and women dressed in yellow bands, a fashion he disliked. "A pox take ye!" he exclaimed and the spectators withdrew, ashamed. In 1624 the king proceeded to parliament "in great state in a chariot of crimson velvet."[4] On some occasions, the king and his entourage made a less splendid entry and came by river in the royal barge to the parliament steps, where the lords met him and all walked through Westminster Hall and the Court of Requests to the Abbey in the same order as if they had ridden.[5]

In the Abbey, tapestries enclosed a private place for king and prince to hear the service. In 1628 William Laud, then bishop of London, left careful directions for the choir and organists. He prayed that God would be present "with the great Counsel of thy gracious servant, our King, and this his kingdom."[6] After the service, the king and his subjects proceeded on foot, and in their proper order, to the parliament chamber.[7] In 1621 James, troubled by weakness in his legs and feet, was carried on a litter. The king retired to his withdrawing room to put on his robes.[8] The lords took their places in the chamber.

At its best, the procession made a strong political statement. Henry VIII quoted his judges as saying, "We at no time stand so highlie in our estate roiall, as in the time of parlement, wherein we as head, and you as members, are conioined and knit togither into one bodie politik."[9] Although commoners took no part in the procession as a group,[10] the king's legal counsel and judges (assistants in the upper House), and the several degrees of lords spiritual and temporal were there, together with the members of the Privy Council. Surrounded by his advisers and the great men of his realm, the monarch moved in state to communicate with his people. The pageantry of the procession exalted both the king and his parliament.

The procession spoke in other ways to those who observed it. In 1614 all remarked (particularly the ambassadors from France, Moscow, Venice, Savoy, and the Netherlands) that the king and the whole procession waited for the arrival of the Spanish ambassador who came late.[11] In 1621 Sir Simonds D'Ewes especially noted the cordiality of the king, "contrary to his former hasty and passionate custom." He observed that James honored Buckingham's wife and mother by speaking to them individually, and that he pointedly bowed to the Spanish ambassador.[12] In 1624 James came to parliament, John Chamberlain wrote, "with greater shew and pompe then I have seen to my remembrance,"[13] a display of ceremony that underlined the royal view of the importance of parliament. By contrast, the king in November 1640 came by water and landed at Westminster stairs, the judges, lords, and bishops walking with him through Westminster Hall to the Abbey.[14] Clarendon, writing long after the event, commented that the king had not proceeded on this occasion "in his usual Majesty," but went privately in his barge "as if it had been to a return of a prorogued or adjourned Parliament."[15]

The Lords met in the White Chamber of the Old Palace of Westminster, a long, dark, narrow room (about 27 feet by 70 feet) decorated in crimson.[16] At the south end was a chair of state for the sovereign. A fireplace in the east wall provided warmth and a tempting gathering place for conversation. A screen for the king protected him from drafts.[17] A small round window high up above the throne and a large medieval lancet window at the north end admitted what light there was. To provide more, the surveyor of the King's Works, Inigo Jones, let four dormer windows into the barrel vault of the ceiling in 1623/4, which was decorated above the windows with black and white fretwork.[18] There were five doors, two in each of the long walls to the east and west, one in the short north wall facing the throne.[19] Tapestries hung on the walls. In 1644 the Lords ordered the Lieutenant of the Tower to deliver the "Suit of Hangings of the Story of Eighty-eight," the famous Armada tapestries, to the officers of the wardrobe to hang in the chamber.[20] Matting covered the floor.[21] To the right and left of the raised throne, a wooden "traverse" or low partition provided a boarded area behind which stood ambassadors and younger sons of peers.[22] A bar covered in crimson marked off the north end of the room.[23]

THE KING

The throne, provided for the monarch, was a conspicuous feature of the chamber. A handsome cloth embroidered with the royal arms hung behind it, a canopy above.[24] On the occasions when the king came to parliament, he occupied this seat. When he was not present, members bowed to it as they entered or made obeisance as they crossed from one side of the House to the other.[25] It symbolized the relationship between the monarch and his parliament.

Writing of the "regiment" or government of England in 1559, John Aylmer noted that the image, "and not the image but the thing indeed, is to be seen in the Parliament House, wherein you shall find these three estates: the king or queen, which representeth the monarch; the noblemen which be the aristocracy; and the burgesses and knights the democracy." Sir Thomas Smith had put the same point in another way when he wrote of parliament that "every Englishman is intended to be there present . . . of what preeminence, state, dignity or quality soever he be, from the prince (be he king or queen) to the lowest person in England."[26] The king was, James I said in 1621, "ever representatively sitting in the Higher House of parliament."[27] In 1646, when it came time for the City of London to present its lord mayor for royal approval, he was brought to the upper House, "where, though His Majesty is not resident in Person, yet present in Authority."[28] It followed that contempt of parliament was an offense against the king, "whoe is the head of the Parliament," which echoed the statement attributed to Henry VIII in Ferrers's case: "Whatsoever offence or injurie . . . is offered to the meanest member of the house, is to be judged as doone against our person, and the whole court of parlement."[29]

If the king was always in parliament in person or "representatively," he was in a sense a member of the upper House. Successive monarchs claimed for their servants the same privilege that the House accorded members.[30] The monarch was, however, a member with a difference. Although it was well known that the king, the Privy Council, and the king's learned counsel prepared bills for parliament and that the king's ministers actively forwarded them on the floor of both Houses, it was considered a breach of parliamentary privilege for the king to notice a bill under consideration or to take cognizance of debate.[31] Charles protested that he saw no harm in doing so since he was presumed to be always present; but the Lords did not sustain his view of the matter.[32] When he came to the House on 24 February 1640/1 to hear the charge against the earl of Strafford, the Lords "commanded the Lord Keeper to resume the House" after he had departed and declared that what had been done in his presence was "no Act of the House."[33] The House set a distance between itself and the monarch and preferred that it should remain.

The king was the alpha and omega of parliament. He summoned it, he determined the length of its sessions, he dismissed it. His death meant its dissolution. [34] His relationship with parliament in the early Stuart period was essentially formal. He came to the House of Lords on particular occasions marked by special ceremonial, when he wore his parliament robes and crown and the lords wore their robes.[35] At such times, the woolsack was vacant. The presiding officer stood at the king's right or, when he was to speak, in his place as a peer.[36] When proceedings were over, the House was adjourned at the king's command. The king usually attended the House for the opening of parliament. He returned on a subsequent day, usually the second, for the presentation of the Commons' Speaker, and once more at the close of a parliament to receive the subsidy and give his answer to bills.[37] At other times he sent messages to the House by the presiding officer, the lords of the Privy Council, or, in 1621 and 1624, by the prince.[38] Occasionally he came to the House in person during a session. In 1621 he spoke concerning patents and monopolies.[39] In 1641 he addressed the House on behalf of Strafford.[40] More frequently, he addressed both Houses or a delegation from both Houses at Whitehall.

THE PRINCE

The prince's position in the House brought the king into closer and somewhat less formal relationship with it. Charles, later to be Charles I, took his seat as a peer in 1621 and 1624; his son, later to be Charles II, in 1640.[41] Summoned as other peers were summoned, he was first in order of precedence, answering to his name when the House was called and ordinarily sitting at the head of the earls' bench.[42] Within the House, the lords remained covered in his presence, something they never would have done elsewhere.[43] Though superficially they treated him like any other member, they could not forget that he was heir apparent. When the king came to the House, the prince occupied a special chair placed below the throne to his father's left.[44] His robes differed from those of other peers.[45] On ordinary days, proceedings took on additional significance if he was there. The earl of Berkshire, who had offended the House in 1621 by pushing Lord Scrope, expressed special grief that he had done so when his highness was present; and after submitting to the House, he knelt also before the prince to acknowledge his fault again. Between sittings, the earl of Southampton testified that "he saw that Heat in the House, that, if the Prince had not been there, they had been like to have come to Blows."[46] In the same year, the House voted that the prince might sit on all committees if he chose to do so. Above all, the Lords recognized that he provided a special and additional avenue of communication to the monarch. He brought messages from the king in 1621. James particularly remarked when he did not do so.[47] He also expressed his father's wishes to the House and delivered the commission for adjournment. In 1624, sometimes called the prince's parliament, he was less the spokesman for the king than for his own policies and those of the duke of Buckingham; but he continued to serve as messenger and go-between.[48] The fact that he had been a member, although rather a special member, had a long-range effect on Charles's later role as king, but did not teach him how to handle his parliaments. In 1626 he sharply reprimanded the House for the tone of its message concerning the imprisonment of the earl of Arundel. "I did little look for such a message," he said, "I have been of the house myself and never knew such a message to be sent from one house to another." He would answer when the House sent "such a message as was fit to a sovereign."[49] More serious was the question raised by the earl of Bristol and by the House whether Charles's testimony given as prince could be used against the earl now that Charles was king. By royal command, the judges declined to give an opinion.[50]

SEATING IN THE CHAMBER

The lords, summoned to the House by the king, sat on wooden forms, made comfortable by linings of canvas stuffed with wool and bright by coverings of crimson say, fastened with crimson tape and copper nails.[51] Two forms ran parallel to the long east wall to the monarch's left, and two opposite them to his right, with a short form on the south side of the fireplace towards the throne. Other forms ran across the lower end of the room inside the bar. In the center of the room, arranged to form a rectangle, were four large "sacks," also covered with crimson say but stuffed with hay.[52]

When the king was not present, the presiding officer sat on the woolsack below the throne, supported by an additional down pillow, the seal and mace beside him.[53] The judges occupied the inner sides of the woolsacks to his right and left. The king's learned counsel sat on the outside of the woolsacks to his left, the masters in Chancery to his right.[54] The clerk of the crown and the clerk of the parliaments shared the fourth woolsack, which completed the rectangle and faced the presiding officer. They had a table before them, with assistant clerks behind.[55] Black Rod, the gentleman usher, sat within the doors of the chamber but beyond the bar.[56]

The order of seating for members was prescribed by act of parliament (31 H. VIII, c. 10) and by the orders and custom of the House.[57] To the right of the monarch, the archbishops of Canterbury and York sat on the short form. Beyond the fireplace, on the two longer forms, sat the bishops of London, Durham, and Winchester and then the other bishops in the order in which they had been appointed. The bishops, as spiritual lords, were differentiated from the temporal lords. They were not considered peers.[58] On the first long form to the monarch's left, the greatest officers of state—the lord chancellor (or lord keeper), the lord treasurer, the lord president of the council, and the lord privy seal (if they were barons of parliament)—took precedence of all other peers save royal dukes. Dukes, marquesses, and earls shared the form with them. Other earls and the viscounts sat on the first form across the chamber, with barons behind them. Barons also sat along the wall behind the dukes and marquesses.[59] Lesser officers of state—the great chamberlain, the constable, the earl marshal, the lord steward, the lord chamberlain, and the king's chief secretary (if they were barons of parliament)—sat at the head of the bench to which their ranks assigned them. Officers who were not barons sat on the sacks in the center of the room.[60]

Within this broad scheme, the peers of each rank (like the bishops) were placed in order of their "ancienties," that is, their order of creation, a matter on which the heralds served as guides, but which was ultimately decided by the lords themselves, as was evident in case of controversy.[61] In 1626 the king, in letters patent to the earl of Banbury, granted him precedence "before other Earls of an ancienter Creation." This the Committee for Privileges found to be directly against the statute of 31 H. VIII for placing and ranking lords. It was a case of prerogative running counter to statute law, a case where prerogative appeared inimical to the dignity of a peer. The statute, the committee reported, was full and clear "that all Lords are to be placed and ranked according to the Antiquities of their Creations." The report continued that the king had sent a message explaining why he had granted the earl precedence and promising "never hereafter to occasion the like dispute." In view of the fact that Banbury was old and childless, the king desired that the earl might enjoy for his own lifetime precedency over other earls whose patents were of a previous date.[62] The House directed the committee to negotiate the matter with the earls concerned. It consulted them, one by one. One by one, out of respect for the king, they gave their consent to this temporary arrangement; and on 10 April 1628, the Lords passed an order putting it into effect, at the same time solemnly protesting that they would never again admit an exception to the statute.[63]

It was not long, however, before a similar question rose, this time concerning the precedency of Lord Mountjoy. Once more the fault could be traced to the king. Mountjoy, by virtue of a patent issued 5 June 1627, claimed precedence over the Lords Fauconbridge and Lovelace. Mount-joy's patent expressly provided that he should have place and precedence before all barons created after 20 May. Fauconbridge had been created on 25 May 1627, Lovelace on 31 May. This time the House did not equivocate or hesitate. The Committee for Privileges reported that according to the statute 31 H. VIII and the decision of the House in the case of the earl of Banbury, Fauconbridge and Lovelace should have place and precedency notwithstanding the provisions of the clause in Mountjoy's patent. The House agreed and so ordered.[64] The case was a ringing affirmation of the Lords' determination to settle matters of precedency themselves. They might pay due deference to the king. They took account of the "marshalling" of peers by the heralds. They laid great stress on the order in which lords were listed in the clerk's book, or journal. But they themselves determined that order; and when difficulties arose on matters of precedence, by 1628 the Lords themselves made the necessary decisions.[65]

Certainly the lords occupied the seats to which they were entitled on days of ceremony, the opening and closing of a session, and in the presence of the monarch. Whether they kept their places on ordinary days is difficult to determine. The arrangements for choosing committees and for voting were predicated on a regular order of seating.[66] Committees were named by benches—the bishops' bench, the earls' bench, the barons' bench. When a vote was taken, the lords began at the "lowest," with the prince voting last. In case of uncertainty about the outcome, tellers took a poll, bench by bench.[67] Bishop Burnet wrote that it was Charles II's habit of standing by the fire "that broke all decency of that house. For before that time every lord sat regularly in his place."[68] It seems probable that Burnet, in making his point about Charles's influence, exaggerated the decorum maintained before his time.

As early as 1621, the Standing Orders of the House admonished the lords "to sit in the same order as is prescribed by the Act of Parlyament."[69] In 1626 each lord was to sit "in his due place" at a committee of the whole House.[70] In December 1640 Lord Montagu had spoken against the disorders of the House and some weeks later the Lords resolved that members were to sit in their proper places.[71] A similar order followed in May 1641.[72] The repetition suggests difficulties. Other sources are more explicit. In April Lord Stamford had referred to the "disorder of the House."[73] In May Lord Rutland, coming to the upper House for the first time, observed that "the Lords . . . sitt so confusedly."[74] Committees were still named by benches. When the bishops left in 1642, the forms that they had occupied were pushed back against the wall.[75] But by 1643 it is noteworthy that earls and barons were named together to committees.[76] The careful ordering required by statute was breaking down. The activities of Charles II underlined a tendency already begun.

PARLIAMENT ROBES AND DAILY ATTIRE

On ceremonial occasions the lords wore special parliament robes—in the parliamentary procession, on the opening days if the king was present,[77] when they formally gave judgment on offenders,[78] and at the time of a dissolution, even if it should be by commission.[79] When a peer was introduced into the House, he wore his robe and his sponsors wore theirs.[80] In 1621, in gratitude for the king's speech concerning patents and monopolies, the House voted that hereafter on 26 March the lords should sit in their robes.[81] When the next occasion presented itself, however, the resolution seems to have been forgotten.[82] In 1646 those lords whose robes were available were to wear them to the funeral of the earl of Essex.[83] The wearing of robes set off important days of special solemnity in the life of a parliament. It was a mark of esteem when the sovereign was present, a courtesy that the king reciprocated by wearing his robes and crown.[84] There were exceptions. Many peers were without their robes during the Oxford session in 1625 and hence none wore them when that parliament was dissolved.[85] On certain occasions, for example, in 1626 and 1628, the precipitous or unexpected action of the king caught the lords unprepared.[86]

The robes were of scarlet English wool, the best in the world, Richard Hakluyt said. None is "lesse subject to mothes, or to fretting in presse, then this, as the old Parliament robes of Kings, and of many noble Peeres . . . may plainly testifie."[87] The design for all lay lords was basically the same, the ranks being distinguished by bars of miniver (or ermine) on the right shoulder: two bars for a baron, two and one-half for a viscount, three for an earl, three and one-half for a marquess, and four for a duke.[88] The bishops wore scarlet robes with white capes that revealed their black chimeres and white lawn rochets and sleeves.[89] The Venetian ambassador particularly noticed their velvet caps, "*a croce*, but black."[90]

Robes represented a substantial investment and probably passed from father to son. A robe stolen in 1607 was valued at £74.[91] Lord Vaux, feeling the pinch of poverty, wrote Burghley in 1592 that he had pawned his robe.[92] In 1601 the bishop of Carlisle inquired whether he should attend without his robe or remain at home.[93] Robes were also a care to the lords because they were awkward to carry about and expensive to store. In 1597 the earl of Rutland paid a carrier 5s. to bring his parliament robes in a trunk from his seat at Belvoir Castle to London.[94] As we have seen, the lords did not take their robes to Oxford. In 1621 a bill for keeping a robe for the seven years since the last parliament in 1614 came to £7.[95] In 1625 the earl of Essex made arrangements to borrow from the earl of Southampton, who was then overseas and also under age.[96] Apparently robes were not left at the House. Messengers brought word when they were needed and the lords brought them to the Painted Chamber where they dressed.[97]

On the most formal occasions, those lords entitled to do so—the dukes, marquesses, earls, and viscounts—wore coronets over soft velvet caps. Barons did not have coronets during this period, but are shown with caps of the same design as those worn by men of higher rank.[98] More frequently the peers probably wore hats.[99] Whether worn with robes or with the ordinary attire in which peers appeared on normal days, the hat was a significant feature of dress, a symbol of status and therefore governed by an elaborate code of etiquette, which was determined by the House.

Within the chamber, save when the king was present and all were uncovered,[100] the lords wore hats and no others were covered, not even the eldest sons of peers unless specifically called by writ.[101] Judges and members of the Privy Council called as assistants were uncovered until granted permission to don their hats. King's counsel, similarly called, were never covered.[102] Members of the lower House, when summoned to the bar of the chamber, stood bareheaded. At conferences with the lords they also stood without hats, while the lords sat covered.[103] When lords spoke in the House or in committee, they removed their hats. When a committee chairman reported to the House, members of the committee stood with him bareheaded. The lord chancellor or lord keeper also spoke to the House uncovered and removed his hat when he read the brief of a bill. But he left his hat on when addressing messengers from the lower House.[104]

Difficulties occasionally arose. When both Houses sat together at Oxford in 1625, "Before the Kinges cominge, the Speaker and divers of the Commons put on their hats, notwithstandinge the Lordes were set, observing some difference betwixt the ordinarye meetinges in the state of a Committee and this where we were in the state of a House."[105] In September 1641 the committee to transact business during the recess had seriously debated whether members representing the Commons could wear hats.[106] A similar problem plagued the arrangements for Strafford's trial. The Commons, wishing to attend on an equal basis with the lords, balked at removing their hats while the lords remained covered. The matter was finally solved when the lower House agreed to come as a committee.[107]

THE WRIT OF SUMMONS

When the king had decided on a parliament, he summoned the members of the upper House individually to attend. A general warrant, which was drawn in English, signed by the king's own hand or signet, and sealed with the privy seal, was directed to the lord chancellor or lord keeper, who in turn sent a warrant to the master of the rolls to direct the clerks of the Petty Bag to prepare the writs (drawn in Latin) for the great seal. The process, which one might suppose to be routine, was fraught with difficulties. The heralds and the masters in Chancery might be consulted.[108] It was not always clear who should be summoned. In 1610 there had been a search for precedents to support a summons to Henry, the king's eldest son, though he was under age.[109] Among the papers of the attorney general are notes concerning the Short Parliament. These raise questions concerning a writ for the bishop of Lincoln, who had been out of favor with the court since 1625; for the earl of Leicester on a mission to France; for Lord Stafford, who had been forced to surrender his barony in December 1639; and for Lord Butler, who was an idiot. Certain peers, still minors, were to have no writs. Sons of earls, summoned to the last parliament, should receive writs; but three, previously called as sons of earls, had since succeeded to their fathers' ranks (one as a marquess, two as earls). Should their sons now be called?[110] Problems of this nature, though perplexing, were resolved without reference to the House. But questions of greater import and with political overtones, like the question concerning the bishop of Lincoln, to which we shall turn presently, could not be so easily determined.

Not only was the list of men to whom summons should be sent subject to question, but in 1621 there was a mistake about the form of the writ.[111] The gentleman usher brought into the House Richard Cammell, a clerk in the Petty Bag office who humbly acknowledged his fault in omitting *Praedilecto et Fideli nostro* before the names of the peers. His apologies did not save him. "Noblemens' titles are incorporated in to their honours, theire honours into their blood," said Francis Bacon, Viscount St. Albans, Lord Verulam, who was presiding in the House, "so as in this default of yours you lose them parte of their right to give them a bare apelacion without these addicions before their names."[112] The Lords committed Cammell to the Fleet, and the episode resulted in the Standing Order that "any difference in the forme or stile of the Writts from the auncient" was to be examined and provision made for "a strict course for punishing the time past, and future amendment."[113] In November 1640 a clerk erred again and the Committee for Privileges undertook to investigate.[114]

A record of writs issued was kept on parliament pawns. These large sheets of parchment, now preserved at the Public Record Office, contain a verbatim example or exemplar of each of the different types of writ: those for archbishops, for bishops, for dukes and marquesses, for earls and viscounts, for barons, and for the various assistants. They further indicate who should be summoned by a similar writ (*consimile breve*).[115] The pawn could likewise be used as a guide for subsequent parliaments. A copy of the pawn for 1539 has survived, corrected to serve as a rough list for 1553.[116] In the same way, a draft of the pawn for 1624 was brought up to date for a later session.[117]

Writs were issued at least forty days before the date set for a meeting. When the writs had been prepared and sealed, they were distributed to various messengers for delivery throughout the kingdom. The crown paid its messengers £20 for the job, the sum to be divided among them. They also received fees from recipients.[118] Delivery was not always prompt and the dates of delivery varied as the men rode from place to place. Following complaints to the lord keeper in October 1640 from lords who had not received their writs, one Thomas Bankes, a deputy to one of the messengers in the Exchequer, described how he had proceeded. At York, late at night on 3 October, he said, he had received forty-six writs (twelve for sheriffs for counties and cities, eleven for earls, four for bishops, five for barons, twelve for judges, one for the attorney general, and one for Sir Charles Caesar, master of the rolls). Bankes stayed at York until Monday, 5 October, to deliver writs in that area and then rode south "with utmost speed." Along the way he received two more writs, one for the earl of Rutland and one for the sheriff of Rutland, which he undertook to deliver since the errand would not take him far out of his way. He confessed he had not asked for a post warrant to enable him to carry out his service more quickly, "nor had any express directions for the more speedy delivery of the writs for London and Middlesex then of the rest."[119] The details of Bankes's journey, with the list of places he went and the times at which he arrived, give a clear picture of the way writs were distributed. There could be a difference of weeks in the date of delivery. It was with men such as Bankes and their problems in mind that the House declared that the privilege of parliament began with the date of the writ itself, not with the date of its receipt, "for that the Delivery thereof may be delayed by the Negligence of the Messenger."[120]

When a lord came to parliament, he presented his writ, which was then filed by the clerk.[121] When a lord was newly introduced into the House, his writ was usually read. Lord Montagu specifically noted that Strafford's writ had not been read, when he was introduced on 23 April 1640.[122] Sometimes the clerk entered the writ at large in the journal, but he later abandoned this practice.[123]

In theory, a writ of summons went to each of the peers (including, when it seemed suitable, the royal heir apparent). Both James and Charles also summoned the eldest sons of certain peers in their fathers' baronies, as other kings had done.[124] Individual writs also went to the archbishops and bishops. A different writ, or writ of assistance, was directed to the chief justices of the King's Bench and the Common Pleas, and to the chief baron of the Court of Exchequer.[125] Writs of assistance normally also went to other judges, such barons of the Exchequer as had attained the order of the coif, the master of the rolls, the attorney and solicitor general, and the king's serjeants. The secretaries of state and certain members of the Privy Council might also be called in this way.[126] However, in case any of these persons were also peers, they were summoned as peers. Masters in Chancery were expected to attend but, like the clerk of the crown and the clerk of the parliaments, received no writ.[127]

Two developments during the early Stuart period markedly changed the composition of the House, which was thus summoned. The first was royal policy in creating and advancing peers; the second was the series of events from 1641 to 1649 that resulted in the expulsion of the bishops and the withdrawal of royalist peers. In 1601, 52 lay lords were called to the House: 1 marquess, 16 earls, 2 viscounts, and 33 barons.[128] The queen had been chary of creating and promoting peers. Taking account of titles that became extinct by failure of the male heir and of those that lapsed by attainder, there were fewer peers at her death than on the day of her accession. James followed a different policy. By 1615 he had increased the peerage from 52 to a total of 81. There were still only 1 marquess and 2 viscounts, but the number of earls had grown to 27, the number of barons to 51. The growth was substantial but not unreasonable, considering the developing wealth and power of the gentry and the prolonged parsimony of the Elizabethan period. Most of the creations and promotions could be justified in terms of birth and substance. The year 1615, with the rise of Villiers and the system of patronage associated with him, marked the beginning of a new policy. With the cash sales of titles, the "inflation of honors" began in earnest. By the end of December 1628, the English peerage had increased from 81 to 126. At the same time, the number of earls had more than doubled, "one of the most radical transformations of the English titular aristocracy that has ever occurred." By 1628 Buckingham had become a duke, and there were 10 viscounts. Shortly after the favorite's death in 1628, the king stopped selling honors. He resumed the practice again in 1641, creating in the last seven years of his life almost as many peers as he had in the first years of his reign. It was a way of raising money and virtually the only means left by which he could reward his followers.[129]

Developments in the years 1641–49 sharply reduced the number of lords who sat and finally brought about the abolition of the House.[130] In 1642 the king gave his assent to the bill for the exclusion of the bishops. On the right side of the House, a visitor observed, there was "a great emptiness."[131] By the time the king summoned peers to attend him at York in May, many had already withdrawn from the chamber and others left soon afterwards. About one-half the peers supported the king, about one-quarter the parliament. Thirty or more remained at Westminster. The failure of peace negotiations in 1643 further reduced the number of peers in the House as men departed to join the army. In 1646 an ordinance declared that all titles conferred since 20 May 1642 were null and void. By 1646 there were twenty-nine peers qualified to vote. Attendance was often less than twenty. These successive changes in the composition of the House from 1603 to 1649 had profound effects, to which we will return later.[132]

The monarch decisively influenced the character of the House by his ability to create and to promote peers and by his right to nominate archbishops and bishops. He was suspected on occasion of using his power to promote political ends. In 1626 the French ambassador reported that the king had recently created five or six barons with the idea of reinforcing his supporters in the upper House.[133] Similarly, Charles was said to have created new barons in 1641 in an attempt to save Strafford.[134] He also sometimes declined to issue a writ of summons to a peer or to a spiritual lord.

There were two traditions that governed the writ of summons and attendance in the House. By one tradition, the monarch determined who was called and who sat. It was he who issued the summons, he who determined to whom it should go, he who excused those unable to attend. As late as the reign of Henry VIII, the sovereign issued summons to some peers and not to others.[135] Conrad Russell has observed that in the period 1621–29, the king, particularly Charles, viewed parliament as an extension of the court from which he could exclude those who displeased him.[136] In 1626 the earl of Suffolk, writing to the duke of Buckingham before the session, implied that the king might exercise his own discretion in summoning members. Suffolk, noting that all Buckingham's friends should be on hand to support him when parliament met, asked for a summons and a command from the king that he should attend despite the fact that he was in mourning.[137] This sycophantic letter was an exception. By the early Stuart period, indeed earlier, peers and bishops expected to be summoned to the upper House not at the king's pleasure but by right. When the king withheld a writ or otherwise interfered with attendance in the House, the matter concerned the House and in Charles's reign eventually became a point of privilege. A second "tradition" was in the making.[138]

In 1621 the earl of Northumberland, imprisoned in the Tower in connection with the Gunpowder Plot, petitioned the House for his writ. It had been "delayed," he said, "though His Majesty was then pleased, and is still so graciously disposed, that he shall enjoy his Right therein." He prayed their lordships to order that it might be sent. When the lord chamberlain had signified the king's assent, the lords ordered that the writ should be drawn,[139] and the case became a significant precedent for the earl of Bristol in 1626. The writ in effect terminated any restraint upon Northumberland and hence upon Bristol.[140] The case of the earl of Hertford in 1621 was somewhat different but also illustrates the interest of the House in the matter of the writ. Hertford's father had recently died and the earl of Essex moved in April for a writ for the new earl. The House so ordered and the clerk of the parliaments addressed a warrant for the writ to the clerk of the crown or his deputy. The king forbade the lord chancellor to proceed with the writ. In May the House chose a committee of six to wait upon the king "to know His Pleasure." Several days later, the committee reported that the king had agreed to call Hertford "so as the Earl do take his Place according to the new Creation of that Earldom, and not otherwise."[141] Although the House had clearly demonstrated a concern for the writ and for the lords' presence, no issue of major constitutional importance had yet arisen. When the king induced the earl of Southampton, who had been examined concerning his activities in parliament, to stay away after the summer adjournment in 1621, the House did not question his "sickness."[142] In succeeding years, when the king withheld a writ or commanded a lord not to obey it, the right to attend became a point of increasing significance to the House and to political observers.

In 1624 John Chamberlain reported that the earls of Northumberland and Hertford and Lords Saye and St. Albans were not called "or yf they had writts *pro forma*, yet they were willed to forbeare and absent themselves."[143] In 1625 the earl of Bristol received his writ; but knowing that he was out of favor with the court, he wrote to Buckingham for advice. The duke replied that the king wished him to offer some pretext for staying away. Consequently Bristol, according to the usual custom, wrote the king for leave to be absent. He received in reply "an absolute prohibition" and was commanded to remain in custody.[144] Neither Bristol nor Bishop Williams received a writ in 1626. Bristol wrote a note of inquiry to the lord keeper, who advised that he had "particular Order to detain it." Bristol then petitioned the upper House, which referred the matter to the Committee for Privileges.[145] The committee reported that it could find no precedent for detaining a writ from any peer capable of sitting in the House and recommended that the Lords petition the king to send a writ to Bristol "and to such other Lords to whom no Writ . . . hath been directed for this Parliament," with the exception of those incapable of sitting because of a judgment against them (for example, Viscount St. Albans and the earl of Middlesex).[146] Before the petition went forward, Bristol had his writ, but with it had gone a letter from the lord keeper to forbear attendance. Bristol, determined to be heard by the Lords, inquired whether the king's writ of summons, issued by authority of the great seal, did not override the commands of a missive letter.[147] In his case, the point was never decided. When Bristol came to parliament, it was not by reason of his writ, but because he had been summoned by the House to defend himself against the king's charge of treason.

In 1626 Bishop Williams, in disfavor since 1625, had also received no writ and was therefore unable to name a proxy. When the king issued the writ and tried to control Williams's proxy, the bishop "strugg'ld," his biographer said, "till he had it his own way" and gave his proxy to the bishop of Winchester.[148] In 1628 the lord keeper had an order to stop Williams's attendance and to force him to accept a proxy proposed by the king. The bishop respectfully refused to obey. When the House met, the earl of Clare brought the matter before the Lords, inquiring if Williams had received a writ. When the lord keeper replied that he had, the Lords called for his presence and he came.[149] In 1640 the bishop received no writ for the Short Parliament. He tried unsuccessfully to persuade John Hampden to move the lower House to intervene on his behalf, arguing that his presence would be of importance to the whole parliament, as it had been in the past.[150] At the time of the next parliament in 1640, the crown attempted to compromise with Williams by sending him a writ of summons with the understanding that he would give bail to return as a prisoner after the session was over. The Lords, as in 1628, sent for the bishop, who took his seat.[151]

The Lords thus directly challenged the tradition that the monarch might summon such lords as he pleased to advise him in parliament. As individuals they claimed for themselves the right to a summons and the right to sit.[152] At the same time, the House claimed this right for them and began to assert control over its own membership by insisting not only that each lord receive a writ but also that he should be free to attend. The case of the earl of Arundel, who was imprisoned in parliament time in 1626, posed this problem dramatically to the House in yet another form and raised the significant issue of a member's right to be free from arrest, a point discussed below with other matters of privilege.

ATTENDANCE

As the king and House both concerned themselves with the writ of summons, so they too were both involved in regulating attendance of members. By custom a lord addressed himself to the king either directly or through an appropriate official for leave to be absent from a parliament, and requested the privilege to constitute a proxy to vote in his place. The king at his pleasure issued a license, which was entered at the Signet Office.[153] Once parliament had assembled, the king attempted to enforce regular attendance through the presiding officer.[154] But the House also took responsibility for attendance, sometimes at the king's behest, sometimes on its own initiative. Thus in 1606 the Lords ordered that the gentleman usher should tell all members who were in London and not present in the House that the king commanded them to attend.[155] Shortly after the opening of a session and at other times (with due notice), the clerk called the House and noted such excuses as might be given by other lords for those who were absent.[156] In 1625 the House declared that members should all attend at the next access to be held in Oxford in August. It requested the king to grant no leaves of absence and declared that his proclamation for the second sitting had determined all leaves given for the first.[157]

In James's first two parliaments, in 1606 and 1614, the House levied a fine on members absent without leave.[158] The Standing Orders of 1621 reversed this policy, providing that there should be no fine but that a lord should "make his excuse, by any Member of the House, which if it be allowed as just, he is excused, if that be not done, hee is to be blamed by the house as the fault requires."[159] By 1626 the House returned to the fine of 5s. per day for those who stayed away without "just excuse."[160] Neither fines nor threats were of much avail. Attendance in the years 1621–29 was rarely higher than sixty and very often less.[161] In 1642, when the king called his subjects to depart from Westminster and to attend him at Hampton Court, York, or elsewhere, the lords were torn between two loyalties. Some turned for advice to the House, which in each case denied a leave of absence.[162] In April 1642 the House refused to honor such royal licenses as had been granted by the king; it had clearly taken over control of dispensations for its members.[163] In 1647 the fine levied on a lord absent without excuse was 100*li*.[164]

PROXIES

When the king granted a member of the upper House a license to be absent from parliament, he also gave him the right to name a proxy.[165] The lord then chose from other members of the House the man who would hold his proxy, but first inquired whether he was willing to serve.[166] By the early Stuart period, it had become customary for bishops to bestow their proxies on one of their own members and for temporal peers to grant proxies to temporal peers.[167] A standing order in 1626 confirmed this usage and limited the number of proxies a single lord could hold to two.[168] A man seeking to place his proxy had then to inquire if the lord to whom he wrote was "full."[169] On occasion there were efforts by the king or his favorite to control the choice of a proxy. This policy was firmly resisted by John Williams, bishop of Lincoln, in his own case in 1626, 1628, and 1640, when it was referred to the Committee for Privileges by the House.[170] In 1626, when Hertford reported that certain peers had not received writs, the earl of Clare moved that the writs should be sent and also "that Proxies of the absent LL. may be lefte freely in the disposicion of him that gyves yt."[171] Men bestowed their proxies on relatives, on trusted friends, on those who could be expected to support causes in which they were interested. In 1607 the earl of Derby was ill, but Salisbury was confident that he would give no proxy to a man who would vote against the union with Scotland.[172] In 1624 Zouche, lord warden of the Cinque Ports, begged the earl of Pembroke, who held his proxy, to protect the privileges of these towns.[173]

A lord might notify the clerk of the parliaments directly of his choice or the man to whom he had given his proxy might register the necessary authorization. Secretary Conway forwarded a "form" to Lord Vere for granting his proxy.[174] Sir Simonds D'Ewes observed that the wisest plan was for lords to have their proxies drawn by the clerk (a duty in fact assigned to the "clerk's man"),[175] "which is the best and most usual course"; but he noted that lords living at a distance and most of the spiritual lords often sent in their own letters of authorization, which thus varied in form.[176]

The proxies came in gradually during a session and were entered by the clerk or assistant clerk day by day.[177] The presiding officer repeatedly urged lords to register the proxies they held. The short sitting in 1614 came to an end before all had been received.[178] The custom of calling the House was a device for hastening this process as well as for encouraging attendance. "It is to be observed," read the Standing Order, "that the first or second day the house bee called, and notice to be taken of such Lords as either have not sent their proxies or are excused by his Majestie for some time."[179] As the clerk called the name of each member who had been summoned, his excuse was entered and his proxy produced.[180] The procedure foreshadowed that more fully developed after the Restoration, as explained by his agent to the earl of Huntingdon in 1672: "The manner of having your proxy accepted is this, the peer whom you appoint to be your proxy, when the House is called over, stands up and gives the reason of your absence and withall declares himself to be your proxy."[181]

Although the right to appear by proxy was a right granted by the grace of the monarch, the House took a strong interest in and undertook to regulate proxies. It ruled that they must be renewed at each session of parliament after a prorogation.[182] It resolved that a lord's return to parliament terminated any proxy he had given and that he could not make a new one without leave from the king.[183] The House, as we have already seen, limited the number of proxies to two in 1626 and directed that bishops give their proxies to fellow bishops, temporal peers to temporal peers.[184] Lords appearing by proxy were subject to the same financial obligations as lords who were present, and also by vote of the House shared some of the same privileges. A lord holding a proxy who was absent from the House without excuse must pay a fine for himself and his proxy.[185] Similarly, he must contribute to parliamentary collections on behalf of the man he represented.[186] When he registered the proxy, he must pay a fee to the clerk, to Black Rod, to the assistant clerk, and to the yeoman usher.[187] A lord absent by license, who had duly appointed a proxy, enjoyed the privilege of parliament for his servants.[188]

The House also controlled the voting of proxies and determined when they should be used. Proxies were not always counted, but "if need bee" the House called for them, probably when an important vote was close, and the clerk produced his book of proxies to check them off.[189] A lord might vote his proxies as seemed best to him: Elsyng, clerk of the parliaments, wrote, "Such lords as gave their own vote, with the question, may give his proxies against it."[190] On the crucial vote in 1626 limiting the number of proxies, the earl of Pembroke was said to have voted four on one side and four on the other.[191] Clarendon noted that in 1641 the earl of Essex often voted the earl of St. Albans's proxy against his own, "but there was no other example of that justice."[192] In 1642 the House instructed the lord admiral to consult Danby, whose proxy he held.[193] Since a lord often gave his proxy to several members of the House, a problem could develop concerning which one should vote on his behalf. Elsyng noted that, at the Committee for Privileges in 1626, the earl of Manchester resolved that the lord first named held the right. The resolution does not appear to have been reported to the House, so possibly the committee took no action upon it. However, D'Ewes declared that proxies were voted in the order in which they were named, and this was probably the case.[194]

In 1641 the committee considered whether proxies might be used in "cases of blood," or capital cases. On its recommendation, the House ordered that they should not be voted in giving judgment in Strafford's trial.[195] There had been no such prohibition in earlier impeachment trials in the seventeenth century, as Elsyng specifically emphasized. He wrote that in an impeachment, the absence of lords cannot invalidate the judgment, "so as the greater number of the Lords be then present (accompting the proxies of the absent Lords) for it is not material whether some Lords do absent themselves, or disassent. The chiefest Matter is the Assent of the Lords, who are present either in Person or by Proxy."[196] In 1645 members disagreed as to whether proxies should be used in a vote concerning the New Model Army; but the clerk reported "upon diligent Search" that there had been no general order "to take away Proxies" and therefore they were counted.[197] The earl of Mulgrave in 1646 pointedly revoked a proxy formerly given to Lord Saye and Sele and asked that his letter to this effect be publicly read and "remain upon the record in the office of the Clerk." When he transferred his proxy to the earl of Essex, the question rose in the House whether this might in fact be done without leave from the king. The House ultimately validated the proxy and upheld Mulgrave's right to reassign it.[198]

THE DAILY ROUTINE: DAYS AND TIMES OF MEETING

The king opened parliament on the first day, the Commons attending at the bar. On this occasion, the monarch traditionally explained why the parliament had been summoned and bade the lower House choose its Speaker. On the second day, the king received the Commons' Speaker, who delivered an elaborate oration. At each of these meetings, the king presided.[199] After two days devoted to matters concerning the whole parliament, the House on the third day turned to its own business and normal routine. The lord chancellor or lord keeper presided. Each morning began with prayers, said by the youngest bishop present, who knelt at the right end of the woolsack.[200] An afternoon session also began with prayers, and those who came after prayers had to pay a fine.[201] After the bishops had been expelled from the House in 1642, the presiding officer appointed his chaplain or another man to read prayers. In 1644 Arthur Needham, a clerk who had been dismissed from the service of the House, petitioned for some allowance. He had, he said, constantly attended for the past seven months "in the reading of prayers, which hath occasioned his residing here to his great expense."[202] The journal for 1646 indicates that a variety of men served the House at that time: Mr. Wilkinson, Mr. Ford, Mr. Ash, Mr. Newcomen, Dr. Burgess, and others.[203]

On the third day the clerk often called the House, noting the excuses offered for those absent and the proxies registered.[204] After 1621 he next read the roll of Standing Orders and then a bill *pro forma*.[205] Beginning in 1621, the House then appointed its "general committees," or committees "which shall stand all that session": first, the Committee for Customs and Orders of the House and for Privileges of the Peers and Lords of Parliament and the subcommittee to peruse the journal; second, the committee to receive petitions.[206] When the presiding officer had adjourned the House with the Lords' acquiescence, members took the oath of allegiance required by law.[207]

After parliament had thus begun, the House set its own schedule for meeting and adjourned itself at the end of each day to the next day and time selected.[208] In the case of a brief recess, it sometimes sought agreement with the lower House.[209] An adjournment was temporary. It kept "a kind of Being" in the parliament. Committees, bills, and other business remained as they were. Privileges continued.[210] The House made no issue of its right to adjourn itself and acquiesced silently in the king's assertion of his overriding prerogative not only to determine the life of a parliament but also to adjourn it. If he was present in the House (as on the opening days), the House was adjourned by his command.[211] If he wished to postpone the beginning of parliament, he adjourned it by writ directed to both Houses. Members of the lower House were then called to the bar of the upper House, where the lord chancellor or lord keeper read the writ and adjourned the parliament.[212] If the king wished to adjourn a parliament already in session, he did so by letting his pleasure be known or by addressing a commission to certain lords of the upper House, who took action upon it and then forwarded it to the House of Commons with word that the Lords had adjourned.[213]

When the Lords themselves chose the days and times they would meet, they often took account of other obligations they might have, but nevertheless insisted on the prior claim of the House upon them. Since many of the lords and the two chief justices sat also in the Court of Star Chamber, it had been the custom in the Elizabethan period, when that court sat on Wednesday and Friday mornings, for the House to avoid those days during the law term.[214] This custom continued in the early Stuart period, although the House occasionally met in the afternoon of a Star Chamber day.[215] In 1626 the House did not sit on the last day of the law term and adjourned for several days because of "the solemnity of Sct. George," the beginning of the next law term, and the meeting of Star Chamber.[216] But the House was careful to declare that such arrangements should "be not drawn into any president, as if this supreem Courte wear to attend any other inferior courte."[217]

Meetings of the House might also conflict with the convocation of the province of Canterbury, which met when parliament met and convened on Wednesday and Friday.[218] When the archbishop of Canterbury formally requested in 1621 that the House forbear to sit on those days, the House voted to honor his request, but retained the right to sit when it chose by providing that the lord chancellor should put the question each Tuesday and Thursday for the next day of meeting.[219] Two weeks later, the Lords voted to sit on convocation days in order to expedite the investigation of charges against Mompesson.[220] A resolution in 1640 not to meet on a convocation day failed on the grounds that "the High Court of Parliament is not subordinate to any other Court."[221] Several days later, Archbishop Laud brought in a report reaffirming the right of the House to meet when it would and suggesting that the bishops ask the lord keeper to inquire each Tuesday and Thursday when the House would next sit so that they could arrange their affairs accordingly.[222] It was essentially the arrangement made in 1621. The House was willing to set its days of meeting to suit the convenience of its members, temporal and spiritual, but did not waver on the point of principle. When business was heavy or haste seemed important, the House might meet daily. In 1641 it sat on a Sunday.[223]

The House usually sat in the morning, convening at nine o'clock and rising before noon.[224] Occasionally the time was advanced to eight and once during the summer of 1641 to six.[225] Observers especially noted when the House continued to sit into the early afternoon without a break. In 1621, for example, a quarrel between the earl of Arundel and Lord Spencer kept the lords sitting without recess until three. During a debate on the Petition of Right in 1628, they sat from eight in the morning until six in the evening, "never stirring from the House."[226] The usual practice when business was heavy was to meet in the morning and reconvene at two or three in the afternoon. This might occur at the end of a session to finish up bills, when the king's business was pressing, when impeachment proceedings clogged the agenda, or when the political situation was tense.[227] In 1642 the French ambassador reported that the House sat until 11:00 P.M., but normally this was not the case and the afternoon was reserved for meetings of committees.[228]

The agenda of the upper chamber and hence its hours of meeting varied considerably. In 1625 or 1626 Elsyng wrote that the House often did not "sit half an hour, and yet as long as they had any business to do, and no longer."[229] Lord Montagu's observations in 1626 and later parliaments bear him out.[230] In 1628 Montagu noted that on several days little was done.[231] On 20 February the House rose so early that committees were ordered to advance their meeting time to the morning.[232]

DEMEANOR

The Lords attempted to maintain an orderly House, but were not always successful in doing so. They expected members to sit according to rank and to remain in their places, not to go to the fire and talk.[233] Any lord who entered when the House was set was "to give and receive salutations from the rest" and to take his seat only after he had made obeisance to the cloth of estate.[234] If he had occasion to cross the House, he was again to bow to the cloth of estate.[235] Members were to remain silent if a lord was speaking. All were to rise when they spoke, to address the House in general, and to refrain from referring by name to other members.[236] Speeches were to be neither "personall, sharpe or taxing." "As nothing offensive is to bee spoaken" either in the House or in committee, "soe nothing is to bee ill taken."[237] If quarrels should arise in or near parliament, they must be reported, for they immediately concerned the House. The House would censure those who offended.[238]

The standard of demeanor that the Lords expected was clear enough; but it was a standard that they sometimes failed to achieve. Indeed, certain of the Standing Orders cited above were made in response to disturbing incidents. In 1604 Viscount Montagu, in speaking to a bill, attacked the established church. He was committed to the Fleet and later made submission at the bar.[239] Some lords were hot-tempered and obsessed with pride of place. In February 1620/1 the earl of Berkshire, when he entered the House, violently thrust aside Lord Scrope, who had preceded him. The House took the gravest view of the offense. The earl was deprived of his sword and committed a close prisoner to the Fleet, "that Posterity might take the more notice thereof."[240] When the earl committed suicide several years later, there were those who believed he had never recovered from this humiliation. but Simonds D'Ewes, who described him as a violent and disappointed man, ascribed his death to other causes.[241]

Private animosities between lords flared up. In March 1620/1 there were quarrels between Buckingham on the one hand and Southampton and Sheffield on the other.[242] In May Lord Spencer cast aspersions on the ancestors of the earl of Arundel. Arundel retorted icily that his forebears had suffered for king and country while Spencer's were tending sheep. Lord Denny defended Spencer's lineage. The bishop of Coventry and Lichfield piously remarked that it was no disgrace to be called a shepherd and hoped for reconciliation. This was made difficult by Arundel's stiff-necked pride; but finally both lords submitted themselves to the censure of the House and the clerk removed their words of altercation from the record.[243]

"Sharpness of Speech" at a committee was reported to the House in 1626, which resulted in the Standing Order against asperity of speech.[244] In 1626, in connection with the debate concerning the imprisonment of the earl of Arundel, "My lord duke, my Lord of Dorset, my Lord of Carlisle, my Lord of Holland, stood all up, one after another to have spoken, but could not be heard."[245] In 1640, when the Short Parliament sat, the lord keeper complained of the difficulty of keeping speakers in line. They stood up simultaneously to speak, he said. They spoke more than once to the question.[246] The tense political situation bred bitterness and sharpened tongues. In April Bishop Hall attacked Lord Saye and was forced to go to the bar and crave pardon.[247]

When the Long Parliament convened in November, difficulties continued. In December Lord Montagu, always keenly aware of procedure, spoke against the disorders of the House.[248] Shortly thereafter he withdrew from parliament, but continued to receive news from his son. Young Edward wrote that Lord Stamford said there had been no order since the elder Montagu left. Edward replied that his father had always maintained there had been none before.[249] In April an open quarrel broke out during the debate on Strafford's bill of attainder.[250] In May Lord Rutland, who had recently entered the upper House, observed that members of the Commons were more orderly than the lords, who "run so up and downe" and "speak by multitudes, so that it is almost a confusion."[251] In July the earl of Pembroke and Lord Maltravers (heir to the earl of Arundel) came to blows at a committee. Pembroke twice struck Maltravers with his white staff. Maltravers hurled an ink standish at Pembroke, but fortunately missed his aim. Both submitted to the House upon their knees.[252] In December Viscount Newark said that it was not honorable for the House to be in such a tumult and noise. He was ordered to withdraw and committed to custody.[253] When the earl of Warwick stood to speak on a point of religion, the archbishop of York cried "hold your tongue" and refused to withdraw until forced to do so.[254]

In 1642 the duke of Richmond drew fire by proposing to adjourn for six months. He sought to excuse himself by saying that since all men were on their feet and out of their places he thought the House had risen when he made this remark.[255] Monmouth and Essex had an altercation in April, and Edward Lord Herbert of Cherbury offended in May.[256] The orders of the House and the role of the presiding officer provided fragile barriers against strong emotions, aristocratic independence, and the bitterness of factional struggles. Even imprisonment and the censure of the House failed to maintain acceptable demeanor.

The ordinary tenor of the House is difficult to gauge. Breaches of decorum appear in the record. Appropriate behavior does not. Despite certain outstanding incidents, it is probable that business proceeded in a relatively orderly fashion in the early years of the century and that the House became increasingly unruly after 1640.

2

THE PRESIDING OFFICER

The presiding officer, the lord chancellor or lord keeper, was both spokesman for the crown and servant of the House.[1] His function was determined by the ritual of parliament, by the personality of the monarch, and by the temper of the times. It was defined also by the wishes of the House, his own nature and training, his influence at court and elsewhere, his parliamentary skills, and the regularity of his attendance.

When he presided over the high court of parliament and specifically over the upper House, he acted and spoke for the crown, calling the parliament into being on behalf of the king, conveying the king's wishes to parliament, and adjourning or dissolving it at his command. On warrant from the king, the lord chancellor or lord keeper directed the clerks of the Petty Bag office to prepare writs of summons and writs for elections.[2] The lord chancellor himself sometimes attended without summons, sometimes was called by a special writ of assistance.[3] Occasionally, as in the case of Bishop Williams in 1624, he received two writs, the writ of assistance and also his writ as bishop or, in the case of Edward Hyde, Lord Clarendon, in 1660, his writ as baron.[4] If the lord chancellor was unable to attend the House, the king normally provided by commission for a substitute, often one of the judges.[5] In August 1641, on the day the king left London for Scotland, the House formally asserted control over its presiding officer, resolving that it might choose its own Speaker and that he was not to depart from the House without leave. After the flight of Lord Keeper Littleton to the king in May 1642, the House regularly chose its presiding officer; and in 1660 the resolution of 1641 was reiterated and entered in the Standing Orders of the House.[6]

Like successive scenes from an illuminated manuscript, the ceremonies of the opening days of parliament graphically depicted the position and duties of the lord chancellor. He wore robes of black velvet, lined with sable. He carried the symbol of his office, the great seal, in a sumptuous purse[7] and was constantly attended by his sergeant-at-arms, who bore a mace.[8] In the great procession to the Abbey and from the Abbey to the parliament House, he immediately preceded the archbishop of Canterbury, the prince, and the king, who also wore their parliament robes.[9] When the king had taken his place in the House, the lord chancellor stood at the right of the throne, still holding the purse.[10] The session began with prayers. Then the king addressed the House. The lord chancellor knelt before him in conference, rose, and delivered his own speech.[11] This formal oration had been carefully prepared. Traditionally it began with praise of the monarch and proceeded to amplify the causes of summoning parliament. The orator asked pardon for his own errors and concluded with directions to the House of Commons to depart to choose its Speaker. He commanded the clerk to read the names of men appointed as receivers and triers of petitions.[12] He once more knelt before the king and, having received word to do so, adjourned the parliament.

Ceremony and ritual also prescribed the activities of the second day. The king, once more wearing his parliament robes, attended the House; the lord chancellor, also in his robes and holding the purse, again stood at his right hand. Members of the Commons, at the bar, presented their Speaker, who modestly disabled himself. The lord chancellor, on his knees, consulted the king,[13] then rose and made reply in the king's name. The Commons' Speaker, he said, by his own performance, had demonstrated his ability. The king would not excuse him. The Speaker of the House of Commons then made a formal oration—praising the king and the English form of government and formally requesting privileges for the Commons and pardon for his own errors. The lord chancellor replied, referring to the points made by the Speaker. He concluded by granting the requests for privileges with due warning that they should be exercised with discretion. Members of the Commons departed to their own House. Once more the lord chancellor consulted the king and finally, in his name, adjourned the House.

Throughout the session, the lord chancellor continued to speak for the king, bringing messages from him. When the monarch was present in the House, he stepped down from the woolsack to take his place at the king's right hand, as he had done in the opening days, knelt before him for instructions, and addressed and adjourned the House in his name. The prorogation or dissolution, like the first days of a parliament, had its own ritual. When the monarch had arrived and the House was set, the Speaker of the House of Commons made an elaborate speech at the bar, thanked the monarch for the general pardon, and presented the subsidy bill. The lord chancellor knelt before the king for instructions, then rose and made reply. He commented on the Speaker's oration and sometimes also on the session. He delivered the king's thanks for the subsidy and ordered the clerk of the crown to read the titles of bills and the clerk of the parliaments the royal replies. Once more the lord chancellor or lord keeper knelt before the king, rose, and dismissed the parliament at his behest.[14]

When the king was not present at the close of parliament, the lord chancellor announced that a commission had been granted to certain lords for prorogation or dissolution. He directed the clerk to read the commission. Then the commissioners, one of whom was always the presiding officer, exercised their power.[15]

This pattern of the opening and final days, clearly established in Elizabethan times, often varied in James's reign, since the king himself frequently addressed parliament, commenting on the session and especially on the Commons' grievances. Charles, by temperament and possibly because of a speech defect, was less fond of doing so.[16] The closing ritual was more seriously disturbed by the exigencies of James's and Charles's relations with their parliaments—few were "happy" or came to a successful conclusion. Many were broken up abruptly and dismissed in wrath, several without accomplishing legislation.[17]

As an officer of the crown, the lord chancellor publicly served the king from the beginning to the end of a parliament. He was a person of considerable dignity and importance, even "grandeur,"[18] as he moved through the solemn ceremonial of the first and last days. His position was enhanced by his rich robes and purse and by his sergeant-at-arms, who carried the mace before him.[19] He had a withdrawing room in the parliament House and apartments nearby, at York House in the Strand in the early part of the century and at Durham House in 1640.[20] As a legal officer, he was paid by the crown.[21] Puckering complained in 1592 that he could not meet expenses on what was allowed him, but the position was generally regarded as lucrative.[22] Although he was not entitled to additional salary as presiding officer of the House, the lord chancellor received a fee of £10 for every private bill. When several individuals were named in a single bill, he could expect £10 from each person.[23] The same fees to the presiding officer were due for ordinances in the period 1642–49. He was probably also entitled to keep books that had been ordered for his use.[24] At the end of a parliament, the lord chancellor may have received some "reward" from the crown. With this in mind, Bacon, Lord Verulam, tried to collect from the king beforehand, but was unsuccessful.[25]

The lord chancellor, when the king was not present, presided over the House and all its proceedings. In this capacity he was, as we have seen, the representative of the king. He was also the servant of the House. The Standing Orders of the House, first drawn up in 1621, provided that the lord chancellor "is not to adjourne the House or doe anything els, as mouth of the House, without the consent of the Lords first had excepting the ordinarie things about Bills, which are of course, wherein, the Lords may likewise overrule, as for preferring one Bill before another, and such like."[26] As Lord Ellesmere said in 1614 in connection with a question about procedure, "My Lords, yow may doe what you will therefore determine as yow please."[27] Although the House thus reserved final authority to itself, in fact many of the duties of the presiding officer were "of course" and determined by traditional ceremony. At all times, he spoke and acted for the House.

He presided over the introduction of newly created peers to the House. On this occasion, the new peer first presented his patent of creation and his writ of summons to the lord chancellor, who then handed it to the clerk of the parliaments to be read.[28] When the lord chancellor himself was raised to the peerage and introduced to the House in his new dignity, he laid his patent of creation on the chair of state and then delivered it to the clerk to be read with his writ of summons. He first took possession of the seat due him as a peer, then the seat on the earls' bench due him as lord chancellor or lord keeper, and finally his place on the woolsack.[29] The presiding officer administered at the woolsack the oaths of supremacy and allegiance required of each member.[30] He interrogated witnesses or delinquents on behalf of the House and pronounced sentence in ordinary cases of contempt or on more solemn occasions on accusation from the House of Commons when both he and the lords wore their robes.[31] He presided over the presentation, reading, and voting of bills.[32] If he was himself a lord, he had the right to vote and stepped down from the woolsack to do so.[33] When messengers arrived from the lower House, he received them at the bar, rising from the woolsack and proceeding uncovered, purse in hand and sometimes accompanied by lords. At the bar he rested his purse before him and returned each of three bows made by representatives of the Commons, who delivered their message and backed from the chamber, again making three bows. These the lord chancellor again acknowledged, then walked back to the woolsack, laid down his purse, and delivered the message to the House.[34] At audiences with the king, the lord chancellor spoke for his own or for both Houses.[35] He took some responsibility for the record of the House.[36] During a recess he embodied the power of the House. He could deal with delinquents and enforce privilege.[37]

The services to the king and to the lords performed by the lord chancellor in presiding over the House went far beyond his role in formal ceremonies and ritual. Just how effective he was in his dual function as spokesman for the crown and servant of the House depended on his own position at court, his relations to the king and to other ministers, his experience in parliament, and the exigencies of the political situation. The man who knelt so humbly before the king to receive instructions was also a privy councillor deeply involved in the plans and preparations for parliament,[38] often an experienced lawyer and judge. The House, as we have seen, reserved to itself ultimate control over its procedure. However, if we consider the record of the activities of the presiding officer found in the journal of the House, the "scribbled books" of the clerks, and diaries of members, or if we search among such papers of the lord chancellor or lord keeper as have survived, the picture of his function in the House that emerges is different. In order to see it clearly, we will examine briefly the career of each of the men who presided over parliament in the early Stuart period.

Thomas Egerton, Baron Ellesmere, was lord chancellor from 1603 until his resignation in 1616/7. He had served as solicitor general from 1581 until 1592 when he became attorney general. In 1584 and 1586 he sat in the House of Commons. In 1596 he rose to the office of lord keeper and joined the Privy Council. His papers show that he was involved in many matters that eventually came before parliament. There were proposals for achieving financial stability, for repealing and amending statutes, for the projected union with Scotland, for modifying economic regulations.[39] Ellesmere was deeply engaged in the decision whether to call parliament[40] and in the preparations for it.[41] He drafted the proclamation for parliament in 1603[42] and worked on some of the legislation to be presented.[43] He labored over the speeches he would deliver, writing them out beforehand and shaping them after the classical models he had studied in school. He spoke, it was said, "after a grave Roman manner."[44]

When the House was in session, he constantly directed agenda. This was done in several ways. With the aid of the clerk, he kept track of bills and their progress.[45] He brought them before the House in an orderly way. He explained the legal implications of certain bills and indicated that commitment was appropriate or delay might be advisable.[46] In the same way, he watched the general business of the session, noting what stages of the great contract should be considered, suggesting that the lords prepare for scheduled conferences with the Commons, recommending that they join the lower House in giving thanks to the king, reminding them what should next be done, and constantly bringing before them proposals to forward business.[47] Far from passively presiding over debate, he was constantly directing its course. Nor did he hesitate to rule on points of procedure or to assert his own opinion concerning a bill.[48] In 1614 he recommended consultation with the judges on impositions and spoke against a conference with the Commons on the matter.[49] He warned the lords that the Commons' complaint against Bishop Neile's speech was an infringement of their privileges.[50] At the end of the same parliament, Ellesmere urged delay in reading the commission for dissolution in the hope that an angry dismissal could be avoided.[51] His experience and his following in both Houses, his many years of service in the upper House, his knowledge of the business at hand, and his record of regular attendance[52] made Ellesmere a useful servant to the crown and an effective presiding officer to the House.

When Sir Francis Bacon, Viscount St. Albans, became presiding officer of the upper House in 1620/1, he had had long years of experience and responsibility in the lower House from 1581 through 1614, nine parliaments in all. He had frequently served as reporter and as spokesman at conferences with the lords. He had worked faithfully and skillfully in the House of Commons to promote the interests of the crown. Long a seeker of high office, he had recommended himself to the king for the post of lord chancellor as early as 1615 on the grounds that he had "been always gratious in the Lower House" and that he had an "interest in the gentlemen of England," which could be useful "in rectifying that body of parliament men, which is *cardo rerum*."[53] He hoped in James's reign to restore the monarchy to the position that he thought it had held under Elizabeth: serene, confident, its prerogative unimpaired, a monarchy to which supply flowed naturally and was not the subject of bargaining. He observed what he regarded to be errors in dealing with parliament: Salisbury's policy of "contribution and retribution" in 1610, the agreement struck with certain members of the lower House in 1614, the evil effects of divided counsels among the king's ministers.[54] He made recommendations to James in a series of letters and memoranda, advising him on calling a parliament, the necessary preparatory steps to be taken, the nature of the proclamation and even of the royal opening speech.[55] The king, he suggested in 1615 when the council seriously considered a parliament, should speak in person and explain his purpose in summoning the assembly. Trade and defense Bacon selected as proper topics, "an argument worthy of the voice of so great and wise a King before his people." The lord chancellor's speech, Bacon thought, should cover "the part which may seem to have any harshness in it," warnings concerning the gathering of grievances, or the "licentious liberty of speaking."[56] Thus the majesty of kingship would shine forth unclouded.

Although Bacon's experience on the Privy Council began only in 1617 when he became lord keeper and finally attained a position of substantial political power, he had long worked in government as solicitor general and attorney general, advising the council in these capacities. He had served on a commission to investigate the management of crown property in the hope of bringing royal revenues and royal expenditures into better balance.[57] He had drawn bills of grace.[58] A favorite project was the review of penal laws and a revision of the common law.[59] His letters and memoranda to the king and to himself concerning parliament involved him in a wide range of foreign and domestic affairs. Matters that came before him during his brief tenure as presiding officer had already engaged his attention over a period of many years.

His formal speeches, which were required by the ritual of parliament, were elegant and well ordered, reflecting many of the ideas familiar from his earlier notes and letters. His address at the opening of parliament in 1621 was shorter than he had originally intended,[60] since he had to take account of the king's own proclivity for public speaking and exhortation. James himself proposed to discuss the institution of parliament and the cause of summons, asking freely for supply and inviting his people to present grievances.[61] Bacon therefore delivered a relatively brief oration, couched in lavish praise of the king. He admonished his hearers to "doe like Mary that was not onely attentive at our Saviour's words but pondered them and layd them up in her hart."[62] The simile, a bit overstrained to modern ears, doubtless seemed less inappropriate in the seventeenth century and was characteristic of Bacon's policy of exalting kingship. His speech of 3 February, after the oration of the Speaker of the House of Commons, followed the usual pattern of an elaborate commentary on that address. However, in giving the king's reply to the Speaker's request for privileges, Bacon worked in some additional remarks, which reflected not only his own experience in the lower House, but also the view that he had expressed in 1615 of the lord chancellor's function. Delighting in the adviser's role, he took to himself what he had called the harsh part. He expatiated on the proper business of parliament, warned against undue attention to private bills, and discussed the way in which grievances should be gathered and presented. For the "husbanding and marshalling of time," he recommended that speakers in the lower House speak as counselors, not orators, that the Commons proceed first to public business and use their committees for "dispatch, not to dispute." Privilege, he urged, was not to defraud creditors or defeat ordinary justice, liberty of speech did not mean license, access should be at times convenient to the crown.[63]

Like Ellesmere, Bacon frequently urged the House forward in its business. He suggested that it prepare for scheduled conferences with the lower House and for an audience of both Houses with the king.[64] He spoke to several bills,[65] to a motion made by the bishop of Durham, and to the enlargement of the earl of Berkshire, who was imprisoned for unseemly demeanor in the House.[66] On several occasions, Bacon tried to manipulate the House and reorder its business. In February 1620/1 he made two attempts to divert the Lords from a petition, known to be offensive to the king, which concerned the precedence of Scottish and Irish peers. First he suggested that the House adjourn. When this move was unsuccessful, he recommended the reading of a bill.[67] Later, in an early morning conference with the lord treasurer and the prince, he laid plans to avoid or postpone a parliamentary investigation of those who had passed on royal patents. The three decided that if a message concerning this matter came from the House of Commons, the Lords would promise a full investigation. Then, to delay the proposal further, Bacon suggested that the archbishop of Canterbury should be encouraged to introduce his motion that parliament should not meet on convocation days. This device was successful. By the time the expected message came from the Commons, Bacon had adjourned the upper House.[68] Bacon's last effort to influence the Lords came in April, during his disgrace, when he tried to escape the sentence the House would pass against him. He had given up the great seal. Was not this sufficient punishment? If the king, he wrote, would indicate as much to those councillors who sat in the upper House, if the prince would make a motion to that effect after Bacon had made his submission, and if Buckingham would use his interest with friends in the House, Bacon might well be spared further disgrace. The king, however, did not intervene.[69]

On 19 March Bacon's brief tenure as presiding officer was over. Sir James Ley, chief justice of the King's Bench, was appointed by commission to take his place.[70] Ley fulfilled the formal functions of the office, which now included the sentencing of Mompesson, Michell, Bennet, Yelverton, and Bacon himself on accusation from the House of Commons. He does not seem to have been so forward in guiding the House as his predecessors had been nor, since he was not then a peer, did he participate in debate.

Like Bacon, John Williams, bishop of Lincoln, tried to manage parliament by advising the king; but he also worked through his personal channels of influence and patronage to manipulate the lower House. Probably Ellesmere, who controlled a block of seats in the House of Commons and a block of proxies in the House of Lords,[71] had done the same thing, but the evidence is not so clear. Before Williams became lord keeper in July 1621 between the two sittings of parliament, he had been chaplain first to Ellesmere and later to James. In 1620 he became dean of Westminster. He was in and around the court and had the ear of powerful men. His advice to the king and to Buckingham concerning parliament showed a nice sense of the temper of both Houses and of the force of public opinion. In 1621 he recommended that the king, in dealing with the Commons' protestation, grant that privileges were now inherent

in the members—the main point of contention. [72] The earl of Southampton, he advised, should be released well before parliament met
again. [73] It was unwise, he wrote Charles in 1625, to issue a substantial
grant to Secretary Conway, "being in the face of that parliament from
which your Majesty is to expect a main supply."[74] He perceived the
dangers to Buckingham in the session of 1625. He suggested that Charles,
in speaking to parliament, promise to consult the council in major actions
and the expenditure of subsidies. [75] He warned the duke to end the session
quickly; but he implored the king not to dissolve parliament entirely, lest
he disseminate so much unkindness through the country. [76]

Williams recognized the power of particular groups in parliament. In
February 1621/2, immediately following the dissolution of parliament,
he boldly held up sealing the royal proclamation concerning a commission for grievances and advised the king to modify it in several points. The
number of men appointed to hear complaints, Williams wrote, should be
enlarged to include certain temporal and spiritual lords who had been
sympathetic to grievances during parliament yet "kept themselves within
the compass of Duty, and due Respect to Your Majesty." Such a move
would favorably impress the subjects. The lords appointed would be
"Witnesses of your Majesties Justice, and good Goverment against the
next ensuing Parliament" and would be won "to side with the State, being
formerly much wrought upon by the Factious, and Discontented."[77] He
also had his eye on the lawyers with whom he had particular influence. [78]
To win their support in May 1623, with another parliament in prospect,
he persuaded the king to issue a call of serjeants. [79] He warned Buckingham in 1624 that the lawyers, especially Sir Edward Coke, would oppose
a bill concerning cathedral lands; he advised him to drop it. Later, in
1628, when he was no longer lord keeper, Williams would advise Charles
to win over the "Puritans."[80]

Williams was constantly aware of the necessity of trying to control the
lower House and usually confident of his own ability to do so. His power
there was based, among other things, on a sure knowledge of members
and their views. He carried a list of members about with him. He was
said to have "Spies . . . in many private Conferences."[81] Although his
"friends" in the House of Commons failed him in his efforts to save
Cranfield in 1624, they repeatedly warned him in 1625 that Buckingham
planned to attack him. [82] In 1624 he "mitigated Discontents, and soft-
ened refractoriness, . . . obliged the leading Voices with benefits."[83] In
1625 he tried to persuade the king to delay the parliamentary writs. It
was better, he thought, to deal with electorates before the actual date of
parliament was known and try to persuade them to vote for royal servants. Later, in the same year, he attempted to dissuade the king from
transferring parliament to Oxford and proposed to deal "with the chief

Sticklers" himself. He spoke to Phelips and to Wentworth on behalf of the duke.[84]

By 1625 Williams recognized that his power was gone.[85] James, who had always liked him, was dead. His frank advice and his stand on certain issues had alienated the new king and the duke. In the second sitting, they assigned the lord keeper's traditional oration on the causes of summoning parliament to Lord Conway and Sir John Coke, a clear signal that Williams had fallen from grace. That the king should command a commoner to speak in this capacity (despite his qualifications to do so) caused some stir in the upper House and even more in the lower.[86] In October 1625, after parliament had been dissolved, Williams delivered the great seal to the king.

He had labored hard as lord keeper. His biographer and friend, John Hacket, who was decidedly biased in his favor, described his long working day. It began at the Chancery, continued in the House of Lords and later in the council or in the Chancery again, and finally concluded at night with further work to prepare himself for the House the next day.[87] His policy was to try constantly to reconcile the king and his parliaments, first by advising the king himself how to handle his parliaments, second to win friends for him behind the scenes. He was also skillful in managing the upper House from the woolsack. In 1621 he succeeded in avoiding a vote on an issue of privilege.[88] During the same debate, when an aged bishop invoked the wrath of certain peers by asking to be excused, "he had another Pass with a Master-Fencer" and successfully parried a thrust at all the bishops by reminding the Lords that license to attend and license to depart rested not with the House but with the king.[89]

Williams carefully prepared his speeches for parliament.[90] At the opening of the second sitting in 1621, when he first presided, he gave an elaborate address, garnished with classical and Biblical allusions, that laid out the cause of summons and the condition of foreign affairs. He concluded by asking pardon for his infirmities.[91] The king, Buckingham wrote, was well pleased with Williams's address.[92] In 1624 he delivered the ceremonial orations customary at the opening of a parliament. With unusual bluntness, he advised the Commons to depart to choose their Speaker, "and whom his Majesty assigns unto you for his liking and presentation Mr. Secretary will declare." When the Commons later presented their Speaker, Williams first disallowed his excuses and then commented at length on his address.[93] His remarks followed Crewe's so closely, even to the allusions, that one suspects the two men had conferred beforehand. Even for an experienced speaker, Williams's well-organized and elegant speech, concluding with a fine flourish regarding privileges, seems too polished a performance to be extempore.

Sir Thomas Coventry became lord keeper in October 1625 and was sworn a member of the Privy Council. He had been solicitor general, attorney general, and, in 1621, a member of the lower House. Although he had some experience with the king's affairs and with parliament when he first sat on the woolsack in 1626, he was not in a position to advise the king as Ellesmere, Bacon, and Williams had done. Nor was he created baron until April 1628. In his first year as presiding officer, he therefore played a modest role. At the opening of parliament, he spoke, as was customary, on the king's behalf. "His Majesty hath called you together," he said, "to consult and advise of provident and good Laws." In conclusion, he bade the Commons choose their Speaker.[94] When the Speaker was presented two days later, we know only that Coventry, as was expected, "went over all the parts of the Speaker's speech, with additions." In the king's name he granted the request for privileges and apologized for the fact that the Commons had not been properly summoned on the first day.[95] At an audience on 29 March, after Charles had spoken briefly, Coventry declared the purposes for which the Houses had been called to Whitehall, chiding the Commons and redirecting them to the chief business of parliament. He continued to speak briefly on behalf of the king throughout the session, delivering messages and royal answers to petitions or requests and finally announcing the commission for dissolution.[96] All his formal speeches were direct and to the point, unadorned with allusions, similes, metaphors, or other figures of speech.

Coventry arranged that the business of the House should proceed in an orderly fashion. Before each day's meeting, he and the clerk of the parliaments went over the agenda together, noting the state of the bills, reports due from committees, and witnesses scheduled to be heard.[97] The lord keeper tactfully suggested these matters to the House, always seeming to defer to the wishes of the Lords, yet moving them on to the business at hand. Would they consider whether a peer might answer charges in the lower House? Would they proceed on a question of national defense? Did the Lords remember the business that had been appointed for the day? Similarly, he seemed to bow to their wishes on points of procedure. Should the Lords speak more than once to a single issue, he inquired in what was surely a rhetorical question. He asked how their lordships wished to proceed against the earl of Bristol, whom the king had accused of treason; at the same time he skillfully put forward some suggestions that were ultimately followed. He was careful to consult the Lords concerning adjournment, even when word to adjourn had come from the king.[98]

He reminded the Lords to return all proxies to the clerk so that they could be entered and to take the oath of allegiance.[99] He arranged that committee appointments should be read aloud to recall the Lords to their obligations.[100] He spoke for the House to prisoners and delinquents at the bar. After the dissolution, he was empowered to imprison or discharge those who had offended the House, according to his own judgment.[101]

By 1628 Coventry had become more experienced. At the beginning of the session in March, he delivered a long oration on behalf of the king, outlining the state of foreign affairs, the need for supply, and the duties of a parliament. Though considerably more elaborate than his opening address in 1626, his speech was still relatively straightforward and simple. Two days later, in replying to the Speaker's request to be excused, he indulged in a metaphor; and in his reply to the Speaker's oration, he waxed quite eloquent, touching on all points in the oration, as was the custom, and permitting himself several Biblical allusions.[102] In April he was formally introduced into the House as a baron, and he thereafter voted in the House and participated in debate, stepping down from the woolsack to his place on the earls' bench before he spoke.[103] With a particular interest and skill in legal matters, he entered freely into the debates leading up to the Petition of Right, the chief business of the first session.[104] Thus his role in the House was greatly enlarged and his influence both there and with the king, to whom he now occasionally offered respectful advice, was probably increased.

In his second parliament, as in his first, Coventry continued the normal duties of the presiding officer, speaking for the king and bringing messages from him.[105] He reminded the Lords of the state of their business and inquired how they wished to proceed.[106] He summed up debate and moved the House to decision and action by framing the question when he felt the House was ready for it.[107] He spoke for the Lords at conferences with the lower House, making his preparations carefully and checking his instructions back with the House before proceeding.[108] He reported from conferences, moving to his seat as a peer when he did so.[109] He addressed and interrogated delinquents and pronounced the censure of the House and its sentence.[110]

In 1628–29 Coventry was more than a successful moderator. He sometimes proposed a course of action for the Lords, several times in the course of the debate on the Petition of Right suggesting conferences with the House of Commons on difficult points, constantly trying to negotiate between the Houses and to prevent the upper House from adopting a firm stance that would make further negotiation impossible.[111] He took an active part in the debate on the royal right to imprison without cause shown and spoke out also on the question of whether a peer should answer in a court of law on oath or on honor, drawing on his own experience in the Court of Star Chamber. He spoke to the case of *Lane* v. *Baud*, which was before the House, and to the case of *Smith* v. *Sher-*

bourne. He did not venture an opinion on other topics outside his professional ken.[112]

A moderate, reserved, and reticent man, he presided with dignity and success. His speeches were "without much ornament of elocution," yet he had "a strange power of making himself believed."[113] He tried to forward the king's business and the king's interests by working for harmonious relations between the Houses and between the king and his parliament. Thus, in his speeches concerning the Petition of Right, he drew a careful line between liberty and prerogative.[114] In 1628 he is said to have persuaded Charles not to dissolve parliament but to assent to the petition. He opposed the dissolution of parliament in 1629. At the end of his life in 1640, he begged the king to "take all Distasts from the Parliament summoned against April, with patience, and suffer it to set without an unkind dissolution."[115] He died before the Short Parliament met.

Sir John Finch succeeded him and served until his precipitous flight from England in December 1640 to escape impeachment. Finch had had extensive experience in the lower House, where he had served in 1621, 1624, and 1625. In the parliament of 1628 he had been Speaker of the House of Commons, on royal command successfully forbidding an attack on Buckingham and negotiating between the House and the king. In 1629 angry members held him in the chair when he refused to put the question on a remonstrance concerning religion and tunnage and poundage. He protested tearfully that he dare not disobey the king. In 1634 Finch rose from being king's counsel and attorney general to the queen to chief justice of the Court of Common Pleas. He joined the Privy Council in 1639 and in January 1639/40 became lord keeper.[116] On 16 April 1640, just after the opening of the Short Parliament, he was introduced into the House as a baron.[117] A high prerogative man, with a reputation for severe sentences as a judge, Finch was not popular,[118] and when he came to preside in the king's name, neither the sovereign nor his policies commanded respect. Finch served as presiding officer in the brief parliament held in the spring of 1640 and during the opening months of the Long Parliament from 3 November through 21 December 1640, when he fled the country.

He carried out the ceremonial duties of his place in the usual way. The circumstances of the times and the king's diffidence in public speaking forced upon Finch the major responsibility for explaining the state of affairs and the king's policy at the opening of each of the two parliaments in 1640. His speech on 13 April was a straightforward account of the state of the north, with a reference to the generosity of the recent Irish parliament, a request for subsidy, a statement about tunnage and poundage, and a promise concerning petitions and grievances. It was garnished, but not extravagantly, with a few classical and Biblical flourishes. On 3 November, at the opening of the Long Parliament, Finch once more made a major address, relating the progress of negotiations with the Scots, the meeting of the council of nobles, and the request for a loan from the City.[119] As was customary, he had opened with praise of the kingdom and its laws, expatiating also on the particular virtues of the present royal family and the various estates of society represented in parliament. On this occasion, he indulged in an elaborate metaphor of a mirror, but on the whole the speech, as it has come down to us, is basically a clear piece of exposition.[120]

Finch also spoke for the House at several conferences with the Commons, once more demonstrating ability to deliver a lucid expository statement.[121] He served on the committees that prepared for these conferences and that drew up the speeches he was to deliver. He reported back from conferences to the House. On certain occasions, he probably wrote his speech out at length.[122] At other times, he may have spoken from notes or "heads." He brought frequent messages from the king.[123]

There is little evidence that he participated in debate in the House or in committee, although he did speak in a committee of the whole House on 29 April.[124] He raised a question in the House concerning counterfeit protections. On one occasion when the familiar issue of whether the House should sit on convocation days had raised the ire of Lord Saye and Lord Brooke, Finch tried to avoid the difficulty by requesting an adjournment because he himself was indisposed. Early in the session when many lords rose to speak at the same time, he reminded them that the first to rise had the floor, that the orders of the House should be kept, and that each man could speak only once unless it were to explain a motion.[125] In the Long Parliament, such glimpses of Finch as a presiding officer are not available.

Sir Edward Littleton became presiding officer in December 1640, when the king sorely needed a strong man on the woolsack. But Clarendon observed that Littleton did not "appear so useful for his service as he had expected." Although he had been an excellent judge, "his learning in the law being his chief masterpiece," he did not have the qualities needed in the present situation.[126] He had seemed a wise choice. He had had extensive experience in the lower House in the parliaments of 1625, 1626, and 1628. His active participation in the attack on Buckingham in 1626 and in the debates that led up to the Petition of Right in 1628, as well as his defense of a close friend, John Selden, who had been arrested for rebuking the Speaker and trying to prevent the adjournment of parliament in 1629, would recommend him to certain powerful parliamentarians in 1640. As solicitor general, he had argued and won the case against John Hampden for refusal to pay ship money, which recommended him to the crown. Appointed chief justice of the Common Pleas in January 1639/40, he was sworn to the Privy Council in the following month on the advice of the earl of Strafford.[127] On 22 December the king deputed him to replace Finch as presiding officer. The following month he became lord keeper and was created a baron shortly thereafter.[128]

He came to his post at a difficult time. The judges were under attack. His predecessor had been impeached. His friend, Strafford, was in the Tower awaiting trial. The judgment in the ship money case, which Littleton had argued so ably, would soon be reversed in the House of Lords, and the records brought in and ceremoniously marked *vacat*.[129] The tide was running strongly against the king. Littleton fell gravely ill and when he returned to his duties he seemed "dispirited." He "had lost all his vigour, and, instead of making any oppositions to any of their extravagant debates, he had silently suffered all things to be carried."[130]

Littleton's loyalties were not always clear. Caught between king and parliament, he seemed to favor parliament. He displeased the king by refusing to seal the proclamation for the arrest of five members and by voting in favor of the militia ordinance.[131] Later he maintained that he had appeared to oppose the crown only to prevent seizure of the great seal and that he had remained at Westminster in the hope of serving the king's interests.[132]

His illness meant that he had been absent from the House for a long period. Even after his recovery, his attendance had been irregular. Since the House in 1641 had asserted the right to choose its own Speaker,[133] Littleton had been replaced by a variety of people and the crown lost the advantage it had had with Ellesmere, Bacon (until his fall), Williams, Coventry, and even Finch (before his hasty flight). It could no longer rely on an experienced man, constantly in attendance in the upper House, to use his influence to manipulate agenda and his voice as peer to support royal policy. Littleton's deficiencies served to emphasize what his predecessors had done.

As spokesman for the crown and chief law officer of the realm, the lord chancellor or lord keeper had been traditionally a figure of importance. The great seal and the mace symbolized his role in the government and in the upper House. In the parliament of the king, he spoke and acted for the monarch.[134] An examination of the careers of successive presiding officers in the early Stuart period has shown that they could be of signal significance in forwarding the king's business. As men in the king's confidence, active and influential members of the Privy Council, they participated in the preparations for parliament, worked on legislation, drafted proclamations, and consulted about the speeches of the opening day and the choice of a speaker for the lower House.[135] Even in the routine business of issuing writs, an experienced adviser could influence the success of a parliament by considering the delicate matter of timing.

Once parliament was in session, the influence of the presiding officer could be very great. He kept an eye on attendance, reminding the Lords that the king expected them to come to the House regularly.[136] The lord chancellor, together with the clerk, arranged the agenda for each day. Thus the presiding officer was in a position to favor certain bills and matters of business, as members and others were well aware.[137] He presided over debate and attempted to manage it, but was not always successful in doing so.[138] Sometimes he stepped down from the woolsack to participate in debate himself.[139] He frequently spoke when the House was in committee. On occasion he served as chairman of a select committee.[140] He regularly managed conferences for the House, spoke for the House, and reported back to it. He could delay business in a variety of ways[141] or move it forward by reminding the Lords of what should come next. He kept track of bills and committees and thus knew what matters were ready for action.

When well instructed, the lord chancellor or lord keeper was in an excellent position to forward royal policies. When he was not in the king's confidence or when policies were confused or not well articulated, as in 1625 or 1640, the king's business faltered. Clarendon remarked that in the Long Parliament men of several opinions entrusted Littleton with their secrets, evidence of the political importance generally believed to adhere to his office; but because Littleton was divided in his loyalties, he found it difficult to serve the king or those who opposed the king. His illness and frequent absences meant that the crown lacked a strong presiding officer in the upper House at a time when he was most needed.

The king's departure for Scotland, the flight of the lord keeper with the great seal in May 1642, and the outbreak of civil war and subsequent events altered the role of the presiding officer. The Triennial Act (passed on 16 February 1640/41) provided that the lord chancellor must on his own authority issue writs for parliament every three years.[142] He took an oath in the House to do so.[143] During the war, orders of parliament were signed by the Speakers of both Houses and both were to act as commissioners of the great seal and the seal of the duchy of Lancaster.[144] In 1660, when the House was restored, the lord chancellor would once more resume his normal duties. But his role in parliament would be greatly altered by the frequent absences of Lord Clarendon from the House and by the presence of the king, not on his throne as in earlier times, but laughing and joking by the fire, drawing his followers to him and moving about on the floor to influence debate.[145]

3

THE CLERK

In a House where members on ceremonial occasions donned scarlet robes trimmed with ermine or on ordinary days wore the elegant dress of peers or the lawn sleeves of bishops, the clerk cut a modest figure in his black barrister's gown. He sat on a woolsack facing the presiding officer. The clerk of the crown sat beside him and to his right. Before them was a table to write on, behind them knelt one or two assistants.[1] If the presiding officer was at one end of an axis upon which the business of the House revolved, the clerk, inconspicuous though he might be, was at the other. Both were present whenever the House was in session. Both had assisted in preparing agenda; both, each in his own way, brought items to the floor in orderly fashion. The clerk read aloud for members' information, recorded what was done and who was in attendance. Although his principal concern was with the House of Lords, his title, clerk of the parliaments, indicated that he served parliament as a whole.[2] In this capacity, after a session was over, he prepared the parliament roll and safely kept the acts, both public and private.[3]

The House was fortunate in its clerks in the early Stuart period, and each left his stamp upon the office. Thomas Smith, appointed clerk in 1597 and knighted in 1603, served until 1609. He had been public orator at Oxford, clerk of the Privy Council, and a member of the House of Commons. He was Latin secretary to James I and, near the end of his life, master of requests. A later clerk, John Browne, observed that Smith had put the records of the upper House "into that order as they now are, and the same order hath been continued ever since."[4] Smith also expanded the journal of the House. Although Sir Simonds D'Ewes and Smith's successor, Robert Bowyer, found flaws in his work, D'Ewes recognized that Smith was "much more careful in observing and setting down the dayly passages" than earlier clerks had been.[5] Smith's journals speak for themselves and will be analyzed in more detail below. Unfortunately he has left few other records of his work. He was gently born, a man of education, experienced in government service; his abilities were recognized and rewarded. He gained the position of clerk in the face of strong pressure from Lord Buckhurst for the appointment of Robert Bowyer, who secured the reversion of the post.

Bowyer assumed office in 1609.[6] He too was gently born and a graduate of Oxford. He had attended the Middle Temple and had been admitted to the bar. In the years 1599–1608, he served as secretary to the lord treasurer, Lord Buckhurst, later earl of Dorset. In 1604 he was appointed keeper of the records in the Tower jointly with Henry Elsyng, a post they relinquished in 1612. He was a member of Elizabeth's last parliament and was elected for Evesham in 1605.[7] Bowyer was a natural record keeper. As a member of the House of Commons, he kept a valuable diary, particularly noting points of procedure. He served on the committee of the lower House that supervised the preparation of its journal. As clerk, he wrote "scribbled books" while the House of Lords was in session—full, running accounts of proceedings later used for preparing the journal and for other purposes. Those that have survived are of inestimable value to the historian. Although he considered much of this material unsuitable for the journal, he used it in studies of procedure and in the preparation of reports on special topics. The journal he prepared for the upper House in his years as clerk reflected both the knowledge of parliament that he had gained from the records in the Tower and his years of experience as a member of the House of Commons. Bowyer also worked to build and preserve the archive of parliament, filing the papers that came across his desk and trying to gather in bills from the hands of committee chairmen. With the preservation of these papers, a fuller picture of the activities of the clerk begins to emerge.[8]

Henry Elsyng, who became clerk in 1621, was Bowyer's friend and nephew by marriage. Elsyng was a Cambridge man and like Bowyer a member of the Middle Temple. Although never a member of parliament, he had long worked with its records in the Tower and had attended the House as assistant to Bowyer since 1610. He made a signal contribution to the preservation of the archive of parliament by acquiring the Jewel Tower of Old Westminster Palace as a safe repository. Thus the Main Papers ceased to be part of the personal estate of the clerk and came into public custody. Elsyng's memoranda and endorsements on the mass of papers filed and preserved present a vivid picture of the duties of the clerk. His "scribbled books," draft journals, and final journal show his efforts to perfect the record of the House, a record he further expanded by an imaginative development of the rolls of parliament.[9]

Thomas Knyvett, nephew of Bowyer and half brother of Elsyng, an Oxford man and also a member of the Middle Temple, probably succeeded to the clerkship in 1635 and held office until his death in 1637. Since parliament was not in session during this period, his career is of little importance in a study of the office. It does, however, serve to underline the strong family connections that bound clerks and assistant clerks together, a tradition that would continue into the eighteenth century. Daniel Bedingfield became clerk in December 1637 but died the following February. In 1638 John Browne succeeded to the office. He was clerk when the House of Lords was abolished in 1649 and resumed the post when it was restored in 1660. He served until 1691, though in later years he was not always in attendance on the House.[10]

John Browne came from a merchant family in London. When his father died, his uncle, a member of the Merchant Taylors Company, adopted him and ultimately left him a large sum of money. This made it possible among other things for Browne to read law. Although not a record keeper by training or perhaps by inclination as Bowyer and Elsyng had been, he shared their connection with the Middle Temple and probably knew both families. Browne had no experience with parliament. He was a man of substance who owned considerable property in Northamptonshire and maintained a large house in Twickenham. In 1650 and 1655 when he was out of office, the Council of State provided employment for him as a commissioner and as an envoy abroad.[11] Clearly he had ability and influence.

The years of the Long Parliament were demanding years for the clerk. The House was constantly in session. The business of the House, which had already grown in the period 1621–29 by the expansion of its judicial affairs, now embraced also the administrative functions of government and the problems of waging a war. The responsibilities of the clerk multiplied. Browne managed a busy parliament office in the Jewel Tower and kept in custody there an ever increasing body of parliamentary papers. Unfortunately he failed to meet modern archival standards in two respects. He loaned to Dr. John Nalson a group of official records that were never returned; he also had at his home in Northamptonshire other original papers, draft journals, and records at the time of his death. These, instead of reverting to the House, descended to his daughter as part of his estate and became dispersed. Elsyng's precautions had saved much, but the concept of the proper care and custody of public records had not yet fully developed.[12] The journal that Browne wrote for the House, as will be seen, reflected his personality, experience, and interests as well as the changes of the time. His parliament roll reverted to its earlier form of a statute roll.

The clerk was appointed by the crown by letters patent. When he assumed office, he took an oath to be faithful to the king, to "well and truly serve His Highness in the Office of Clerke of his Parliaments, making true Entries and Records of the Things done, and past in the same." He swore to "keep secret all such Matters as shall be treated in his said Parliaments" and to "do and execute all Things . . . appertaining to the Office of the Clerk."[13] Robert Bowyer took the oath together with the oath of supremacy at York House where Ellesmere, then lord chancellor, resided. Henry Elsyng arranged to be sworn in the House itself and entered the words of the oath in the journal.[14] This public ceremony may have been part of an effort by the Lords to control the office or it may well have been Elsyng's own scheme and a natural plan when parliament was in session.

This chapter will consider first the activities of the clerk on the floor of the House, then the general work of his office and his responsibilities for the papers of the House, and last his duties as record keeper. Each morning before the House convened, the clerk met the presiding officer to arrange the business for the day. He suggested which bills could be read, which committees were ready to report, what other business might be introduced or which witnesses were scheduled to appear.[15] In 1621 Bowyer seems to have overstepped himself and actually called for the reading of five private bills on the floor. Possibly he was trying to carry out the usual formality of reading a bill on the first day of business.[16] When the House was sitting, the clerk, with very few exceptions, was present. John Browne, as he grew older, came less frequently; and in the eighteenth century, the clerk regularly performed his duties by deputy. But in the early seventeenth century, the clerk was faithful in attendance.[17]

One of his duties in the House was to read aloud. This required special skill. The Lords were critical of one who did not read *ut clericus* and Bowyer's appointment as clerk may have been delayed because he had a slight speech defect.[18] If parliament was not held on the day appointed in the writ of summons, the clerk read the king's patent of prorogation. On the first day of parliament (that is the day on which the king or commissioners for him appeared), he read the names of the receivers and triers of petitions in French.[19] Usually on the third day of parliament, he called the House by reading the name of each member, beginning with the puisne lord and ending with the prince.[20] Each rose as his name was called. After 1621, when the Standing Orders were first established, the clerk read the roll.[21] As the Lords appointed committees, he jotted down the names called and then read aloud the list chosen from each bench. He read each bill as it came before the House, standing at his table, then delivering the bill to the presiding officer. When a committee reported a bill, the clerk read any amendments or other changes.[22] He also read such other documents as the House needed for its information. He administered the oath when witnesses were sworn in the House.[23] He read the oaths of supremacy and allegiance required for certain private bills.[24] At the close of a parliament, when the clerk of the crown read the titles of bills, the clerk of the parliaments pronounced the king's replies.[25]

Reading was an arduous task and could be physically exhausting even in an age when men were more used to standing than they are today. In 1641 the reading of the subsidy consumed three hours. The reading of other documents, such as the charges in impeachment proceedings, might take even longer.[26] Neither Bowyer nor Elsyng delegated the responsibility for reading. Elsyng's treatise, "The Moderne Forme of the Parliaments," clearly describes reading as the clerk's function. In 1624 Elsyng read the list of lords to call the House. In 1628 he "reade all and soe coulde wryte no more." Possibly John Browne used an assistant for some of this work. His notes of excuses offered for lords during a call of the House suggest that he was sitting at the table when the names were read.[27]

Behind these activities on the floor lay careful preparatory work, which was carried out by the clerk or by assistants under his direction in the Jewel Tower or elsewhere in the Old Palace. He was responsible for ordering and receiving supplies—paper, parchment, ink, needles and bodkins, sand, and reference books.[28] He maintained a roll of members that was compiled from a list of those summoned and was kept up to date as creations occurred, as bishops were appointed or translated from see to see, as peerages passed by descent. Lords delivered their writs to him as they entered, and new peers, after 1621, their patents of creation as well.[29] The clerk or his assistant also had to register lords' proxies as they came in during a session and to keep his list current.[30] He was concerned with bills at every stage. His lists and "books of bills" enabled him to advise the presiding officer on agenda. From the books of committees, with members' names and the place and time of meeting, he knew when to expect a report.[31] He gave lists of members to committee chairmen. The clerk arranged to deliver the bill itself for the committee's use, making a note so that he could retrieve it.[32] He saw that bills were engrossed. After a third reading, he inscribed the proper phrases of transmittal on them and sent bills that had originated in the House of Lords to the lower House. Later he took successful bills to the king and made a note of the monarch's wishes. At the close of a session, when the clerk had read the royal replies, he entered each at the head of the act. He kept a calendar of acts. Public acts he sent to the printer and then had them copied on the parliament roll.[33] Bills that had failed or were incomplete he filed with other papers of parliament.[34]

The clerk assisted the presiding officer in carrying out the decisions of the House and became involved in drafting a variety of orders and war-rants.[35] He summoned parties to a dispute and called witnesses. He is-sued warrants in cases of privilege and orders for delinquents to appear at the bar. He called in documents and in 1640 had a warrant from the House to search the office of the Court of High Commission himself for its books of orders.[36] He supplied copies of examinations and deposi-tions to defendants and arranged for copies of documents required or requested by other persons.[37]

Hearings on bills, the investigations of committees, the judicial activi-ties of the House—all generated statements, certificates, depositions, pe-titions, and legal records that crossed the clerk's desk.[38] He held a trunk of records brought in connection with the case of *Withypoole* v. *Dever-eux* and money deposited as security for payments to be made on order of the House.[39] He had a "rich cabinet" offered as evidence. He also had to keep and file messages from the king and documents transmitted from the lower House. For all this mass of material, as well as the journals and other records of proceedings, the House held the clerk respon-sible.[40] He must keep them safe and at the same time accessible. He must be able to produce the papers the House required, check his records to verify its decisions, and on short notice provide precedents from earlier parliaments.[41]

In 1621, at the suggestion of the clerk, the House had taken over for its use the Jewel Tower in Old Palace Yard. Up a flight of stairs, an inner room, made safe from fire by a brick vault and secured by a heavy iron door, provided good storage space. The royal initials on the door empha-sized that records and papers were in public custody.[42] It was to this office that Sir Simonds D'Ewes repaired in 1629 to copy the journals of the Elizabethan House.[43] Here also the clerk stored the acts of parlia-ment, public and private; the subsidy acts were placed in special trunks. Occasionally we catch glimpses of his filing system and his difficulties. He numbered acts. He assigned numbers to petitions and also arranged them alphabetically. He docketed papers as they came to the House, noting the date and the action taken. In 1621, when impeachment pro-ceedings against Michell brought a flood of material, he asked for help in sorting depositions.[44]

A major responsibility of the clerk was to record the proceedings in the House and to prepare an account of the decisions of parliament in the parliament roll. As we have seen, he was bound by oath to make "true Entries and Records of the Things done." John Pym referred to him as "Clarke of Register," a term usually applied to the clerk of a court and thus reflecting the concept of the high court of parliament as well as the judicial capacity of the upper House.[45] The clerk's record was the official

record of the king's parliament as well as the upper House of that parliament. Both the journal and the roll of parliament changed and developed during the early Stuart period. Different clerks worked in different
ways and their concept of a record varied. The expectations of the House
also changed and the nature of the proceedings in parliament modified
the record that was made of them.

We know very little about the way Sir Thomas Smith prepared the
journal. The principal evidence is the journal itself. Fortunately two additional sheets, originally pinned to it, have survived to indicate how Smith
may have taken notes in the House. One sheet recorded the words of
apology spoken on 5 June 1604 by the bishop of Bristol. The other sheet
contained an account of Viscount Montagu's speech inveighing against
the established church on 25 June in the same year, as well as a report of
the lord chancellor's reproof and the Lords' debate on how to proceed.[46]
Robert Bowyer's comments are interesting. Bristol's acknowledgment, he
observed, "so pinned to the proceedings of this day in the Journall booke,
yt seemeth Sir Tho. Smith . . . did for some private respect, or direction
forbeare to enter into the booke purposinge upon exception taken to
such negligence, to excuse his slackenes by pretence of presente busines,
the rather for that under the briefe note which he had entered is lefte
space at more leisure to adde or wright the other." In the same way,
concerning Montagu's speech, Smith "for some private cause, or negli-
geance forebore to enter havinge fastened it . . . to the booke."[47] Whether
Bowyer's interpretation is correct or not, Smith made notes of proceedings on loose sheets of paper at his table in the House, perhaps occasionally, perhaps as a regular custom. From these he later drew up the
account he entered in the journal. At two points he was uncertain how
much to include in his narrative and the unfinished account gives a brief
glimpse of the way he worked.

In composing the journal, Smith shaped his material to the constraints
of an older form.[48] To the left of the page, he listed the lords present, in
two columns. To the right of the page, he wrote a brief account of proceedings, including the titles and readings of bills. At the bottom of the
page, he noted the adjournment and the continuation of the House to the
next day of meeting. When there was insufficient space for his narrative,
the account of proceedings spilled over into the left-hand side of the
page, below the "presents" or continued on the back of the sheet. "Sir
Thomas Smyth . . . did allwayes sett downe the continuance of the Court
or Parlament in the bottome of the first page or side wherein the proceedings of that day began," Bowyer observed, "and yf the whole busi-
nesse, and matters of that day coulde not be entered or wrighten upon
that same page, then did he wright the rest or residewe on the page fol-

lowinge: Perhaps yt had been more fit to have entered the Continuance of the Court last though on the second page."[49] By 1606 Smith frequently but not invariably did so, subsequently reverting to his former practice.[50] Possibly an assistant first entered the "presents," the reading of bills, the names of committees, and the adjournment and continuation, and Smith later added such narrative of proceedings as he thought suitable in the space available.[51] His account of 9 November 1605 was incomplete and included only part of the king's speech and no other proceedings, "but tenne leaves and one side of cleane paper lefte to enter (as it seemeth) at more leisure what for the present the said Clerke could not entende to finish."[52] Only the "one side of cleane paper" now remains. Probably the "tenne leaves" were omitted when the manuscript journals were bound.[53] Bowyer complained that on this same day Smith omitted the continuance of the House, but this was in fact entered.[54]

Smith seems to have put his journal together after a day's sitting was over. Although Lord Burghley had moved in 1597 that a committee of lords should check the journal,[55] there is no record that such a committee was appointed and no indication that the House supervised Smith's work or helped him to resolve his perplexities as to what he should include. Burghley's concern had been for the "presents" and for the "true Record" of the order of placing the lords in the House. The same interest, shared by the Lords, doubtless prompted the full entry of the Neville-Bergavenny decision in 1604.[56] To a closer supervision of the narrative of proceedings and the entry of orders, the House would turn later in 1621. In addition to a journal, Sir Thomas Smith also prepared parliament rolls that registered the text of public acts and the titles of private acts, essentially statute rolls following the pattern established in the reign of Henry VIII.[57] The roll was prepared and certified into Chancery after parliament was over. A member in 1593 complained that the clerk delayed in order that men would have to come to him and pay his fees for copies of bills.[58]

When Robert Bowyer became clerk, the way in which he carried out his work as record keeper appears more clearly than it does with Smith. During a sitting, Bowyer kept full notes of proceedings and he believed that other clerks had done so. In his collections of earlier journals, he wrote: "The Clerke of the Parliament, doth every day (sitting in the House or Court) write into his rough and scribled Booke not onely the reading of Bills and other proceedings of the House, but as farr forth as he cann, whatsoever is spoken worthy of observation."[59] Bowyer was a student of parliament and parliamentary procedure. In the lower House, as we have seen, he had kept an elaborate diary. In the upper he recorded as much as he could while the House was sitting. His notes were for his own instruction and went far beyond what he needed or thought he needed for the journal. In preparing the journal, he used his "scribbled books," some notes also taken in the House by Elsyng, who was his assistant, and drafts of reports and speeches, as well as bills, petitions, and other papers that came across his desk as clerk. He wrote a clear account of the decisions of the House, but excluded much that he considered "unfit"—particularly debate.[60] "Into the Journal book which is the record he [the clerk] doth in discretion forbear to enter many things spoken, though memorable, yet not necessary nor fit to be registered and left to posterity to record." He recorded when the House met, who presided, what lords were present, the business transacted, the adjournment of the House, and the day and time set for the next meeting. He did not record motions that failed nor did he register votes.[61] He recorded the decisions the House had made, not the process by which it had come to those decisions. His picture was not of a House divided but of a House united. In working over earlier journals, he read with a critical eye, noting omissions, errors in nomenclature, and mistakes in the listing of the reading of bills. He observed that one of his predecessors had failed to check the work of his assistant.[62] We may assume that Bowyer did not make the same mistake. His account was coherent and complete. His journal reflected painstaking care and his respect for the House that he served.

The parliament roll prepared under his direction followed the form used by Sir Thomas Smith and included the text of public acts and a list of private acts. The clerk might, Bowyer wrote, copy the public acts himself from the book of acts issued by the king's printer at the end of a session, or assign the job to an assistant; but he usually turned to one of the underclerks of the Petty Bag ("because they write the Chancery hand best") and paid him to do the job. The clerk of the parliaments then checked the copy back against the original acts, subscribed the roll, and transmitted it to Chancery.[63] Bowyer's parliament roll for 1610 included the general pardon, as requested by the attorney general, and the subsidies of the temporalty and of the clergy, as commanded by the lord chancellor. This departure from earlier custom was not Bowyer's idea nor did it wholly meet with his approval.[64]

Robert Bowyer trained Henry Elsyng, who shared his interest in parliament and procedure. Like Bowyer, Elsyng made running notes or "scribbled books" in the House, both for his own information and for assistance in preparing the journal. More of Elsyng's preliminary work for the journal has survived than was the case with Bowyer, together with many queries and notes that reveal his uncertainties as he prepared early drafts. In 1621, for the first time the Lords appointed a committee—thereafter a subcommittee of the Committee for Privileges—to supervise the journal. Thus the "scribbled books," formerly a private exercise of the clerk, came to have official status; after Elsyng took office in March, they were regularly checked week by week by the lords themselves.[65] Elsyng's "scribbled books" differ from Bowyer's and record less detail. As the years went on and he became surer of what he needed for his journal, his notes became sketchy and he probably relied more heavily on notes taken in the House by his assistants.

The second stage in preparing the journal, the writing of a draft journal, was entirely Elsyng's work. As Bowyer had done, he used his own notes, the notes of assistants, and reports, texts of speeches, orders, and petitions. It was not easy to assemble what he needed. Marginal jottings indicate his efforts to do so. Although he began his draft promptly ("I must make up my journal book every day," he wrote), sections of the account for 1624 were not completed until May 1625. Often he made several drafts of particularly difficult or novel proceedings before he and the Lords' committee were satisfied. Like Bowyer, he omitted votes in the House, the details of debate, the story of an altercation. The final stage of Elsyng's work was the "fair, written book" copied by an assistant from the corrected draft and engrossed in parchment at the Lords' order. Elsyng checked some of the copy himself, his deputy clerk the rest. As the years went on and Elsyng and his assistants became more experienced, the three stages of his journal became less distinct. The "scribbled books" were less detailed and Elsyng fell back on the archive of parliament to supply what he needed. In 1628 he merely indicated in his draft where his assistant should enter these items; the entries were actually made only in the "fair written copy."[66]

Elsyng's journal reflected his training and his own high standards of workmanship. It also reflected the Lords' own concept of an appropriate record. Their committee read the "scribbled books" and checked the draft journals. It suggested corrections and deletions. The final product was a journal that the Lords themselves had designed, with the assistance of an able clerk.

The parliament rolls were Henry Elsyng's most original creation and an important addition to the record of the parliaments for which he worked. In preparing the rolls, he followed the form established by his predecessors. He registered the public acts in full (including the general pardon and the subsidies of the temporalty and of the clergy) and listed private acts.[67] But he went farther and prepared additional rolls that related the extraordinary proceedings of the years in which he served—the impeachments of Sir Giles Mompesson, Sir Francis Michell, and Lord Chancellor Bacon; the complaints against the bishop of Llandaff and the attack on Edward Floyd in 1621; the narration of the Spanish marriage negotiations and the impeachment of Lord Treasurer Cranfield in 1624; the text of the petition of religion in 1625 with the king's answers; the impeachment of the duke of Buckingham in 1626; the text of the Petition of Right in 1628 and the royal reply. In composing these rolls, Elsyng returned to the form of the medieval rolls that he had known as keeper of the records in the Tower, especially the rolls made in the reign of Edward III, whom he greatly admired.[68] He found there a narrative form suitable for the events he wished to describe. To this he added details of procedure that reflected his own interests and those of the Lords. He may also have found precedents from more recent times. The clerk who recorded parliament's proceedings concerning Mary, queen of Scots, in 1586 had prepared a roll that included the speeches at the opening of parliament, the address of the lord chancellor on 5 November announcing the sentence passed against her, the Lords' proceedings, the proceedings of the Commons, the preparation of a petition from both Houses to Queen Elizabeth, its presentation, and Elizabeth's several replies. The roll concluded with the Commons' requests that the petition and "theire whole actes and proceadinges in this present Session of parliament touching the saide greate cause might be entred of recorde in the Rolles of the same parliament," to which the Lords agreed. The lord chancellor promised that certain lords would beg the queen to accede.[69] It is uncertain whether this roll, now at Hatfield House, was ever deposited in the Rolls Chapel. However, Elsyng could have known of it through the copy in the library of Sir Robert Cotton.[70]

John Browne, who became clerk in 1638, was new to parliament. He had had no experience on the floor of the House, no training as a record keeper or archivist. When he first sat at the clerk's table during the Short Parliament of 1640, he kept or tried to keep the full "scribbled books" characteristic of Bowyer and Elsyng. What he managed was rather garbled and reflected both his own inexperience and the confusing complexities of the session itself. He wrote a draft journal according to Elsyng's early pattern, which the Lords' committee examined at intervals.[71] From this the "fair written book" engrossed on parchment was drawn up under his direction.[72] Since no acts passed, he prepared no parliament roll.

With the Long Parliament, the record gradually changed. Browne continued to take notes, usually rather brief notes, in the House, in books or on single sheets.[73] He wrote his draft journal as rapidly as Elsyng had done in later years, indicating in the margin where an assistant should enter the text of documents. Sometimes these entries have been made as directed. Sometimes they have been grouped together at the end of a day's proceedings, sometimes merely laid in. The subcommittee for the journal checked Browne's work from November 1640 through June 1641 and for some months in 1646, 1647, and 1648. In several significant ways, Browne's draft journal differed from those that had gone before. His lack of historical or clerical training cropped up in entries made partially in English, partially in Latin. He was less interested in the procedure of the House than Bowyer and Elsyng had been. Generally he continued the convention of omitting the record of a vote, although some appear or he noted a majority vote. But his draft did not, as earlier journals had done, reflect a House united. This convention the Lords broke themselves. After 1642 they insisted on a record of those who dissented or protested against the vote on certain measures brought before them. Another innovation, beginning in September 1643, was the fact that Browne began to include in his draft a list of lords present. Earlier clerks had included the "presents" only in their final version. Browne gave not the customary full list of lords summoned, marked "p" for those in attendance on a given day, but a shorter list of lords actually in the House.

Probably in the first years of the Long Parliament, Browne assumed that he would perfect his draft as had been done before. Later he may well have abandoned the idea. Perhaps the inclusion of attendance in his draft is a clue that Browne came to realize that there might never be another version. No fair engrossed copy of Browne's journal for the Long Parliament has survived and it is doubtful if it was made. What we now have in print is not a finished composition but Browne's draft journal, hastily composed from notes in the House, often incomplete, with his directions to his assistant as to what further should be done and his numbers reordering committees by precedence. The "great parliament book" engrossed in parchment of Bowyer's and Elsyng's days was a casualty of the times.[74]

Browne prepared a parliament roll in three parts, which resumed the earlier form of the statute roll used by Smith and Bowyer. It registered public acts passed in 16, 17, and 18 *Car.* I. Browne abandoned Elsyng's narrative form, although it might well have been suitable for the judicial proceedings against Strafford, Laud, and others. This form would reappear in an account of the trial of Charles I, which was engrossed and certified into Chancery in 1651.[75]

THE CLERK'S REWARDS

The clerk drew a salary of £40 per annum from the crown, and by 1641 and probably earlier he had the use of a house in Old Palace Yard.[76] He also received other payments. In 1604 Smith was paid for attending the commissioners for the union.[77] In 1605 he received £40 for preparing and certifying the parliament roll into Chancery, a sum that may correspond to the £40 rather grudgingly paid to Robert Bowyer in 1610. "I allow this," the lord treasurer wrote at that time, "because he hath taken extraordinary pain, but I see no precedent these 40ti years of any and therefore until I see it and what the next session will prove I can allow no more." At the end of a session, the clerk took his desk as perquisite (or its equivalent in coin) and also perhaps the books ordered for the parliament office.[78]

A substantial portion of the clerk's income came not from the crown or the perquisites of office but from members of the upper House. In 1626 the lords made a collection for the clerk at the end of the session, "for his paynes in this and former Parlements." If all paid up, he would have received well over £150. The resolution was repeated in 1628. The difficulty was the collection of what was due. In 1628, doubtless at Elsyng's suggestion, the House ordered that those who had not paid in 1626 should do so.[79] Each of the lords who first entered the House paid a fee to the clerk. Lords who rose in rank and bishops translated from see to see were also liable.[80] Since a duke paid £10, an archbishop or a marquess £6 13s.4d., an earl £4 10s., the bishops of London, Winchester, and Durham £3 6s.8d., and other bishops and the barons £2 10s. apiece, the clerk realized a considerable amount.[81] The fees for registering proxies varied. The clerk received 30s. for registering each proxy in 1597, 20s. in 1610, and 30s. in 1640, but on the whole, over the years, his fees changed remarkably little.[82]

The amount the clerk received from the lords also included the fees paid by members of the House in forwarding their private parliamentary business. In a pattern familiar in other courts and offices in Elizabethan and Stuart England, much of the clerk's income came from those who transacted business in parliament. For public business, he received no fee; but for each private bill, he received £5 at or before the first reading, 2s.4d. for preparing the committee sheet, and £2 for a proviso before it was read.[83] Certification of a private bill brought in £1 6s.8d. for the first sheet, 13s.4d. for subsequent sheets. The total sum might run to £8 or £9.[84] The clerk charged £1 for reading a private petition reported from committee or a judgment on it.[85] For copying an order, he collected 10s. if it were not long, 5s. a sheet for each additional sheet.[86] He charged a delinquent when he was released by the House £3 6s.8d. To search a record for a private individual, the clerk received 2s.6d., to supply copies 1s. a sheet, to sign or authenticate a copy 2s. When a case came to the House on writ of error from King's Bench, the charges were similar to those for a private bill. The clerk received £5 for comparing the transcript with the original record, the first step in the procedure, and other fees for each subsequent step in the case: 10s. for issuing an order for a writ of *scire facias*, 10s. for the return of the writ, 10s. for a short order, 5s. for each additional sheet, and 1s. a sheet for a copy of the record.[87]

Probably the clerk gathered in more than these schedules indicated. In June 1610 Mr. Justice Walmsley wrote to Bowyer asking his help in forwarding a bill. If, Walmsley wrote, Bowyer would show those who followed it what "lawful favor" he could, "that wch I told you should be paid shall be paid if the bill take effect."[88] Similarly the earl of Bath wrote to Bowyer concerning a bill in which he was interested. He asked Bowyer to give his agent a copy of the bill, a copy of the committee sheet, and a note concerning the Lords' proceedings, "for wch this bearer shall content you and I will thank you."[89] In 1641 the attorney for the queen testified that the clerk should have no fee for a private bill concerning the queen's jointure, but a gratuity "in the end."[90] The earl of Leicester wrote his London agent from Paris in 1640 asking him to obtain a weekly journal of proceedings in each House from the respective clerks. "You may assure them you will recompense them very well for theyr paines and kindeness."[91] In October 1644 Richard Culmer, who had entered a petition for presentation to a living, wrote a note to John Browne asking him to speed the order, which would be to his advantage;[92] and in 1647/8 a note, probably addressed to the clerk in a similar case, urged him to "get these two presentations moved this morning if you find opportunity and I will wait upon you in the afternoon."[93] The clerk was in a position to dispense favors and consequently to receive rewards.

THE CLERK'S ASSISTANTS

The clerk appointed his own assistants. Owen Reynolds worked for Sir Thomas Smith. A brief but jaundiced glimpse of Reynolds's situation comes from a letter in which his brother urged him to better himself. Reynolds was, his brother asserted, "in perpetual servitude." He had no "certain provision" for his life, nor could any be hoped for "when your Master is all for himself, and maketh his servant but as a post horse to serve his present terms." In return for "infinite labours," Reynolds had only the "bare fees" of his place "and those sometimes pared and curted to the uttermost."[94] Nothing came of these exhortations. Possibly Reynolds was satisfied with his position, and the fees were not as poor as his brother believed them to be. In 1610 Reynolds made an agreement with the new clerk, Robert Bowyer, to continue as "underclerk" and clerk's deputy for £10 per annum and one-third "of all such money as shall be received for all such copies" he should make. "For engrossing private acts, transcripting of them into chancery, writing of proxies and orders of the house" and the like, Reynolds was to "receive such due fees" as Smith had allowed him.[95] There is no indication that Reynolds took notes in the House. His agreement with Bowyer suggests that his work was in the office rather than on the floor and that he was chiefly engaged in copying and in the preparation of routine papers and orders. Together with Bowyer, he signed the list of acts for 1610 in the "long Calendar."[96] When he died in April 1610, Henry Elsyng, although not formally appointed until later, seems to have taken his place. Unlike Reynolds, Elsyng assisted Bowyer in the chamber. He was in the House in June 1610 and took notes of the king's speech in 1614.[97] He was officially admitted by the House as deputy clerk in March 1620/1 when Bowyer became too ill to carry out his duties. It is interesting that in this instance the House itself confirmed an appointment that usually was arranged privately by the clerk. Although this departure from previous practice may be explained by the fact that Elsyng, as deputy, must immediately function in the chamber as clerk, it may also have wider significance. Not long after, the Lords devised an oath for assistant clerks, whether in the House or in the office, which provides additional evidence of the growing interest of the House in its clerical staff.[98]

When Elsyng became clerk at the end of March 1620/1, John Throckmorton probably stepped into his place as "clerk's man" and deputy.[99] His figure would long be familiar at Westminster.[100] He served for many years and saw the abolition and restoration of the House. Persons who did business with the House were accustomed to address requests to him,[101] and when Browne, the clerk, was away in 1646, Throckmorton took on his duties.[102]

Although Elsyng and Browne both relied on several assistants, and two benefited by collections made in the House in 1626 and 1628, only the "clerk's man" appears on the fee rolls. We know that Reynolds, by private agreement with the clerk, received fees for engrossing, copying, and writing out proxies and orders, as well as one-third of the money the clerk himself received for copies.[103] By 1621 the clerk's man had chalked out a list of fees that corresponded to those of the clerk. He collected or tried to collect 5s. from each "nobleman as for entering his writ," 3s.4d. for every proxy, 5s. from "every Nobleman that hath sat in the House formerly and made no proxies." He claimed fees for private business in the House, 10s. "upon entring of every private bill as for breviating it," 3s. for every committee, and 2s. for entering a petition.

Fees for engrossing came to 3s.4d. for each skin; fees for copying, 3d. per sheet. He received 2s.6d. for an order if it were not long, 5s. at the release of a delinquent. Throckmorton noted that he had been paid on this scale in 1624 "though since I am informed I wronged myself much thereby." He wrote up a new scale of fees that tied the fees of the clerk's man to those of the yeoman usher—to be paid at the entrance of a lord, for proxies, and for the release of delinquents. The sums were not given. For a committee, the fee was not 3s. but 1s. (the clerk himself to have 2s.6d. apiece), for engrossing 10s. per skin, for copying 1s. per sheet.[104]

By 1640 the fees of the clerk's man were spelled out in even greater detail and corresponded item by item with those of the clerk, though in each instance they were less. He claimed fees graduated by rank at the entrance of each lord: £1 5s. for an archbishop or a marquess, £1 10s. for a duke, £1 for an earl and a viscount, 13s.4d. for the bishops of London, Winchester, and Durham, 10s. for other bishops and for barons. The fee for a private bill was now £2, for a proviso 10s., for "making up the committee fixed to a private bill, attending at the commitment and reading the same there" 10s. The fee for entering a writ of error was £2, the same as for a private bill; each order upon the writ or upon a petition cost 2s.6d., an order upon a judgment 10s. Fees for engrossing increased to 13s.4d. for the first skin, 10s. for additional skins (engrossing of public bills he did "at his owne charge"). The fee for a search in the office was 1s.[105] The office of the clerk's man had developed greatly since the days of Owen Reynolds and probably became consolidated in Throckmorton's long term of office. He claimed a wide range of fees, which were listed in detail and confirmed in 1640 by the Lords themselves.[106] Although the fees of the clerk did not change greatly from 1610 to 1640, those of the clerk's man markedly increased in almost every category. He had established himself as an officer of parliament.

Like the clerk, he received some of his income from members of the House: at their first entrance, from the registration of proxies, and from those lords who had private business in the House. Collections made in 1626 and 1628 included 5s. apiece for each of the clerk's two men.[107] The rest of the assistant clerk's income came from the fees for private business and from the extensive demand for copies.[108] He probably did well when parliament was in session, but even then would need other means to maintain himself. John Throckmorton held a position in the customs house, which he had filled in person before the constant sitting of the Long Parliament forced him to provide a deputy. Probably others made similar arrangements.[109]

Some of the duties of the "clerk's man" are suggested by the fee rolls. It would be a mistake, however, to take them too literally. He did not himself necessarily perform all the duties for which he collected a fee, but he was probably responsible for them. The assistant, like the clerk, was concerned with members of the House and with their business. He received and entered the writs of summons. He registered proxies.[110] He was deep in the paper work of the House: he prepared or supervised the preparation of breviates and of committee sheets. He attended a committee to read the charge and the bill. He copied or arranged for the copying of orders, judgments, and other material the House required. By 1621 he assisted the clerk in the House as well as in the parliament office, a fact that was recognized by the Lords in drafting his oath.[111] Elsyng wrote that "the clerke of the Parliament hath one or two Clerks who kneele behind the Woolsack."[112] From 1621 on, an assistant clerk regularly kept minutes in the House and had a particular responsibility to record attendance[113] and list committees.[114] There is some slight evidence that during the Long Parliament he assisted the clerk, John Browne, in reading aloud, a duty that Bowyer and Elsyng did not delegate.[115]

It would be misleading to look for any further differentiation of the assistant's duties. We can only say that in the House itself he took notes and possibly did some reading. Doubtless he also supplied any papers the clerk might require and assisted him when he was ordered to produce a record or search a precedent. He collected fees due the clerk and the gentleman usher.[116] In the office, he did what was necessary to prepare business for the House, carry out its directives, answer inquiries, search the record, and supply the heavy demand for copies of all kinds. An assistant like Throckmorton who remained long in the position was a trusted experienced man who could serve as the clerk's alter ego and deputy.

Only one assistant appeared on the fee rolls, although two benefited by the Lords' collections in 1626 and 1628 and two are pictured kneeling behind the clerk's woolsack. Elsyng referred to several assistants, including his son, and others, notably Thomas Ken, appear in Browne's regime.[117] In 1626 Will Harrison and in 1641 one Smith served as clerks for the Committee for Petitions and presumably received some regular income.[118] Others indiscriminately called "clerks" may have subsisted or partially subsisted on piece work. Henry Morris in 1641 was doing copying for Smith and submitted an itemized account of orders, petitions, and other writings.[119] In 1645 he was termed "underclerk to the Clerk of Parliament." By 1646 he was called "a Clerk belonging to the House of Peers." He was to have his house rent free and was declared "a diligent, painful and deserving Man, whose long Pains, in his way of Clerkship, hath been very serviceable to the State." The House urged the Committee of the Revenue to look out for him "for his better Subsistence in the future."[120]

An altercation between John Throckmorton and Sir Richard Wiseman gives a brief glimpse of assistants in the office in the Jewel Tower. Wiseman followed Throckmorton "up the stairs in the clerk of Parliament's office" and Throckmorton made a search "in the inner office where the records remain."[121] An affidavit made in 1650 lifts the curtain a bit more. One Morris, alias Poyntz, who was said to have forged an act of parliament, brought forward the testimony of Thomas Elslyott in defense. "Hee happened . . . ," Elslyott said, "to be present with some of Mr. Brownes Clerks above in the Tower where the Records of Parliament were transcribed when Mr. Browne came in and asked wch of them had made a Coppie of the said Acte and given [it] to Mr. Morris to use . . . who answered that they came for itt, as other folkes did for Coppies of their busines, and that they had made itt and examined it with the Record as they did other things, and gave it to his man, Mr. Farmer [Browne's servant] to get it signed by himselfe, and with his owne hand, which hee accordingly did, and therefore they were not to be blamed." Nevertheless, Browne rebuked them, called for the record, and went off with it down the stairs in great displeasure. Poyntz was said to have paid 12d. a sheet for the copy.[122]

CONCLUSION

The clerk of the parliaments with his various assistants had many masters. Like the presiding officer, he was at once a servant of the crown and a servant of the House—roles that were not incompatible in the king's parliament. He also served individual lords in the House. As clerk, he kept the records of parliament, forwarded the business of the House, and maintained its archives. Continuing in office from session to session, he drew on a fund of parliamentary experience. He was consulted on points of procedure and provided precedents for the House and its committees. His greatest power lay in his ability to advance or retard measures by his influence on the preparation of daily agenda. He could move business along for individuals who sought his favor and equally could delay action for those who asked him to do that. Although technically proceedings were secret, he might discreetly release information. In 1628 the "ancient" at Banbury who had called Lord Saye a "puritan dog" "came early one Morning to the Clerk's Office" to discover the charge against him and subsequently fled justice.[123] Browne made the journal available to the earl of Leicester's London agent, Hawkins, who drew a weekly account from it to send to the earl in Paris. Hawkins observed, "I send your Lordship the passages of the Upper house as particularly as the Journall booke will afford them, but I am not so well skilled in making and mending particulars as some are."[124] In the lower House, Hawkins reported that "the Clerk there is much to seek, and not suffered to doe as the last clerk did." He fell back on newsletters supplied by Captain Rossingham.[125] For a price, the clerk supplied copies of parliamentary papers of different kinds to members of the upper House and copies of bills to a wider public. On occasion he passed information along to members of the lower House.

Subject to constant pressure from a variety of sources, the clerk sometimes had to defend the honor of his position. Sir Thomas Dawes in 1644 alleged that the order of the House (drawn by Browne) in the case of *Dawes* v. *Jenyns* ran contrary to the agreement he, Dawes, had made. This, he complained, "tends much to the derogation of this House and to the scandal and imputation of him which is a sworn officer of this supreme court."[126] During the Long Parliament, Browne came to share the popular resentment against the House aroused by its political stance or by the administrative and judicial powers it had assumed. He complained in 1645 that his property at Twickenham had been despoiled because he was said to be "a Roundhead."[127] Workmen, felling timber at Mimms Commons in 1648 in accordance with an order of the House, were set upon by a mob of two hundred men and women, some of them armed. Being shown the order, one "did publicly wipe his Breech" with it, "saying, That he cared not a fart for it, there was but a Jacke Browne to it." In the case cited above, Browne accused John Morris, alias Poyntz, of forging an act of parliament and also Browne's signature authenticating the act. "All which being Crimes of a very high and transcendent Nature," Browne declared, "and do concern the Public Justice of the Kingdom, and of this Honourable House, the Supremest Judicatory of this Kingdom, that Acts of Parliament, the highest Records in this Kingdom, should be framed, invented, forged, and given in Evidence, and published as true Acts of Parliament, and the Hand of the Clerk of the Parliaments, a sworn Officer, forged, counterfeited, and subscribed to the same; as that, if such bold and audacious Acts should not be severely punished, no Man can be safe, in his Life, Person, or Estate." Poyntz in turn petitioned the House.[128] Mary Poyntz, implicated with her husband, complained in a further petition that Browne and Throckmorton, his deputy, were "in so great office with your honors" that they "draw up what orders they please." She said that she and her husband could obtain no counsel "in regard of Mr. Browne's potency." The House heard the case and handed down a decision against Poyntz and his associates, who were ordered to pay damages to Browne.[129] The act was canceled and vacated. Nevertheless, the case continued and was "appealed" to the House of Commons, to Lord Fairfax as general of the army, and finally to the lord protector before it was again dismissed.[130]

These rather bizarre episodes serve to underline the importance of the position of the clerk and his assistants. During their terms of office, Bowyer and Elsyng perfected the journal and Elsyng developed an interesting additional record of proceedings in the rolls of parliament. Both worked to establish the archive of parliament, Elsyng arranging for a secure place in which it could be kept. Browne's signal contribution was to maintain successfully the smooth and efficient operation of the office in times of heavy pressure upon it. His journal was unfinished. He continued the archive. Although he did not attain modern standards in this regard, he managed to file and preserve a vastly enlarged and diversified mass of parliamentary papers, at the same time regularly attending the House and drawing and issuing the growing number of orders that stemmed from its extended judicial and administrative activities. The clerks during this period were key men in the effective functioning of the House and in the preservation of its record and its papers.

4

OTHER OFFICERS OF THE HOUSE

The parliamentary duties of the gentleman usher of the Black Rod began long before the opening of the session. It was his responsibility to provide many of the furnishings for the chamber and for the other rooms used by the king and lords, and also to order stationery and books for the officers and clerks. The care of Old Westminster Palace and the area around it fell within the jurisdiction of the lord chamberlain, a responsibility that began to pass to the lord great chamberlain by 1641. Maintenance of the buildings and construction of desks, tables, stools, benches or forms, and other "joined work" were the province of the Office of Works.[1] But for other furnishings an order went to the master of the great wardrobe, who in turn issued a warrant to the gentleman usher of Black Rod for what was needed: 160 ells of canvas to make sacks, 22 pieces of crimson say to cover them, 14 tods of good wool to pad the forms, hay to fill the sacks, tape, nails, fire tools and andirons, screens, down pillows, chests, sunshades, pewter chamber pots, and close stools.[2] Substantially the same warrant went forth before each parliament and sometimes before each session; but an account of who ultimately claimed the heaps of wool sacks and pillows or the regiments of fire tools, andirons, screens, and chamber pots does not appear. The clerks probably used most of the stationery ordered for them, the paper and parchment, as well as pens, sealing wax and sand, glue, cotton and thread, tape, needles, and bodkins. On the other hand, the gentleman usher, like the other officers, probably appropriated the books that he requisitioned year after year.[3]

He oversaw the cleaning of the House both before and during the session and authorized the payment of bills for it. This work was actually carried out by the yeoman usher, whom he appointed and who collected 3s. per diem for himself and his servants and 12d. per diem for the cost of his brooms and other tools.[4] In 1628 the yeoman usher provided boughs, herbs, and roses for sweetening the rooms. He was also in charge of cleaning the chimneys and making fires.[5] When fuel became a major item of expense during the Long Parliament, the House directed Black Rod to look into the charges for providing it and report.[6]

During the sitting of parliament, Black Rod was generally responsible for order about the House and its surroundings. When Old Palace Yard became too crowded or noisy, he was authorized to clear out a canvas "tent or booth lately erected."[7] To keep out carts and wagons, he hired one Charles Best to tend a chain to block the way.[8] He was in charge of and probably appointed the groom porters (2od. per diem), the door-keepers, the waiters, the messengers and pursuivants, all of whom assisted him in his work.[9]

His chief duty, as defined in the Statute of the Order of the Garter of 1522, was "the Care and Custody, and the Pre-eminence of keeping of the doors of the High Court of Parliament."[10] He sat inside the doors of the chamber but outside the bar. In addition to taking the oaths of allegiance and supremacy, he also swore that "with faithfulness and secrecy" he would serve in his place and "neither . . . discover or report to any person or persons (not a member of that House) anything" that he should hear in the House.[11] He assisted the House in enforcing attendance. On several occasions he was ordered to inform all lords in London that the king commanded their presence in parliament.[12] He kept strangers out of the House and lobbies and took into custody any who presumed to listen at the doors when the House was sitting.[13] When a lord was introduced, the gentleman usher and the Garter King at Arms led the little procession into the chamber.[14] He announced the arrival of messengers from the House of Commons.[15] He informed the Lords when the Commons were ready and waiting for them in a conference room.[16] He summoned the Commons to the bar of the upper House to hear the king or to hear the judgment of the Lords. On these occasions, the sergeant of the lower House gave no notice of Black Rod's arrival but admitted him immediately.[17] Usually he carried his black rod. D'Ewes wrote on 1 May 1641, when the House was summoned to hear the king speak concerning Strafford, "Mr. Maxwell came in bringing in his hand a white stick that we might perceive hee came not about a dissolution (for then hee must have come with his blacke rodd) and after hee was come to the middle parte of the howse, he said with a cheerful countenance, Feare not I warrant you."[18] The Commons called him "screech-owl."[19]

The gentleman usher sought out and brought to the House those who offended against its privileges, particularly those who arrested the servants of peers in parliament time. In 1641, on order of the House, all warrants for apprehending delinquents were to be directed to him, an order that was immediately challenged by the sergeant-at-arms.[20] In practice, both men performed these duties and both had custody of prisoners or took bail for their appearance.[21] Black Rod brought the earl of Bristol to the House in 1626 when he was charged with treason by the king.[22] He reported the value of goods seized from George, Lord Digby. He searched for and apprehended printers working against the law or the ordinances of parliament.[23] During a quarrel in 1646 among the heralds, he sealed off the door of the Office of Arms.[24]

Constantly in attendance on the House, he was useful in a number of minor ways.[25] He held the Bible when lords took the oath of allegiance. He delivered messages to them.[26] Certain citizens of London, eager to have their petition read, asked him to jog the memories of three of the lords.[27] During the Protectorate, he gave notice to ministers who were to officiate at ceremonies for fasting.[28]

The gentleman usher was well paid for his services in parliament. He received an allowance of 5s. for each day the House sat, for himself and his men. At the end of the session he could take all the joined work (desks, tables, cupboards, and the like) of the upper House, with the exception of one table that belonged to the clerk. Rather than accumulate so much furniture year after year, he often settled his claim by composition: 53s.4d. in the last parliament of Elizabeth, 50s. in 1604, 6li. in 1628.[29] He and others apparently tried to appropriate the "timberwork of the court made for the trial of the Earl of Strafford in Westminster Hall," a claim that the House disallowed in the case of Maxwell.[30] As noted above, he took for himself the books that were charged to his office.[31] Did he also appropriate fire tools, woolsacks, and similar furnishings of the House, which were ordered and reordered for each meeting?

Even more lucrative than these perquisites and possible perquisites was his share of the fees. At the first entrance of a lord into parliament or at the translation of a bishop from one see to another, Black Rod was entitled to receive a fee: £6 13s.4d. from an archbishop; £10 from a duke; £6 13s.4d. from a marquess; £4 10s. from an earl; the same from a viscount; £3 6s.8d. each from the bishops of London, Durham, and Winchester; £2 10s. from other bishops and from barons. A lord who was absent by permission must pay him £1 10s. for a proxy. For each private bill, he received £5. For many private bills, if several persons were named, he received double this amount. A naturalization bill could be particularly profitable, because each person concerned in it must pay separately. The usher collected £2 at the passing of the bill, presumably for hypocras and wafers for the Lords' committee. He received £3 6s.8d. on the release of a delinquent. His assistant, the yeoman usher, received comparable but slightly lower fees.[32]

Black Rod's duties also put him in the way of receiving other income to cover his expenses and probably more. There were constant complaints in parliament concerning his charges for bringing up delinquents and witnesses from the country and for keeping delinquents in custody. The earl of Newport asked for confinement in "some private place" where the charges would be less.[33] Black Rod handled a good deal of money in furnishing parliament and in the provision of books and stationery.[34] He was a groom of the chamber with lodging at Whitehall and an annuity.[35] In 1628/9 he received a New Year's gift of £6.[36] He was entitled to livery. Fifteen yards of crimson satin lined with five ells of white taffeta made him a splendid robe in 1640.[37] During the civil war, he lived at St. Martin's-in-the-Fields and was assessed £10 on his lands and 13s.4d. on his goods in 1644.[38] Like all officers, he was protected by the privilege of parliament.[39]

THE SERGEANT-AT-ARMS

A sergeant-at-arms, bearing a mace, attended the presiding officer of the House of Lords.[40] His primary obligation was to accompany the lord chancellor at all times. As part of the daily ritual of parliament, he ushered the presiding officer into the House, carrying the mace up to the "very chair of state"; there he made his obeisances, laid the mace on the first woolsack by the presiding officer, and left the chamber, until summoned once more to attend him when the House rose.[41] Often accompanied by the gentleman usher, he brought others to the House: for example, the earl of Middlesex to hear judgment on his impeachment. On occasion he went with the usher to summon the Commons at the dissolution of parliament.[42]

Aside from these ceremonial functions, the chief duty of the sergeant was to apprehend and present delinquents or other persons, such as witnesses, to the Lords, and also to supervise the execution of punishments that might be ordered for any of them. He was held liable for the performance of his duties.[43] The assignment of these tasks to the sergeant was continually disputed by the gentleman usher or Black Rod. In November 1601 the gentleman usher, Sir Richard Coningsby, requested the Lords to confirm his right to bring before them those who had violated the privilege of the House. "In the last parliament (by some mistaking as he thought) the Serjeant at Arms was employed therein." A committee was appointed to look into the matter. Before it had completed its work, the "mistaking" was repeated and the sergeant-at-arms was dispatched to bring in those who had arrested a servant of the earl of Shrewsbury.

However, the House took the precaution of declaring that the incident should not serve as a precedent.[44] No committee report was made and the quarrels between the two officers continued into the reigns of James I and Charles I, when Sir Richard Coningsby, George Pollard, James Maxwell, and Alexander Thayne served successively as Black Rod, and Walter and Humphrey Leigh as sergeant.[45] In 1621 the Lords charged the subcommittee for privileges to review the records by which the sergeant claimed 20s. per diem as his fee for bringing up a delinquent.[46] In 1641 the House ordered that "all warrants for apprehending of delinquents, and bringing them before this honourable court" should be directed to Black Rod. Leigh at once entered his petition against this decision.[47] In July 1660 the whole matter was aired once more. After a formal hearing of both parties and "serious" debate, the Lords satisfied neither contender and reserved "the power to themselves to employ what persons they shall think fit for the apprehending delinquents and keeping them in safe custody as they shall see cause." In 1689 this order was confirmed.[48] The ultimate solution was reached only in 1971 when the office of sergeant-at-arms was combined with that of Black Rod.[49]

An examination of the activities of both officers reveals that their duties in this sphere did indeed overlap. Both employed messengers and agents to bring in delinquents. Both held offenders in custody or remitted them to prisons in London. Apparently, the House issued warrants for these activities indiscriminately to both and did not clearly differentiate the duties of the two.[50] In 1621 there was confusion in the House as to whether Black Rod or the sergeant should take the earl of Berkshire to the Fleet. In 1626 Lord Montagu, a stickler for procedure, assumed that the sergeant should bring in the earl of Bristol, who had been charged with treason by the king; this point was later decided by the House in favor of the gentleman usher.[51]

However, some efforts were made to distinguish between the responsibilities of the two men. In 1626 the ultimate decision that Bristol should be brought in by the gentleman usher was made because he was "the proper servant to the house, and the Serjeant but as to the Lord Keeper."[52] Elsyng, clerk of the parliaments 1621–35, made another distinction. If a peer is committed to prison, he wrote, the gentleman usher had charge of him thither. "But if a Commoner be Committed, the Serjeant at Arms attending on the Great Seal doth usually carry him to prison, and he also hath the Charge of him, and to see any Corporal punishment inflicted on him."[53] Pettus, writing after the Restoration, divided the duties of the two men in somewhat the same way, assigning the commitment of "Delinquents without door" to the sergeant and commitment of members "within doors" to Black Rod.[54]

Such distinctions, however, seem to have been largely theoretical. Although it is true that the gentleman usher usually had custody of peers, he also apprehended and held many who were not peers. The real issue was not the persons each officer could arrest and hold, but the matter of fees.[55] As an officer of the Order of the Garter as well as an officer of the House of Lords and often a member of the royal household, the gentleman usher outranked the sergeant, had a wider range of duties, and drew on a greater variety of perquisites and fees that were entered on the fee roll and approved by the House.[56] Payments to the sergeant were not. He received 12d. per diem[57] and relied for additional income on what he could claim for fetching and keeping delinquents and for carrying out other warrants of the House and the lord chancellor. If these payments were to be taken over by the gentleman usher or even shared with him, the effect on the sergeant's income could be serious. In a single year, 1642, following the Lords' order in his favor, Black Rod presented a bill of £603 12s. for the expense of delivering orders to individuals and performing similar duties. Presumably this sum did not include the usual payments met by the men served with orders and so represents only a portion of Black Rod's gross income.[58] Although 1642 was in many ways an extraordinary year, the figures serve to indicate how much money was at stake. The sergeant was determined to have his part.

5

THE ASSISTANTS

THE JUDGES

The role of the judges in the House of Lords was debated and defined in the early seventeenth century, sometimes by the judges themselves, sometimes by the peers, sometimes by the king and, less appropriately, by the House of Commons. In the reign of Edward I and for many years thereafter, judges had been summoned in much the same way that other members of the council were summoned—as full members of the parliament. Just when they assumed a position subordinate to the lords spiritual and temporal is not clear, but this change may have occurred in the reign of Richard II. Certainly the act for placing the lords, passed in the reign of Henry VIII, does not mention the judges. By that time their position in parliament had been transformed, they had lost their vote, and they were referred to as "attendants" or "assistants."[1]

In the seventeenth century, as in Tudor times, judges were summoned to the upper House by writs of assistance. With others of his council ("nobiscum ac cum ceteris de concilio nostro"), they were to advise the king concerning the difficult and urgent business for which he had called his parliament ("pro quibusdam arduis et urgentibus negotiis").[2] Thus, although they were generally regarded as assistants to the peers and prelates of the upper House, the judges were in fact summoned to assist the king[3]—a point that was not always recognized or accepted.

They sat "in the middest" of the parliament chamber upon the inner side of those woolsacks that lay before the earls' and bishops' benches.[4] On ceremonial occasions, they wore "gowns and hoods of scarlet, lined with a white fur called miniver."[5] Judges remained bareheaded until the lords gave them leave to cover. They did not speak unless required to do so by the House, a decision reached by majority vote "in case of difference about it." At committees, judges were not to sit or be covered "unless it be out of favor for infirmity, some judge sometimes hath a stool set behind, but never covers, and the rest never sit, or cover." Though infirm, Popham, lord chief justice in Elizabeth's reign, would "very hardly ever be persuaded to sit down, saying it was his duty to stand, and attend."[6] Lord Montagu, who had been a member of the House since 1621, was surprised to find that in the Short Parliament of 1640 judges were sitting with their hats on at committees, but learned that they had been given permission to do so.[7] In such cases they sat behind the lords of the committee at a distance from the table.[8] Although clearly differentiated in these ways from the lords, the judges could claim the usual privileges of parliament.[9]

In the early seventeenth century, the judges faithfully attended the upper House. Commentators and members of parliament observed that legal business moved slowly when parliament was in session. In 1621 the king advised a recess since "the Term Businesses have been hindered these Two Terms by the Businesses of the Parliament."[10] In 1624 John Chamberlain remarked that parliament had "retarded all manner of proceedings" at law.[11] Part of the difficulty lay with the king's learned counsel, also attendants in the upper House and sometimes members of the lower House, and with the lawyers' preoccupation with parliament; but the parliamentary obligations of the judges also created serious difficulties. In 1614 the lord chancellor requested the House to determine how many judges it required, in order that the rest might attend the courts.[12] The House frequently arranged not to sit on Star Chamber days so that judges and others might attend that court, and in 1621 the absence of the lord chief justice was specifically excused since a great cause was to be heard.[13] In 1641 judges were sometimes refused and sometimes granted permission to attend other legal business in time of parliament.[14] After 1660 the judges seem to have been much less faithful in attendance. They were warned on numerous occasions to be present and several times threatened with the displeasure of the House because of their continued absence.[15] The Lords' insistence on the judges' attendance was an index of their value to the House. In 1610 proceedings on the bill for the king's safety was postponed because the judges were on circuit.[16] On other occasions, as will be seen, the Lords relied heavily upon their services and advice.

Some of the duties of the judges were ceremonial. At the opening of a parliament, they were invariably nominated as receivers of petitions, a function no longer performed.[17] They also served as messengers on important occasions. They accompanied "bills of greater moment" to the lower House, where, when they were admitted, they came "up close to the table, where the clerk sitteth, making three congees; and there acquainting the Speaker, that the Lords have sent unto the House certain bills, doth read the titles, and deliver the bills to the Speaker, and so again departed with three congees." According to John Browne, clerk of the parliaments in 1640, they "give an account" to their own House "at their return."[18] Thus, the Lords in 1604 sent down the bill for the recognition of the "immediate right of the crown" to the Commons by four judges and the attorney general.[19] All bills concerning the royal family were customarily honored in this way.[20]

These ceremonies marked the judges as servants of the House, but should not obscure their more substantial services. Their influence on legislation had long been profound, both in and out of parliament. In the fourteenth century, they had been responsible for framing statutes. The chief justice in 1305 interrupted counsel, who was arguing for a certain construction of a statute, "Do not gloss the Statute; we understand it better than you do, for we made it."[21] In the reign of Henry VII, judges had frequently convened before parliament assembled to expound the principles of laws to be enacted.[22] Michael Graves has stressed the importance of the judges in shaping the legislative program of the government and in guiding and assisting the House of Lords in the reigns of Edward VI and Mary.[23] At all periods, the judges in their courts explicated statutes. In the seventeenth century, their advice was sought on proposed legislation before a parliament was summoned and they often did preliminary work on bills.[24] While parliament was in session, they were intimately concerned with bills in all stages. As Henry Scobell observed in his book of procedure, they were to assist committees with bills, draw bills, and prepare amendments suggested by debate.[25]

In the reigns of Henry VIII, Edward VI, and Mary, a bill had sometimes been referred to a single law officer of the crown to check its legal form.[26] Keen observers of parliamentary procedure like Robert Bowyer, clerk of the parliaments 1609–21, the fourth earl of Bedford, and Sir Simonds D'Ewes remarked that in the Elizabethan period, the judges had served on committees as members.[27] But in James's and Charles's reigns, the judges served only as assistants to committees, a role clearly demonstrated by the order that they should stand. Their influence, however, may well have remained undiminished. Judges were almost invariably named to assist committees early in James's reign, but somewhat less frequently after 1621 when king's counsel and others shared the task of providing legal expertise.[28] If delegated by a committee to investigate a specific point, judges reported back to the committee, not to the House.[29]

Judges might assist in drawing bills. Thus, in 1604 two judges were to attend the subcommittee to frame a bill for the commissioners for the union, and in 1606 judges and learned counsel were asked to draw a new bill for sea-coals.[30] In 1621 the Lords consulted judges about the effect upon prerogative of the proposed bill against monopolies and, after rejecting the bill, nominated judges to aid the committee in drawing a new one.[31] The judges' assistance might take other forms. In 1606, for example, certain judges and the king's learned counsel were to consider the bill of purveyance from the lower House before the Lords' committee on the bill met, in order to be able to inform them about its provisions. Possibly for the same reason, the bill against dividing tenements was delivered by the clerk to the lord chief justice. In 1610 the lord chancellor suggested that the judges should study selected statutes to consider which should be retained and which repealed.[32]

Sometimes the judges as a group were required to settle legal points raised by impending legislation, and in these instances their resolutions were often solemnly recorded. In 1621, for example, at the third reading of the act for the restraint of the transportation of ordnance, the Lords were concerned that the penalty clause might affect their right to be tried by their peers. The judges conferred "in private amongst themselves" and declared: "That, in all Cases, the Lords are to be tried by their Peers, unless they be excepted by particular Words." The Lords commanded the clerk to enter this opinion in the journal and, being reassured, passed the bill.[33] A similar problem arose in connection with the subsidy bill of 1624, and was solved in the same way. By order of the House, the judges' resolution was to be "fair engrossed" and signed.[34] Similarly, the judges ruled on a bill for Wales and its possible effect on the jurisdiction of the Council of Wales. The eldest judge present reported "that they are all of Opinion (save One only, and he not directly on the contrary Opinion)" that the bill did not affect the jurisdiction of the council. Their resolution was, by order, recorded in the journal.[35] In 1624 a bill that had passed the House was found to be imperfectly drawn. After due consultation, the judges agreed. The Lords transmitted the bill to the lower House, together with the judges' opinion of its defects, and left the Commons to provide remedy.[36] In each of these instances, the formal record of the judges' opinions is of particular interest, and the weight given to their resolutions seems to go beyond that of an "assistant" in the upper House. They never wholly forsook nor did the peers forget their role as judges of the king's other courts.

The judges' duties as legal advisers on bills led to their participation in conferences with the lower House. In April 1621 the Commons had refused the Lords' suggestion for a subcommittee to confer with the judges on the bill of informers. Alford, a member of the lower House, regarded it as "inconvenient" and possibly unprecedented that "when a Conference is desired by us with the Lords, or by them with us, that then the young Lawyers, Members of this House, should be put to debate with the learned Judges there, and with the King's Attorney, who are no Members of that House, but only Assistants there."[37] Sir Edward Coke, at that time also a member of the lower House, took a similar position in the Floyd case, which involved the question of judicature in the House of Commons. He would not, he said, admit "any to confer with us, who is but an Assistant of the upper House; for that we are all Judges, and so are not Assistants."[38] But in May of the same year, Judge Houghton and Judge Chamberlain carried the full burden of the conference on the bill for writs of *supersedeas* and *certiorari*.[39] In April 1628 Alford and Phelips returned to the earlier objection, that judges were not members of the House of Lords, that they should not "argue with us" as sometimes they had been brought to do at conferences. "Let us reason with the Lords but not with the judges."[40]

In the judicial and quasi-judicial business of the upper House, the judges' role was of particular importance. They frequently assisted committees for private bills. In 1641 the committee to consider a bill for the sale of certain lands of the earl of Cleveland received several petitions concerning the rights of individuals affected by the bill. These petitions were referred to two of the judges to consider and certify the true state of the cause to the committee. For example, were the claims of one Woodward sufficiently protected by the general proviso in the bill?[41] In 1624 the judges' responsibility had gone farther. A private bill for reversing a decree in the Court of Requests was referred by the House to three judges "to end the same if they can" or else to certify their opinion at the next session of parliament.[42]

In proceedings on writs of error that came before the House in increasing numbers from 1621 onwards, the role of the judges was usually decisive. In 1608 in the case of the *post-nati* (that is, of those Scots born after James had acceded to the English throne), Lord Chancellor Ellesmere had said that the Lords in examining errors "are informed and guided by the judges, and doe not follow their owne opinions or discretions otherwise."[43] The opinion of Sir Matthew Hale followed the same line. Although he wrote after the Restoration, his experience carried further back to the Long Parliament, where he had apparently worked in the 1640s. On 4 January 1646/7 his note appears on the transcript of a record in a case brought by writ of error, indicating that he could not do the legal and clerical work required since he had previously been involved in the case in question.[44] In his treatise on the judicature of the House of Lords, Hale deplored the procedure by which the House, whose members were for the most part inexperienced in the law, decided legal questions in cases of error by majority vote. "It is a great inconvenience, that men's estates and interests, and the judgments of learned judges given with great deliberation and advice, should be subject to be shaken, and it may be overthrown, by, it may be, one single content or not content." It would be wiser, he thought, to return to earlier usage by which such cases were generally tried by the judges in parliament. Nevertheless, Hale continued, despite the drawbacks of current procedure, in the House the judges' opinion in cases of error was "held so sacred, that the lords have ever conformed their judgments thereunto," except in cases not fit for the determination of the judges or in those where (as in the ship money case) they were parties to the former judgment. "He, that considers the great reverence that hath been in all cases of law given to the resolution and opinion of the judges by the lords in parliament, and how conformable regularly the judgment of the lords hath been to the opinion and advice of the judges upon matters in law transacted in the house of lords . . . will find, that though for many years last past they have had only voices of advice and assistance not authoritative or decisive; yet their opinions have been always the rules, whereby the lords do or should proceed in matters of law."[45]

The record in cases of error bears out Hale's statement. In 1586 plaintiffs came in person to parliament and assigned errors. Afterwards the Lords, "per Consilium Justiciarorum, post longam et maturam Deliberationem, uno Consensu" judged that the decision should be reversed. Other cases were heard privately by the judges and reported to the Lords, who sustained their opinion. This procedure continued in the Stuart period.[46] A case in point is that of *Haughton* v. *Harris* in 1646. The errors were argued on both sides in July. It was then ordered that all the judges "except those before whom the judgment was" should consider the record and report their opinions to the House, and the parties were to attend the judges. Having met and heard counsel on both sides, the judges reported in October that they were of the opinion that the errors alleged were insufficient to justify reversal. The House then ordered the judgment confirmed, the record remitted, and execution taken out accordingly.[47]

In addition to cases of error from King's Bench and Exchequer Chamber, cases of the first instance and appeals in civil cases greatly increased the judicial business of the House after 1621.[48] These matters came to the House by petition and most of them were referred to the Committee for Petitions. At the outset, the Lords were primarily concerned with investigating alleged complaints, and it is interesting to note that judges or other legal counsel were not assigned to the committee when it was first appointed in 1621.[49] If a case came from an inferior court, the Lords might request the judge of that court to certify whether there were sufficient cause for review, and if not, what course should be taken; but it was not until several months later in 1621 that the House ordered that judges and other legal assistants might be added to the committee as needed.[50] In 1624 the committee was again initially appointed without legal assistants. In 1626 and 1628/9, assistants might be added as seemed necessary.[51] In the Short Parliament of 1640 no assistants were appointed, but in the Long Parliament two judges were assigned to the committee from the beginning of the session,[52] and judges were frequently employed in handling petitions.

Committees charged to consider petitions used the services of judges in various ways. The judge of a court might be asked to certify how the case stood in his court.[53] A committee might refer a petition to a judge or judges, asking them to conduct a hearing and report the state of the case.[54] Judges who had been present at a hearing before a House committee might be asked to draw up the case in writing and certify it to the committee or to offer their opinion.[55] In other cases, judges were to certify the equity of a decree[56] or the validity of a pardon,[57] or to examine deeds or other documents offered in evidence.[58] In certain cases, judges were asked to provide remedy, but this was always subject to the confirmation of the specific committee and the House.[59] The variety of duties assigned to judges in handling petitions reflects the variety of problems these cases presented to the Lords. The upper House moved slowly and rather tentatively from examination and investigation to judgment. As petitions came to raise serious technical and legal questions, committees turned to judges and other legal attendants for assistance; but the role of the judges was never as influential or decisive in these areas of judicial and quasi-judicial activity as it was in the proceedings on writs of error.

In the daily business of the House and in assistance with bills, writs of error, and petitions, the function of the judges was generally accepted without comment and the House relied heavily on them. When their opinion was sought and given on matters of broad public policy under discussion in parliament as a whole, their role became more controversial. The major issues of James's first parliament—the questions of the union with Scotland, purveyance, wardship and feudal tenures—all involved legal problems of great complexity on which the judges were called to rule. Thus, although they were technically assistants in the upper House, their decisions came to be the center of debate and drew fire from many sides.

The question of the union must be referred to parliament, the judges advised the king in April 1604. They had no precedent for it "and rare and great matters whereof there is no Precedent are to be referred to the Parliament, and if the Parliament of England do agree to accept of the Union of Scotland, we will obey."[60] However, when the question had been brought before parliament, the judges' opinions determined the course of debate. Their first declaration of April 1604, that the adoption of the name Great Britain would invalidate all legal processes, displeased the king and delighted members of the lower House.[61] It effectively ended one phase of the discussion and made it necessary to proceed by other steps toward union.[62] A further opinion of the judges concerning the *post-nati* had even more serious implications. The judges this time pleased the king but bitterly antagonized many members of the lower House. In February 1606/7, in preparation for a conference with the lower House on the point of naturalization of Scots born after 1603, the Lords sought the opinion of the judges. Eleven spoke in the House of Lords on 24 February, "beginning at the youngest or lowest," with the lord chief justice of England speaking last. All concurred (save Mr. Justice Walmsley) that "such of the Scottish as have been, or shall be, born in Scotland, since His Majesty's coming to the Crown, are not Aliens, but are inheritable in this Realm by the Law (as it now stands in Force), as native English." Two days later, committees of both Houses met together to hear the judges, who reiterated their opinion.[63]

The question at once arose of the force of their resolution. Was the point of law still open to debate, as some of the lords maintained? Or had the judges, in fact, spoken the final word for the upper House and perhaps for parliament and the realm?[64] The Commons preferred to think that they had not. Indeed, if the Lords should urge the judges' opinions, the Commons decided to take the line that the judges' words in parliament were not as weighty as when they sat "Judicially in Courts of Justice," for there they were bound by oath. Further, one judge had disagreed and none had heard the Commons' opinions. "Therefore are we not so much bound in this Case to their Opinions, as to their Judgements when they are in their Tribunalls."[65] It was a difficult point. The Commons, Salisbury wrote, desired a resolution that the judges' opinion was invalid, "as may make them dainty hereafter to judge the question, or make the judgment less acceptable." If such a resolution seemed ready to come to the question on the floor, the Speaker had instructions to adjourn the House and feign illness so that it could not reconvene. A direct confrontation between the lower House and the judges must be avoided. It "could neither be good for this present time, nor for hereafter."[66] Ultimately the point of law was dropped in parliament and settled in Calvin's case in the Court of Exchequer Chamber in 1608.

Lord Chancellor Ellesmere, who had been presiding officer of the House of Lords in 1606/7, took care in delivering judgment to affirm the significance and validity of the opinion of the judges previously given in parliament. There, Ellesmere asserted, the judges are bound by oath "as much . . . as in their proper courts: for, that is the supreme court of all:

and they are called thither by the kings writ, not to sit as tell-clockes, or idle hearers." In the past, he recalled, judges' opinions in parliament had been highly regarded. Although some men were not satisfied with their "grave resolution" in parliament concerning the *post-nati*, he himself "must always valew and esteeme [it] as a reale and absolute judgement."[67] In December 1608 a rumor circulated that the king, probably on Ellesmere's advice, would seek further confirmation for the judgment in Calvin's case by means of a writ of error in the upper House; but nothing came of it.[68]

The role of the judges was equally important in the vexed issue of purveyance (the royal right to requisition supplies) and that of feudal tenures and wardship (the right to control minor children of tenants-in-chief). By special order of the Lords, judges attended a conference with the House of Commons concerning purveyance in February 1605/6 and ultimately assisted the Lords in drawing up nineteen objections to the Commons' bill.[69] At a further conference on 12 April, the judges took an active part. Fuller objected. They were not, he said, "competible for Conference with the Lower House."[70] He made the point later repeated in 1607 in the case of the union: when judges spoke in their courts, they were bound by oath. If the Lords wished to hear them in parliament, they might do so, but members of the Commons should withdraw.[71] In the same month, as Dudley Carleton wrote to John Chamberlain, the judges again took part in a conference. They "overruled all on the prerogative side, and gave it out for law that the King had both prising and preemption and that he was not bound to payment but upon these terms *quand bonnement il peut* and delivered one judgment in all men's opinions of dangerous consequence, that the prerogative was not subject to law, but that it was a transcendent above the reach of parliament." The Lords terminated the conference by promising that the king himself would provide the remedy that parliament could not supply.[72] Once again, the judges closed the door to a legal approach to a major problem, forcing the House of Commons back to the point of conveniency. Similarly, in the proposal to abolish feudal tenures and wardship, the judges' opinions had blocked off one possible way of proceeding. Although feudal service to the crown might cease, they insisted, "the King's profit must continue."[73]

In the fourth and fifth sessions of James's first parliament in 1610, the judges played a less spectacular part. The Lords once more sought their help when the matter of tenures and wardship was again raised and propositions came forward for a great contract by which feudal obligations might be transmuted into annual payments. "For matters legal," Salisbury remarked, "without further information I think this House not sufficiently able to meet with the lower House."[74] Thus, before going to a conference with the Commons, the Lords inquired of the judges whether the king might part with his tenures and still retain the fealty of his subjects and whether the subjects might be eased of wardship and other burdens. The judges, who were prepared in advance, replied at length in the affirmative.[75] On this major issue of public policy, the judges' opinions served to forward the business of both Houses; and the Commons, no longer intent on denigrating the position of the judges, sought to incorporate their names and resolutions in an act to guarantee the terms of the bargain,[76] again suggesting that their opinion carried special weight, like that of a fourth estate.

By 1614 some of the lords themselves came to question the function of the judges. The judges, in turn, by refusing to give their opinion on the vexed question of the king's right to levy impositions, sharply defined the area of their competence. Impositions were additional customs duties, over and above the usual rate, levied by the crown. The royal right to levy impositions had been debated at length by the lower House in 1610. It was several times suggested that this right, which had been confirmed by the decision in Bate's case in 1606, might be retried in parliament.[77] In 1614 the House of Commons raised the issue of impositions again and asked for a conference with the Lords. On 23 May the upper House debated whether it should hear the judges in preparation for this conference. Ellesmere, lord chancellor, was much in favor.[78] Other peers demurred but were ultimately overruled. Lord Spencer objected to consulting the judges concerning impositions. They are called by writ to attend us, he said, "beinge but our assistans, we make them not assistans but Judges in Parlament, wch president will be dangerous in future ages, that such a thinge cannot be resolved betwixt the houses, but we must heare the Judges opinions first."[79] In view of the judgment in Bate's case, there could have been little doubt about the judges' position. At the same time, debate in 1610 had left even less doubt of the opinion of the majority of the Commons. The situation was similar to that in the session of 1606/7 with the *post-nati*. In 1614, however, the judges resolved the issue by removing themselves from a difficult situation between the Houses. Chief Justice Coke, speaking for all the judges, declined to give an opinion. They would, he said, be willing to do so had the cause been argued. "For my part I will not argue the case, it beinge against our othe soe to doe: we are called by our writte to advise the Kinge when it is his pleasure to have us speake, and to advise and assist your Lops when you please to have us speake, but not to dispute. . . . If that your Lops will undertake to dispute the matter we will upon the hearinge of it argued on both sides if it be your pleasures to deliver our opinions."[80] Having failed to elicit support from the judges in one way, Ellesmere sought to do it in another, by suggesting that the king's right to levy impositions come to the House on writ of error. From experience he knew that this would throw the decision into the lap of the judges. Once more he failed.[81]

In subsequent parliaments, the Lords continued to confer with the judges on matters of public policy. The bill against monopolies was of particular importance to the House of Commons in 1621 and, as previously noted, the judges were several times consulted by the Lords as the bill came up for their consideration.[82] In 1628 there was a brief flurry of indignation in the House when the judges hesitated to give an account of their proceedings in the Five Knights case before gaining permission from the king to do so.[83] In the debates leading up to the Petition of Right, the judges were frequently consulted. In April they agreed that the Great Charter of England and the six statutes guaranteeing the subjects' liberty were still in force.[84] On several occasions in May, the Lords debated turning to the judges, particularly for their opinion concerning the effect of the petition on royal prerogative;[85] but at no point did the judges' opinions significantly affect decisions in parliament or relations between the Houses, as had been the case earlier.

In 1641 the judges on several occasions gave technical advice in Strafford's trial, in the matter of hearing further witnesses, for example;[86] and they finally delivered the crucial opinion that the treason alleged against Strafford fell within the statutes covering treason.[87] But in the case of Laud, they were more careful, saying that they could deliver no opinion in point of treason by law except what was particularly expressed to be treason in the act of 25 E. III. They must therefore leave the application to Laud's case to their lordships.[88]

The judges in parliament, particularly under the leadership of Coke in 1614, attempted to restrict their advice concerning matters of public policy to judgments on specific, previously argued cases. A similar restriction was placed upon them by the king. In 1626, as noted above, in connection with charges brought in parliament by the crown against the earl of Bristol, the House sought the opinion of the judges as to whether the king's testimony might be admitted, whether words spoken to him as prince could make any difference in the case, whether he could in fact be at once witness and judge. The attorney general informed the judges in the king's name that they were not to answer such a general question with broad implications for the future, but confine themselves to speaking freely in particular matters that might arise in the case at hand.[89]

In the main, the judges also eschewed consideration of matters of parliamentary procedure and privilege, although there were exceptions. As Chief Justice Fortescue had said in Thorpe's case in the reign of Henry VI, they "ought not to make answer, for it hath not been used aforetime that the Justices should in any wise determine the privileges of this High Court of Parliament. For it is so high and mighty in its nature that it may make law, and that that is law it may make no law, and the determination and knowledge of that privilege belongs to the Lords of the Parliament and not to the Justices."[90] Coke said in the *Fourth Institute*: "Judges ought not to give any opinion of a matter of Parliament, because it is not to be decided by the Common Laws, but *secundum legem & consuetudinem Parliamenti*: and so the Judges in divers Parliaments have confessed."[91] The judges were said to have been consulted about proxies in Elizabeth's reign.[92] At the suggestion of the king, they participated in a conference concerning a disputed election case in 1604.[93] In 1621 the judges were asked to advise members of the House concerning privileges during a parliamentary recess. They sidestepped the issue, asserting that they could find no precedents for such a long adjournment, and the Lords decided the matter themselves.[94] In 1626 the House inquired of the judges whether the earl of Bristol, having been accused in parliament of treason by the attorney general on behalf of the crown, should be committed.[95] The judges withdrew to consider the precedents offered. On their return, they explained the method of proceeding in other courts and also referred to the possibility of procedure by bill of attainder. However, they "desired to be excused to deliver any Opinion of the Precedents of Parliamentary Proceedings" and "how the Proceedings ought to be in this Case, they humbly left to their Lordship's Considerations."[96] In 1628 the Lords consulted the judges concerning one Willoughby, servant of Lord Delawarr. If he were delivered by privilege of parliament, what inconveniences would result to his creditors and others? The case touched on privilege, but the question addressed to the judges did not, as one of the peers was careful to point out: "The Judges may attend," he said, "to answere the questions as demanded but not to referre any thing to them."[97] The judges' opinions were also sought in peerage claims and questions of precedence that stemmed from them.[98]

The relation of the judges in parliament to the king was complex. As we have seen, they were technically called as the king's assistants. They were certainly appointed by the king and bound by oath to serve him. On two occasions they declined to obey the Lords' orders before obtaining the king's permission, and on each occasion members of the House reacted with indignation. In February 1620/1 the judges refused to give an opinion on the Lords' claim to the privilege of testifying in courts of justice upon honor rather than oath. They took the line that the issue affected the prerogative and that they therefore would not answer until they knew the king's pleasure. Lord Houghton asserted that he had examined the judges' writs and that they were to give the Lords advice if asked to do so.[99] The matter was finally resolved in March when the Lords sent a delegation to the king.[100] In 1628, as we have seen, the judges were initially reluctant to report on the Five Knights case until the king had given them leave to do so. "We are the Kings Judges, and sworne trewly to accompt to his Majestie. . . . Doubted whether by the Kings warrant and lycence."[101]

The judges were at the service of the king both as assistants in the House and in their capacity of judges of his courts of justice; sometimes they were members of his Privy Council as well. The king was therefore accustomed to consult them about parliamentary affairs. In preparing for a parliament, he or his ministers frequently turned to them for advice. In 1614 the chief justices and the lord chancellor met several times about propositions for parliament and the lord chancellor recommended amendments to the proposed bill for preservation of woods.[102] In 1620 the king requested Bacon, then lord chancellor, to confer with the two justices ("old parliament men") and with other judges "touching that which mought in true policy, without packing or degenerate arts, prepare to a Parliament."[103] The king consulted the judges in 1628 about the effect of the Petition of Right before he gave his answer to it. He consulted them in 1629 on points of parliamentary privilege and in May 1640 on the power of convocation to make canons without parliamentary confirmation.[104]

In yet another way the judges' activities out of parliament tended to affect their function in parliament. Possibly, as W. J. Jones noted, their value to the House of Lords would decline as their role as assistants to the king, rather than to the House, was increasingly emphasized.[105] Certainly their decisions in important cases involved them in political controversy. The decision in Bate's case, which reinforced the king's right to levy impositions, was bitterly attacked by members of the House of Commons.[106] In accusing the judges in 1641, Waller, speaking for the House of Commons, linked their decision in the ship money case with the king's offer in the Short Parliament to cease his call for ship money in exchange for twelve subsidies. Waller asserted that the judges had usurped the function of parliament by presenting his Majesty with twelve subsidies.[107]

In sum, the judges served parliament and the king in parliament in a variety of ways. They advised the king on matters to be laid before parliament, drafted bills, reviewed obsolete statutes, and gave legal opinions on which royal assent to legislation could be based.[108] In parliament they assisted committees for bills, drafted amendments, explicated points of law and defended them in conferences with the House of Commons, conducted hearings, reviewed cases on writs of error, assisted with the dispatch of petitions, and performed such ceremonial functions as the House requested. In an age when the great issues of public policy and public complaint were so frequently cast in legal terms, the influence of the judges could be all-pervasive. The Commons might well object to debating against them, the king might restrain them on occasion, they might and did withhold their advice on certain matters; but, whether in their courts in Westminster Hall, in other parts of the Old Palace (the Lords Chamber, the Painted Chamber where conferences were held, the committee rooms), or in their own chambers at the Inns of Court, the judges' work was a significant element in the life of a parliament. Bacon's characteristic suggestion that some course should be taken "to ingage and assure the Judges *in omnem eventum*, for any points of law or right which may be foreseen as likely to come in question in Parliament" was the ultimate tribute to their importance.[109]

THE ATTORNEY GENERAL

Others were called to the House by writs of assistance: the master of the rolls, the attorney general and solicitor general, the king's serjeants, the secretaries of state, and, on occasion, certain members of the Privy Council.[110] Of particular interest in this period is the role of the attorney general. Like the judges, he and the solicitor general served the king and the House in a number of ways. Evidence from Sir John Bankes's papers indicates that the attorney took some responsibility for the writ of summons.[111] He drafted and redrafted bills such as the recusancy bills for James's first parliament and bills of grace offered by the crown.[112] After the terms had been agreed in parliament, he or other members of the king's counsel drew the bill of subsidy.[113] He drew the preamble and confirmation necessary to enact the subsidy of the clergy. He drafted the general pardon.[114] He approved a bill of restitution and a bill for the queen's jointure on behalf of the crown.[115] He explained bills to members of the upper House, for example, the bill of attainder against offenders in the Gunpowder Plot and the bill concerning purveyors in 1606.[116] He served as an assistant to committees in the House of Lords and carried important bills to the House of Commons.[117]

A peculiarity of the attorney's position in the early Stuart period was that in some parliaments he sat as a member of the lower House while serving as an assistant in the upper. In 1606, between sessions of James's first parliament, Sir Henry Hobart, then a member of the House of Commons, was appointed attorney. A brief discussion in the House concerning his eligibility to remain in his seat produced no decisive results.

Hobart continued to do so.[118] In 1614 the Commons raised the point again and were clearly ready to exclude Bacon, then attorney general. The king suggested a compromise by which Bacon would remain in the House for the present but would not serve there in the future. On this basis, the House excluded Sir Thomas Coventry in 1621, Sir Robert Heath in 1626, and Sir Edward Herbert in 1641. After the Restoration, the rule seems to have lapsed. Sir Heneage Finch and others took their seats in the lower House as members.[119] The Commons also objected, as they did in the case of the judges, when the attorney went beyond what they regarded as his proper role as assistant in the upper House and spoke on behalf of the Lords at conferences in 1621 and 1628. "This Conference is between the Two Houses," one member said. "Mr. Attorney is no member of your House. He attends you." During a debate on the Petition of Right, another member distinguished between legal counsel of the crown "perpetually maintained by fee" and the members of the House of Commons who spoke for the commonwealth.[120]

The attorney's withdrawal from the House of Commons after 1614 enabled him to be in constant attendance in the upper House. The growth of legal and judicial business underlined his importance as an assistant there. He was frequently appointed to attend committees. He assisted with their deliberations and also when they reported to the House. In 1621 he explicated the defects in the bill concerning informers and drew up a statement of the points that he had made for the use of the lord treasurer in conferring with the Commons. He read various drafts of the statement concerning the breach of treaties with Spain to the House in 1624, and the king's answer. When the committee for the petition against recusants reported in 1624, he read the petition. Later he read it again, clause by clause, for the consideration of the House, then the amended version and the king's reply. He presented the judges' resolutions concerning clauses in the subsidy bill said to affect the judicial powers of the House.[121] He drew or redrew bills when this seemed desirable.[122] With the development of impeachment proceedings, he became involved in presenting charges against Mompesson, Bacon, Sir John Bennet, and Sir Henry Yelverton in 1621 and Lionel Cranfield in 1624.[123] It is noteworthy that he did so on behalf of a committee of lords. In 1624 the House specifically provided in Cranfield's case that king's counsel should not draw the heads of charges or consider "with what to charge a member of this house."[124]

It was Sir Edward Coke who most clearly differentiated the position of the attorney general as an assistant in the upper House from that of the judges, although they performed many of the same functions. Speaking for himself and his fellow judges in 1614, he had, as discussed above, declined to give an opinion to the Lords concerning the king's right to levy impositions. If the matter had been argued before them by king's counsel and by representatives of the lower House, he observed, then he and his fellows could judge what had been said. "The Kinge is much preiudized that he hath no councell heare, as the Atturney and Soliciter, whose place and dewty it is that the[y] should attend this house, and not be of the lower house."[125] The attorney and other members of king's counsel were called to the upper House primarily as the king's legal representatives and advocates.

There is plenty of evidence that they carried out this function. The attorney was "heard for the King" on the bill for free trade in 1604 and on the terms of the great contract in 1610. In the same year he defended the king's right to levy impositions.[126] When the House heard rival claimants to the office of lord great chamberlain in 1626, the attorney reserved the right to set out the king's title to the office if it should later appear.[127] In 1628 he spoke for the king concerning the "Liberties and Freedoms" claimed by the House of Commons.[128] In 1640 he presented the royal claims to the baronies of Ruthin and Hastings, and in December 1641 he "made a long Argument" for the king on the bill for pressing soldiers for service in Ireland.[129] In the judicial proceedings in parliament, he sometimes served as assistant, sometimes as prosecutor for the crown. In 1621 Floyd, who was not a member of parliament, was said to have been condemned by the Lords at the suit of the king's attorney; and in 1626 in the case of the earl of Bristol, the attorney general specifically brought charges in the king's name.[130] In 1624 Elsyng maintained that the suit against Cranfield was brought *ex parte Domini Regis*; but the journal indicates that the attorney presented charges on behalf of a committee of lords.[131] When he brought charges of treason against Lord Kimbolton and five members of the House of Commons in 1642, he was caught between king and parliament. The Lords ordered a committee to determine whether such a proceeding were lawful and "whether an Accusation of Treason may be brought into this House by the King's attorney against a Peer in Parliament." Herbert's plea that he had acted on royal orders did not protect him.[132]

The attorney, summoned as an assistant to the upper House, performed a variety of valuable functions there. It may well have been that he was more useful to the crown in James's first two parliaments as a member of the House of Commons, occasionally attending the upper House.[133] After 1614, when he was deprived of a seat in the Commons, his time and his legal expertise were more regularly available for the king and the Lords. Like the judges, he assisted with the daily concerns of legislation and the legal business of the House. When committees reported at which he had served as assistant, he often took on a considerable portion of the reading that otherwise would have fallen to the clerk.[134] In 1626 the House assigned him as counsel for Lord Willoughby, who claimed the earldom of Oxford; in 1641 he was ordered by the House to prosecute one Fowler in King's Bench for false weights and to proceed against two persons for seditious sermons.[135] But his primary and distinctive function was to present the case for the king, whether in a claim to land or title, in a charge of treason, or in a matter of prerogative right.

6

COMMITTEES

Both the king's council and the House of Lords had long used committees to prepare and expedite business.[1] It was an old and natural way of proceeding. A fragment of the Lords journal indicates that bills were committed in 1461.[2] In the Tudor period, although many bills were referred to an officer or officers of the crown, committees of lords were used for particularly significant or controversial bills and for other matters of importance.[3] By the early seventeenth century, much of the work of the upper House was assigned to committees and the committee structure had developed in an interesting way. During this period, the House established and used extensively the device of the committee of the whole House and, beginning in 1621, it increasingly delegated responsibility to standing committees. Committees in the House at this time may be divided into two groups, depending on their membership.[4] Select committees were composed of "particular persons named for that purpose."[5] A committee of the whole House, as its name indicates, was formed when the House adjourned and reconstituted itself as a committee. It was thus composed of all members of the House then present. This section will discuss select committees, including standing committees, which were also select committees. Successive sections will analyze the committee of the whole House and joint committees.

SELECT COMMITTEES

The way in which committees were chosen helped to determine their political significance. In the reign of Henry VIII, members of some committees seem to have been approved by the Lords; but the records do not make clear just how these members were selected.[6] John Hooker, alias Vowell, writing in 1571 and 1572, noted that the lord chancellor or lord keeper chose committees for bills. However, Hooker was a Commons man and had no special knowledge of procedure in the upper House.[7] The advice that Anthony Mason, clerk of the parliaments, gave to Sir Christopher Hatton, who had newly become lord chancellor in 1587, indicates that at that period the House chose its own committees. "The Lordes," he wrote, "if occasion soe require use to speke to the bill, and either commit it or commaund it to be engrossed; if it be committed, the Lord Chancellor askethe to whome they will have it committed."[8] Henry Elsyng, clerk of the parliaments 1621–35, writing sometime before 1630, described in detail the way in which the House chose select committees in his time.

> The Lord Chancellor demands of the lords, how many of each bench shall be of the committee. . . . The number of each bench being agreed, they are named *promiscue* by any of the lords, but the clerk is to be careful to set down those whom he hears first named; which is done in this manner: First, the earls are named, and those that sit on that bench. The clerk having written them, stands up and reads their names. Then the bishops, and then the barons, in like manner. And, if the clerk happen to set down more than the number agreed on, it is in the liberty of the House to take out the latter, and so to leave the just number, or to admit them. Then, the House names the attendants, which are of the judges, the king's learned council, and the masters of the chancery. The clerk reads their names also. The last is the time and place, where to meet; which being agreed on, and set down, the clerk reads that also.[9]

Accounts of proceedings and notes of the clerk and the assistant clerk confirm Elsyng's description. There is ample evidence that "the number of each bench was first agreed on," and some evidence that the practice was older than Elsyng believed it to be. He ascribed it to 1614 or later; but on a number of occasions in Elizabeth's reign and in the early years of James, there was an effort to choose an equal number from each bench, surely an indication that a number had been set.[10] Robert Bowyer, clerk of the parliaments 1609–21, in his "scribbled book" of notes taken in the House, indicated the number to be chosen from each bench for committees in 1610.[11] In more than half the committees selected in the years 1610–29, the same number of members was chosen from two of the benches.[12] In 1641 a specific number for each bench (three earls, four bishops, and a baron) was to constitute the committee for a conference.[13] On some occasions certain committee names have been struck out of the clerk's notes; these may have been deleted to bring the committee into line with the pattern previously agreed upon by the House. "If the clerk happen to set down more than the number agreed on, it is in the liberty of the House to take out the latter." On other occasions, deletions indicate that a lord declined to serve.[14]

In the notes taken by the clerk in the House and in the "minute books" kept by his assistant, it is clear that lords were usually named by benches, but as Elsyng had indicated, they were nominated *promiscue*, not in order of precedence.[15] The clerk jotted names down, bench by bench in three columns, in the order in which he heard them called from the floor. Thus, in preparing the draft of the journal, it was necessary for him to renumber them in order of precedence so that they would be properly arranged when copied into the final manuscript journal.[16] Great officers of state, who sat on the earls' bench according to the statute for placing the lords (31 H. VIII, c. 10), counted as earls, even the lord keeper when he was a bishop.[17] The exceptions to this procedure, though they are few, should be noted. Possibly the convention of naming committees by benches had not been wholly accepted until after Bowyer's death. In the last months of his clerkship, there are indications in his notes that the names of some men were called out as they came to mind, irrespective of the benches on which they sat.[18] The House apparently named two large general committees, the Committee for Privileges in 1621 and a committee to go to the king in 1628, without regard to benches at all.[19]

In 1621 Lord Montagu, who had a keen eye for procedure, observed that it was customary for the House, in naming a committee, to provide an equal number from the earls' and bishops' benches and twice that number from the barons'.[20] It is interesting that he should have thought so, for the custom, honored both in the breach and in the observance, was by no means followed regularly. Elsyng, who had examined precedents of committees in the reigns of Edward VI and Elizabeth, believed that this custom too had begun in 1614.[21] "Sometimes the number of each is equal," he wrote, describing the committee structure as it was in the House in 1610, "and sometimes the barons are the greater number. But they seldom double the number of the other bench, unless in the committees of a small number."[22] While investigating the "ancient manner of selecting committees" in 1679, the Committee for Privileges found that formerly committees had indeed been named by benches, but that the proportions had varied. It reported that committees chosen on 6, 7, and 9 April 1624 were composed of an equal number of earls and bishops with double the number of barons, but this had not been the case for those chosen on 14 April in the same year.[23] Nevertheless, a check through committees in the early Stuart period reveals that, as the period advanced (although 1614 does not seem to have the special significance Elsyng assigned to it), committees were increasingly composed of an equal number of earls and bishops and double that number of barons through the parliament of 1626.[24] The wisdom of these proportions was questioned in 1628 as the number of earls expanded, and the custom began to die out.[25] It was followed in only two of the seventy-four committees selected in 1628–29. By the time of the Short and Long Parliaments, it had been abandoned.[26]

The pattern of committee membership for the Long Parliament was complicated by the fortunes of the archbishops and bishops. Laud went to the Tower on 19 December 1641, followed by twelve other bishops on 31 December. The bishops of London, Winchester, Rochester, and Worcester continued to be appointed to committees until the end of January 1641/2.[27] Their service was finally terminated when the king gave his assent to the bill excluding bishops from the House on 15 February 1641/2.

Even before these events had occurred, the participation of bishops in committees in the early years of the Long Parliament had been selective. In 1640 and 1641, no bishops sat on committees connected with the impeachment of the earl of Strafford.[28] They were also omitted from other committees, such as one to inform the king of the House's resolutions concerning the treaty with the States-General of the Netherlands, one to forward a request to the king concerning the ecclesiastical offices held by Archbishop Laud, committees concerning northern affairs, and those negotiating with the City for loans.[29] Despite all these precedents, when bishops were omitted on 5 May 1641 from a committee to examine persons implicated in the Army Plot, the Lords declared that this omission should constitute "no Prejudice to the Lords the Bishops."[30] Thereafter, without further comment, bishops were omitted from committees to inspect foreign letters (on 11 May), draw up heads for a conference concerning Jersey and Guernsey, and request the king to disband five regiments, and frequently from committees to wait upon the king or the queen.[31] There were no bishops on committees to draw an order to prevent quarrels in the House, examine witnesses concerning incendiaries in Scotland, make plans for disbanding the army, or compose a letter to Scotland. Bishops were included, however, in the Lords' committee to confer with the lower House about the bishops' exclusion bill and in a committee concerning the execution of laws against recusants.[32] They were not represented on the committee to draft a bill for restraining particular recusants named by the House of Commons, but were named to the committee that studied the bill when it came into the House. They did not serve on the committee to amend an ordinance securing a loan from the City.[33]

Generally, bishops did not sit on committees for the negotiation of treaties or for settling affairs with Scotland (though this was not true of Ireland). They were not included on committees for military arrangements or for financial transactions with the City.[34] By the end of December 1641, their numbers in the upper House had been sharply reduced, which further affected their committee membership, and by the middle of February 1641/2, they were gone. Political events and the onset of war also reduced the number of peers in attendance. In the period from 1640 to February 1641/2, the House continued to appoint an equal number of members from two of its benches, sometimes the first (earls) and second (bishops),[35] sometimes the first and third (barons),[36] less often the second and third.[37] Occasionally all three benches were equally represented.[38] No other significantly consistent pattern based on rank appeared in this parliament in the naming of committees. By 1643 it became common for the House to name earls and barons together.[39]

The original balance of a committee had been disturbed on occasion by the addition of lords later in a session. Thus, when a bill was recommitted in 1606, certain lords were added to the original committee; and in the same session, others were added to the committee for the government of Wales.[40] In 1610 a committee had been chosen for the bill against pluralities. When another ecclesiastical bill was referred to the same committee, it was augmented by "such other lords as this day have spoken to the bill."[41] In February 1620/1 the policy of adding to committees was debated in the House. Buckingham's name had been suggested by Bacon, then lord chancellor. Lord Darcy promptly suggested three others. The earl of Southampton, doubtless trying to block Buckingham's nomination, stated categorically that "the Committie beinge chosen allreadie it hath not beene the manner of the howse to add any." He suggested a committee of the whole House instead. Dorset cryptically remarked that "the addinge of one alters the forme of the howse as well as all and therefore it comes all to one to add them all." The final decision, proposed by Buckingham, was to add only the prince.[42] In the early months of the second meeting of parliament in November and December 1621, several committees were enlarged; and in 1625, 1626, and 1628 lords were also added.[43] In November 1640 the Committee for Petitions had clearly originally been designed to include twenty from the earls' bench, eight bishops, and sixteen barons. The addition of the earl of Bridgewater and Viscount Saye and Sele altered these proportions.[44] In March 1643/4 five lords were added to a committee that had been appointed in April 1642, "in regard many of the lords committees are now absent."[45]

In addition to rank, the Lords applied other criteria in choosing committees and ordered that a lord when named should be present in the House. "No absent lord is to be of any committee," Elsyng wrote, "unless officers of state, when the bill or business concerns their office."[46]

Lords attending other committees near the parliament chamber were considered present in the House for the purpose of nomination.[47] Two studies have demonstrated how this order linking attendance and committee membership came to have political ramifications. Mrs. Flemion has shown that certain groups of lords in the 1620s, whom she calls "opposition" lords, were more faithful in attendance than lords aligned closely with the king and hence were able to dominate committees and gain power in the House.[48] In his study of the lay peers between 1640 and 1644, Mr. Crummett noted that, although attendance and nomination to committees were of course related, in the first and second sessions of the Long Parliament an inner group of those who attended dominated committees.[49] During the remaining years covered by his study, he found a clearer correlation between attendance and committee appointments, without the operation of any other determining factor.[50] An analysis of committees during the four years 1640–44 led him to conclude that the affairs of the House were in the hands of a few individuals regularly in attendance. Either their colleagues generally recognized them as capable or a well-organized group put their names forward quickly and regularly when committees were nominated. Possibly both factors were at work. Significantly, those most frequently named to committees were also those first named.[51]

A further requirement of the House was that a lord who had spoken against the body of a bill should not be named to the committee to consider that bill.[52] However, one who "moveth any doubt concerning the bill" ought to be named, if present. "This is . . . a received opinion," Elsyng observed, "and often in practice, and the clerk ought to be attentive, and hearken after the names of such lords." The House completed a committee by choosing attendants, who, as Elsyng had said, were "of the judges, the king's learned council [counsel], and the masters of the Chancery," all assistants in the House. The clerk read out their names, and, when they had been agreed upon, he read the time and place of meeting.[53] It is difficult to believe that the House itself arranged these details and yet such seems to have been the case.[54]

When the task of naming a committee had been completed, the clerk delivered the bill to "the first of the committee then present," that is, the first in order of precedence.[55] Possibly this custom was new. D'Ewes observed that in 1601 one bill had been delivered to Lord Howard of Walden, "being the puisne baron of the committees," and another to the "third" of a committee. "By which it is plain," he wrote, "that as well in the Upper House [at that time] as in the House of Commons, after any Bill is committed upon the second reading, it may be delivered indifferently to any of the Committees."[56] In 1604, on the same day, bills were delivered in one instance to the first of a committee and in another to the fifth.[57] In 1606 bills had been delivered to the first committee, the third committee, and the lord chief justice, an assistant.[58] But as the years went on, the usual procedure came to be that described by Elsyng.

With the bill, the clerk also delivered a sheet, which may be called a committee sheet for convenience. Many of these committee sheets have survived. They were sometimes copied out for other members and for interested parties as well. The clerk's assistant received 10s. for drawing up the committee sheet for a private bill and attending the committee. He collected 2s.6d. for "a Copy of a Committee delivered to a private person."[59] Committee sheets state the charge to the committee or, in the case of a bill, its title. They list committee members in due order of precedence with the first committee sometimes set slightly apart. They list attendants and the time and place of the initial meeting. Together with these sheets in the Main Papers of the House of Lords and elsewhere are filed bills, briefs of bills, related petitions, sketches, and rough notes, which indicate the kind of material a committee had at hand and sometimes the way it worked.[60] The clerk listed all committees in a committee book and kept a schedule of the days to which they were assigned.[61] He had been ordered to read at each meeting of the House the names of committees appointed for that afternoon; and on a number of occasions he seems faithfully to have read these and also the meetings scheduled for subsequent days —"that the Lords may know, when and where to meet, and when a Committee is *sine Die*, appoint a new tyme of meeting."[62]

The first committee, the lord first in order of precedence, was the chairman of the committee.[63] Early in James's reign, when a chairman could not serve, he returned the bill and other material he had received from the House to be redelivered to the successor whom the House should appoint.[64] In 1621 the House designated Huntingdon, second in line of precedence, to act in Arundel's absence.[65] Later, the member next in line seems to have taken over with less formality. The minutes of the Committee for Privileges in 1660 show how the chairmanship shifted at meetings of the committee, depending on the members present, and suggest the way it may have done so earlier.[66]

In 1621 the House discussed the question of a quorum for committees. Southampton moved that the committee for the bill concerning the Sabbath might proceed "yf a considerable number appeare," though not the majority of the members. Sheffield alleged that in the upper House it had not been customary to meet unless the major part was present. The House ordered the committee to meet if a third of its members came.[67] Later in the same sitting, the House set a general quorum, ordering that a committee should proceed if ten members appeared though they might be less than half those named.[68] In subsequent years, it became the custom when naming certain committees to set a particular quorum for each. "They, or any Four of them" were to meet in 1625, "they, or any Eight" in 1626.[69] This plan was followed more frequently in 1628 and quite regularly by 1640.[70]

Committees usually met at eight in the morning and two o'clock in the afternoon and were assigned to rooms near the parliament chamber: the "little" room, the Painted Chamber, and the prince's chamber. Sometimes they met in the council chamber at Whitehall or in the lodging of a committee member. Large committees met in the parliament chamber itself.[71] Except on these occasions, the lords probably sat around or at a table.[72] Other lords in addition to those specifically named to the committee could be present and could speak but not vote. Such lords were to "give place to all that are of the Committee though of lower degree, and shall sitt behind them."[73] Judges and other assistants assigned to the committee remained uncovered and stood.[74] At meetings for private bills, refreshments (hypocras and wafers) were provided.[75]

Proceedings at a committee varied with the matter at hand; but the basic function of every committee was to prepare business for the House.[76] In the case of a bill, "the nature of a committee is to speak unto the parts of the bill, to bring the matter to a head."[77] A committee permitted greater freedom of debate, and a man might speak more than once on the same topic in a given day and with less formality than in the House. He removed his hat, but need not rise from his place.[78] To start the committee's work, one of the attendants read the bill or part of it and later such amendments as were proposed.[79] When a committee considered a private bill, the assistant clerk read the bill and collected a fee for doing so.[80] By 1626 some standing committees had their own clerks.[81]

The committee called and heard all parties known to be concerned with a bill or with the business that it had in hand. They appeared in person or by counsel. Those who testified on oath were sworn in the House, since committees did not have the power to administer an oath.[82] Parties opposed to the bill were traditionally heard first, "for it is already understood, what the bill desires." Often hearings were quite long and a committee might adjourn itself from day to day as seemed necessary, setting a new time to meet before the end of each day's session.[83] Committees that did not do so, or that did not meet at the time originally set for them, were considered to be *sine die* and must return to the House for a new assignment.[84] There are some records of vote in a committee; and on certain occasions there is evidence of bitter disagreement and even of violence when tempers ran high. In June 1626 the archbishop of Canterbury reported to the House that there had been "some Sharpness of Speech between two Lords" at the Committee for the Defense of the Kingdom.[85] The House, on the recommendation of a subcommittee for privileges, ordered that "all Personal Sharpness, or Taxing Speeches" should be forborne in the House and in committee. The House declared that it would censure any offender. In 1641 it committed both the earl of Pembroke and Lord Mowbray and Maltravers to the Tower as a result of the altercation between them at a committee.[86]

When a committee or the greater part of it had come to an agreement, the results were reported to the House. "The first of the committees, that was present [at the committee], makes report thereof standing, and uncovered, with the bill in his hand."[87] In many instances the reporter, as one would expect, was the first committee or its original chairman.[88] In other cases he was "one of the committees."[89] Sometimes this suggested that the original chairman had not presided at the meeting of the committee. Sometimes it meant that the original chairman was not present in the House when the report was given.[90] Other variations are difficult to explain. Why did the bishop of Bangor, seventh in line of precedence, report from a committee in 1624? Had so few lords attended the meeting?[91] Although tenth in line of precedence, Lord Saye reported on a bill in 1625; and in 1644 Lord North, last in line of precedence, reported on a petition, although other members of the committee were in the House.[92] The reporter had not therefore always served as chairman, but was sometimes selected for another reason. While the reporter spoke, Elsyng wrote, "all the rest of that committee, then present, stand up, and are uncovered; whereby, they signify their assent unto the said report."[93] Despite this symbolic act, a committee member was free to speak in the House against the body of a bill or its amendments, even if the bill and its amendments had been reported favorably to the House. In an unusual case in 1624, the archbishop of Canterbury reported a bill concerning York House as fit to pass, but said frankly that "his heart goeth not with that bill."[94] The House was not in any way bound by a committee report nor by any order taken by a committee, but was free to alter or vary from it as seemed best.[95] Sometimes bills or other business were recommitted. On the whole, however, the House followed the recommendations that its committees brought in.

When the House adjourned itself, all committees remained in being and some continued to meet.[96] Thus, during the usual Easter recess in 1621, the House empowered committees to examine witnesses in Bacon's case; and in 1624 the Lords named a committee (which later became a joint committee with the lower House) to work with the king's secretaries to draw a manifesto concerning the breach of treaties with Spain.[97] Similarly, during the Long Parliament, the Committee of Both Kingdoms met during a recess in 1641.[98] When the king adjourned parliament, all committees were said to cease until parliament reconvened.[99] However, it is noteworthy that in both 1624 and 1628 the House subcommittees for the journal book were to meet after the end of the session to "peruse and perfect the journal" and to distribute the money in the poor box. In 1628 the subcommittee was also to examine what fees were due to officers of the House and report its findings at the next session.[100] Surprisingly, the Committee for Petitions appointed in the Short Parliament of 1640 continued to meet and transact business even after the parliament had been dissolved. This remarkable constitutional innovation seems to be unique.[101]

STANDING COMMITTEES

The Committee for Privileges

The Orders of the House defined a standing committee as "a committee to bee chosen out of the House, which shall stand all that Session."[102] It was also sometimes called a "generall Committee."[103] Standing committees of the House were "select committees" because they were chosen by the House from its members. However, standing committees differed from the select committees described above in that they were designed to handle any matters during a session that might arise within a broad subject area and were assigned to them by the House. Other select committees had been chosen to investigate a specific topic or to make recommendations concerning a specific bill or bills. Standing committees in the upper House first came into general use in 1621. Two were of major importance in the years 1621–49: the Committee for Customs, Orders, and Privileges and the Committee for Petitions.

The concept of a standing committee evolved gradually, as may be seen in the case of the Committee for Privileges. On 5 February 1620/1 the Lords named a committee "to take Consideration of the Customs and Orders of this House, and of the Privileges of the Peers of the Kingdom, and Lords of Parliament." On 8 February the committee reported on a number of points and also indicated that it needed further time to complete its business. The House then agreed "that the Power and Direction formerly given to the said Lords Committees . . . shall not at this Time cease and be determined, but shall continue further, so long as shall seem fit to this House." Although the committee's report was approved, it was to be held until the committee should, "towards the End of this Session of Parliament, present and tender a further Report, and Note of their whole Proceedings and Opinions in the Premises."[104] From that time forward, the committee was a standing committee, chosen regularly in each parliament.

The Committee for Privileges was selected early in a parliament.[105] In 1621 it had been chosen on the third day of the first sitting. The names were read again on the third day of the second sitting. In 1624 the committee was again chosen on the third day, and in 1625 and 1626 on the fourth. In the parliament of 1628, the House selected the committee on the third day of the first session and on the first day of the second. In the Short Parliament of 1640, the committee was again chosen on the third day and, on the insistence of Lord Montagu, before the House was called. In the Long Parliament of 1640, it was nominated on the second day, and other names were added later in the month.[106]

The committee was relatively large, ranging from 32 and 33 in 1621 and 1624, 26 in 1625, 35 in 1626, 34 in 1628, 45 in 1628/9, to 65 and 64 in the two parliaments of 1640. In 1626 and in the Long Parliament, it was called a "grand committee."[107] In the Short Parliament, Lord Montagu wrote that "the great committee for privileges mett and in regard of the greate number they removed into the parliament house."[108] The terms "great committee" and "grand committee" were used not only to indicate the size of the Committee for Privileges, but also to differentiate it from its subcommittees. In February 1620/1 the Committee for Privileges had requested that the House appoint a subcommittee to search and view such records as might seem necessary to its work. The House did so.[109] In March the House selected a committee of fifteen "to view and examine the Entries of the Journal Book,"[110] which was renewed in the second sitting; but in subsequent years this duty was assigned to a subcommittee of the Committee for Privileges.

The Committee for Privileges and the committee or subcommittee to view the journal were not always selected in the way that other select committees were chosen. In 1621 the Committee for Privileges was named without regard to benches. The House chose a different committee for the journal.[111] In 1624 the House voted to retain the same Committee for Privileges named in 1621 (with the addition of Lord Montagu). The subcommittee previously charged to search records was now a subcommittee to view the journal. The clerk was instructed to omit all lords who were absent. His revised list was then read and passed by the House.[112] In 1625 the House chose the Committee for Privileges by benches. This committee chose its own subcommittee.[113] In 1626 the Lords returned to the procedure they had used in 1624. They retained the committee and subcommittee chosen in 1625, but made some additions.[114] They continued the same committee in 1628 with five additional names. Absent lords were dropped, and the committee chose its own subcommittee.[115] For the Short Parliament of 1640, the House once more selected a committee by benches and the subcommittee in the same way. It followed the same procedure in November 1640 for the Long Parliament.[116]

Beginning in 1625 and 1626, the House set a quorum for both the grand committee and the subcommittee.[117] The chairman was the first committee, and he also served as reporter to the House. The committee met regularly on days usually established by the House when it was first appointed and also on such other days as it might select.[118] It had the power to search records without fee and summon such persons as it pleased.[119] It seems to have had a definite agenda—some agenda sheets have survived[120]—chiefly handling business referred to it by the House. This comprised a wide range of topics, covering the whole spectrum of privileges of peers and lords of parliament as individuals and their privileges as members of parliament as well as the customs, orders, and rights of the House itself.[121] The committee's first charge was to examine the form of the writ of summons.[122] As cases of privilege or general problems of procedure subsequently arose, they were referred to the committee. It dealt with the matter of protections issued by lords to their servants.[123] It inquired whether goods as well as persons were privileged.[124] It examined such complex questions as that presented in 1648 by the earl of Thanet, who complained to the House that the servants and farmers of his land had been attached and restrained for nonpayment of some arrears of rent by force of a decree in Chancery. The decree, the earl maintained, was of no force against him and his lands and constituted a breach of his privilege.[125] It was the Committee for Privileges that studied the problems raised by the denial of a writ of summons to the earl of Bristol and by the imprisonment of the earl of Arundel in time of parliament.[126] It made recommendations to the House concerning the precedence of peers.[127] In 1641 it considered a protest from the Irish parliament when members were summoned to answer in the parliament of England.[128] It investigated the unsuitable conduct of lords in the House or in committee and of others near the parliament chamber, in the lobbies, or in adjacent taverns. It was charged to study a proposal for an academy for noblemen's sons.[129]

The committee recommended orderly forms of procedure for the House, the seating of members, and the way to handle bills and conduct conferences with the lower House.[130] It reported on the procedure for bringing in a writ of error and studied the questions of jurisdiction and procedure raised by Sir John Bourchier's petition in 1621 concerning a decree in Chancery.[131] It set out the role of the officers of the House and its assistants and attendants: the lord chancellor, the judges, the king's counsel.[132] It investigated the powers of the gentleman usher. For instance, in pursuit of his duties of attaching persons on order of the House, had he the right to break down a door locked against him?[133] It reported on fees paid to officers of the House and recommended that fees for private ordinances should be the same as those for private bills.[134] In 1625 a subcommittee was asked to consider bills "begun, and not dispatched" during the previous session and "to order which of them shall be presented to the House."[135] This unusual assignment constituted this subcommittee, but probably only temporarily, as a kind of "steering" committee for the House.

In carrying out their work, the committee and subcommittee studied the ways in which parliament had proceeded in the past and relied heavily on precedent. For this inquiry in 1621, the committee engaged the services of two experienced antiquarians, William Hakewill and John Selden, who were familiar with legal research and with the records in the Tower.[136] It also used the talents of the clerk. Both Robert Bowyer and Henry Elsyng were experienced in searching records and had compiled collections of precedents.[137] Thus, in reporting the committee's recommendations concerning a lord's right as defendant to answer upon protestation of honor only "and not upon common oath," the earl marshal explained that "they had perused all the Precedents."[138]

The committee also investigated a problem by conducting hearings; and, when the question of testifying on honor arose again in 1640, the committee summoned officials of various courts. Each witness was assigned a day and time and required to answer why he had put peers on their oaths and refused averment on honor.[139] Having heard them all and "divers learned men of both laws" and examined such certificates as were presented, the committee then recommended that the House declare its earlier order to be in effect, and that the lord keeper should give notice accordingly to all courts of justice and see to its enforcement. Similarly, the committee investigated a case concerning respite of homage. On 1 July 1641 the House ordered that all process against peers of the realm concerning relief and respite of homage should be stayed until it had heard the cause. The matter was referred to the Committee for Privileges for consideration at its meeting of 12 July. The king's counsel were to have notice and the clerks of the Court of Exchequer were to attend to inform the lords of the committee by what means a recent judgment in the Exchequer had been gained on this point against the nobility—whether by a judgment or by *nihil dicit*.[140]

With the records that have survived, it is difficult to examine the work of the committee in further detail. There is no evidence that it had a clerk and no regular minutes are known. There are a few notes of committee meetings, but they are slight. Elsyng sketched out the charge for the committee meeting of 5 May 1628 and phrased a question. The question has been corrected, the vote entered, and a further question noted in another hand.[141] The careful minute books kept for the Committee for Privileges in 1660 and the years following clearly indicate how the committee operated at that time and are worth looking at. By 1660 the committee had its own clerk.[142] The chairman for each meeting, usually indicated in the minutes, seems to have been the premier lord present in order of precedence, a point also suggested by the fact that there is no indication that the committee *chose* a chairman. Thus the presiding officer varied from meeting to meeting, presumably depending on the attendance at each. Unfortunately, the minutes do not indicate attendance, except when there is a question concerning a quorum.[143] The committee met in a variety of places in and about the House. When it convened in the Painted Chamber, there was a table, and this was probably true of other rooms.[144] There was also a "bar." All parties who attended the committee were to stand "without the bar." Counsel was to be heard "at the bar and not elsewhere."[145] The committee established its own agenda in advance, determining which item referred by the House it would consider. Interested parties were given notice to appear and relevant documents were called in.[146] Each day's committee session began with a reading of the order of reference or charge from the House and any petitions or other relevant papers. In 1661, when the duke of Richmond complained to the committee concerning the arrest of his servant, he was referred back to the House for an order summoning those who had offended.[147] Those who presented petitions took the House's order of reference from the clerk of the parliaments and delivered it to the committee.[148] The committee heard testimony from plaintiffs, defendants, and their counsel and witnesses. It called some on its own authority, but on occasion returned to the House for power to do so. The committee voted formally, first on whether to put the question and finally on the question itself.[149] Sometimes several lords were asked to assist in drawing the report for the House, and sometimes the committee's clerk may have done so.[150] Normally the chairman presented it to the House.

Perhaps the formality of these proceedings stems in part from the way in which the clerk kept the minutes. But it cannot be entirely attributed to clerical influence. The fixed agenda, the regular days of meeting, the orders of reference, the summons to persons to appear,[151] the use of a bar, the record of votes, and the presentation to the House were the committee's own doing. Even its debates may have been formal. In 1667 a committee was "adjourned during pleasure" and later "resumed," the phraseology used when the House went into a committee of the whole House in order to free debate of the usual restrictions.[152] Although one cannot verify all details, many appear earlier. The main features of this procedure after the Restoration probably stemmed from the tradition before the civil war and make it possible to visualize more clearly how the committee may have operated in earlier years.

The Committee for Petitions

The Committee for Petitions was also a standing committee that developed in 1621. When originally instituted near the end of the first sitting on 29 May, it was a small committee containing eight members who were apparently chosen by benches.[153] It gradually increased in size over the years and came to be regularly established early in a parliament following the selection of the Committee for Privileges. In 1624, two weeks after the beginning of parliament, the House voted to continue the committee selected in 1621 with a few additional members. Others were added later.[154] In 1625 no committee was appointed. On the fifth day of the next parliament in 1626, the House chose a committee of twenty-four, selected by benches, with power "to divide themselves into several Parts," any five having authority to act.[155] On the fourth day in 1628, the House voted to retain the same committee it had chosen in 1626; the omission of members who were absent and the addition of a few names resulted in a total of twenty-nine. The earls' bench was heavily represented with seventeen members, four of whom were great officers of state (as against one in 1626). The quorum was seven.[156] In the Short Parliament, the committee, again chosen by benches on the third day of parliament, was even larger: seventeen of the earls' bench, eight bishops, and sixteen barons, with a quorum of seven. With a few exceptions, men were chosen who had served in 1628, but no court officials were included.[157] A similar committee was selected for the Long Parliament, again on the third day.[158]

The charge for the committee varied. Initially, in 1621, it was limited: it considered all petitions that had been exhibited in the House and had not yet been answered, save those concerning Sir John Bennet. In the next sitting of this same parliament, the House enlarged the committee's charge to include consideration not only of all petitions that had formerly been received, but also those presently in the House or that might come to the House (save petitions concerning Bennet, as before). In 1624 the committee was to receive petitions only at regular sittings and to have the power by majority vote to reject those it considered unfit. In 1626 recommendations to reject petitions were to be referred back to the House, but later in the session this restriction was removed. In the Short Parliament the committee was again instructed to receive and answer petitions only when formally sitting and only if they were signed and personally delivered.[159] Probably the same practice continued during the Long Parliament. Despite the press of business in this parliament, the Lords on several occasions specifically required that petitions must come first to the House, but the repetition of the order suggests that this was not in fact the case. The Lords also ordered in 1641 that petitions could be dismissed only on the authority of the House as a whole.[160] The committee soon fell behind in its work, and the House at frequent intervals issued orders that no more private petitions should be received.[161] A committee "for all abuses in matter of imprisonment and courts of justice" was chosen early in the session. This large standing committee also handled petitions and its work overlapped with that of the Committee for Petitions.[162] In March, the two committees coalesced.[163]

The Committee for Petitions relied on the assistance of attendants in the House: the king's learned counsel and the judges. In the second sitting of the parliament of 1621, on the motion of the earl of Bridgewater, who was then first committee, the House ordered several serjeants and the attorney general to assist the committee, together with such judges as the committee itself should be pleased to call from time to time. In 1626 both learned counsel and judges were again called to assist.[164] In April 1640 two judges were appointed by the House to attend; the committee could choose such other assistants as it might require, a pattern also followed in November in the Long Parliament.[165] The House usually set regular days of meeting for the committee, but also provided that it might meet on such other days as it chose. It was to report weekly.[166]

In the early years, the clerk of the parliaments provided the committee with clerical assistance. He docketed and numbered petitions as they were received, scheduled them for reading in the House, and noted the date and reference to the committee. He notified interested parties and the counsel that had been assigned. He summoned witnesses. After the committee reported and the House had come to a decision, the clerk drafted and drew the necessary orders and was sometimes involved in their execution.[167] In 1626 the clerk assigned to the committee an assistant, Will Harrison, who prepared catalogs and lists of petitions that were similar to the catalogs and lists of bills prepared for the House. He provided rudimentary agenda sheets for the committee and occasionally took notes of proceedings. He kept two "books" of petitions, one in which to enter petitions as they were received and the other to record answers given to them. What purports to be a book of orders for 1628 also contains accounts of committee proceedings.[168] For the Short Parliament, the petitions themselves tell most of the story. The clerk or his assistant noted when petitions were received by the committee and numbered them accordingly. The clerk of the committee continued to work in the same way in the Long Parliament. He numbered petitions and filed them alphabetically; he also kept a book of the committee's orders on petitions, usually orders of referral or rejection.[169] For other orders the committee normally relied on the authority and resolution of the House. When such action occurred, the petition was sometimes endorsed by the clerk of the parliaments as a bill was endorsed, with the date of reading and the action taken. Orders were also registered in the Books of Orders and Judgments, which have survived from 1640.[170]

These records, the recommendations of the committee, and the reports in the House and the orders of the House (both noted in the journal) provide glimpses of the way the committee worked. Like other committees, it received much of its business from the House. Petitions were read in the House and regularly referred to the committee for consideration.[171] However, the House also seems to have expected that petitions could come directly to the committee since it provided that they should be received only at formal meetings. Some petitioners addressed themselves to the House, some to the king, some to the lower House. Occasionally a petition was before both Houses at the same time.[172] Sometimes a petitioner's case was already pending in another court.[173] Some petitioners sought an individual sponsor among the lords in the hope that he would expedite a hearing in the House or in committee or otherwise would promote the cause in question.[174]

When the committee had formally received a petition, it set a date for a hearing. The normal schedule followed the order in which petitions had been received.[175] Sometimes the House intervened and required that a cause be heard "peremptorily."[176] In 1628 it ordered that the petition of the earl of Warwick against the East India Company should have "Precedency before all others."[177] Occasionally the first committee or another lord intervened or was asked to intervene to set a date for a hearing;[178] the clerk of the parliaments or the clerk of the committee also may have done so or tried to do so.[179] All interested parties received notice. They might appear in person or by counsel. In 1626 the House itself summoned defendants and witnesses.[180] Later, in 1640 and 1641, the committee took over most of this responsibility.[181] It ordered the gentleman usher, with the aid of all mayors, sheriffs, justices of the peace, constables, and other officers, to bring in John Stiles, who had neglected to appear, as he had been told to do, to answer the petition of Thomas Flanner.[182] Sometimes the House called in deeds, court records, or other documents it deemed necessary; sometimes the committee was empowered to do so or acted on its own authority.[183] All who were to testify were sworn first in the House, normally by the clerk of the parliaments.[184] A complainant must offer security to pay charges if he failed to make his case.[185] Counsel and usually the expenses of witnesses were paid by the individual in whose behalf they appeared.[186] All parties enjoyed the privilege of parliament while a petition was pending.[187] Prisoners were released from day to day by writ of *habeas corpus*.[188]

The committee met regularly once or twice a week and sometimes more frequently. In 1641 a subcommittee was to meet daily. Of those present, the first lord in order of precedence presided. Sometimes he took notes of proceedings. Clearly there was a fixed agenda. Possibly members of the committee had copies of the petition to be considered.[189] Both parties and their witnesses were heard, often at length. On some occasions, depositions of witnesses taken in the country or elsewhere were admitted and on some occasions depositions taken in other courts.[190] A decision was reached by majority vote.[191] The clerk of the committee recorded what was done and drew up the orders of the committee.[192] Remarkably, as noted above, there is firm evidence that the committee continued its meetings after the Short Parliament had been dissolved on 5 May. One petition was endorsed "*lecta 11⁰ Maii* 1640"; another was dated 20 May, and an original order, signed by the clerk of the parliaments and dated 25 May, indicates that the committee not only met then but also planned to meet again on 17 June. It required the presence of a defendant at a hearing scheduled for that day.[193]

The business of the Committee for Petitions developed in significant ways in the years 1621–49. It considered many original causes or "cries for help" of different kinds. In 1621 a group of prisoners in the Fleet complained of the "wrongs and violences" of their warden. Their petition was ultimately turned over to the committee.[194] So too was the petition of the Glovers of London for incorporation, a petition from Lady Yelverton concerning her husband's imprisonment and fine and that from Lord Morley's tenants for relief.[195] The committee also received and considered or at least contemplated considering petitions concerning cases in other courts. On 4 June the committee reported to the House that, in view of the imminent adjournment, they had agreed on replies the clerk could make to such petitions as had not yet been answered. He was to inform petitioners that suits in other courts would not be stayed "upon pretence of petition exhibited in parliament and unanswered" and also that parliament would not reverse decrees without hearing counsel on both sides.[196] Thus, early in its career, the committee handled a variety of complaints, some of original causes and others of causes already pending or already decided in other courts. But in the second sitting of the parliament of 1621, on recommendation of the Committee for the Privileges and Customs of the House, not of the Committee for Petitions, the House specifically declined to entertain an appeal by Sir John Bourchier against a decree in Chancery. The House examined the matter of fact in the petition—Bourchier's allegation that his case had been hastily heard—but did not hear his appeal against the decree of which he complained. Bourchier, in fact, was brought before the House, forced to apologize to Williams, the lord keeper, and threatened with imprisonment, a procedure not likely to encourage further petitions of this sort.[197] In 1624 the House declined to support an order proposed by the Committee for Petitions concerning an appeal in equity, recommending instead that the lord keeper apply to the crown for a commission of review.[198] In 1626 and 1628, however, the committee recommended and the House ordered further hearings on cases previously determined in both temporal and spiritual courts; but at the same time, the customary procedure for reversing decrees in Chancery by private bill continued.[199] There had been no clear decision concerning the scope of the committee's work, a situation that continued through the Short Parliament of 1640 and was abundantly demonstrated in the years of the Long Parliament.

In the Short Parliament, the committee considered a petition against Sir John Ipsley, a servant of the crown who had seized merchandise belonging to one Nicholls and his partners. It heard and dismissed a petition from John Harrison, stationer, to sell supplies to the clerk of the parliaments. It handled a petition concerning payment of alimony, a claim to privilege, a complaint concerning customs duties, and a request to be free from charges imposed by the commissioners of sewers of the Isle of Wight, as well as appeals from a verdict of the Court of Admiralty and from a decree in the earl marshal's court.[200]

With the Long Parliament, a flood of petitions of many kinds came to the committee. The accumulation of grievances in the long intermission of parliaments, the heavy schedule of business in the lower House, and the precedents and practice established by the Lords in receiving and hearing petitions in the years 1621–29 led petitioners to submit their complaints in increasing numbers to the upper House. Sir Matthew Hale, who was thirty-one years old in 1640, wrote: "When the Long Parliament came after intermission of parliaments, and the grievances of the subjects by the reason thereof were very many and importunate, such a throng of complainants pressed into parliament, especially into the lords house, as transported proceedings in that house beyond the known ancient and regular bounds thereof. Complaints of decrees sentences and judgments came in apace, and were promiscuously heard."[201] Some petitioners complained of delays below. Anthony Wither spoke of "the multitude of business in the . . . Commons house" in referring his case to the Lords.[202] Others noted the abolition of the Courts of Star Chamber and High Commission (both in the summer of 1641).[203] In 1642 there was a complaint concerning Chancery, since the lord keeper "was absent," and in 1643 a note that no other court of equity (save parliament) was open.[204] Some petitioners claimed poverty and the inability to go to law.[205] Such statements were of course designed to induce the upper House to take jurisdiction of the petitioner's case and may be discounted accordingly.

Nevertheless, the increase in litigation, the overcrowding of the courts, the cloud cast upon the judges by impeachment proceedings, and the dislocation caused by the civil wars, as well as the hope for cheap, speedy, and possibly final justice, doubtless led many to look to the House of Lords for relief.[206]

The petitions were of many kinds and involved the Committee for Petitions (and the House) in a variety of business. The committee continued to handle original cases between party and party, often cases of little consequence such as that of Frances Collyer, who complained that the lord privy seal had torn down her wall and outhouses and encroached upon her land, or that of Mary Weoly, who petitioned for support from her husband. The latter was finally dismissed as "too mean for their Lordships recognizance."[207] The committee undertook to hear complaints concerning judgments in many courts (which were in effect appeals) and also some complaints that were specifically phrased as appeals:[208] from the Court of Requests,[209] the Court of Wards,[210] Star Chamber,[211] the Court of High Commission[212] and other ecclesiastical courts,[213] Exchequer, and Chancery.[214] It heard numerous complaints about the church, its courts and officials, the presentation to livings, the personal lives of ministers, the railing of communion tables.[215] It also became involved in investigating complaints concerning the administration of government: the pressing of soldiers and the collection and payment of coat and conduct money,[216] the awards of the commissioners of sewers,[217] the difficulties of a constable,[218] the quarrels over ship money,[219] and the problems of the fens.[220] It even assisted an ambitious father to place his son at Winchester and considered whether a Latin grammar was worthy of publication.[221]

From its earliest days in 1621, the House had empowered the committee to come to certain decisions on its own authority. As we have seen, the House had voted that the clerk of the parliaments, on behalf of the committee, might refer petitions to appropriate courts and might inform petitioners that parliament would not reverse decrees until both sides had been heard and would not stay proceedings in other courts.[222] In 1641 the House voted that the committee should reject petitions that could be relieved either at common law or in courts of equity, retaining "such as are fit for their Lordships' consideration," and presumably leaving the necessary decisions to the committee itself.[223] The committee's orders on individual petitions in 1640 and 1641 indicate just how far it went in handling cases on its own authority in those years.

It submitted some cases to referees either for a preliminary hearing before further examination by the committee or if possible for final determination. Thus Dr. Potter's complaint was to go to the lord keeper, to "settle the business if he can or otherwise to certify" the state of the case to the committee; the committee would then "take such further order therein as the justness of the cause shall require." The case of Dame Anne Mollineux was referred to the barons of the Exchequer for "speedy consideration." If they could not end the matter, they were to certify the true state of the cause to their lordships. Similarly, the petition of Jonas Legg was referred to merchants, "to end" or "to certify to their Lordships," and a commission under the great seal was to be issued to examine the misdemeanors of justices of the peace of Middlesex and report to the committee. The lord admiral was to examine Margrett Medcalfe's case "and to do the poore woman justice therein."[224]

It recommended a number of complaints to trial at law. Sir William Monyns, who claimed the right to an advowson, was to seek remedy in this way, and the committee requested the archbishop of Canterbury to waive his privilege of parliament so that Monyns might proceed. Likewise, Thomas Bushell was to waive his protection so that Lady Middleton could commence an action against him. Archibald Mackeller and Dr. Shipsea, who each claimed by separate patent a right to the Church of St. Peter's in the Tower of London, were to try their case at common law and were further referred to the lord keeper, "who is Visitor of the place." Edward Noye's petition was referred to the lord keeper, "to admit him *in forma pauperis*" and to expedite a hearing. Edward Mayne's petition was dismissed, to be heard by the lord keeper if he saw cause. On the advice of referees, Tobias Martin's complaint concerning a decree in Chancery was referred to the lord keeper, who was to hear the cause in case it had not been fully heard the first time.[225]

In a number of instances, the Committee for Petitions referred petitions to other courts with directions as to what should be done. Thus the judge of the prerogative court of Canterbury was to entertain an appeal from Martin Browne and others concerning the administration of the estate of John Browne, despite the fact that the usual time limit for such appeals had long passed. The lord keeper was to review a decree made against George Beare and to give the petitioner such damages as he thought fit.[226] The committee directed Bassett Cole and his wife to prefer a bill in Chancery for the discovery of a trust for the office of register. If the trust should appear, the committee ordered that "the said Court of Chancery give authority" to the bishop of Lincoln to sequester the profits of the office of register for payment of debts due the Coles.[227] The committee ordered that Lord Fauconbridge should bring a bill of review in Chancery upon a decree made against him, the execution of the decree to "be respited until the cause be reheard . . . according to the course of that Court." In the case of Henry Fisher and the dean and chapter of Christ

Church, Oxford, the committee recommended that the judges and barons of the Court of Exchequer Chamber should expedite the case of error depending before them and certify their judgment to the committee so that it might proceed further. The committee referred petitions from the Winstanleys, Mary Roth, and Margaret Whithorne to the lord keeper for "speedy hearing" since they were already plaintiffs in Chancery in the same matters. Sir Richard Strode petitioned that the lord keeper should call the register of the Court of Chancery to examine an order made in the twelfth year of Charles I's reign. The Lords' committee recommended that the lord keeper do so, "and to certify the said order if by his law it shall be thought reasonable." The commissioners of the Court of High Commission were ordered to appear before the committee to defend their sentence against Lady Purbeck.[228] When Sir Robert Hamilton complained about a decree made against him in Chancery and about the dismissal of a cross bill that he had preferred, the committee declined to hear him but referred his petition to the lord keeper, "to be set down to be heard notwithstanding the said dismission" provided that it was reviewed "before the end of Trinity term next." Otherwise decree and dismission should "stand firm and good."[229]

In some instances, the committee ordered a stay of proceedings in other courts or in the execution of a judgment. In considering the petition of Charles and Mary Stanford, the committee ordered certain ecclesiastical officials to appear, the cause in the ecclesiastical court to "stay in the meantime." A petition from Jane Gibbons, wife of a mariner, resulted in a committee order deferring the execution of a sentence in the Court of Admiralty against her husband until the lords of the present parliament had determined the jurisdiction of the court or had themselves heard the cause.[230]

Sometimes the committee itself or members of the committee virtually decided a case, but still under the umbrella of the authority of the House. For example, in 1624 the House ordered the earl of Bridgewater and Lord Russell (both members of the committee) to consider the petition of Widow Rogers and to settle the matter if they could.[231] In the case of the earl of Cleveland and Phillip Lord Herbert in 1641, the committee had ordered that counsel for both parties should agree upon an act of parliament for the sale of certain manors before "our Lady Day then next ensuing." If such an agreement were not reached, the manors should be delivered to the trustees of Lord Herbert. The day passed without agreement. The House therefore required Cleveland to show cause why the committee's order should not be performed and voted to confirm the order if he should fail to do so.[232]

In certain instances, the committee came to a resolution on its own authority. Thus Thomas Austen was ordered to take the profits of the parsonage of Grafton, allowing ten pounds per annum to the curate and leaving him in peace. The committee proposed a settlement concerning debts between Lady Dyer and Sir Robert Pye, to which both agreed. It dismissed Thomas Gratwick's petition and decreed that Lyming Dickenson should continue to receive the rents that had been in question. The committee declared void a sentence that had been passed against John Ward and ordered that the archbishop of Canterbury, the bishops of Ely and Rochester, and other high commissioners should attend to show cause why Ward should not receive damages. The committee found that Mary, Judith, and Abigail Stoddard deserved "much pity and commiseration" and directed their brother to pay their annuities and allow them to enjoy the tenement that they had inherited or else "show cause better to the contrary then yet he hath done." In the case of Hugh and Mary Gwynne, the committee ordered that a decree made in Chancery should stand unless the petitioners found good cause of review upon new matter not expressed in their petition.[233] The vice-chancellor of Cambridge and the heads of the colleges were to admit Robert Medcalf as fellow of Trinity College with the seniority "which shall appear to be his right."[234]

The committee was required to report regularly to the House, usually through its first committee. In 1621 the responsibility of reporter often fell to the earl of Bridgewater, in 1624 to Bridgewater and Essex, in 1626 to Bridgewater and Manchester.[235] When two peers reported on the same day, each may have handled cases considered when he had served as chairman.[236] In 1628 a number of lords served as reporters: Devon, Clare, Warwick, Saye, and the bishops of Lincoln and Norwich. This variety may have reflected shifts in the chairmanship from meeting to meeting, or reporters may have been chosen for other reasons.[237] In the Short Parliament, only one report was recorded, by Dorset, although there is other evidence that the committee continued to meet.[238] In the early years of the Long Parliament, the committee met and reported with fair regularity.[239]

In general, the House confirmed and approved the committee's recommendations. The House thus denied a petition in 1628 from Lady Packington for a hearing on the grounds that her counsel had already been fully heard in committee.[240] Occasionally, however, the House reheard a case itself before coming to a vote.[241] It also assigned petitions to other committees,[242] and in 1644 directed the judges to decide which cases could be relieved at law.[243] It continued to handle some petitions directly itself.[244]

Many of those who had hoped for speedy or cheap justice were destined to be disappointed. Robert Lane presented a petition to the House in 1624, complaining that he had been debarred by a decree in Chancery from suing at common law. Hearings were scheduled in 1626 and 1628. The case was still unsettled in 1648.[245] Archibald Nicholls's petition against Ipsley had come first to the upper House and was heard in 1628. In May 1640 the House confirmed a decision reached by the committee that the crown owed Nicholls £2,575 and the earl of Dorset was delegated to present the matter to the king. By November 1640 Nicholls had still received no payment and once more petitioned the Lords.[246] Hearings were regularly scheduled, rescheduled, and postponed. Plaintiffs, defendants, their counsel, and their witnesses all had to attend on numerous occasions, often fruitlessly. Symon Plychar complained that fourteen several days had been appointed for the hearing of his case. He had attended each day with counsel at great charge and had pawned goods worth 120*li.* "to follow his just complaint."[247] Witnesses who appeared for Robert Partridge said that they were very poor men who had attended at their own expense "and spent their money here, and no ways able to get home, their habitation being 43 miles off, without the benevolence of good people."[248]

The significance of the work of the Committee for Petitions goes far beyond the limits of a discussion of the standing committee as an institution. During the years 1621–49, it in effect took over the ancient role of receivers and triers of petitions. These, though still formally appointed at the opening of every parliament, no longer served any purpose.[249] Through the work of the Committee for Petitions and other committees of the same sort (for abuses of imprisonment, for Star Chamber, for trade, and the like), the House became involved in the redress of grievances, a function traditionally claimed by the lower House. "Members of the House," Sir Edward Coke had said in 1624, "were inquisitors of the realm, as coming from every part of it and being more sensible of grievances than the Lords in the Upper House were because they were once liable unto them."[250] By 1640 members of the House of Commons were no longer the only inquisitors of the realm. Grievances flooded into both Houses and were considered by both.[251] The activities of the committee also raised the problem of the jurisdiction of the upper House (which will be considered at greater length elsewhere) and laid the foundation for later quarrels between the Houses concerning the judicial powers exercised by the Lords. Writing after the Restoration, Sir Matthew Hale reflected that Selden's investigation of the privileges of the Lords in 1621 had given "the lords occasion of looking into the *Placita Parliamenti tempore E.I.* which they applied singly to the house of lords," so that they began to enlarge their jurisdiction not only to appeals but to almost all kinds of cases of the first instance.[252] The work of the committee and the House in dealing with a large and undifferentiated mass of petitions does indeed recall the parliaments and great councils of Edward I; but this result was brought about not so much by the influence of Selden and the early precedents that he avouched as it was by the pressure of events. Further problems resulting from the committee's work, which will also be considered in a later chapter, arose from the execution or attempted execution of orders recommended by the committee and confirmed by the House. In a period when the very position of a lord was increasingly challenged, difficulties of enforcement tested the power of the House.

THE COMMITTEE OF THE WHOLE HOUSE

On 1 December 1606 the clerk of the parliaments first recorded a new procedure in the House of Lords—a procedure to be known later as the committee of the whole House. The occasion was a debate on the proposed articles of the instrument of union between England and Scotland. The clerk wrote:

> It was thought the best and readiest Means for Speed, not to insist upon the usual and formal Order of the House, according to the Manner of speaking to Bills (where the Order is to speak but once to a Bill at one Time of Reading), nor to make a several[253] Committee for the preparing of the Business to the House (which seemed to restrain the Liberty of Discourse and Debate, that would probably be enlarged if every one of the Lords were present, and had his free Speech); but to confer all together, and yet after the Manner of a Committee, and with the same Liberty of Speech that is usual in Committees, that every one may deliver his Mind and Meaning upon any Point as Occasion may serve, by as often Speech as he will; and that it should be done every Morning (according to the Manner of Conference in a Committee), some while after the usual Form of Sitting in the House were holden and observed.[254]

Michael Graves has spoken of the "cross-fertilization" in matters of procedure between the Houses. This may well be an example of it. When the House of Commons first used the same procedure is not entirely clear, perhaps in April 1606 but certainly by the following spring.[255] In the lower House, scholars have traced the gradual evolution of the committee of the whole House from "general committees" of the Elizabethan period.[256] Unfortunately, the record of the upper House does not permit speculation about earlier forms of the committee there, nor is there any further indication of its use by the Lords until February 1609/10.[257] Thereafter it was employed fairly frequently.

First this section will describe the procedure itself, then discuss its use and significance. In normal practice, the initial step was taken when the House agreed to go into committee to discuss a specific topic, bill, or other measure. Often there was debate; at least once (March 1625/6) there was a formal vote before this decision was reached.[258] Finally, a standing order, said to have been made shortly thereafter, provided that the House must go into committee if a lord so desired.[259] Sometimes the decision to go into committee carried over for several days, as in 1606: "that it should be done every Morning."[260] Similarly, in July 1610, the committee of the whole House, which met to consider the bill for the king's safety, scheduled meetings for subsequent days.[261] When the committee had first met in 1606, it was "some while after the usual Form of Sitting in the House were holden and observed,"[262] that is, after the House had formally convened. But in 1610 the committee assembled, by prearrangement, in the early morning before prayers were said.[263] On some occasions, the House went into committee several times in a single morning.[264]

When a committee had been decided upon, the lord chancellor (or presiding officer) adjourned the House (if it was in session), stepped down from the woolsack, and (if he was a baron) took the place on the earls' bench to which his office entitled him. If one of the other judges was presiding, he went to his place with the assistants. Because he was not a peer in 1625, Coventry, lord keeper, also removed to the judges' woolsacks.[265] Unlike the practice in the House of Commons, no chairman or moderator was chosen. In April 1640 a speaker for the committee was proposed, not to keep order but "to recollect and gather together the Heads of those Matters that are propounded, the better to prepare Business for a Conclusion." The suggestion followed long and bitter debate on whether the Lords had infringed on the Commons' right to initiate money bills.[266] There is no convincing evidence that it was carried out until after the Restoration, although Lord Wharton recalled in 1660 that he thought chairmen or moderators had been appointed "anciently" and Lord Robartes said in 1679 that there had been no chairmen until 1642.[267]

When the House went into committee in James's first parliament, the clerk was sometimes directed to depart, sometimes ordered to stay to take notes or to read a bill.[268] Henry Elsyng, clerk from 1621 to 1635, usually remained and took notes in his "scribbled book."[269] John Browne, a later clerk, did the same.[270] No formal record appeared in the journal. The judges left unless required to stay.[271] The lords were "to sit in Order, as at other Times of Sitting."[272] They might speak freely, even (in the years after the Restoration and possibly before) referring to each other by name.[273] They were expected to stand when they spoke.[274] If two men rose at the same time, apparently the committee ruled who should speak first.[275] Often resolutions emerged naturally from debate.[276] Sometimes, as previously noted, there was considerable difficulty in formulating the committee's opinions or in reaching a decision. Perhaps the committee of the whole House occasionally voted, as other committees did, but there is no clear record that it did so during this period.[277] A committee of the whole House might create a subcommittee to study matters under debate or suggest ways to implement decisions.[278] Such a subcommittee reported back to the committee. When the committee of the whole House dissolved and the House was "resumed," it was the duty of the lord chancellor or presiding officer of the House to report to the House what had occurred and what decisions had been reached, in this way performing some of the duties of a chairman.[279] The House was then free to confirm what had been done or to reject it.[280]

The clerk's careful description in 1606 (repeated several times) and the Standing Orders indicate that the chief purpose of the committee of the whole House was to free the lords from the usual rules governing debate.[281] Remarks on the floor and a consideration of the circumstances when the House went into committee underline the same point. In 1621 Lord Sheffield, beginning to speak for a second time, was reminded by the prince that he could speak only once to the same matter, "Whereupon the E. of South[amp]ton and Lo. North moved that the House should be adjourned, that in this case every man might have freedome of speech." A similar situation arose in 1626: "Divers Lords speaking twice or thrice . . . contrary to the ancient order, it was moved the house might be put into a committee." The order to speak only once to the same matter was reconfirmed on 9 May 1626, with the addition that "if the Cause required much Debate, then the House [was] to be put into a Committee."[282]

A committee of the whole House could move business along, particularly in a vexed question (*vexata quaestio*) that might require "upon some Occasion, Reply, or one Man oftener to speak."[283] The lords could "answer one another if occasion served," or one man might explain himself by speaking several times.[284] The committee of the whole House was used on numerous occasions when the Lords were trying to work out ways of proceeding. In 1621 the House thus went into committee to discuss how to move against delinquents such as Yelverton, Mompesson, and Michell; to debate ways to proceed in Bacon's case and whether his submission "were a sufficient Confession for the Lords to ground their Censure on";[285] to consider problems raised by Floyd's case and the Commons' claim to judicature; to discuss arrangements for a hearing on a petition; and in 1626 to debate the procedure for trying the earl of

Bristol.[286] A committee was appropriate, the Lords specifically stated, for matters of importance that the whole House should discuss, whether framed as bills or in other form. Thus the bill against nonresidence and pluralities of benefices in 1610 was referred to a committee of the whole House, "the rather because the same is of much Importance."[287] Similarly, the bill for the king's safety went to a committee of the whole House.[288] In 1614 the Lords, in order to debate whether to confer with the lower House concerning impositions, went into committee "because they were to treat of Matter of great Importance"; and in 1626, in reporting a petition from the countess of Bristol, whose husband had been charged with treason before the House of Lords, the Committee for Privileges "thought it to be of so great consequence as more fit to be treated of by the whole house."[289] In the years between 1621 and 1629, much of the weightiest business of the House was handled in this way: in 1624 the advice to the king on the Spanish match,[290] the charges against Lord Treasurer Cranfield and his sentence,[291] petitions against recusants in 1624 and concerning religion in 1625,[292] in 1626 the king's imprisonment of the earl of Arundel in time of parliament and other matters of privilege,[293] and in 1628 the great questions of "ancient liberties," which culminated in the Lords' approval of the Petition of Right.[294]

Early in the Stuart period, the committee of the whole House was used occasionally for important bills. In the Long Parliament, the committee of the whole House continued to be used for bills and later for ordinances.[295] It was natural, as attendance declined during the civil war years, that committees should be composed of all the remaining members of the House, but at the same time select committees continued to be appointed. For example, on 8 June 1644 thirteen peers were listed as present. A select committee of seven was nominated for one ordinance, while another was referred to a committee of the whole House.[296] By the eighteenth century, all public bills were referred to committees of the whole House.[297]

Gradually it became the practice for both Houses to use committees of the whole House in conferences with each other. This arrangement first began in 1610 and was not employed again until 1621. By 1628 the custom was fully established and was so general by 1641 that the Houses were careful to specify when smaller committees were intended. After the Restoration, all conferences were between committees of the whole House. Similarly, when the Houses jointly presented addresses to the crown, they went as committees of the whole House.[298]

The committee of the whole House served the Lords well. It did indeed promote free debate, swift rebuttal, prompt explanation, and more expeditious proceedings. Although the rule against speaking more than once in the House was sometimes broken,[299] the clerk's "scribbled" notes and other accounts show that lords did speak more frequently when the House was in committee.[300] It is perhaps significant that the first use of this form of procedure in the upper House should have been in 1606 in a discussion of the instrument for union. This was a measure promoted by the crown through its chief ministers, Salisbury and Ellesmere. The committee of the whole House may well have been their device. Both had sat in the Elizabethan House of Commons and were well acquainted with the "general committee" and its uses.[301] A similar committee in the upper House would enable proponents of the instrument to explain it article by article, answering such objections as might well be put forward by lords who were said to be opposed.[302] In February 1609/10, when apparently the committee of the whole House was next used in the House of Lords, it was clearly done at the motion of the lord chancellor, Ellesmere, who was working closely with Salisbury in forwarding business.[303] The issue was again one of great complexity—the first stages of the discussion of tenures and wardship that would lead to the proposed contract—a project in which Salisbury was particularly concerned and where he would welcome an opportunity to promote his ideas free of the usual restrictions on debate. The consideration of this subject during both the fourth and fifth sessions of the parliament, like that of the union earlier, also proceeded with royal approval under Salisbury's aegis; and it was largely handled in a committee of the whole House, where one man or a handful of men could more readily put their points across and answer questions and objections as they arose.

For the same reasons, Salisbury pushed again and again in James's first parliament for a "free conference" with the House of Commons, where proposals could be discussed between committees of the two Houses.[304] He was surely seeking the opportunity to rebut and to negotiate an agreement. Not unreasonably, members of the Commons, who wished to hear what was said and then to retire to debate among themselves, preferred to give "audience," where they came to hear the Lords' propositions and remained silent.[305]

The Lords themselves quickly perceived the benefits and disadvantages of procedure by committee of the whole House and on several occasions debated whether to adopt it or not. There were times when free debate and hence a committee might be inadvisable. In May 1621 the House discussed a message from the king concerning Sir Henry Yelverton. Several lords spoke more than once and tempers rose. It was moved that the House should go into committee. Lord North objected, "Noe, for the reason of not twyce speaking, leaste they be driven into a heate." Mandeville, lord treasurer, agreed.[306] There was a sharp exchange in 1628.

The duke of Buckingham, opposed to joining with the House of Commons in the Petition of Right, tried unsuccessfully to block a committee of the whole House.[307] His instincts were right. Writing in 1640, Bishop Williams recalled that "when the Petition of Right had passed the lower House, there was but 4 lords for certain days, that stood for the same. And the Bishop [Williams himself] came in to be fifth. If either these 5 lords had been then away . . . the Petition of Right had been cast forth, upon the first reading. As it had been howsoever, if the Duke, who opposed it, had had so much parliament craft as to keep the House from being a committee (which gave the Lords opportunity to speak so often) and to put it suddenly to the voices."[308] Similarly, proponents of the Irish cattle bill in 1666 pushed for a committee of the whole House so that they could speak more frequently.[309] The procedure could be a powerful weapon for ministers of the government with a program to expound or for a small group of articulate lords determined to swing a majority to their ways of thinking.

From the beginning, the committee of the whole House in the upper House developed differently from that in the lower. It was always distinct from the general committee by its lack of a moderator. It had probably initially been instituted by ministers of the crown to forward royal policy. It served also as a vehicle for conferences and addresses. But its primary function was to promote expeditious and free debate, and it became a useful tactical procedure for lords outnumbered on the floor.

JOINT COMMITTEES

In November 1666 the House of Commons sent a message to the House of Lords desiring that a committee of both Houses might be appointed to examine the accounts of royal officers. The Lords consulted their Committee for Privileges and the lord great chamberlain reported that although many precedents for committees of lords and commoners had been found, they "conceive that all those Precedents are only of such Committees as are usually called Conferences," with the exception of one in 1640 and one in 1661.[310]

What we today call joint committees had in fact been frequently used in the early Stuart period, and both Houses had relied heavily on them in the years of civil war. It is often difficult, however, as the Committee for Privileges discovered, to differentiate between joint committees chosen to carry on discussion by way of conference and hence called "conference committees" or "conferences," and joint committees chosen to work in other ways. The term "conference" was frequently applied to committees, the term "joint committee" rarely. Both were committees chosen from both Houses and thus were technically joint committees. In the present discussion, however, the term "joint committee" will be used to designate relatively small committees from both Houses selected to carry forward the detailed work that a larger body could not conveniently execute. These committees were smaller than conference committees (no more than twelve lords and twenty-four commoners) and indeed were sometimes subcommittees of the larger conference committees. Such small joint committees might draft bills, examine witnesses, or prepare and deliver addresses from both Houses to the king.[311] During the civil war, joint committees carried forward the executive responsibilities of government taken over by parliament.

It is difficult to differentiate the conference and the joint committee in Tudor times. In the Tudor period, the Lords on several occasions selected committees to join with committees of the lower House. In 1542 a group was to confer with members from the House of Commons; and in 1544 twelve lords were to meet with an equal number of commoners to discuss a bill. In Mary's reign, a joint committee drafted an address to the crown. Another met in a number of sessions to draft an act repealing the Act of Supremacy and later a small joint committee worked on the revision of another bill. Under Elizabeth, the Houses continued to work together in both conferences and in joint committees.[312]

In the reigns of James and Charles, the work of conferences and that of joint committees were distinguished on a number of occasions and thus the particular role of the joint committee became clearer. In 1604 fifty lords and one hundred members of the House of Commons met together in conference on the matter of the union with Scotland. After five meetings, they were at last ready to draft a bill. This was work for which a joint committee was appropriate. The Lords chose two earls, two barons, two bishops, two judges, and a member of the king's learned counsel. The Commons chose twenty of their leading members, voting on each individually. Similarly, a small joint committee (a subcommittee of the conference committee) met in 1621 to negotiate amendments to a bill concerning informers. In the same parliament, when precipitate action by the House of Commons in punishing Floyd, who had spoken disparagingly of the queen of Bohemia and her husband, threatened good relations between the Houses, the matter was considered first by both Houses meeting together as committees of the whole House at a conference. Later several lords suggested a small joint committee. As the earl of Southampton said, "A general conference wyll not well ende this matter." He therefore moved "that a small Committee of theirs may meet with a small Committee of ours. . . . At a small Committee we may argue yt more freely, and sett downe a course between us both for the friendly endeing of this buissines." Both Houses agreed to appoint members for a subcommittee and the matter was indeed successfully ended.[313]

In the Stuart period, as in the Tudor, joint committees fulfilled a variety of functions. In 1621 a joint committee discussed a bill and prepared a message of thanks to the king. In 1624 a joint committee negotiated the amendments to the bill of monopolies, and another drafted addresses to the king, asking him to break relations with Spain. In 1625 a joint committee prepared and delivered an address concerning recusants. However, in 1628, when the House of Lords requested a joint committee to discuss a proposed addition to the Petition of Right, the Commons refused. Initially they objected to both the addition and the suggested procedure, but ultimately they were forced to drop their objection to a joint committee. Such old parliament men as Sir Thomas Wentworth, Sir Nathaniel Rich, and Sir Edward Coke easily refuted the contention that a joint committee was unparliamentary by citing precedents from their own experience.[314]

The Long Parliament relied heavily on joint committees. In 1641 it appointed eighteen joint committees and in 1642 sixty, some permanent or semipermanent in character. The work of some of these committees followed the familiar pattern established earlier: they drafted addresses to the crown, messages of thanks to military leaders, and declarations of parliament for public consumption. Joint committees waited on the aldermen and the Common Council of London. They examined letters, petitions, and other documents to prepare them for parliamentary consideration. As the Houses took on the responsibilities of government administration, the joint committee was increasingly used in an executive capacity and its powers grew with the powers of parliament. In May 1641 a joint standing committee was charged to plan the disbandment of the armies and to "settle and perfect the Account between the Scotts and the Northern Counties." In the following month, a joint committee was to meet from time to time to consider the Commons' proposals for dealing with the times. In August two lords and four commoners were to accompany the king to Scotland and to keep the parliament informed. Subsequently, similar committees to gather and relay information were dispatched to Hull and to York. In September 1642 a "Standing Committee of Assistance" advised the earl of Essex about military operations. Joint committees thus developed as necessity demanded; but their activities were, for the most part, specifically limited and none as yet had powers independent of parliament itself.[315]

With the establishment of the Committee of Both Kingdoms in 1644, the joint committee entered a new phase of development. It assumed wider jurisdiction and became virtually independent of the Houses that had voted it authority. These changes did not come about suddenly. A gradual extension of the activities of joint committees may be seen in the appointment of a joint committee for Irish affairs in March 1641/2. Appointment of several committees for defense culminated in July in the Committee for the Safety of the Kingdom (five lords, ten commoners), which became the principal organ for carrying on the war.[316] It could commission officers, issue warrants for the payment of money, assume powers of the commander in chief in his absence, administer oaths, handle correspondence, and do what was necessary to frustrate royalist hopes of aid from abroad. The treaty with Scotland in November 1643 provided for a committee to represent both kingdoms.[317]

The Committee of Both Kingdoms was the most important committee established by the Houses. There were many others with extensive authority and heavy responsibilities that took over the work of running the war and governing the realm: the Committee for the Advance of Money, the Committee for the Sequestration of Delinquents' Estates, the Committee for Compounding with Delinquents, the Committee for Plundered Ministers.[318] In April 1645, after the passage of the Self-denying Ordinance, the Lords recommended that since the places in the kingdom usually held by nobility were now entrusted to committees, a proportionable number of lords should be represented on them, particularly on the Committees for Revenue, the Admiralty and the Navy; the House also desired that the great seal should continue in joint custody.[319] Joint committees with more limited power also continued to be chosen for matters of less weight. There were joint committees to supervise the king's children,[320] consider county petitions, draw up an answer to the king, consider the excise,[321] inquire into the office of heralds,[322] and consider the king's propositions in October 1647.[323]

Joint committees were thus established to perform a great variety of functions. They might operate for a brief time with a limited charge or serve as standing committees over a long period with extensive responsibilities. Despite this wide range of activities, certain basic forms of procedure seemed to govern them all. The exception was the Committee of Both Kingdoms, to which we will return.

The Houses appointed joint committees in response to messages sent from one House to the other, in response to requests made at conferences, or, after 1640, as required by bills or ordinances that made provision for such committees or granted them power.[324] Generally the upper House named joint committee members in the same way that it named members for other committees and insisted that it was the right of each House to name its own members. In the early years of the joint committee, no fixed proportion of lords to commoners seems to have prevailed. In the reign of Henry VIII, twelve lords met with an equal number of commoners to discuss a bill.[325] A committee to wait on Queen Elizabeth was composed of seven prelates, seven earls, and seven barons (twenty-one from the House of Lords), and forty-four members of the Commons.[326] By the reign of James I, it had become the custom for the House of Commons to name twice as many members to a joint committee as the House of Lords. This is what was meant when the Lords set a number for themselves and requested that the Commons choose "a proportionable number."[327] The same proportion was usually followed in setting a quorum.[328] The House of Lords was said to have the right to choose the place of meeting, as was the case with conferences. By 1644 the Lords ordered that all joint committees should sit in the Painted Chamber.[329] (Outstanding exceptions were the standing committees that met at Derby House, Haberdashers Hall, and elsewhere in Westminster and London.) The Lords set the time for the first meeting. Thereafter a joint committee could adjourn itself from time to time.[330]

It is difficult to visualize a joint committee meeting. At conferences the members of the House of Commons stood, uncovered, and the lords sat, covered.[331] In 1661, when a joint committee was established to investigate a plot against the crown, the members from the House of Lords were empowered to "dispense with all usual Forms, Ceremonies, and other Things, as they shall find it necessary for the carrying on the Public Service."[332] Members from both Houses sat together and the commoners were covered.[333] Possibly the occasion was particularly remarked because it was unusual. Yet there had been earlier indications that the ceremonial usually observed at formal conferences might have been abandoned when the Houses met together as committees of the whole House or at meetings of joint committees, particularly joint standing committees. On 21 September 1641, among the notes of proceedings at the joint committee appointed to transact business during the recess, there is a memorandum that "it was long debated by the lords committees whether the Commons should be permitted to put on their hats at the meeting and the question was put." Unfortunately, the decision was not recorded and the note has been scratched through.[334] At Strafford's trial, members of the Commons sat, although they were uncovered because they attended as a committee of the whole House. In 1644, when arrangements were made for a committee of both Houses and representatives of the Scots to receive the duke of Richmond and the earl of Southampton as emissaries from the king, it was decided that the lords should sit on one side of the table, the Scottish commissioners on the other, the duke and the earl at the upper end of the table, and "the Committee of the House of Commons to sit upon a Form behind the Lords."[335] There was, Clarendon recalled, some problem about hats. All were in fact bareheaded, "for though the lords used to be covered whilst the Commons were bare, yet the Commons would not be bare before the Scots' commissioners; and so none were covered. But as soon as the two lords came thither they covered, to the trouble of the other; but, being presently to speak, they were quickly freed from that eyesore."[336] When a question had been raised in 1644 concerning precedency to be observed in the Committee of Both Kingdoms, the Lords replied that in all public audiences the representatives of the House of Lords should go first. "In other Private Meetings," however, "the Lords are left to the Rules of usual and common Civility."[337] There is no firm evidence as to what was done in meetings. We know that judges and assistants sometimes sat with committee members despite the Standing Orders.[338] It is possible that as joint committees met regularly during the years of civil war a number of formalities were dropped; and it may well have been that particularly at small committees, lords and commoners sat together, with or without hats.[339]

The chairman of a joint committee was invariably a lord.[340] The Committee of Both Kingdoms chose its chairman to serve for a fortnight. Committees generally arranged their own agenda within the charge given them by the Houses. Some, like the Committee of Both Kingdoms, set up a list of orders to govern procedure. A minister was to pray daily when the committee convened and when it rose. Clerks, one of each nation, were to keep books of entries. Members were to meet at 3:00 P.M. and depart at 7:00 P.M. No new motion was to be made without leave after six, and no member was to depart at any time without the permission of the committee. Other civil war committees also had clerks, messengers, and other assistants, all salaried and several drawing fees as well.[341]

It is a question just how joint committees voted. Many probably did not do so at all but reached agreement by consensus, particularly committees concerned with drafting, negotiations between the Houses concerning bills, and similar business. But on some occasions joint committees certainly voted.[342] Sir Edwin Sandys reported in 1624 that the reasons to be presented to the king in breaking with Spain had been "approved by the general vote of both Committees." Possibly this meant that the committee had voted as a whole, possibly it meant that the lords and commoners had voted separately.[343] On other occasions it was the custom for the representatives of the two Houses to vote apart from each other, a logical proceeding in a group where the lords might be outnumbered two to one. On 18 March 1646/7 the upper House ordered that all things transacted between the Houses of parliament "shall be done by way of a Committee," with the "Peers to vote apart from the Commons, according to the ancient Custom."[344] The report from a joint committee was usually made by a lord to the upper House and by a member of the House of Commons to the lower.[345]

In 1644 debates on the ordinances providing for the Committee of Both Kingdoms raised important questions concerning the constitution of a joint committee and the procedure that should govern it. The first question was the charge for the committee and its relationship to parliament. This discussion was highly colored by the political struggles among groups in both Houses and between the Houses themselves.[346] But what concerns us here is its significance in the development of the joint committee. An ordinance providing for a committee of both Houses was introduced into the House of Lords and passed on 1 February 1643/4. It named fourteen commoners and seven lords to advise and consult with the Scottish commissioners, and with them "to order and direct whatsoever doth or may concern the managing of the War . . . and whatsoever may concern the Peace of His Majesty's Dominions, and all other Things in pursuance of the Ends expressed in the . . . Covenant and Treaty."[347] This ordinance, which had in fact been drafted by two members of the House of Commons, Sir Harry Vane and Oliver St. John, had apparently suffered no criticism in the upper House, but was hotly debated in the lower.[348] A revised version was finally voted by the Commons on 7 February.[349] In this the committee was empowered to consult with the commissioners of Scotland and to "propound" to them "whatever they shall receive in Charge from both Houses" and likewise to "report the Results to both Houses." It was to "advise, consult, order, and direct, concerning the carrying on and managing of the War, . . . to hold good Correspondency and Intelligence with foreign states" and to consult concerning matters in the covenant and treaty. The revised ordinance specifically provided that the committee should not treat for peace "without express Directions from both Houses" and further that it should endure for three months only.[350] The House of Lords refused to accept this version of the ordinance. It now desired even stricter limitations on the committee's powers than the Commons had proposed and deleted "order and direct," leaving "consult and advise." The Commons declined to alter their position. The upper House, perceiving that the authority of the lord general might be threatened, voted that he could suspend such directions from the committee as he thought necessary, "until he have acquainted both Houses of Parliament therewith." It also voted to limit the committee's life not to three months but to six weeks.[351] Again the Commons refused to accept the amendments and on 16 February the ordinance was passed in the form voted on 7 February.[352] In May 1644 the ordinance expired. In its place the Commons passed the ordinance initially forwarded to them by the Lords on the first of the previous February. This parliamentary sleight of hand meant that the Committee of Both Kingdoms now operated under a very generous mandate to order and direct whatever concerned war and peace and that no time limit had been set to its powers.[353]

A second question debated was the authority for naming the committee. The procedure used for selecting representatives from the two Houses to negotiate bills or draft addresses might well not be appropriate for the selection of lords and commoners who would serve as a standing committee to transact business involving two kingdoms in time of war. The fact that the joint committee was constituted by an ordinance further complicated the problem. The draft provided by Vane and St. John and passed by the Lords on 1 February 1643/4 had ignored the custom that each House selected its own members and had listed the names of both lords and commoners for the proposed committee. In debate on 7 February, the Commons objected not only to the persons named but also to the fact that commoners had in effect been named by lords.[354] The Commons proceeded to choose their own representatives, one by one, as they had done in 1604 and further voted that the lords named should be confirmed by the lower House, thus suggesting another exception to established procedure.[355]

On 6 April 1644, when the Lords proposed a joint committee for peace to be independent of the Committee of Both Kingdoms, they resolved to return to the "ancient custom" by which each House named its own members. They explained to the Commons that the custom in proposing a joint committee was for the upper House to set the number of lords who should be represented and to ask the House of Commons to select a "proportionable" number before the Lords actually named their own committee members.[356] The issue arose again in May when it was necessary to review the powers of the Committee of Both Kingdoms. The Lords presented a new ordinance for this purpose, naming their own members. This the House of Commons amended, "both for the Persons and the Number, which the Lords find contrary to all Precedents." The Lords, in view of the exigencies of the times, voted to compromise and to agree to a change in the number of peers and to such commoners as the lower House would suggest, provided a blank was left in the draft of the ordinance "for the Lords to nominate their own Members." The Commons acknowledged that each House might nominate such persons as it thought fit, but denied that "either House hath a severed and particular Right so to name their own Members in a Bill or Ordinance, as that the other House shall be thereby concluded," for bills and ordinances were made "by the Legislative Power, which is not a distinct Privilege of either House, but a common Right of Parliament."[357] It was a nice point, although it had never arisen early in the century because joint committees at that time had not been established by legislation. This particular impasse was resolved when the House of Commons returned to the ordinance originally passed by the House of Lords on 1 February, in which lords and commoners had both been named, and voted it into effect.[358]

A further question concerning procedure in the Committee of Both Kingdoms followed from its charge and from the particular circumstances of 1644. The House of Commons believed that members of the committee should take an oath of secrecy, to be administered by the chairman. The Lords rejected this plan, stating that it was the right of any peer to come to any committee of the House of Lords, to any committee of both Houses, and especially to the Committee of Both Kingdoms.[359] They resolved that an oath was "inconvenient and inconsistent with the privileges of this House" and spelled out their reasons. Members of both Houses named to the committee were "of such unquestionable Integrity" as to need no oath to bind them to secrecy. All members of both Houses had "an equal Liberty to offer their Reasons in all Debates" at committees. The oath would deprive the upper House of the power to "call for an Account of their own Members" on the committee without consent of the lower House. The oath was inconsistent with the duty of parliament to give advice and counsel, for it kept information concerning the safety of the kingdom from the members of both Houses. Peers should not "preclude themselves from all Knowledge of the Condition of the Affairs of the Kingdom" and should not "be implicitly led by the Conduct of a few chosen for this Service," who were bound by an oath of secrecy.[360] Throughout the spring, the upper House maintained its opposition to the oath under heavy fire from the lower House. Not until 19 July did the Lords finally accept it.[361]

Another issue debated in these months that affected the concept of a joint committee was the Lords' resolution for a separate committee to consider propositions for peace. The House of Commons wished the propositions referred to the Committee of Both Kingdoms.[362] The House of Lords voted to adhere to its original position on the grounds that the power to deal with propositions of peace was a new power and therefore required a new committee. The Lords did not agree that a new committee would breed delay, but observed that "the usual Practice of Parliaments hath been to make several Committees for Expedition."[363] Ultimately the upper House capitulated, but took the occasion to maintain its right and privilege to name its own representatives on a joint committee and to assert that its plan, though abandoned, would have been the better.[364]

The Lords' opinions in these debates reflect their experience with joint committees over the years. It did not seem to them necessary or advisable to devise a new procedure for the new kind of joint committee that emerged in 1644, a joint committee with broad, independent powers. Characteristically, the upper House preferred to continue to use the procedure developed in earlier times and in a different context. On many of these points it had to compromise or accept defeat. Its position was finally undermined by the march of events. On 3 February 1648/9 the House of Commons voted that all joint committees might sit and act even though the lords should absent themselves.[365]

7

CONFERENCES

Parliament had long relied on conferences to forward business that required agreement between the Houses: bills, petitions, and major projects of various sorts. In the medieval period, the Lords used the conference primarily to instruct the Commons and came to the lower House to do so. As time went on, the rise of the position of Speaker and the election of members of the Privy Council to the lower House provided more acceptable means of instruction and persuasion.[1] By the Elizabethan period, the Houses frequently met in conference, to iron out difficulties with bills or to communicate royal wishes or other information that one House desired to share with the other.[2]

The nature of conferences varied. Some were formal audiences or meetings at which the representatives of one House spoke and those of the other listened. At some conferences there were replies. Some conferences were wholly oral. At others documents, charges, or written reasons were exchanged. Some were working sessions to accommodate the texts of bills to the wishes of both Houses. Conferences may also be distinguished by the degree of control exercised by the Houses over their representatives. Certain conference committees in the Elizabethan and early Stuart periods were charged to reach agreement, an undertaking that implied a broad mandate. Examples are the conferences concerning the bill of monopolies in 1601, three conferences in 1605 concerning the union, and a conference in 1607 concerning the bill for free trade. At other conferences, committees were more limited in power. They might debate, but were to maintain only such positions as had been earlier agreed on by the House from which they came. When the representatives of one House were the sole speakers, they might follow an outline or "heads" of argument previously agreed upon. At other conferences, members were merely empowered to deliver or receive documents.[3]

During the early Stuart period, the conference developed in interesting ways and the Lords' procedure governing conferences became more firmly established. Both the evolution of the conference and its procedure were directly influenced by the attitude of the upper House toward the whole conference process, which in itself was a reflection of the Lords' view of the lower House and of the projects on which it was proposed that the two Houses should confer. In the first parliament of James's reign, the earl of Salisbury made heavy use of conferences in an attempt to guide both Houses from his seat in the Lords. He had two great projects to forward: first, the king's desire for a union of his two kingdoms, Scotland and England; second, the proposal for a contract to ensure fixed revenue for the crown in exchange for certain feudal rights. Relatively sure of support in the upper House (despite the rumors of opposition to the union),[4] Salisbury repeatedly pressed the Commons to enter freely into debate at conferences. "I assure myself," he said in 1610, "we should never fail were it possible we might often meet and exchange mutual thoughts, prevent jealousies and not precipitately project causes." "Conference ripens and hastens dispatch of business."[5] He deplored the limitations that the Commons imposed on their representatives, who often came only to listen and were not empowered to reply. These were "meetings," Salisbury insisted, not conferences. "We have had many meetings," he complained, "never yet a conference, and a better device to keep men in difference can never be found out than never to have conference."[6] In October 1610 he said despairingly, "If you resolve all within your own doors, if all our conferences come under the style of meetings, if we come open-hearted and stand not upon punctillos and meet not you so, if we have not yet spent days enough, but must spend more, then I shall have cause to fear the end will be worse than the beginning."[7] Throughout the fourth and fifth sessions of parliament in 1610, Salisbury professed great faith in the power of free discussion and constantly strove to convince the Commons to enter into it with the Lords. A conference did not bind either House, he maintained. All advantages lay with the Commons. More lawyers sat in the lower House. It boasted more eloquent speakers and surely had no need to fear the greatness of the lords in a cause where reason would ultimately prevail.[8] The lord chancellor, Ellesmere, and Nottingham, lord admiral, also deplored the formality on which the Commons insisted.[9] Archbishop Bancroft recalled the benefits of the "collations" of the early Christian church. Salisbury remembered earlier sessions of the parliament when he believed both Houses had freely debated the Godwin-Fortescue case, the union, and other matters.[10]

Consistent with its belief in free discussion, the House of Lords in 1610 sent its representatives uninstructed to meet with the Commons and hoped in vain that the lower House would follow its example.[11]

"The upper House," Salisbury said, "trust their committee better than the lower House do theirs, who had only to deliver a message."[12] The bishop of Peterborough complained that at a conference the lords disputed among themselves while the commoners presented a united front. He moved that the lords might do likewise. But Bowyer, the clerk, noted that the motion was not followed up, for it restricted "liberty of speech and freedom of conscience."[13]

By 1614 the Lords held a less favorable view of free conferences. In his opening address, the king clearly disavowed Salisbury's reliance on the conference, whether free or formal. "I like not," he said, "that you shoulde come as heretofore and to speake in conferences and sometymes to come wth eares and other some tymes wth eyes." Each House, he declared, had its own proper business.[14] After Salisbury's death in 1612, no single man spoke for crown and council and controlled the upper House in the way that he had done. The failure of his policies cast a long shadow over the type of conference he had so vigorously advocated. Further, the chief topic on which the Commons requested a conference in 1614—impositions—was not one the majority of lords wished to discuss with them.[15] In Bate's case in 1606, the judges had held that the king had the right to levy impositions. In 1610 the Commons had debated the point at length. Parliament was dissolved before the issue was settled to the Commons' satisfaction; and they therefore determined to press it further in 1614.[16] The subject, involving the royal prerogative, was not one on which all the lords wished to venture. Bishop Neile of Lincoln declared, "It is a *Noli me tangere*." It was a topic, he said, that those who had sworn to uphold the privileges of the crown could not in all conscience address.[17] Impositions were not a project proceeding from king or council, like the union or contract, but rather a matter the king declined to have discussed. Further, the Commons had already treated impositions in a full-dress debate, calling forth their finest legal talent as well as the efforts of the king's counsel. The Lords who had not investigated the subject felt themselves at a disadvantage.

The House was seriously divided on what to do. One group of lords pushed for a preliminary "meeting" at which they would listen to what members of the lower House had to say and possibly receive reasons for the Commons' position in writing. A meeting, these lords maintained, would not be binding.[18] Throughout the debate, they clearly differentiated such a meeting from a conference.[19] At a meeting the lords would only hear or receive documents. At a conference they must "dispute the matter." Ultimately the vote was to do neither.[20] The upper House turned its back on both the free conference that it had previously so vigorously promoted and the more restricted meeting that the Commons had advocated in James's first parliament.[21]

The attitude of the Lords toward conferences moved in subsequent years between the extremes illustrated in James's first two parliaments. In 1621 the Lords again espoused the free conference, but at the same time they limited or events limited their liberty to negotiate. In the Floyd affair, the House of Commons had condemned and voted punishment for one who was not a member of their House, an action that the House of Lords thought an infringement of its own powers of judicature. Dissatisfied with the Commons' first attempt at a conference to justify what they had done, the Lords arranged to meet with them again. The Lords proposed a free conference. Anything might be propounded "that may tende to a gentle Ending."[22] But the subcommittee of the House chosen to confer subsequently with a similar committee from the Commons received a more limited charge. It was not to yield to any point that might become a precedent for the Commons to infringe upon the privileges of the Lords in the future.[23] In the same parliament the Houses held a series of conferences to discuss agenda. When they received word of the king's intention to adjourn parliament, the Commons requested a free conference with the Lords to join with them in petitioning for a longer sitting. The Lords agreed to go to the conference as a committee of the whole House. Just before they did so, the prince brought a message from the king asking the Lords not to come to any decision with the Commons until he sent further word.[24] The Lords' freedom to negotiate was thus effectively curtailed.[25] The Houses continued to seek agreement on business to be completed. On 31 May, when the Lords requested a free conference, they laid down the rule for themselves that if the Commons brought in any new propositions, the Lords would give no answer until they had had an opportunity to discuss the matter among themselves.[26] On another occasion the Lords voted to meet at a "free conference," which was defined in much narrower terms as a meeting at which they would first hear what members of the lower House had to say but at which they themselves were not "bound . . . to yeld opinion."[27]

In 1628, in the negotiations between the Houses on the Petition of Right, the Lords returned to a more generous view of the free conference and added another dimension to it when they took care to avoid a preliminary vote in their own House on matters to be discussed. John Glanville expressed the Commons' appreciation: "The House of Commons cannot but observe that fair and good respect which your Lordships have used in your proceedings . . . by your concluding or voting nothing in your House until you have imparted it to them, whereby our meetings about this business have been justly styled free conferences."[28] This concept of the free conference persisted in the Short Parliament of 1640, but did not prevail. On 24 April King Charles asked the Lords to urge the Commons to vote subsidies before investigating grievances. During the debate in the committee of the whole House that ensued, several lords spoke for a "conference without prelimitacons." They hoped to avoid a vote in the upper House before the attempt to negotiate with the Commons, but they were defeated.[29]

Early in the Long Parliament, the Lords requested a free conference concerning the Commons' proposal that their representatives should be present at the examination of witnesses in the trial of the earl of Strafford.[30] The Commons defined a free conference as one at which their representatives had "liberty to speake" only to "what hath passed before the house," and no "new matter."[31] There is no indication that the Lords so bound their members at this time. They seem to have gone to the conference uncommitted; by 1641, however, the Lords had laid it down as a rule that when the House had determined on a conference and had agreed on what should be said, no lord was to speak "contrary to what was the general Sense of this House."[32]

The nature of the "free conference" varied, but it was well understood by both Houses during the early Stuart period and clearly differentiated from the more formal, restricted conference (earlier called a meeting). Although on some occasions the upper House limited the powers of its representatives and on others refused to confer altogether, it stood generally committed to the free conference as a way of doing business and interpreted "free" in broader terms than did the lower House.[33]

The procedure of "adhering," which developed during the Long Parliament, modified the free conference as originally conceived. The term came into use in 1643/4 or possibly earlier and described the situation when one House submitted a proposition to the other and the second House replied with an alteration, amendment, or rejection.[34] The original House might accept the changes or "adhere" to its first suggestion. On occasion each House protested the procedure of the other in this regard. In 1643/4 the House of Commons objected when the Lords sent a message concerning their continued opposition to the oath of secrecy for members of the Committee of Both Kingdoms.[35] The usual way, the Commons said, was to proceed at a conference, where the Lords could state their position and give their reasons for it. Similarly, the Commons protested the Lords' message in 1645 concerning certain clauses in the proposed treaty with the king. The Commons could not, they said, give an answer because they were not possessed of the papers. Further, it was not usual to send "a positive Answer of Adherence with Reasons given." The Lords then voted to arrange a conference at which they could deliver the necessary papers and state their reasons.[36]

Either House might adhere to a proposition at any point. While such adherence usually put a stop to negotiations, this was not always the case. Having voted to adhere on 5 April 1644 concerning the appointment of a special committee to treat for peace, the Lords ultimately accepted a compromise on 13 April.[37] The stage of negotiations when a House determined to adhere and its method of doing so (whether by message or by conference) remained flexible until the end of the century. In 1689 the principle was first asserted that there must be two free conferences before either House should vote to adhere. But this principle was not generally accepted by the Lords.[38]

The procedure followed at conferences was relatively simple and flexible. Either House might request a conference by sending a message to the other, stating the specific subject to be discussed; but in the case of a bill or a project drawn up in written form, the House in possession of the papers initiated the request. This custom was generally accepted by 1576 and not afterwards questioned.[39] The time and place of meeting was set by the Lords.[40] At the earliest conferences in the Stuart period, the Houses were represented by select committees. The Lords indicated how many they would send and invited the Commons to select an appropriate number from their own House, which was understood to be twice the number of lords, as in the case of joint committees. Although this proportion was not always accurately observed, generally speaking there were at least double the number of commoners named as lords and sometimes more.[41] The Lords chose their representatives as they chose other committee members.[42] After the rise of the committee of the whole House, it became common by 1621 for both Houses to meet together at conferences. By 1641 committees of the whole House were generally used for this purpose. Subcommittees continued to be chosen to work out specific points.[43]

For some formal conferences, the upper House made careful preparations, laying out what it would say and who would say it.[44] The usual place of meeting was the Painted Chamber, which was provided with a table surrounded by a double row of benches (or forms).[45] When the conference was between select committees, the Houses might remain in session.[46] When the conference was between committees of the whole House, the Houses were necessarily adjourned. The Lords also adjourned if their presiding officer went to a conference.[47]

The Standing Orders of the upper House provided that the commoners should enter the conference chamber first. The lords were to come in together as a body and take their seats. There was some question whether they should sit in order of precedence, but there is no clear indication that they did so.[48] The lords may have removed their hats briefly in greeting as they entered but remained covered throughout the conference, while the commoners stood bareheaded.[49] On certain exceptional occasions, the lords ignored these rules and entered the chamber first. At the session in Oxford in 1625, Lord Montagu observed that there were many small errors, of which this was one. In 1626, at a conference between the two Houses concerning charges against the duke of Buckingham, the lords deliberately made provision to precede the commoners, "to avoid the great thronging."[50]

The House that had requested a conference opened the session.[51] None were to speak but members chosen for the committee. Others might attend but must sit behind.[52] To the free conferences of James's first parliament, the lords had gone uninstructed. At formal, prepared conferences, the Lords expected their representatives to speak as the House had planned. In 1621 the House rebuked two lords who spoke on their own initiative.[53] At a conference on the Petition of Right in 1628, Lord Saye disavowed certain words spoken by the earl of Manchester: "That wch the president spake was his own he had no direction from the House."[54] Similarly, in February 1640/1, the House reprimanded Bristol for taking an independent line at a conference.[55]

Sometimes the lord keeper or lord chancellor reported a conference between committees of the whole House;[56] but usually the House chose reporters from its members.[57] They were assigned a place at the table, which enabled them to take notes conveniently.[58] When a report was made to the House from a select committee for a conference, the committee stood bareheaded.[59]

On a number of occasions, procedure became an issue between the Houses. In James's first parliament, the Commons protested the long weary hours of standing uncovered. "Heretofore," an experienced member observed, "the Course of Proceedings was by Bill, so as when any Conference was required the Same was only for Satisfaction, and examining some one Point: Now the whole body of the business is of late discoursed and debated at Conferences which maketh the Attendance long." Members, especially older members, "found themselves sicke and lame long after."[60] Undoubtedly the commoners suffered discomfort and resented the conference procedure that emphasized the difference in status between members of the two Houses. They noted that this had not always been so and pointed out that on commissions of the peace and at the assizes, lords and commoners sat together as equals. The Lords' only response was Salisbury's suggestion that the commoners stop jostling each other in the conference chamber.[61] Protests concerning procedure also reflected the Commons' dislike of the project for the union and their uneasiness with Salisbury's reliance on the free conference as a way of transacting business.[62] Members of the lower House were fearful of engaging in open debate with the lords, just as the majority of lords in

1614 declined to debate with the commoners. Similarly, during the Long Parliament, disputes concerning the procedure of adhering sprang from the underlying disagreement between the Houses on broader issues such as the powers of the Committee of Both Kingdoms and the terms of a proposed treaty with the king.

After the Restoration, conferences became increasingly formal and increasingly concerned with legislation. The long series of more widely ranging conferences preceding legislation declined. By 1704 the free conference of early Stuart times had disappeared.[63] John Relfe, an eighteenth-century clerk who collected precedents from the reigns of James I and Charles I, found it difficult to discover consistent patterns of procedure. He was looking back to a time when the Lords tended to favor the free conference, used the conference in a variety of ways, and developed appropriate procedure year by year.[64]

PART TWO

THE BUSINESS OF THE HOUSE

8

PRIVILEGE

The king summoned the lords to give advice on the urgent affairs of the realm. At the opening session of the parliament, he or his lord chancellor or lord keeper explained the specific purposes for which it had been called and thus emphasized that the king's parliament met to transact the king's business and the business of the commonwealth. Parliament applied judicial and legislative remedies to public and private ills. Lords and Commons also devoted a portion of their time to the definition and protection of their own privileges and the privileges of their House.

Unlike the House of Commons, the upper House presented no formal request at the opening of parliament for the privileges generally considered essential for an advisory or legislative body—the right of freedom of speech or debate, freedom from arrest, and access to the sovereign. The claims of privilege that the lords made for themselves and for their House arose out of the proceedings of the House in individual cases. Not until 1621, long after the House of Commons had done so, did the House of Lords appoint a Committee for Privileges.[1] In proposing this committee, the earl of Arundel observed that "there are many privileges belonging to us and divers orders which weare anciently observed in this house that by disuse and want of puttinge in practise are now almost lost."[2] For remedy, the committee brought in the first draft of the "Remembrances for Order and Decency to be kept in the Upper House of Parliament," the basis of the Standing Orders to which the House continued to add thereafter and which were customarily read early in each parliament.[3] The committee also engaged John Selden and William Hakewill to investigate privilege and presented to the House Selden's study of the privileges of the baronage of England.[4] A subcommittee was charged to check the journal each week and see that the orders of the House were properly entered.[5] Thus, individual cases and the general orders and principles that emerged from them were carefully recorded, while Selden's treatise provided historical background and definition.

Just what the House meant by privilege is not always clear from the work of the committee, the "Remembrances for Order and Decency," or Selden's treatise. The charge of the committee in 1621 and in subsequent years was extremely broad: "To take Consideration of the Customs and Orders of the House, and Privileges of the Peers of the Kingdom, or Lords of Parliament."[6] The committee thus concerned itself as much with matters of procedure and the individual privileges of peers and lords as it did with the lords' rights as members of parliament or the rights of the House as a collective body. In matters of procedure, for example, it searched precedents concerning the form and manner of adjournments.[7] In the area of individual rights, it investigated the claim of peers or noblemen to answer on honor rather than oath and the question whether a peer, after he had done homage at the coronation, owed further homage to the king.[8] The committee considered parliamentary privilege for both lords and their servants in terms of freedom from arrest and from suits at law during a session.[9] The word "privilege" was also used to designate certain functions of the House that were thought to be distinctive and its special prerogative; these included its right to assess its own members, initiate bills of restitution, and act as a judicial body.[10] The fruits of the committee's work in 1621 reflect the same broad view of its functions. The Standing Orders (first presented as a report on 8 February 1620/1) cover procedure, individual rights, and the privilege of the House.[11]

So too does the study of the privileges of the baronage made by John Selden on behalf of the committee. Selden used the term "baronage" to comprehend all those "who as *Prelati* or *Magnates* and *Proceres Regni* by common right are to be summoned to everie Parliament, wherein allso they have place and voice, as incident to their dignitie."[12] Baronage thus included temporal lords (who were peers and lords of parliament) and bishops (who were not peers but lords of parliament and who held their lay fees as baronies).[13] Selden divided their privileges into two sections: "things which concerne them either as they are one Estate together in the upper house or as every of them is privatelie a single Baron."[14] The rights that Selden thought concerned barons as "one estate in the upper house" were, briefly, the right to make proxies, privileges in suits for themselves and their followers during a parliament, the right of a baron not to be questioned before the House of Commons without a hearing in the upper House, the right of the House to judge offenses both capital and not capital "wch tend to anie publique mischief in the state" and cases brought on writs of error, and the right of lords' tenants of ancient tenancies to be free of the obligation to pay knights who represented a shire in parliament. Also included was the right of temporal lords to pass bills and give judgment without the assent of the spiritual lords.[15] Privilege thus concerned not only members' rights but also certain functions of the House (as judicature).

Selden also explained and documented the individual rights of lords or barons of parliament. Many concerned their privileges in relation to courts of law. Barons of parliament testified on honor rather than on oath. In all cases of treason, felony, or misprision of either of these offenses, barons, other than spiritual lords, were entitled to trial by their peers. Barons could not be arrested by *capias* upon action of debt, account, trespass, or the like, but were subject to distraint only. If a baron refused to answer a *subpoena*, it was questionable whether an attachment could be issued against him. Amercements were set by a baron's peers, although in fact they came to be fixed sums. A knight was to be returned upon every panel where a baron was party. No day of grace was permitted in an action where a baron was either plaintiff or defendant; and finally, he might claim benefit of clergy for a first offense without demonstrating ability to read. As individuals, barons or lords of parliament had other rights. They were protected by a special statute (*scandalum magnatum*) against any who should spread false tales against them and cause dissension between them and the Commons or other subjects of the realm. They were permitted a certain number of chaplains under the statute of pluralities. They could retain in their households more "strangers" than the average citizen. A baron might make a deputy to perform the duties of an office entrusted to him. On his way to parliament, he might take two deer in the royal forest.[16]

Selden's summary reflects learned opinion as it stood in 1621 and came also to have official status in the House. However, the clearest statement of what privilege meant to the Lords is discovered in the proceedings of the House. Although the House of Lords relied on the Committee for Privileges for investigation of precedents and for certain recommendations, it continued to handle complaints concerning privilege itself, one by one. As general orders were made on these cases, they were added to the roll of Standing Orders, which is a useful guide; but to place the orders in their proper context and to understand what privileges the Lords considered important, one must examine the complaints themselves and the decisions made upon them, day by day.

This chapter will be concerned with the individual rights of peers and lords and with their privileges as members of parliament. The two types of privileges overlapped, and the House in the early Stuart period did not clearly differentiate between them. It was intent on defining and defending them both. Among individual rights, it thoroughly investigated the question whether a lord should answer on oath or testify on his honor.

Trial by their peers also deeply concerned the lay members of the House. Bishops were not entitled to trial by peers.[17] In 1604, for example, the Lords offered a proviso to the bill against conjuration and witchcraft ensuring that peers who offended should be tried by their peers, "as is used in cases of felony, or treason." Similarly, the House questioned certain provisions of the subsidy bill of 1624, declining a final vote until there was reassurance that it did not affect the right of peers to be judged by peers.[18] In a number of instances, the House defended members against *scandalum magnatum*, an offense that it interpreted to cover a wide range of activities. In 1624 one Morley was condemned for preferring a petition in which he was said to have cast aspersions on the lord keeper. Gardner, who was punished in 1626 for an offense against the House, was sentenced again for criticizing the lord keeper and "scandalizing the Justice of this House."[19] Anthony Lamplugh in 1628 risked the wrath of the Lords in his petition against an injunction issued by the lord keeper; he saved himself only by admitting his fault and craving pardon.[20] Several cases had their roots in local quarrels. Sir Henry Sherley was condemned in 1628 for publicly accusing the earl of Huntingdon of oppressive actions in Leicestershire, and one Bowyer suffered for speaking out against the lord president and the Council of Wales.[21] The earl of Danby brought a charge of *scandalum magnatum* and secured a judgment against Sir William Sanravy in 1642. The two had clashed over forest administration in Oxfordshire. Danby accused Sanravy of saying that Danby was disloyal to king and country and would "undo them all."[22]

A number of cases reflected the bitterness of war. In 1643 one Simpson was punished not only for arresting the earl of Holland's servant, but also for calling Holland himself a "Roundhead."[23] In 1646 the Lords examined Richard Lloyd, Esq., on the charge of saying that the earls of Northumberland and Pembroke had furnished money to the king.[24] In a dramatic encounter, Colonel John Lilburne was brought to the bar and charged with attacking the earl of Manchester in two of his books, casting aspersions on the earl of Stamford, and finally challenging the jurisdiction of the House of Lords. Lilburne declined to recognize its right to try him for his offenses and "stopped his Ears" so as not to hear the charge.[25]

Certain privileges pertained to lords as members of parliament and were thought necessary for the effective functioning of the House. It had long been recognized that, in order to carry out the king's business, councillors, both lords and commoners, must be excused from certain obligations to which ordinary citizens were liable. They should be free from arrest in civil processes during the time of their attendance at parliament and also immune from civil suits. Those serving in the high court of parliament should not be subject to call from lesser courts, except in matters of treason, felony, or breach of the peace. The first privilege, freedom from arrest, pertained to lords at all times. As traditional advisers of the monarch, their persons were held to be "forever sacred and inviolate." Besides, it was assumed that their estates were sufficient to satisfy any debt by distress.[26] Although this privilege was inherent in the persons of lords, it came also to be viewed as a parliamentary privilege. Complaints were brought to parliament when it was in session and the privilege was enforced in parliament.[27] The second privilege, freedom from being impleaded in civil suits, applied to lords only in time of parliament, which was held to begin with the date of the writ of summons and to run for twenty days before and after each session.[28] Lords were also to be free from attachment. In Elizabeth's reign, Lord Cromwell, who had been attached for not obeying an injunction in Chancery, had been released by vote of the upper House.[29] In 1629 the Lords cited this precedent and voted to maintain the same principle in another case.[30]

All peers and their families (even their dowagers, widows, and younger sons) and all spiritual lords during a session claimed privilege for themselves and their property against arrests and suits in other courts.[31] The House granted most requests for privilege; but since each case was decided individually, exceptions were of several kinds and the House was not always consistent. Francis Bacon, Viscount St. Albans, and Lionel Cranfield, earl of Middlesex, were both impeached in 1621 and 1624 and forfeited their privilege of parliament.[32] When Cranfield tried to protect himself in 1643 against outlawry for debt, the House denied his request. Thus, as Lord Robartes remarked, he had in effect been deprived not only of his parliamentary privilege but also of his privilege as a peer.[33] The nine lords impeached in 1642 also forfeited their privileges of parliament, but the House upheld one of them, Lord Rich, in defending himself against arrest and hence in retaining his privilege as a peer.[34] The House had voted in 1625 that privilege should not bar a suit for recusancy. But in 1640 Viscount Montagu and others, who had been indicted for recusancy while parliament was sitting, were granted privilege.[35] In 1642 the earl of Bath succeeded in protecting his horses while he was a prisoner in the Tower.[36] In 1644 the House finally resolved to deny privilege to lords "voluntarily deserting and absent from Parliament"; but in 1647 it granted protection to the servant of a lord "beyond the seas."[37] Finally an ordinance was drafted in 1648 depriving "delinquents," or peers who had joined the king, of privilege, although there is no evidence that it was passed.[38]

According to a standing order entered in 1624, which confirmed earlier practice, the Lords extended the privilege of freedom from arrest in time of parliament to their followers, their servants, the servants of their families, "as also those imployed necessarily and properly about their Estates, as well as their persons." "The ground of this priviledge" was, they explained, that "they should not bee distracted by the trouble of their servants from attending the serious affaires of the kingdome."[39] In 1614 the House had voted that lords who were licensed to be absent from parliament and who had appointed proxies could also claim privilege for their servants.[40] In writing on freedom from arrest for his book on parliament, Henry Elsyng could scarcely contain his indignation at this extension of privilege, which seemed to him unwarranted.[41]

For the purpose of identifying their servants and dependents, lords issued "protections" or certificates to them that indicated their privileged position. This practice seems to have begun in the early seventeenth century and was not finally abandoned until the middle of the eighteenth.[42] It was easily abused. Irresponsible lords issued protections freely to those who had little or no right to their protection or to privilege.[43] Counterfeiters pushed a thriving trade, and forged protections brought anywhere from 40s. to 6*li.*, a good price.[44]

In addition to lords and their servants, all officers and servants of the House itself, as was customary in other courts, also claimed privilege for themselves and their property, for example, the clerk of the parliaments and the gentleman usher.[45] The same was true of assistants (judges and legal counsel)[46] and of those who supplied the House. Even Fitchett, the man who delivered fuel, asked protection for himself, his servants, his carts, and his horses. His certificate was renewed periodically.[47] The printer and the man who supplied stationery for the House claimed freedom from arrest.[48] The upholsterer, an officer of the wardrobe, and the clerk of the King's Works all asked immunity from military service on the ground that they were necessary to parliament.[49] A collector of the Lords' subsidy in 1621 was unsuccessful, however, in establishing his claim to protection.[50]

The king was entitled to privilege. He was, he said, a member of parliament and his servants and their property should be protected in the same way as the servants of other members. This claim had been made by Henry VIII. It had been recognized under Elizabeth and was upheld in cases in 1604, 1621, and 1624.[51] In 1625 Charles declared that Richard Montagu, who had written a book that the Commons found offensive, should be free from censure because he was a royal chaplain.[52] Events in 1641 and 1642 severely strained this privilege, but as late as 1643 the House was still extending it to servants of the king and his family. It only declined to do so in 1644.[53] The Prince of Wales, also a member of par-

liament, claimed privilege for himself and his servants. Thus, all suits in
the Stannary courts were stayed in 1641 during time of parliament because of his special relation to them. His servant was freed from arrest in
1642. In 1647, however, when the case of another servant arose, the
House called for the "Diurnal Book . . . to see whether the said Prince
was entered amongst the Presence of the Peers."[54] Parliamentary privilege
also protected servants of the state such as military commanders holding
commissions under parliamentary authority.[55] Those to whom the state
owed money were protected from their debtors.[56]

All persons with petitions or cases before the House, their witnesses,
and their counsel were protected from arrest and from other suits while
their business was pending.[57] Those who held sureties for such persons
were also privileged, as were persons summoned to parliamentary committees.[58] During the Long Parliament, numerous cases were brought
before the Committee for Petitions and the committee for courts of justice, and many were long continued. Plaintiffs, defendants, and witnesses
remained in and about Westminster and London for weeks or months.[59]
As the business of parliament expanded, so too did the number of those
privileged.

The lords had ever been watchful of their privileges as peers and their
privileges as a House. However, the increase in the number of peers
during the early Stuart period (and hence the increase of their families
and dependents), their irresponsibility in extending their protection to
a wide circle of people, the expansion of parliamentary business, and
especially the duration of the meetings of the Long Parliament over a
period of years meant that the question of privilege came to assume an
increasing proportion of the time of the House.[60] Writing in the 1620s
about the privilege of freedom from arrest for lords' servants, Henry
Elsyng noted that "in all the parliaments of Queen Elizabeth there are
but 5 recorded who were released by the benefit of this privilege in the
upper House, and but 4 in the first 3 sessions of the first parliament of the
king [James I], now in the parliament of 18 of the king, 22 had the benefit thereof. . . . In so much that it seemed very grievous unto the lords,
and they took much pains how to restrain the benefit of this privilege to
their menial servants only." Elsyng attributed the increase in cases to the
enactment of a statute (1 *Jac.* I, c. 13) providing that those whose suit
had been stopped by privilege might, after parliament was over, bring
new executions. This provision, he believed, undercut the sense of responsibility previously felt by lords for their servants' debts.[61] The times
were indeed changing. Less than twenty years after Elsyng wrote, certain
forms of privilege, notably freedom from arrest and from civil suits, had
become a public scandal.

In 1641 and 1642 constables in Westminster and London complained that they could not carry out the duties of the watch when arrogant peers, returning late at night, refused to stop or identify themselves.[62] Clarendon wrote that lords freely granted protections, which were then sold by their servants to bankrupt citizens and those who did not wish to pay their debts, to the "interruption of the whole course of the justice of the kingdom." Counting members of both Houses in the Long Parliament, Sir Roger Twysden noted that "they and their Retinue could not be less than five thowsand protected from all manner of Justice."[63] It was a common plea that defendants falsely claimed privilege.[64] Lord St. John was known to have been called to the upper House in November 1640 during the lifetime of his father to enable him to escape his debts.[65] In October 1641 a committee of the Common Council of London estimated that debts owed to citizens by the nobility came to over a million pounds. As parliaments now are, it said, "these privileges, protections and privileged places are a greater burthen to the City of London, a greater grievance and of worse consequence to the general trade of the kingdom, then the patents of soap, leather, salt, or that great and insupportable burthen of Ship Money."[66] The overall proportions of the problem were very great. Individual cases also show the hardship that privilege laid upon tradesmen. Robert Stevens petitioned the House in 1641 for relief against Lord Stafford, who, he alleged, had owed him 450*li.* for four years.[67] A shirtmaker in Ireland begged payment of 43*li.* due him for seven years for "linen shirts, bands and other necessaries."[68] The difficulties that Elsyng had observed in 1621 seemed insignificant compared to these.

In May 1641 the City of London petitioned against protections and the House once more tried to limit them to persons who were actually the immediate servants of lords.[69] Those who advised Edward Nicholas about the tenor of a royal speech designed to win over the City suggested that Charles offer to diminish the number of protections for royal servants and to move parliament to part with its ancient privileges "in so far as they are a stop of trade and hinder justice."[70] In the Grand Remonstrance in December the House of Commons promised relief.[71] In fact, however, nothing was done to ameliorate the situation, which became worse with the onset of war.[72]

The House used privilege to protect its members, servants and families of the members, and its officers and assistants against military demands: the seizure of their horses, the use of their homes as garrisons, service in the army, billeting, and financial assessments.[73] Hence the reaction against privilege was also colored by political passion. In October 1642 the House heard a complaint against one Molesworth who had arrested an embroiderer, servant to the prince. Molesworth defended himself on the ground "that the Case was now altered" and that the king's and prince's servants "had not now those Privileges they were wont to have"; but the decision went against him.[74] When in 1643 the earl of Bridge-water's steward showed his protection to a quartermaster who came for hay, the quartermaster was reported to have cried "Pish and ofered to lay wagers that it was gained for 5*li.* of John Browne [clerk of the parliaments] and said they did not value it anything. They came for forage and forage they would have."[75] The protection of Lord Campden's servant was ignored in 1646 because "my Lord Campden cannot protect himself."[76] In 1647 a bailiff refused to release John Halsey, solicitor to the earl of Lincoln, despite a protection signed by the earl and a note in Lincoln's hand for his discharge. "He cared not a fart for the protection," he said, "and that when the Earl of Lincoln sat again in the honorable House of Lords he would yield obedience to his protection."[77] Protests like these, though they were directed to members of both Houses, had added asperity to the drive against the bishops and significantly exacerbated the growing resentment against the peers because of their special claims.[78]

An enraged public, fighting abuses of freedom from arrest and the right to postpone civil suits until after parliament had adjourned, saw these privileges only as an effort to set a particular and ever-expanding group outside the operation of the law. Indeed, in their efforts to enforce these privileges, the Lords themselves often seem to have lost sight of the principles that justified them. Members of the upper House, however, did not entirely neglect the wider constitutional significance of privilege and their gradual recognition of its broader importance is a marked characteristic of the early Stuart period.

In the case of the earl of Arundel in 1626, they asserted the right to freedom from arrest and imprisonment even directly by the king. Imprisoned in the Tower during time of parliament, Arundel controlled five proxy votes as well as his own.[79] The House protested the loss of their member, the loss of the proxy votes of other lords, and the infringement of their privileges. The king replied that he held Arundel for reasons personal to himself, unconnected with parliament.[80] The House nevertheless continued to petition for his release and finally declined to proceed with business until he should appear.[81] Charles ultimately capitulated and the earl took his seat in the House, thanking the Lords for their efforts in his behalf.[82] In November 1640 the bishop of Lincoln was also a prisoner in the Tower. The House was informed that he had received a writ of summons to attend parliament on condition that he give bail to "render himself a prisoner again after the end of this parliament if his Majesty do not in the interim extend his grace further to him." On behalf of the bishop, the earl of Dover raised a question of privilege in the House. The bishop was called before the Committee for Privileges, which voted that he should sit in parliament "without any restraint upon his person"; the House so ordered.[83] Arrest was also an issue in 1642, as well as freedom from suit, when the king charged Lord Kimbolton and five members of the House of Commons with treason. Once more, when the House protested, Charles gave way and dropped the case.[84]

Freedom of debate in the upper House, a privilege also involved in the attack on Kimbolton, had been threatened earlier by both king and Commons.[85] When the Commons in 1614 protested a speech made by Bishop Neile in the upper House, the lord chancellor warned the Lords to look to their privileges or they would lose them.[86] Between the two meetings of parliament in 1621, the Privy Council interrogated the earl of Southampton concerning his parliamentary activities. He was said to have offended "my Lord of Buckingham" in debate.[87] The House did not take the matter up, but Bishop Williams warned the king that Southampton should be released well before parliament reconvened.[88] In 1640, after the Short Parliament but within the time of privilege, the Lords vigorously objected to the fact that a clerk of the council had searched the pockets of the earls of Bedford and Warwick for parliamentary papers.[89] Another aspect of freedom of debate was the concern for secrecy. The Lords called to account unauthorized printers who reported parliamentary proceedings.[90] Members also protested the king's comment on a bill pending in the House, although he reminded them that he too was a member;[91] they vainly objected to the public pressure brought on their debates and their decisions by the London mob in 1641–42.[92]

Within certain limits, the House controlled its own membership. The king created peers and appointed bishops. However, during the early Stuart period, the House successfully insisted that a lord had a right to a writ of summons.[93] The king regularly referred peerage claims to the House, which examined them at length and presented its recommendations to the king.[94] Matters of precedence were also ultimately decided by the House within the limits of the statute (31 H. VIII, c. 10), though the influence of the heralds was very great. The king licensed those who were absent; but the House controlled the number of proxies a single lord could hold, whether they should be held by spiritual or temporal lords, and the method by which they should be voted. During the civil war, attendance became a difficult issue when the king commanded certain peers to join him at York or elsewhere and the parliament required their presence at Westminster.[95]

Other matters of privilege were connected with the House's view of its own function and its defense of this opinion. It jealously guarded its claim to judicature against encroachment by the House of Commons.[96] It protected the right to investigate charges and take action against its own members and others.[97] Lord Savile regarded the bill of attainder brought up by the House of Commons against the earl of Strafford as a breach of the privileges of the House of Lords.[98] The question whether a lord should answer charges in the lower House raised special problems. In 1624 an order of the Lords forbade any members from appearing to testify in the House of Commons without leave; but thereafter, on several occasions, the House left the decision to the individuals involved.[99] The House insisted on the right to initiate bills of restitution.[100] It consistently asserted the right of members of the House to assess themselves, not only in the subsidy as was traditional, but also in the myriad taxes and levies voted by the Long Parliament and by the localities. The defense of this right invoked serious resentment, especially in time of war.[101]

A final privilege, unchallenged, was the right of the House to manage its own affairs. It prepared and stored its own records. Its Standing Orders guided procedure. It maintained order in the chamber and in the adjacent rooms.[102] On occasion it corrected the demeanor of lords. It forbade challenges or duels between members in time of parliament.[103] It punished violent behavior and inappropriate speech.[104]

The right of access to the king was not a problem to the Lords. At certain periods the crown prince sat in the House and regularly transmitted messages from the House to the king. Royal favorites, great officers of state, and members of the Privy Council performed the same function. The king readily granted audience to individuals, groups of lords, or the House as a whole.[105]

The Lords entered slowly into the discussion of privilege. Rather than requesting or debating it in broad general terms, they examined each case as it arose. Privilege for them meant both their rights as peers and lords and their rights as barons of parliament. After 1621 the Committee for Privileges assisted the House in maintaining its privileges, and the Standing Orders as well as the journal (now supervised by a subcommittee) registered decisions made. Selden's treatise was officially adopted by the House. Certain privileges (freedom from arrest and freedom from civil suits in time of parliament) were extended far beyond limits that could comfortably be justified to the protection of people who did not attend parliament at all and had only the most tenuous connection, or none at all, with those who did. The abuse of privilege by both Houses led inevitably to the strong reaction against it in the middle of the century, including the petitions against privilege from the City of London during the Long Parliament,[106] the complaint of men such as Richard Overton and John Warr that prerogative and privilege, including privilege of parliament, were inconsistent with true freedom,[107] and ultimately, after the House of Lords had been abolished, the stripping of all members of parliament of special privilege in 1649–50.[108] During the preceding years, however, the Lords' view of privilege had matured. They came to perceive its wider constitutional implications and the need to protect not only their rights as individuals, but also those that were necessary for the effective functioning of the House: the right to receive a writ of summons, the right to speak freely without being questioned elsewhere, and the right of members to be free from arrest, particularly against the king.

The House defined its privileges and the privileges of its members case by case. It also arrived at certain general principles, such as the right of a peer to testify on his honor, by searching precedents, consulting learned men, and conducting investigations. It protected its privileges in several ways. Some have already been suggested. Others will be analyzed in the following chapter. In defending these privileges against the king, the upper House addressed itself directly to the monarch, pleading for Arundel's release and protesting the withholding of writs of summons. Other questions that affected membership, such as peerage claims and the right to hereditary offices, it examined at the request of the crown and tendered its advice; but on the matter of precedence, it finally acted independently. In defending its privileges against others, the House of Lords issued direct orders to correct offenses, stayed suits in other courts, released prisoners, called culprits to the bar, conducted hearings, and meted out punishment. Even royal officials did not always escape. Although he held warrants from the secretaries of state for what he had done, Sir William Beecher, a clerk of the Privy Council, was called to the bar as a delinquent for searching the pockets and studies of members for papers; he was then imprisoned.[109] The House was asserting its authority as a court.

9

JUDICATURE

The most revolutionary changes in the business of the House of Lords during the early Stuart period occurred in its judicial activities. A treatise on the judicature of the House, written in or about the year 1630, is often ascribed to John Selden, but it was actually composed by Henry Elsyng, clerk of the parliaments. As an observer of many of the processes he describes, his account is of particular value. He analyzed the judicature of the House in the following categories: (1) trying peers for felonies or capital offenses; (2) making judgments against delinquents for capital crimes or misdemeanors on complaint of the king, the Commons, or private persons; (3) reversing erroneous judgments in parliament or in King's Bench; (4) deciding suits long depending in other courts; (5) hearing complaints of particular persons; and (6) setting at liberty members or their servants and staying proceedings at common law against them during time of parliament.[1] In Elizabeth's reign and the years 1603 to 1621, the House of Lords judged no cases on impeachment. It heard a few cases of error from King's Bench but no appeals from other courts. It accepted no cases of the first instance except those that affected its own privileges. In 1621 and the years following, however, impeachment cases at times became the chief business of the House.[2] Cases in error, which earlier could have been counted on the fingers of one hand, rose to number in the hundreds. The House heard appeals or reheard cases earlier heard or still pending in Chancery, the Exchequer, the Court of Requests, Star Chamber, the Court of High Commission, and other ecclesiastical courts.[3] It accepted a wide variety of cases of the first instance. Cases of privilege greatly multiplied. Judicial hearings occupied a major portion of the Lords' time. The high court of parliament became a working reality.

DEFENSE OF PRIVILEGE AND THE RIGHTS OF PEERS

The House of Lords had long been prompt to protect its members or other privileged persons from arrest or suits during parliament time. This process was well defined and, except against the king, was conducted on the authority of the House itself. In the case of privilege for a lord or his family or for an officer of the House, his complaint was sufficient to institute action. Other persons must prove they were entitled to privilege. In the case of a lord's followers or servants, the Standing Orders provided that, before any action was taken, the lord, either in person or otherwise, must "certifie the howse upon his honor, that the person arrested is within the lymitts" of privilege.[4] The House then issued the necessary orders for release of the person or property or for the stay of suits directly;[5] or it instructed the clerk of the parliaments to sign a warrant for the clerk of the crown to draw a writ of *habeas corpus cum causa* or a writ of privilege if the case involved arrest. In case of suit, he was to draw a writ of *supersedeas* to stop proceedings. The clerk of the parliaments also notified all concerned of a hearing. Those who were said to have offended were brought to the bar of the House and examined.[6] The House voted whether they were innocent or guilty and released or sentenced them accordingly. Punishment could be both humiliating and severe. John Clarke, a bailiff responsible for arresting a servant of the earl of Salisbury, who also spoke contemptuously of the earl's privilege in 1640, got off rather easily. He was "to ride upon a jade, with his face towards the horse tail, from the new palace in Westminster to the old Exchange in London, with a paper on his head, declaring his offense."[7] For counterfeiting and selling protections in the same year, Edward Bradshaw was to stand in the pillory, be fined £100, and be sent to the house of correction until he could produce sureties for good behavior. In 1621, for a like offense, John Blunt had been publicly humiliated and sent to Bridewell for life.[8] The same procedure was followed in the case of members of convocation, who had to apply to the House of Lords for the enforcement of their privileges.[9] During a recess, the presiding officer of the House had the power to deliver upon *habeas corpus* any member's servant imprisoned contrary to the privileges of parliament.[10]

Scandalum Magnatum

When parliament was sitting, the House also undertook to defend its members against *scandalum magnatum*. On 29 December 1640 the earl of Newport complained of James Faucett, who had on several occasions "given out most insolent and abusive Speeches against him." The House, "being the most proper Place to afford him Reparation, being a Peer of this Realm, and a Member," sent the sergeant for Faucett. Faucett was required to give security for his appearance. The earl produced witnesses who testified on oath to Faucett's words. Faucett, in turn, requested copies of the depositions, which were granted him. Finally, on January 13, the last hearing was scheduled. Sworn depositions of witnesses for the earl were read. Counsel for Faucett indicated that his client was ready to deny on oath all the allegations. He also noted that "there was but a single Witness to prove he called the Earl of Newport a base Knave and Fellow." The Lords, commanding Faucett and his counsel to withdraw, "fell into Debate of the Business." They ordered and adjudged that Faucett should be imprisoned, should kneel before the earl and make submission to him at the bar as well as at the sessions at York, and also should pay him £500 damages.[11]

In 1642 the earl of Danby, in a case mentioned above, specifically cited the statute of *scandalum magnatum*. He requested the House to permit him to prosecute his case against Sir William Sanravy, "as well for the Reparation[12] of your Petitioner's Honour, as the Recovery of such Damages as your Lordships in your honourable Wisdom and Justice shall think fit to award." The House appointed a day for hearing and notified Sanravy. When the day came, Danby's counsel presented his petition with specific charges against Sanravy attached. Sanravy replied in writing but did not appear, either in person or by counsel. "After a serious Consideration of the whole Business, their Lordships gave . . . Judgement" against Sanravy. He was sentenced to pay a fine of £100 to the king and damages of £500 to Danby. He was to make submission at the bar and be imprisoned in the Fleet during the pleasure of the House. Further, the Lords declared that the earl was free of all "Aspersions, Falsities, and untrue Reports and Speeches" and ordered the whole judgment to be publicly read at the grand assizes in Oxfordshire.[13]

In 1645 James Whinnel was brought to the bar as a delinquent, charged with speaking scandalous words against the Viscount Saye and Sele. Two witnesses testified against Whinnel. Whinnel denied the allegations, but the House declared him guilty. He knelt at the bar and the Speaker pronounced his sentence. He was to pay £50 fine to the king and £100 damages to Saye and Sele, be committed to the Fleet during pleasure, and be put out of his place in the excise office and out of all committees. The judgment was to be publicly proclaimed at Wisbech.[14] As in cases of arrest, seizures of property, or suit in time of parliament, the House judged and pronounced sentence on its own authority.

Claims for Peerage and Hereditary Offices

Questions concerning peerage claims and the rights of peers to hereditary offices came to the House on reference from the crown.[15] The House conducted hearings and came to a decision, but presented its conclusions to the king for his consideration. In 1604 both Edward Neville and Lady Mary Fane laid claim to the barony of Bergavenny (or Abergavenny). James referred Neville's petition to the House, where it was agreed "that Hearing shall be given unto the said Cause by the Court of the Higher House." Neville and Lady Fane were warned "to attend the Court" and "to proceed by their Counsel learned."[16] The first hearing took place on 12 April. After counsel had been heard on both sides, Serjeant Altham (on behalf of Lady Fane) requested a postponement so that he might pursue earlier precedents. On 19 April, when counsel was again heard, the attorney general advanced a royal claim to the castle of Bergavenny. In consequence, the Lords sent a delegation to the king, who bade them proceed.[17] The hearings continued on 7 and 16 May, but were not completed. Finally, the earl of Nottingham suggested that the king might ennoble both contestants. After consultation with commissioners of the lord marshal's office and with the heralds, the Lords voted to support this plan and to request that the king, by way of restitution, allow Lady Fane the barony of Le Despenser and Edward Neville that of Bergavenny. James proceeded accordingly.[18]

The House handled the rival claims in 1626 for the earldom of Oxford and the office of lord great chamberlain in the same way. The petitioners, Robert, Lord Willoughby of Eresby, and Robert Vere, who called himself earl of Oxford, were referred by the king to the House. "Seeing these Petitions concern so great an Honour and Office of Inheritance," Charles said, "and that it falls out so opportunely during the Sitting of our High Court of Parliament; We think it fit to take the Advice of Our Lords and Peers of Our Higher House of Parliament, who have the Judges with them, for their Assistance in any Point of Law which may arise."[19] One of the lords, probably Lord Spencer, took offense that the king had asked only for advice "without giving power of judicature." He "thought it a great diminution of the power of the house and to abridge them of their liberties." The earl of Pembroke replied that since the petition had been directed first to the king, "it was in the King's pleasure how far he would authorize the house . . . without any diminution of their power and liberty." The Lords agreed.[20] The king also referred to the Lords a further petition, from the earl of Derby and his wife, setting aside the claims of Willoughby.[21] Counsel represented all three contestants, with the attorney general and Serjeant Crewe being assigned to Willoughby by the

House. After three lengthy hearings, the House referred the two questions at issue to the judges, who reported their unanimous opinion that the honor of the earldom rightfully belonged to Robert Vere, the heir male.[22] The House concurred. The judges, however, were divided on the question of the office of great chamberlain and desired further time. The Lords directed that they were to consider specific questions posed by the House concerning the office. Again the judges reported a divided opinion, three for the claims of Willoughby, two for Vere. "After much Debate and long Consideration of the Opinions and Arguments of the Judges," the House voted in favor of Willoughby against both Vere and Derby. Last of all, king's counsel was heard "for His Claim and Right" unto the office of great chamberlain. Richardson and Crewe conferred with the attorney general (all three now acting for the king). The attorney general reported that they had discovered some doubtful points in the title to the office and therefore suggested a *salvo jure Regis*, "as is usual in all other Cases of like Nature in Courts of Justice" should any royal title appear thereafter. The House agreed. A committee, assisted by the attorney general, prepared a certificate concerning the whole affair, which was read in the House, voted, and sent to the king.[23] The Lords thus recommended a settlement of both the claim to the earldom and the claim to the hereditary office of great chamberlain. Charles followed the advice of the House, but the final act was his.

IMPEACHMENT

Sir Giles Mompesson

In 1621, at the instigation of the House of Commons, the Lords for the first time in many years undertook to try delinquents on accusation from the lower House. The first case that came to them was that of Sir Giles Mompesson, who held a patent for surveying inns, a patent for licensing alehouses, a patent for making gold thread, and a grant for concealed lands. Each of these the Commons had examined and condemned. At a carefully prepared conference with the Lords, the lower House showed the particular ways in which Mompesson had offended, declaring in sum that he had wronged the honor of the king, the justice of the kingdom, and the livelihood and liberty of the subject. In a grand conclusion, Sir Edward Coke asked for redress. With a formidable array of historical precedents, he reminded the Lords of parliament's judicial powers. "I leave you," he said, "to tread in the steps of your progenitors."[24] Henry Elsyng, who had been present, wrote that the Commons had "accused and impeached" Mompesson; he thus applied the characteristic medieval phrase to the action.[25] Whether this was indeed an impeachment or just what the procedure had been to which Coke and others looked back with such assurance is not, as Colin Tite has shown, entirely clear.[26]

In his treatise on judicature, Elsyng confidently explained what impeachment had meant in earlier centuries. He differentiated impeachment from complaint. In a complaint, he said, the Commons exhibited "no articles, neither in writing nor by word of mouth, by their Speaker at the Bar." Proceedings were left to the House of Lords, which in turn acted *ex parte Domini Regis*. Except in capital cases or on special request, the Commons had no further part in the case. In impeachment, on the other hand, the Commons exhibited articles, either in writing or by their Speaker. The suit belonged to the lower House and it was "privy to all proceedings." It listed witnesses and provided interrogatories, copies of examinations taken in the House, and such proofs of articles as it possessed. The Commons heard the party's answer and the examination of witnesses in the upper House, or had copies of what had been said. The Commons, Elsyng wrote, acted "instead of a Jury." They demanded judgment and judgment was given in their presence. The role of the Lords was not to try but to judge the delinquent.[27]

This pattern does not readily apply to all cases handled by parliament in the years 1621–49.[28] Procedure changed and developed from case to case. The procedure initiated in 1621 in cases involving misdemeanors was further developed in 1624 and would significantly affect the procedure used in capital cases in 1626 and 1640–41. It will therefore be more fruitful to examine in detail what the House of Lords actually did in several important cases before drawing general conclusions as to the nature of its procedure.

The Commons' charges against Mompesson were presented orally, at a conference, by members of the House. The Lords requested the evidence in writing. The Commons complied. In the upper House, three committees examined Mompesson's patents, each interrogating witnesses on oath.[29] The defendant himself had fled and did not stand trial. When the upper House had satisfied itself of the truth of the Commons' accusations, it was ready for judgment and sentence. After debate, it resolved that Mompesson had been guilty of misdemeanors, voted to punish him accordingly, and determined on a sentence.[30] It sent word to members of the Commons that if they would with their Speaker "according to the ancient Custom of Parliament come to demand" judgment, they would be heard.[31] On the appointed day, the lords wore their parliament robes, the commoners came to the bar and demanded judgment through their Speaker. The lord chief justice, who was then presiding officer of the upper House, pronounced judgment and gave the sentence. Later, the king approved of what had been done, and the clerk of the parliaments, at the order of the House, drew up a full account of the case for the parliament roll.[32]

Sir Francis Bacon, Viscount St. Albans

In the case of Sir Francis Bacon, Viscount St. Albans, the role of the House of Commons was less important.[33] The House was concerned to present the evidence it had against Bacon to the Lords "without prejudice," being fully conscious that Bacon was not only a peer but lord chancellor and custodian of the great seal.[34] At a conference between the Houses on 19 March, the Commons informed the Lords of abuses in the courts of justice and "accused" the lord chancellor "of great Bribery and Corruption" in his office, alleging two specific instances and offering proofs of what they said. When the report of this conference was made in the upper House, the lord admiral, Buckingham, presented a letter from Bacon requesting that he might advise with counsel and reply, and that in the matter of witnesses he might take exception to some, move questions for cross-examination, and produce those who would testify on his behalf. He asked that he might answer any further petitions brought against him, one by one.[35]

The Lords moved to investigate the case. They consulted with the House of Commons concerning the examination of such of their members as were involved, resolved to send for others, and asked Bacon to prepare for his defense. They appointed a committee to receive letters and other documents from the Commons and three committees to take examinations. Witnesses were sworn in the House and examined both in committee and in the House itself. Several presented depositions in writing.[36] The House resolved that "none be urged to accuse himself" and that examinations should not be used in any other case or any other court. These provisions meant that those who had given bribes might testify without incriminating themselves and that those whose Chancery decrees had been obtained by bribery could still benefit by them. Without these safeguards, it would have been impossible to make the case against Bacon.[37]

During the usual Easter recess, Bacon had a private audience with the king. He asked for the particulars of the charge against him. Where his answers were "fair and clear," he desired to stand on "his Innocency"; where they were not so "fair and clear," he wished to extenuate the charge; and where no answer was possible and the proofs were full and undeniable, he declared that he would confess and put himself on the mercy of the Lords.[38] The king made no answer but referred him to the upper House.

On the basis of their committees' examinations, the Lords began to draw up particulars of the charge. Before the House had completed its work, Bacon sent in a submission. This document the Lords found unsatisfactory. It was not "fully nor particularly set down." The House proceeded to hear the committees' reports of the "Corruptions charged upon the Lord Chancellor" at large and resolved that he should specifically answer each point. In deference to his position as lord chancellor, the Lords resolved to send the charge to him, not to require him to appear at the bar. "He is only accused, not condemned," Pembroke observed.[39] Bacon did not defend himself, but confessed to every point except one. The House sent the gentleman usher and the sergeant armed with his mace to bid Bacon come to hear judgment and sentence.[40] On the appointed day, he failed to appear. Nevertheless, the Lords voted to proceed. The attorney general read the charge and the confession. The House voted that Bacon was guilty and, after debate, determined his sentence. The Lords sent a message to the House of Commons indicating that they were ready to give judgment if members of the Commons with their Speaker would come to demand it. The lords put on their robes, the Commons came, and the lord chief justice, as presiding officer of the upper House, pronounced the judgment and sentence. The House requested the prince to inform the king.[41] As in Mompesson's case, the clerk, on order of the House, drew up an account for the parliament roll.[42]

Sir John Bennet

Sir John Bennet, judge of the prerogative court of Canterbury, was a minor figure compared to Bacon; but the Lords came to certain decisions concerning the procedure appropriate in his case that give it significance in the history of their judicial activities. The Commons accused Bennet of corruption in 1621 and expelled him from the House. They presented accusations against him to the Lords at a conference. "We have given nothing but an opinion," Sir Edward Coke concluded, "your lordships must give the judgment."[43] Bennet was imprisoned and sent a petition to the upper House to be bailed. The Lords began the examination of witnesses in the case. Serjeant Crewe and the attorney general, as assistants in the House, presented further charges against Bennet at the bar and Bennet in turn made certain requests.[44] In reply, the Lords granted bail and allowed Bennet time until the next sitting to make answer. He was allowed to have a copy of the charge, but not a copy of the proofs or the names of witnesses. He might have counsel to advise him, but not to defend him in the House. Although king's counsel opened the charge and proofs, they were "not to inform any Thing against him at the Hearing."

Bennet's witnesses were to be sworn in the House upon such interrogatories as he had prepared and the House would permit. He might examine them, but not upon cross-interrogation. During the hearing, Bennet might take exception to witnesses produced against him and at that time he might have their names. He was free to search the records of his court and to look among his own writings.[45] The case never came to judgment.[46] It had been a useful exercise for the House, however. The Lords' orders concerning counsel and the witnesses and documents permitted to the defendant would reappear in 1624 in the trial of Lionel Cranfield, earl of Middlesex.

Lionel Cranfield, Earl of Middlesex

Mompesson had fled. Bacon had confessed. Parliament did not pursue the charges against Sir John Bennet. But Lionel Cranfield, earl of Middlesex, offered a defense and stood upon his justification. Thus his case is of particular interest in the development of the judicature of the upper House. The attack upon Cranfield began simultaneously in both Houses and committees collected evidence against him in both.[47] At a conference with the Lords at Whitehall on 16 April, Sir Edward Coke spoke for the Commons. He reminded the Lords that members of the Commons constituted "the Representative Body of the Realm" and were therefore "Inquisitors General of the Grievances of the Kingdom." In their inquisition, they had found "many great, exorbitant, and heinous Offences against . . . the Lord Treasurer." Coke then proceeded to present three charges against Cranfield in detail and to cite the proofs. In conclusion, he demanded justice on behalf of the lower House.[48] Although carefully prepared and examined, the charge was oral, not written. Elsyng, discussing the case in his treatise on judicature, made much of the fact that the charge was delivered at a "committee," not in the open House and not in the presence of the accused.[49]

The Lords divided themselves into committees to examine witnesses. When this had been done, a committee of lords prepared part of the charge against Cranfield in writing; the charge was then read in the House and forwarded to him. Although this procedure had also been followed in Bacon's case, the Lords noted that it was unusual and dictated by the fact that the House was thin because of ceremonies attendant upon the feast of St. George. By ancient custom, they observed, "the parties accused and complained of are to receive their Charge at the Bar." The upper House notified Cranfield that he was indeed to answer at the bar at a future date and to send in the names of his witnesses to be sworn and examined before that time.[50] Cranfield did so; but he delayed sending the interrogatories for his witnesses until he had prepared his answer. He requested counsel. After consulting its Committee for Privileges, the House replied that he might have assistance of counsel in preparing his defense, but not in pleading at the bar. Cranfield asked for copies of the depositions of witnesses, but was denied these until he had made his answer. On 29 April the attorney general read an additional charge against Cranfield, which was voted by the Lords and forwarded to him. On 1 May Cranfield replied in writing to this and earlier charges and sent in the interrogatories upon which his witnesses should be examined. Again he asked for copies of the depositions on both sides. The House once more consulted the Committee for Privileges; on the committee's recommendation, it resolved "that, in all Cases, it is thought fit and just, that Publication [that is, the showing of depositions openly] be made a reasonable Time before the Party accused make his final Answer; and that, after Publication, he may have Copies freely of all Witnesses, as well against him as for him."[51] By 4 May the examination of witnesses in the upper House was complete.[52]

On 7 May Cranfield was brought to the bar. He came without his staff of office as lord treasurer and, by specific vote of the Lords, knelt until the lord keeper bade him rise. Serjeant Crewe opened the charge against him. As "general Inquisitors" of the realm, the Commons had presented a complaint, "whereof, and of other Misdemeanors, their Lordships have taken Cognizance." They charged Cranfield with "Violation and Breach of Trust, in defrauding the King, who trusted him, with Bribery and Oppression." Crewe presented first the charge concerning the office of the wardrobe. The clerk read the depositions of witnesses as proof. The lord treasurer spoke in reply. The House granted his request for ink and paper. In the afternoon, Cranfield appeared at the bar again, neglecting to kneel until reminded to do so by the lord keeper. The attorney general opened the next section of the charge. The clerk again read the depositions of witnesses as proof. Before Cranfield replied, the House granted his request that if he forgot anything it should not be a disadvantage to him. Cranfield complained that counsel was not permitted to speak in his behalf, although he claimed to have precedents that this should have been the case. He requested the right to reexamine some witnesses and to produce proof concerning a particular point in question. Both requests were denied. Cranfield then proceeded to his answer and his proofs. The attorney in turn replied and Cranfield answered him.[53]

On 10 May Serjeant Crewe proceeded with the next charge. Cranfield answered. Crewer replied and Cranfield spoke again. The Lords agreed that he might have a stool to rest upon at the next session while the charge was given. In the afternoon and the following day, the procedure was the same. Cranfield complained that he had been "injuriously dealt with" because the attorney had opened the "Proofs by Parcels" and had directed that parts of depositions should be read, "which should have been wholly and together." He replied to the charge. The attorney answered him and presented proof. Serjeant Crewe then delivered the charge concerning the administration of the Court of Wards and offered proofs. The lord treasurer replied with his proofs. In conclusion he once more protested that by precedent he should have counsel and should not be brought to answer at the bar. The Lords' proceedings had been just and honorable, but king's counsel had been "unchristianly." When he had withdrawn, the House cleared king's counsel of these aspersions and gave them a vote of thanks.[54]

On 12 May Cranfield recapitulated his defense. When he had retired, the House considered his guilt or innocence of each of the charges, resolving into a committee of the whole House for debate and resuming the House to vote. On 13 May, using the same procedure, the Lords debated and agreed upon the sentence.[55] They sent a message to the House of Commons that they were ready to give sentence, if the lower House, by its Speaker, "will come to demand it." The gentleman usher and the sergeant summoned the lord treasurer. The lords wore their robes; the lord treasurer was brought to the bar and knelt there until the lord keeper asked him to rise. The Commons came with their Speaker, and the "Serjeant attendant on the Speaker presently put down his Mace." The Speaker spoke of the offenses committed by Cranfield that had been transmitted to the Lords and of the other misdemeanors laid to his charge, and demanded judgment on them.[56] Cranfield tried to speak, but was not permitted to do so.[57] Curiously, the lord keeper did not pronounce judgment, but proceeded at once to sentence.[58] As before, the clerk drew up an account for the parliament roll.[59]

Throughout this case, the House was still feeling its way in the matter of procedure. As King James had said, "Precedents there are none of many Years, before this and the last Sessions."[60] The Lords turned to the Committee for Privileges on the question of counsel for the defendant, and Cranfield disputed their decision.[61] Similarly, they were uncertain concerning the publication of witnesses. When Cranfield asked if he might have copies of the depositions of witnesses appearing against him, the Lords first resolved that he should have those of his own witnesses only. When the lord keeper inquired why not for all, the Lords again turned to their Committee for Privileges, and, upon its recommendation, resolved to proceed as Williams had suggested.[62] There were specific resolutions that Cranfield should kneel at the bar and that the gentleman usher should summon him.[63]

The accusation had been prepared and presented by the House of Commons orally at a joint conference. To these charges the Lords had added other charges of their own. They examined witnesses on all the matters in question, for and against the defendant. They prepared the final written charges forwarded to Cranfield. There is some difficulty in determining at whose suit the case was brought. Serjeant Crewe and the attorney general presented the charges at the bar. Both served as counsel for the king and as assistants in the House.[64] Elsyng noted in his treatise on judicature that the accusation was by the Commons but the suit was brought on behalf of the king, *ex parte Domini Regis*. "Touching the Lord Treasurer," he said, "First the Commons did swerve from the Ancient Course in this, they delivered not their Accusation in writing (he being absent;) Had it been in the open House, an Impeachment by word of mouth had been sufficient, and the Suit had been theirs: but it being at a Committee, how could the Lord Treasurer take notice of their Impeachment? wherefore the Lords of necessity did draw up a Charge against him out of their Accusation, and then it became the Kings Suit, and they were abridged of their power to reply, or demand Judgment."[65]

However the case is finally classified, it had significance for the future. As Colin Tite has shown, the Commons were far from satisfied with the sentence given, regretting that it had not been based squarely on the charges they had presented. They chose a committee to search out how such decisions had been made in the past. They realized with dismay that they had no independent record of the charges they had sent up to the Lords.[66] The Lords, on the other hand, seem to have been well content with what they had done. They summed up their experience in Standing Orders concerning judicature, which would guide them in the future. The Standing Orders dealt first with the general problem of judicature. The Lords resolved that proceedings in their high court should be "most cleere and equall," both in discovering offenses and in providing for defense. Defendants should have copies of all depositions, as had been resolved in Cranfield's case. They should have counsel to assist in their defense, provided no exception had been taken to those they chose. If counsel should refuse to serve, they were to be assigned by the court. "This their Lordships doe, because, in all causes, as well civill, as criminall, and capitall, they hold that all lawful helpes cannot, before just Judges, make one that is guilty avoide Justice, and on the other side . . . God defend that an Innocent should bee condemned." Finally, a member of the House should be called to the bar only after the most serious consideration. Precedents were to be searched and the matter was to be further considered at the next meeting.[67]

At the end of the parliament, James reminded the upper House that its actions were not final. As the royal assent to bills gave life to bills passed by the two Houses, so the king would implement the sentence passed against Cranfield. "I gave my Lords admonition in general concerning my Lord of Middlesex," he said, "that they should make the punishment no greater than his crime and therefore advised them to hear all things patiently and so to determine judicially and not to condemn in him what I had willingly assented unto, for that was mine own fault. And now how far I find that they have proceeded according to my rules, so far I will punish."[68]

Conclusion

What had the Lords accomplished? In these and other cases, they had tried, judged, and sentenced delinquents on accusation of the Commons and had established procedure for doing so. In each instance, the Commons presented their accusation orally at a conference. In each the Lords examined the substance of the Commons' complaint, calling and questioning witnesses on oath and finally drawing up their own detailed charge. Out of deference to Bacon's position, the Lords sent him the charge. They promised Bennet a copy of the charges against him and Cranfield received the first part of his. At the same time, the Lords asserted that Cranfield should properly hear his charge at the bar. When the articles against him were complete, the Lords carried out that ceremony. In Bacon's case, the Lords insisted on a particular answer, point by point. They expected the same from Cranfield. Defendants might be advised by counsel, but must plead for themselves. They might call witnesses and take exception to those who were to testify against them. The type of sentence varied. It included degradation, outlawry, imprisonment, and fine. Men were disabled from sitting in parliament, coming near the court, or holding public office. The Lords protected themselves from hasty decisions. They resolved to review fines before they were finally imposed[69] and to consider over a period of several days any sentence that went beyond imprisonment.[70] A gentleman should not be whipped unless he abused the royal family.[71] When the Lords had voted judgment and sentence, they sent word to the House of Commons to come to demand judgment with its Speaker. They dispatched the gentleman usher and the sergeant to fetch the defendant. On the appointed day, the lords wore their robes. The Commons came and made their request, and the sergeant accompanying the Speaker laid down his mace at the bar. The presiding officer of the House of Lords declared the judgment and announced the sentence. The king was informed of what had taken place.

The royal role in this procedure varied and might be of major importance.[72] The role of the Commons also varied and would later increase. In succeeding years, the Lords continued to act as judges in cases on impeachment, but it is not necessary to pursue their judicial activities in this area further. The procedure that they had established in 1621 and 1624 did not greatly change. They had worked it out in considerable detail and had taken care to record what had been done. The procedure would serve as a precedent and model for the future.

TRIAL BY PEERS

The methods that the Lords established for trying delinquents on accusation from the House of Commons influenced their judicial proceedings in other types of cases. This interaction may be clearly seen in the development of their procedure for the trial of peers in 1626 and the years following, a procedure that drew on their experience with Bacon in 1621 and Cranfield in 1624.

A peer charged with treason, felony, or misprision of treason or felony had the right to be tried by his peers. When parliament was in session, this meant a trial by the House of Lords at which a lord high steward, commissioned by the king, presided. When parliament was not in session, a peer was tried by a court comprised of a lord high steward and a body of peers selected by the king.[73] It is this first type that concerned the upper House and that will be discussed here. When the Commons accused a peer of treason, as in the cases of the earl of Strafford in 1640–41, Lords Finch, Digby, and Strange in 1640–42, and seven lords in 1647, the two types of trial—impeachment and trial by peers—came together and became one.

In his treatise on judicature, Henry Elsyng described the way peers had formerly been tried. In all capital cases of this nature, the king's steward (made, Elsyng said, at every parliament) sat in the chancellor's place.[74] The lords were both triers and judges.[75] The form of judicature depended on the nature of the complaint. Accusation might be brought by the king, by the Commons, by private persons, or by appeal of some of the lords in parliament, a procedure that Elsyng believed had been abolished by the statute 1 H. IV, c. 14. The articles of accusation were read by the clerk of the crown.[76] The defendant, a prisoner, was called to the bar to answer. Counsel was not permitted. The practice concerning witnesses seemed to Elsyng (though the evidence was sparse) to be the same as in his own day. Witnesses were sworn in open House and examined either there or in committee upon interrogatories previously prepared. The demand for judgment came from the party who had brought suit.[77] Judgment belonged only to the Lords and in capital cases only to the temporal lords.[78] After the case had been heard, the lords retired to debate the decision among themselves. When the lord high steward finally put the question, they voted one by one, "content" or "not content," beginning with the puisne lord.[79] The king's assent was necessary in a capital case.[80] When the lord high steward pronounced the judgment, the king might be present, but the Commons and the judges must be present in order that the parliament might be "a full court."[81]

The procedure thus outlined was drawn from Elsyng's investigations of the records of parliament. In his commentary on this procedure, he drew also on his experience as clerk of the parliaments in the years 1621–29. In considering capital cases in his own day, however, there was no clear example of procedure for him to follow. "In cases Capitall," he wrote, "I cannot say what is now in use, for none such have proceeded these hundred years."[82] Although the earl of Bristol and the duke of Buckingham were charged with treason in 1626, both trials were abortive. After Elsyng's death, the trial of Strafford for treason in 1641 would be cut short by an act of attainder. Lord Finch was charged with treason in 1640/1, Lord Kimbolton, Lord Digby, and Lord Strange in 1642, and seven lords in 1647, but none of these ever came to trial.[83] Neither did Lord Morley, who was accused of murder in 1641.[84] Nevertheless, in connection with these events, the Lords raised problems and came to decisions concerning procedure. In the trial of peers, as in other areas of judicature,[85] the early Stuart period is a time when the upper House was exploring ways in which it should carry on its business. Procedure was not fixed but developing.

The Earl of Bristol and the Duke of Buckingham

The case of the earl of Bristol in 1626 is of particular interest in this regard and merits examination in some detail. In this instance, the Lords either explicitly declined to follow traditional forms of procedure or postponed the adoption of them. The case was initiated by the king. In a letter sent to the House in April, he requested the Lords to summon the earl, as a delinquent, to answer to offenses committed in Spain and England.[86] The earl, previously under restraint by the king, had been forbidden to come to parliament.[87] However, the House long debated whether he should be sent for and answer in his place freely as a peer or remain in the custody of the gentleman usher.[88] Finally, the House ordered that the gentleman usher should bring Bristol to the bar and that Bristol should "kneel at his coming, in respect he is accused of High Treason." The attorney general opened the charge at the clerk's table. The earl interrupted and reminded the House that he himself had previously sent a petition requesting to be heard concerning his accusation of the duke of Buckingham. He asked not to be "impeached until his Charge of so high a Nature be first heard" and offered the House articles in writing against the duke and against Lord Conway.[89]

After Bristol had been withdrawn, the House was plunged into debate and finally agreed to hear first the king's charge against the earl and then the earl's charges against the duke and Lord Conway. A motion to commit the earl and proceed to an indictment was presented. As noted above, the judges retired to examine precedents offered in support of this procedure; when they returned, they explained the various ways of handling a case of treason, but declined to give an opinion on Bristol's case in particular. The House was not satisfied to commit a peer "upon a bare Accusation." As a compromise, it ordered that he should remain in the custody of the gentleman usher, that the Committee for Privileges should peruse "the Precedents of this Nature," and that the earl's testimony against the duke should not be "prevented, prejudiced, nor impeached" by the king's charge against him.[90] Several days later, the House declined to vote on a motion to indict Bristol and proceed to trial.[91] On 4 May a subcommittee of the Committee for Privileges reported. It cited the precedent of the earl of Northumberland (5 H. IV), who had been tried by the Lords and acquitted of treason and felony.[92] Once again, several ways of proceeding against Bristol were suggested: (1) by bill in parliament (presumably meaning a written complaint, not a bill of attainder); (2) by bill of indictment, remitted to parliament, upon which the peers would then proceed; or (3) by presentment or information from the Commons.[93]

The lord keeper moved that the attorney should prepare an indictment in King's Bench to be returned to the House of Lords.[94] But the House still held back, preferring to hear proofs of the charges first before resolving upon a course of action. If the Lords should go by way of indictment in King's Bench, it was said, they would be forced to contravene the Standing Orders adopted on 28 May 1624, which governed judicial proceedings in the House and provided that defendants should have "all lawful helpes." Such an indictment would mean that Bristol could have no counsel, that he could use no witness against the king, that he could not know the evidence against him "in convenient time to prepare himself for his defense." Further, the House would not be able to keep him from arraignment and he would be "disabled to make good his charge against the Duke."[95] It was finally determined that the attorney should prepare the heads of charges in writing and that Bristol should receive them. The Lords would then decide when he should reply and, after he had done so, would decide "into what way of proceeding to put this cause." It was, however, "to be retained wholly in this House."[96] There was to be no indictment in King's Bench at this juncture and presumably no royal commission and lord high steward. There was to be no role for the clerk of the crown in King's Bench. When the attorney general asked that the clerk might attend because of the nature of the crimes, the request wás denied. The clerk of the crown in King's Bench "is no Minister of this Court," the Lords said; and it had been ordered "that this Cause shall be retained within this House."[97]

Bristol's request for counsel caused further debate. In the Standing Orders adopted in 1624, the House had resolved that "in all causes, as well civill, as criminall, and capitall," defendants should have counsel.[98] Accordingly, it voted to accede to Bristol's request.[99] On the following day, the king reminded the House "that the not using of Counsel for a Defendant, in cases of Treason and Felony, is an ancient Fundamental Law of this Kingdom" that he desired should receive "no Prejudice nor Blemish."[100] The House maintained its position, alleging that it was not yet proven that Bristol would be tried for treason.[101] Later the matter was debated at length and the Lords agreed on an answer to the king, indicating that their resolution permitting Bristol counsel had been taken before Charles's message had come. They conceived that their order did not "prejudice any fundamental Law of the Realm" and reminded the king that in 1624, when he had been present in the House as prince, the Standing Orders concerning counsel had been passed.[102]

Bristol raised a question concerning the king's testimony. If Bristol were to be convicted of treason, his land would be forfeit to the crown. The king would provide the testimony on which this decision would be made and the king would also serve as judge.[103] The Lords turned to the judges for advice.[104] But, as discussed above, Charles forbade the judges to respond.[105]

On 19 May the earl answered the charges against him in writing, requesting that his reply might be engrossed. He denied that he had committed treason, asked the Lords to reach a decision on this point, and requested the opportunity to examine witnesses. His witnesses and those testifying for the king were sworn in the House and examined by committees who also considered the proofs offered by both parties. On 8 June the House again heard Bristol at the bar. He asked for a speedy trial by parliament. No man, he said, would serve him as counsel if parliament should end. He besought the Lords to declare whether the charge against him were treason or not.[106] Once more the Lords declined to reach a decision concerning the charge until they had completed their examinations. They were loath to declare judgment upon the bare charge of the attorney before hearing proofs. Further, they reminded Bristol that if his case were judged to be treason, the decision would weaken his testimony against Buckingham.[107] The House continued to swear and examine witnesses. Bristol continued to ask the House for expedition; but the parliament was dissolved on 15 June, before the charges had been proved or dismissed.[108]

What in fact had the House been doing? The attorney, the lord keeper, the king and Buckingham, and Bristol and his friends had all attempted to influence its proceedings.[109] The Lords had refused to come to a decision. They had acted neither as triers nor judges. They had rather cast themselves in the role of a grand jury investigating the charges against Bristol in order to determine whether to bring an indictment against him or not. At every point in their proceedings they declined to look upon Bristol as a traitor, even by implication. For this reason they refused to define the nature of their procedure or to adopt any of the limitations on the defendant customary in treason trials. Although they continued restraint upon Bristol and required that he kneel at the bar, they refused to commit him to the Tower. They allowed him free use of counsel even in the face of the king's protest.[110] They accepted his charges against the duke and began to act upon them. They would not admit the clerk of the crown in King's Bench or take any of the steps usual in a trial for treason. Everything they did was preliminary to a trial. It was a hearing upon charges, a hearing in which the House never came to a resolution. Clearly showing the political pressures to which the House was subject at this time, the case is an admirable demonstration of the Lords' determination to chalk their own way in judging offenses that came before them. As the earl of Clare had remarked in one of the debates on Bristol's case, "The Parliament is not tyed to any forme."[111] The earl of Cleveland made the same point, "We may gyve a rule for tryalls here in this House."[112]

The first formal charges against the duke of Buckingham were brought by the earl of Bristol in a petition to the House on 19 April 1626, followed by written articles on 1 May.[113] Elsyng had written in his treatise on judicature in parliament that historically accusations were brought by the king, the Commons, private persons, or, before 1 H. IV, c. 14, by appeal of some of the lords in parliament.[114] It is interesting that Elsyng did not refer to Bristol's procedure in any way, either as an example of accusation by a private person or as an example of appeal, even though he thought this form of action had been forbidden by statute. In 1626 Sir Dudley Digges looked upon Bristol's action as an appeal.[115] Years later in 1663, when Bristol's son, George Digby, the second earl, brought charges of treason against the earl of Clarendon, Judge Forster reflected whether Bristol's articles against Buckingham in 1626 had indeed constituted an appeal. Could these articles serve as a precedent for the charge in 1663? Forster concluded they could not, because the impeachment of Buckingham had not proceeded and there had been no indictment. On his advice and that of the other judges, the House ruled that "a Charge of High Treason cannot by the Laws and Statutes of this Realm be originally exhibited by any one Peer against another, unto the House of Peers."[116] By 1663 the House was ready to rule out accusation by an individual peer. In 1626 this was not the case.

The House took great care that the king's charge of treason against Bristol should not invalidate Bristol's accusation of Buckingham.[117] Thus, the two investigations proceeded together. Bristol continually pressed his accusation of the duke, persistently asking that the two men might "be put into equal Condition." On 1 May he declared his articles against the duke "to be Treason" and demanded that the attorney general bring in an indictment.[118] On 6 May he observed "a great difference between Buckingham whoe is at large, and in the King's favor" and himself.[119] "The Duke is accused of Treason, and yet at large," whereas he, Bristol, was a prisoner. On 8 June he reiterated his requests.[120] Finally, on 9 June, the House ordered king's counsel to confer with Bristol, consider the "heads" he had delivered against Buckingham, and draw them up as a formal charge.[121] The case proceeded no further, for parliament was dissolved on 15 June.

The House of Commons also accused the duke, not of treason, but of "Misdemeanours, Misprisions, Offences, Crimes, and other Matters," bringing formal charges of impeachment on 8 and 10 May.[122] This effort was also abortive, but raised an interesting point concerning the use of counsel. In answering the Commons' charges, Buckingham requested that he might use some of king's counsel, who served as assistants in the House, if the king would give him leave.[123] The Committee for Privileges acceded, but the serjeants in question demurred. Serjeant Davenport explained that they were bound by oath not to act against the king.[124] The House moved to examine the oath, but two days later Buckingham announced that he declined to use king's counsel.[125] On 8 June he answered the Commons' charges at length.[126] Shortly thereafter, the king dissolved the parliament. Neither the case against Buckingham nor that against Bristol had proceeded to trial.

Sir Thomas Wentworth, Earl of Strafford

In the case of Bristol, the House did not proceed beyond preliminary examination. With Bristol's charges against Buckingham, it did even less. The earl of Strafford was the first peer in the years 1603–49 actually tried in parliament for a capital crime. Although his trial was incomplete, being interrupted by an act of attainder, it provided an example of the procedure thought proper at that time and briefly served as a model for future trials of the same kind.

The proceedings against Strafford began on 11 November 1640, when the House of Commons presented a general charge of treason against him at the bar of the House of Lords and requested the Lords to sequester him from the House and commit him. The Lords so resolved and the gentleman usher at once took the earl into custody.[127] The proceedings may be divided into three stages: (1) the accusation, (2) a preliminary testing of the validity of the charges, and (3) the trial of Strafford upon the charges. At each stage the Commons conferred with the Lords on procedure and the decisions on these points reflected both the determination of the Commons to maintain an influential position in an impeachment and the efforts of the Lords to retain their traditional role in the trial of a peer.

The accusation, as we have seen, came from the lower House. It was presented first in general terms. The Lords refused to examine witnesses until the Commons offered particulars of their charge. On 25 November the Commons brought seven detailed articles to a conference with the Lords. The lower House requested that the Lords call Strafford to answer, that his answer should be made known to them, that they might also be acquainted with the depositions of witnesses, and that they might add to their charges "as Occasion shall serve." The Lords ordered Strafford committed to the Tower. He was to have a copy of the charges against him, "to prepare a Speedy Answer," and to have free access to counsel after the names of such legal advisers had been passed by the House.[128] As Buckingham had done in 1626, Strafford included in his list the names of three members of the king's counsel. This "was not liked of." His other choices were approved.[129] The examination of witnesses began. Under heavy and persistent pressure from the lower House, the Lords granted representatives of the Commons the right to be present during these examinations,[130] accepted the demand that not only commoners but also peers and assistants in the upper House might be examined on oath, and bound themselves to secrecy. The proviso that these arrangements were for this case alone served to emphasize how unusual they were. Lords who testified as witnesses questioned whether they could later serve as judges. The House left them to decide this matter for themselves. Despite Strafford's protest, the depositions of witnesses were made available to the Commons, which based the last articles of the charge upon them. They presented these on 30 January.[131] On 24 February Strafford entered his formal reply. The king came unannounced to the upper House for the occasion. He requested the lord keeper to call

Strafford to the bar and put "off his hat graciously" to him in greeting.[132] Charles commanded the clerk to read the charge against the earl and Strafford's counsel to read his answer to every article.[133] After the king had left, the Lords disavowed what had been done in his presence and ordered Strafford to come to the bar and present his answer in writing. At this point, the bishops withdrew, "it being *in Agitatione Causae Sanguinis*." Strafford's counsel once more read his answer. Thus ended the first two stages of the proceedings. On 6 March the House of Commons announced that it was ready to prove its charge against the earl.[134] On 22 March his trial began.

The question of the proper role of the bishops in the proceedings had first been raised in the House of Commons in November; in the House of Lords it was raised in December and February. After debate on the floor, the House referred the matter to the consideration of the bishops themselves. Bishop Williams served as their spokesman and maintained their right to participate. Then, having made this point, he led the bishops on the prudent path of disassociating themselves from the proceedings concerning Strafford. This, Clarendon asserted later, was what "the governing party" in the House of Commons had counted on him to do. Doubtless the growing hostility to the episcopacy recommended the policy. Whatever the motivation behind it, the procedure established was to persist in much the same form in later trials: a protestation by the bishops and then their withdrawal, not before the trial as in this case, but before judgment was given in a capital case.[135]

In the arrangements for Strafford's trial, as in those for the preliminary proceedings, the influence of the lower House was significant. This influence, characteristic of impeachment, set a distinctive stamp upon the procedure in Strafford's case and differentiated it from that used for other peers during this time. The Commons insisted on being present at the trial, which necessitated the use of a larger chamber.[136] Members stated "that of Right they may come as a House if they please," but agreed to come as a committee of the whole House. In this case it was deemed appropriate that they should remove their hats in the presence of the lords.[137] The Lords accepted this arrangement "with a Saving to the Rights" of the upper House "as either by Law or by Parliamentary Proceedings belongeth" and the further statement "that this shall not be drawn into a Precedent for hereafter, on either Side."[138] Not content with accusation and with attending the trial, the Commons also cast themselves as prosecutors. They said that they would manage the evidence, which they interpreted to mean "the ordering, applying, and inforcing the Evidence, according to the Truth of the Fact."[139] They further insisted on their right to demand judgment.[140]

The Commons persistently attempted to limit Strafford's use of coun-

sel. On 22 February they prayed the Lords "to admit . . . no further Use
of Counsel than is agreeable with the ancient Course of Proceedings in
Parliament and the Rules of Law." The Lords replied in the same vague
terms. On 8 March the Commons stated that no counsel should be allowed Strafford in giving evidence at the trial. The Lords, however, accepted a report from their Committee for Privileges and ordered that in
matters of fact the earl could not use counsel, but in matter of law he
could. Further, the upper House would make the decision between fact
and law.[141] In reply, members of the Commons reserved "all Rights that
do pertain to them, according to Law and the Course of Parliament," and
indicated that they understood the Lords' order to mean that "during the
whole Time of giving the Evidence," Strafford should have no counsel,
nor should his counsel at any time "interpose." It would not become
those who managed evidence for the Commons "to plead against Counsel." The orders for the trial incorporated all of these points. Strafford's
counsel were not to speak or interrupt members of the House of Commons until all evidence had been given. They were not to stand at the
bar and were to speak only in matter of law "when the Lords shall think
fit."[142]

The final arrangements for the trial were made by the Lords.[143] They
chose as presiding officer or lord high steward the earl of Arundel, steward of the household, not the lord keeper, who was ill.[144] The Lords
resolved that Arundel was to be Speaker of the House during the trial,
"and to do all offices belonging to the Speaker."[145] The Lords also chose
the place and time of trial. Prompted by the Commons, who had pressed
for a larger chamber, they settled on Westminster Hall.[146] The master
of the great wardrobe provided for furnishings: 22 pieces of say of the
largest size, 160 ells of canvas, 12 tods of wool, hay, lyor (or tape), and
nails. He also arranged for the workmen to set all in place. These were
the usual provisions for the upper House, but on this occasion the pre-
dominant color was green instead of red. Green say was to cover the
forms and stools for the lords; as in the upper House, these were set
down two sides of the room. The forms were padded with wool. Those
for some of the barons ran across the room just before the bar, which
was also covered in green. Green say covered the "woolsacks," filled with
hay, provided for the lord high steward and the assistants in the House;
these were set inside the rectangle created by the forms.[147] To the left of
the chair of state there was a chair for the prince, and on either side of the
throne were two latticed boxes for the king, queen, and other observers.
"The tirlies, that made them to be secret, the King brake doun with his
own hands."[148] The clerk's table was slightly sunk in the floor to allow a
clear view of the prisoner from the woolsack.[149] For Strafford, a parti-

tioned box or desk had been built behind the center of the bar. Behind him was another box for his secretaries and counsel, to the right of this a place for witnesses, and beyond it a place for the managers of the evidence.[150] "The Lords and Judges all sate in the same posture as in the upper House," Sir Simonds D'Ewes observed, "only the Spiritual Lords were not there." Behind the lords, on either side, sat members of the Commons on ten "stages" of seats built on scaffolds like bleachers.[151]

The Lords determined further details of the trial, which was to take place daily in the morning. They ordered guards for the general area. The lord great chamberlain was to see to the security of the building.[152] Members of the Commons were to take their places first,[153] while the lords assembled in their own House. After prayers had been said there by one of the bishops, the lord high steward was to adjourn the House to the place of trial. The lords, wearing their robes and hats, were to proceed two by two to Westminster Hall, led by the gentleman usher of the Black Rod and the lord high steward. Within the hall, none but peers were to be covered.[154] When they were set, the lieutenant of the Tower was to bring forth the prisoner, "to be tried for his Life: and his whole Impeachment is to be read, and then his Answer."[155] The lord high steward was then to tell the Commons to proceed with their evidence. He was to explain that the defendant could use no counsel at this time. When the Commons had been heard, the lord high steward was to tell the prisoner to "come to his Evidence." Questions from any of the participants must be directed to the presiding officer, who would then address them to the appropriate persons. Peers who were witnesses were to be sworn at the clerk's table by the lord high steward and to testify in their places. Commoners were to be sworn by the clerk at the bar and deliver their evidence there. Strafford might cross-examine witnesses viva voce at the bar, but not upon oath. If any doubt should arise concerning the conduct of the trial, the matter was to be resolved in the House, not in the hall. When the daily session was over, the lord high steward was to adjourn the House from the hall to its own chamber.[156]

The charge of treason, which the upper House had accepted, determined the nature of the whole trial. It meant that at an early stage the bishops withdrew. It meant that Strafford could use counsel only in matters of law, that none of his witnesses could testify on oath, and that the last word at every session was spoken by the Commons as prosecutors for the crown.[157] In vain did Strafford plead that he should be allowed counsel and the privilege of examining his witnesses on oath in defending himself against articles that concerned misdemeanors.[158] He also took exception to the appearance of certain witnesses—Sir Pierce Crosby, for example, whom he had imprisoned. When the lords retired to their own House and considered the question, they denied the exception on the grounds that Crosby himself would not benefit if the charge against Strafford were made good, and reserved to themselves the right to evaluate the validity of Crosby's testimony. "This was a precedent; so that hereafter no exception of wrongs, either received or alleadged, did sett any witnes."[159] For matter newly introduced into the trial, the Lords ruled later, both prosecutors and defendant should waive new proofs or equally have the right to call more witnesses. The Commons, regarding this as a decision in Strafford's favor and foreseeing that it would prolong his defense, withdrew in indignation and began to prepare their act of attainder.[160]

Still the Lords persisted with the trial, determined to proceed with or without the Commons. On 17 April they heard Strafford's counsel in point of law. The Commons' managers, though present, were silent and did not present their side of the case. This was the last day of the trial. It was never completed. The Commons did not come to demand judgment, nor did the Lords proceed to judgment and sentence. The Commons shifted to procedure by bill of attainder. The two Houses met together informally for a conference on 29 April in Westminster Hall. "So curious are we . . . about Formalities," a reporter wrote, that the lords did not wear their robes. The Commons' managers did not resume their usual places, but sat with their fellows. The king, queen, and prince were present and Strafford "sat behind the Place where he used to sit before." St. John alone spoke for the Commons, taking the occasion to reply to Strafford's counsel in point of law and explaining to the Lords why the Commons had drafted and passed an act of attainder. The following day, Strafford petitioned the Lords to be heard again, but was denied "because the House [of Commons] were to have the last speech." On 1 May the king addressed both Houses. He had not had, he said, "any intention" to speak of the impeachment of the earl. "But now it comes to pass, that of necessity I must have part in that Judgment." He reminded members that he had been present throughout the trial "from the one end to the other." He could not, he declared, find Strafford guilty of treason. On 8 May the upper House passed the bill of attainder. The king finally gave his assent and Strafford went to the block.[161]

Lords Finch, Digby, and Strange

The case against Lord Finch, keeper of the great seal and presiding officer of the House, did not proceed beyond the general charge of treason brought by the House of Commons to the House of Lords on 22 December 1640, a charge followed by detailed articles of accusation and impeachment some weeks later.[162] Finch fled to Holland on 22 December. The Lords issued a proclamation ordering him to appear and made arrangements to examine some of the judges as witnesses.[163] Nothing further was done.

The cases against George Lord Digby in February 1641/2 and James Lord Strange in September 1642 were likewise abortive. In each instance, however, it was clear that, as in the case of the earl of Strafford, the Commons intended to go beyond their role as accusers to participate in the proceedings of the trial itself. In Digby's case, the Commons prayed that he might answer in their presence. In the cases of Finch and Strange, they reserved the right to rebuttal.[164]

Lord Kimbolton

In the case of Lord Kimbolton in 1642, an accusation was presented by the attorney general in the upper House on behalf of the king. He brought articles of high treason in writing against Kimbolton and five members of the House of Commons and requested that a select committee of lords "under a Command of Secrecy" examine the king's witnesses, "as formerly hath been done in Cases of the like Nature, according to the Justice of this House." He further asked the Lords to secure the persons charged.[165]

The House at once resolved itself into a committee to debate the significance of what had taken place and the proper procedure to follow. Was the accusation that had been presented a "regular Proceeding, according to Law?" Were there precedents for it? Could the king's attorney legally bring an accusation of treason against a peer in parliament? Should the House commit upon a general accusation, whether from the king or from the lower House?[166] Unable or unwilling to arrive at a resolution of these tangled questions, the Lords chose a select committee to continue the investigation and to peruse precedents and records.[167]

The House ordered the attorney general, Sir Edward Herbert, to justify the legality of his proceedings.[168] Herbert based his defense primarily on the fact that he had carried out the orders of the king. He also cited the case of the earl of Bristol in 1626. When he had to defend himself later against impeachment, he enlarged his precedents to include the case of the earl of Arundel in the same year, particularly the remonstrance of 19 April, which by implication admitted that a peer in case of treason or felony might be restrained or imprisoned in time of parliament.[169] On both occasions, his defense failed. The House voted that the attorney's action in accusing Kimbolton constituted a "High Breach of the Privileges of Parliament."[170] Despite the king's efforts to stop what he had begun, both Houses asked that, since their members had been charged, there should be a "Legal and Parliamentary Proceeding" against them so that they might have justice. In reply, the king inquired how, with due regard for the privilege of parliament, he should proceed, whether by impeachment in parliament or by preferring an indictment at common law. There was no recorded answer. Parliament attempted to clear the accused members by a bill. The king objected to its terms, which he felt reflected on his honor, and declined to assent to it.[171]

As the king quickly realized, the whole undertaking had been a mistake and politically disastrous.[172] Whether the charge against Kimbolton in the upper House constituted a breach of privilege, as the House declared, or was in fact illegal is another matter. Neither precedents nor the events of recent years provided a clear line to follow. Charles and his advisers were as uncertain of the proper procedure as the Lords themselves. Sir Matthew Hale, writing later in his treatise *The Jurisdiction of the Lords House or Parliament*, noted that impeachments of treason by the king's ministers or attorneys were against the law and particularly against the statute 25 E. III, st. 5, c. 4. "And though it were a turbulent time," he remarked, "yet it was so granted by the lords themselves in the impeachment presented by mr. attorney Herbert against Lord Kimbolton . . . and the prosecution thereby desisted from, and the accusation withdrawn. And indeed the statute of 1 H. 4. seems to include this case."[173]

The Seven Peers

In September 1647 the House of Commons entered a general charge of treason against seven peers for levying war against the king, the parliament, and the kingdom, and requested that they should be sequestered from the House and committed. Those accused were the earls of Suffolk, Middlesex, and Lincoln, Lord Willoughby of Parham, Lord Hunsdon, Lord Maynard, and Lord Berkeley.[174] The grand phraseology of the charge covered their activities when they had continued to sit at Westminster from 26 July to 6 August after the two Speakers and other members of parliament withdrew to the protection of the army. The Lords of the upper House put the peers in custody. As time went on, the Lords became uneasy about the affair and appointed a committee "to consider of Precedents; and to offer somewhat to the House, for preventing the like Precedent for the future." In January six of the accused peers addressed a letter to the House. They had been long restrained, they said. Since the charge against them had not been prosecuted, they asked for their liberty and were promptly released. On similar petition, the seventh, Lord Hunsdon, was freed shortly thereafter.[175] The House, still concerned about what had taken place, charged another committee to consider a declaration for the journal concerning the general question of commitment of peers upon impeachment.[176] Finally, in February, the House of Commons presented the detailed articles of its charge.[177] The House of Lords debated whether the release of the peers in January had constituted a dismissal of the charges against them. It resolved that there had been no dismissal of charges and proceeded with arrangements for trial. The accused peers were to have copies of the charges against them, to be sequestered from the House, and to put in bail. Each came to the House, knelt at the bar, and heard the charges read at length. Each put in bail and desired that counsel be assigned. Two requested that they might "have recourse to the Journal Books" in preparing their defense. Nothing further took place. In June the House of Commons sent word that it would not proceed.[178]

Lord Morley

The case of Lord Morley was of quite a different nature. Morley, who had been indicted in King's Bench for the murder of Captain Peter Clarke, first brought the matter to the House in January 1640/1 in a petition for privilege. The House ordered that all parties should appear and that all indictments and proceedings in King's Bench and elsewhere should be stopped.[179] Elizabeth Clarke, the widow of Captain Clarke, responded with a counterpetition.[180] The House set a date for a hearing, called in the records from King's Bench, and notified both parties to be ready with their witnesses.[181] In June 1641 the House ordered the Committee for Privileges, with the assistance of the judges of King's Bench, to consider how Morley should be tried—whether in the House by his peers "or have a Commission."[182] After several meetings, the committee recommended to the House and the House ordered that Morley should be tried at the bar, that a writ of *certiorari* should be directed to the lord chief justice of the King's Bench to bring into the House indictments and examinations against Morley still remaining in that court, and that the king's attorney and learned counsel should give evidence against Morley on the king's behalf. Morley was to have counsel in point of law, but not in matter of fact. Complainants could be heard by counsel at the bar. Several times the House asked the Committee for Privileges to set a day for trial and to consider how it should be conducted.[183] The lord chief justice brought in the indictment as directed. King's counsel were ordered to prepare themselves.[184] Finally the trial was set for mid-August, with the House repeatedly bidding the Committee for Privileges to consider how it should be conducted.[185] In August, when the trial was further postponed, Mrs. Clarke asked for a deferment until after Michaelmas. She and her counsel and witnesses had attended, she said, since 4 July. Five of her witnesses had lately returned to the country.[186] The trial was next set for February 1641/2. Again the committee was to consider how to proceed and king's counsel were to prepare themselves. On 7 February the trial was postponed until April and then until May, each time with further directions to the committee to consider the manner of proceeding. Finally, on 14 May, the committee made its report and the House, accepting its recommendation, resolved that in a capital case in parliament time, "a Peer ought to be tried in Parliament by his Peers and no where else; and the Impeachment or Accusation must be brought from the House of Commons." Therefore, the order continued, Mrs. Clarke should petition the House of Commons concerning the death of her husband.[187]

The House of Lords had not acquitted itself well. In June 1641 it had ordered that Morley should be brought to trial at the bar. In May 1642, despite the fact that he had been indicted in King's Bench, it declared that he must be impeached by the House of Commons before the Lords could proceed to try him. Fortunately for the justice of England, this extraordinary ruling, after so many months delay, did not establish a binding precedent. In 1677, in the case of the earl of Pembroke, who had been charged with murder in a coroner's inquisition, the Committee for Privileges recommended and the House ordered a different, more equitable procedure. The earl's trial, the House said, "ought to be by commission of Oyer and Terminer first issuing under the Great Seal to commissioners before whom the said Earl may be indicted, and the said indictment committed to a grand jury empanelled for that purpose." If the indictment was found, the record should be returned to parliament, where the earl should be tried by his peers. This was in fact what took place. The earl was tried and found guilty of manslaughter. Though he escaped the death penalty by claiming benefit of clergy, a privilege he could exercise but once, as the lord high steward reminded him, he had at least been brought to trial.[188]

Conclusion

The procedure of the House of Lords in the years 1603–49 in the trial of peers had been varied. It established certain precedents and raised some questions to be resolved in the future. Accusation, Elsyng said, might be by king, House of Commons, or private persons. In 1626 the king accused Bristol of treason and the House solemnly undertook to investigate the charge. In 1642, when Charles accused Lord Kimbolton, the House protested the accusation as a breach of privilege and considered it possibly illegal. Again, in 1626, the earl of Bristol, whether as a private person or as a peer presenting an appeal, accused the duke of Buckingham and the accusation stood unquestioned. In 1641 the House refused to prosecute Lord Morley on petition from Elizabeth Clarke, although he had been indicted for the murder of her husband in King's Bench. The Lords ultimately rejected this petition from a private party and insisted that she address herself to the House of Commons, which could then bring the accusation. Only accusation by the lower House or impeachment seems to have gone unquestioned against the earl of Strafford, Lords Finch, Digby, and Strange, and the seven peers.

In the next stage of proceedings, the Lords' practice also varied. The treatment of the defendant was inconsistent. When charged in 1626, Bristol was sequestered from the House and restrained. Buckingham was not. Strafford was sequestered on the general charge of treason and restrained. After the House of Commons had offered particular charges against him, he was committed to the Tower. Lord Morley and Lord Kimbolton continued to attend the House. The seven peers were at first committed on a general charge, then liberated, and later, when the Commons brought in detailed charges, required to give bail. In 1626 the House allowed the earl of Bristol counsel though he had been charged with treason. Strafford was permitted counsel only in matter of law, not in matter of fact. His request for the use of some members of the king's counsel was refused. Morley, who was accused of murder, was also to have counsel only in matter of law. In every case, witnesses were to be heard on both sides. In Strafford's case, all witnesses for the crown, commoners and lords alike, testified on oath. Witnesses for the defendant did not. The interesting question of admitting the king's testimony arose in 1626 in Bristol's case, the question of the lords' testimony arose in 1640/1 in Strafford's.

In 1626 the House insisted on retaining Bristol's case within its own walls. The Lords refused to seek an indictment in King's Bench, but investigated the charges against Bristol themselves, declining to accept the implications of the charge of treason in determining their procedure. In 1640/1 the upper House admitted the representatives of the House of Commons as participants in the proceedings against Strafford in a pattern very much like that outlined in Elsyng's treatise. Members were present at the examination of witnesses and received copies of depositions.

Strafford's case was the first to come to trial. The House had carefully debated the procedure it would follow.[189] Traditionally the presiding officer for the trial of a peer in a capital case was the lord high steward, who was appointed by the king. In 1641 the House itself chose the lord high steward and there seems to have been no royal commission. The

Lords provided a dignified and colorful setting for a solemn occasion. The red robes of lords and judges contrasted sharply with the green of the forms and woolsacks and the long black robes of the clerks. Strafford too was all in black, "as in doole." The behavior of participants did not always match the occasion. While Strafford prepared his answer to the Commons' charges, the lords rose and walked about. Bristol whispered to the lord high steward. Food and drink were openly consumed. Men urinated between the forms.[190] When problems arose concerning procedure, the exceptions against witnesses, or the admission of new evidence, the lords returned to their own chamber for debate. The trial moved along as had been planned and provided a concrete precedent that the House could use in the future as it saw fit.

However, the House was not long satisfied to use Strafford's trial as a model. It would serve for the trial of Archbishop Laud, even though Laud was not a peer. It would provide precedents concerning the use of counsel and the participation of the Commons for other trials in the period.[191] After the Restoration, when the political climate had changed, the reference to Strafford's case seemed less appropriate. In November 1667 the House of Commons cited it when it charged Clarendon with treason and requested that he be sequestered from the House and committed. The Lords observed that it was dangerous to commit a peer on a general accusation[192] and discredited the use of the case as a precedent because it was of "an ill time" and "not allowable." The House noted that Strafford's attainder had been repealed in 1663 by an act of parliament, which also provided that the record of all proceedings connected with the attainder should be effaced from the journal of the House of Lords. The record of Strafford's impeachment was also obliterated, although later it was restored.[193] The arrangements in 1677/8 for the trial of the earl of Pembroke, who had been indicted for murder, were certainly based on those for the trial of Strafford;[194] but thereafter Pembroke's trial itself became the model. In determining the procedure to be used in trying five lords accused of high treason in 1679, the Committee for Privileges examined both the order of proceeding in Strafford's trial and that in the trial of Pembroke. It used the latter for its guide.[195]

The pace of proceedings in trials by peers varied. In the cases of Bristol and Buckingham, the House spun preliminaries out as long as possible to avoid trial. It postponed and delayed the trial of Lord Morley. With Strafford, the Lords finally came to trial, but moved with such deliberation that the House of Commons lost patience.

The variety of efforts, though often abortive, in which the House engaged in these years indicates that there was no fixed procedure in trial by peers. Sometimes the House applied the rules of law to its proceedings, sometimes it declined to do so. As Strafford himself said, "this is a Court of Honour, which is a Rule to itself, and no other Court is a Rule to it."[196] In trial by peers, however accused, and in trial of delinquents accused by the House of Commons, whether peers or not, procedure was evolving case by case.[197] It did not achieve consistency until later in the century; the House of Lords, though subject to heavy political pressure and bound by its own Standing Orders, was thus free to shape procedure that seemed appropriate in the individual instance.

PROCEDURE IN ERROR

The judicial activities of the House of Lords in cases of error from King's Bench and Exchequer Chamber posed no jurisdictional problems and required no major procedural innovations. The significant point to consider is the vast increase in the number of cases that came to the House during the years 1621–49. The jurisdiction of the House of Lords over cases of error in King's Bench had long been recognized, but does not seem to have been frequently used before 1640. Only five cases were recorded in the journal for the years 1514–89.[198] In 1585 the statute of 27 Eliz., c. 8 spoke of delays in reforming erroneous judgments that resulted from infrequent meetings of parliament and from the press of business when it did convene. The statute confirmed and reinforced parliament's jurisdiction, but also provided that certain cases from King's Bench (which did not involve the monarch) might be brought before the judges of the Court of Common Pleas and the barons of the Exchequer, sitting in Exchequer Chamber.[199] Their decision need not be final, for the aggrieved party could then take his case to the high court of parliament, that is, to the House of Lords, which traditionally exercised these powers.[200] A subsequent act in 1589 (31 Eliz., c. 1) addressed additional obstacles that had arisen concerning the continuance of writs of error and once more stressed that those discontent with their treatment in Exchequer Chamber might sue in the high court of parliament. Cases begun in King's Bench, except those specified in the statutes, were still referred directly to parliament.[201]

No cases were in fact recorded in the Lords journal in the years between 1589 and 1621.[202] Whether they came to the House and the clerk failed to take note of them or whether no cases were brought, it would be difficult to say.[203] The Lords' jurisdiction was known to lawyers and judges. It was discussed in law reports and noted in abridgments. In 1614 the king had authorized the consideration of a case, but there is no record that it proceeded.[204] In the same parliament, as already noted,

Lord Chancellor Ellesmere suggested that those who wished to test the king's right to levy impositions might do so by seeking a writ of error for the examination of the judgment against Bate.[205]

The first clear case of error in the Stuart period came to the House in 1621, the same year that the Lords undertook impeachment proceedings and began to accept civil cases in petitions.[206] During the years 1621–29, the Lords received four or five others, continuing a well-established jurisdiction and clarifying details of procedure. During the Long Parliament, the number of cases greatly increased. The House set time limits to guard against the use of the process for the purposes of delay, but in other respects procedure remained the same.

Cases from King's Bench or Exchequer Chamber came to the upper House in two ways. In the first or older form, the plaintiff presented a petition or bill to the king, setting forth his complaint and praying that the record of his case might be removed to parliament. If the king endorsed the petition to the effect that justice should be done, the chief justice was commanded to bring the record into parliament (i.e., into the upper House) and the endorsed petition served as a special commission for the Lords to proceed.[207] The second method of bringing a case to parliament, more commonly used in later years, was to petition the king, who then authorized a writ of error addressed to the chief justice of King's Bench, who had custody of the record.[208] The writ directed him to bring the record to parliament. Hale wrote, "It ought not pass the seal without a petition or bill to the King and that bill signed by him," and should be *"per regem, or per warrantum domini regis."*[209] The writ was returnable in parliament. In accordance with his instructions, the chief justice brought up the record and a transcript of the record. This record, it should be understood, did not include everything written or said in the progress of a case, but only certain parts of it: the arraignment, plea, issue, and verdict. It was usually prepared by the clerks of a court and rarely seen by the judges unless called into question.[210] When record and transcript had been compared, the record was returned to the court from which it had come. The plaintiff assigned errors and prayed a *scire facias* directed to the defendant.[211]

The errors were errors in law based on the record. Since the Court of King's Bench had power to correct errors in fact, such matters did not come to parliament. Errors in law might be either general or specific. A general plea might be that, on the basis of the record, judgment that had been given for the defendant should have been given for the plaintiff. Specific errors in law might be that the declaration differed from the original writ, that the verdict differed from the complaint, that more damages had been recovered than originally claimed, or that the case was insufficient in point of law to sustain an action. Coke cited a case where a recognizance was said to be imperfect, Dyer a case where the writ of *habeas corpus* had no *teste*. In criminal cases, error might be alleged if a man was found guilty of one offense and judgment had been given for another.[212]

In earlier times, Hale observed, the *scire facias* was returnable in the next parliament; but by Charles's reign, it was customary to designate the "present" parliament. Sometimes the defendant appeared without a *scire facias*, merely on the orders of the House, and pleaded to the errors. This was the usual course after 1660.[213] If the plaintiff alleged a "diminution," that is, that the record was in some way incomplete—lacking, for example, the original writ or bill—then a writ of *certiorari* was issued that ordered the lord chief justice to complete the record.[214] The defendant pleaded *in nullo est erratum* and the case was heard in the House. As we have seen, the lords relied heavily on the opinion of the judges, but reserved the final decision to themselves. When they had come to a decision, the case was returned to the court from which it had come, for execution of the judgment, if it had been confirmed.[215]

This basic pattern of procedure remained unchanged throughout the Stuart period. The House decided on certain details as questions arose and made certain modifications required by the exigencies of war. In 1621, when the chief justice was serving as presiding officer of the House, he inquired whether he should "arise and fetch the record (wch is at the door)." The Committee for Privileges considered the matter and, fortified by a precedent from the reign of Edward III, recommended that he should do so. Consequently, he rose from his place and went to the door. Before he came to the bar, he "made three obeisances, and then after, 3 obeisances more." He laid the roll "on the Lo. Chancellor's woolsack, the clerk received the record and the transcript and brought it to his table."[216] A further question in 1621 involved procedure in bringing a case from Ireland. A *scire facias*, on warrant from the House, was directed to the chief justice of King's Bench in Ireland, requiring him to command the sheriff of county Wexford to give notice to the defendant to appear in Westminster.[217]

Many cases in error were brought for the purpose of delay and both plaintiffs and defendants proved dilatory at every stage of the proceedings.[218] In 1641 the House of Lords ordered that costs should be paid by the plaintiff in cases brought merely to delay justice and execution and such a case should be remitted to the court from which it came so that the defendant could take out execution upon the judgment.[219] In 1646 the Lords ordered that errors should be assigned within eight days after the writ of error had been brought in. If this was not done, the case should be returned to King's Bench.[220] After the king had retired from London, the problem of obtaining his signature caused difficulty.[221] It was solved initially by the attorney, who authorized the cursitor to draw writs of error endorsed *"per warrantum attornati domini regis generalis."*[222] In 1646 the Lords finally considered a general order authorizing cursitors to prepare writs of error.[223] Other problems occurred when the judges no longer met in Exchequer Chamber and when the commands of the great seal were inadequately executed. An ordinance passed in 1644 provided that writs of error brought from any court and sealed with the great seal should be recognized in parliament.[224] In May 1646 both Houses passed an ordinance regulating and confirming the whole procedure on writs of error. This ordinance became the foundation for Standing Order 54 and the basis for subsequent practice.[225] It provided that plaintiffs, in prose-cuting their writs of error, should repair to the clerk of the parliaments and pay the necessary fees. They should assign errors within eight days or lose their writs. If they alleged diminution and asked for a writ of *cer-tiorari*, the clerk should enter the award accordingly. Before the defendant had pleaded *in nullo est erratum*, the plaintiff might sue forth his writ of *certiorari* in ordinary course, without order from the House. If he did not prosecute the writ and procure its return within ten days of his plea of diminution, he would lose the benefit of it and the defendant could proceed as if no such writ had been awarded.[226]

In his discussion of judicature, Elsyng had referred to the power of the House to consider cases of error made by parliament itself, but this jurisdiction was of no importance during the early Stuart period. One petition in 1647 in which the House was asked to reconsider its own earlier judgment recalled its obligation to correct "erroneous judgments in parliament" and would have necessitated research into medieval pre-cedents, but this case does not seem to have proceeded beyond the initial petition.[227]

Judicature in error developed relatively slowly in the early Stuart pe-riod and reached a climax in the Long Parliament. There had been four or five cases reported in the upper House between 1621 and 1629, twenty-six cases in the early years of the Long Parliament, and several hundred from April 1646 through December 1648.[228] For the causes of this enor-mous growth, we may look in part to the successive orders and ordi-nances that removed obstructions from the process of error and in part to the decline of the Court of Exchequer Chamber set up in the Elizabethan period.[229] Procedure in Exchequer Chamber had been "lengthy, cum-brous, and expensive." A contemporary wrote in 1602 that the abuse of the statute for reforming errors in King's Bench "hath frayed the clients from their suits, when they can have noe judgment certaine or speedy."[230]

The route from Exchequer Chamber to parliament was not an easy one. Hale wrote that if a man "once make his election . . . to bring [his case] in the exchequer chamber, it seems he has concluded himself, and shall not waive it and bring a writ of error in parliament, but at best, if he do it, it shall be no *supersedeas*."[231] During the years after 1640, the House was constantly in session. With the impeachment of the judges and the attack on other courts, men turned increasingly to parliament for remedy. To some it offered yet another way to cause delay, to others the hope of speedy and final remedy and an end to a weary round of suits.[232] Long after it had refused to undertake private business in the form of petitions,[233] the House continued to hear it on writ of error. By the constant exercise of its judicial authority in this area, it confirmed its jurisdiction over cases of error and the forms and methods of its proceedings.

SUMMARY AND SIGNIFICANCE

The judicial activities of the House of Lords were extensive and involved different kinds of procedure. Slowly the House built up a body of precedent for the trial of peers and the judgment of cases brought before it on impeachment. The chief change in the matter of privilege was in its definition. The procedure for protecting privilege remained the same. The handling of cases in error also followed a traditional course; but in hearing suits that had long depended in other courts and complaints from individuals, the House worked in a variety of ways.[234] Both came to the House by way of petition and many were handled initially by standing committees. Certain cases the House heard, tried, and judged. Others it referred to appropriate courts, fact-finding commissions, or arbitrators.[235] In some cases, it intervened in the normal operation of the courts. For example, it transferred an indictment from a court of quarter sessions to the Court of King's Bench on petition from the defendant, who said he was too feeble to make the required journey.[236] In yet other cases, the House took on judicial and administrative functions usually associated with the Privy Council or other institutions of government. Probably under the general umbrella of privilege, it summoned printers of unlicensed books (particularly books concerning proceedings in parliament) and authorized the Stationers Company to search for illegal presses.[237] In 1641, with the general breakdown of public order, it became involved in putting down anti-enclosure riots in Huntingdonshire on petition of the bishop of Lincoln and in protecting property in the fens on petition of the earl of Lindsey. In 1642 it took similar action on behalf of the earl of Sussex, who sought to maintain his fishing rights on Burnham River against an angry, well-organized group of local fishermen.[238]

The extension of the judicial and administrative activities of the House was not unaccompanied by difficulties. A technical problem arose when the keeper of Ludgate prison questioned whether an order from the House was sufficient warrant for release of a peer's servant. The House referred the matter to the judges. In reply the judges suggested that it might have been "more formal" to proceed by writ of *habeas corpus*. However, they declared that the Lords' order was in fact sufficient, since the upper House was not tied to "regularity of proceedings" as inferior courts were. Moreover, they recalled that business was often brought before King's Bench by court order. Finally, the judges advised the Lords to pass a specific resolution in this instance to protect the keeper against a charge of escape.[239] The point arose again in 1646, when the sheriff of London declined to discharge Edward Allen on the Lords' order. Allen wrote the House suggesting a writ of *habeas corpus* or other procedures that might be effective, citing in each instance a precedent in which the Lords had used the procedure he described.[240]

More serious than these procedural matters were problems of execution. In 1621 creditors of the Muscovy Company were successful in winning an order of the House for payment. When parliament had been dissolved, one creditor, the Scottish East India Company, turned to the Privy Council for relief. Only part of the money, it claimed, had been paid.[241] There were further complaints from creditors in 1624, 1626, and 1628, and the House referred the execution of its order to the Court of Chancery.[242] The continuous sitting of parliament in the years 1640–49 alleviated some difficulties, but others of greater moment arose. In attempting to enforce enclosure agreements, property rights in the fens, and fishing rights in the rivers, the House encountered serious hostility that was strongly colored by disrespect for the bishops and peers and by contempt for the House.

In each of these cases, the House had passed an order confirming the lord in possession. There is no record of a preliminary hearing, though the earl of Sussex had had a verdict confirming his fishing rights in the Court of Common Pleas. In each case, local people protested the order and the House summoned them as delinquents. The bishop of Lincoln reported that the men of Huntingdonshire had refused to obey and had answered "with contemptuous words." While imprisoned in the Fleet, they thought better of the matter, submitted to the bishop, and promised good behavior.[243] In Lindsey's case, the House issued a similar order. The sheriff, the earl reported, did not carry it out but spoke "scornfully and irreverently," as did others present. The House sent for the sheriff. The next report was of rioting and destruction of corn on the earl's

lands, encouraged by a justice of the peace.[244] He and his fellow delinquents were sent for. Again the orders of the House were "disobeyed and
slighted," the messengers were threatened and ill-treated. One man said
the Lords' order "was not worth a pin, but if any order came from the
House of Commons he would obey it." Another added that "there needed
no obedience to be given to the Lords' order for it was not under seal and
for ought he knew it was made under a hedge."[245] The problem with the
fishermen continued for several years. In 1645 Serjeant Finch, on behalf
of the House, had negotiated an agreement. The fishermen refused to
comply and were imprisoned for contempt.[246]

Certain defendants openly questioned both the procedure and the jurisdiction of the House. In 1643 Clement Walker, brought to the bar for
printing a book that cast a slur on Lord Saye, raised a fundamental objection to the judicial activities of the House. He said that it had not the
right to try his case. He refused to submit to its judgment, "because it
was against the Liberty of the Subject." When the presiding officer inquired what he meant, Walker went on to explain that judgment had
been given against him "without Original Writ or Record of his Crime."
He was a member of the House of Commons and a "Commoner of England" and "ought not therefore to be judged by the Lords, without their
hearing of him."[247] John Lilburne made the same point in 1646. He
denied the jurisdiction of the Lords. "Your Lordships," he said, "by
Magna Carta and the Law of this kingdom have nothing to do with me
(being a commoner) in any judicial way."[248] In April 1648 an alderman
of London also refused the jurisdiction of the House;[249] and in August
John Pendred, whose associates had been condemned by the Lords for
forging an act of parliament, gave printed petitions to the guards at the
door of the House and told them that "he wondred they would be such
fooles as to be made slaves by those they came to Guard . . . They will
even serve you as they have done these poore wretches ready to starve in
Prison, nay (said he) looke on this petition, you shall be sure to be made
slaves, as these poore people are. And moreover, he said, that this Court
was now made, as badd as ever the Starr Chamber was, the high Commission or the Spanish Inquisition."[250]

The judicial activities of the House consumed a large proportion of
its time and were a matter of pride to the Lords. In 1621 and the years
following, the judicature of the House came to be regarded as its unique
function. When the king first turned the case of Sir Henry Yelverton over
to the Lords in 1621 and then determined to resume control of it himself,
the House was quick to defend its right to proceed with the trial.[251] The
irresponsible enthusiasm of the House of Commons in passing sentence
on Edward Floyd in the same year for speaking disparaging words of the

Princess Elizabeth again threatened the judicial function of the upper House. In the compromise that settled the matter, the House of Lords was careful to preserve its right to judge delinquents.[252] Later, disturbed by certain clauses in the subsidy bill of 1624, it had turned, as noted above, to the judges for advice before voting the bill. The judges' interpretation reassured the House and was filed with the act and included in the journal as part of the permanent record.[253] As the right to initiate money bills was unique to the lower House, so judicature was held to be unique to the upper. "Judicature proper to us," Lord Brooke declared in 1640, "subsidies to them."[254]

The House of Lords also prided itself on its judicial procedure. When questioned before the Privy Council in 1622, Lord Saye asked his accuser to come forward that "he might not be made both witness against himself and his own accuser and . . . this he told them was the course that they always took in parliament never to put any man to speak that which might give a ground of accusation against himself."[255] In 1624 the Lords declined to join with the Commons in a petition to the king naming individual recusants. "Our Way in Judicature," they said, "is, to proceed upon Oath and to hear the Parties Defence, which the Shortness of Time in this Case can in no Means permit."[256] To the same end, they voted the general Standing Order concerning judicial procedure. "As this Court is the highest from whence others ought to draw their light," it read, "so the proceeding thereof should bee most cleere and equall, as well on the one side in finding out offences where there is just ground, as on the other side affording all just meanes of defence to such as shall bee questioned." Therefore defendants should have copies of all depositions and should be allowed counsel.[257] In the trial of Strafford in 1641, as we have seen, peers who had appeared as witnesses questioned whether they might properly serve as judges; in the same year the House resolved that a judge of appeal in a superior court should not hold a place in an inferior court from which an appeal might lie to himself.[258]

For a number of reasons, the years 1621–49 were years of exuberant growth in the judicial activities of the House. At the outset in 1621, the Commons encouraged the Lords in this expansion.[259] The Commons regarded judicature as yet another manifestation of the role of parliament to redress grievances. Each House had different judicial powers. The two were not in competition. The House of Commons was limited to cases of privilege or cases involving its members. When the Commons attempted to claim a wider jurisdiction in the Floyd case in 1621, they suffered a sharp rebuke from the king and the Lords.[260] Though the Commons accepted complaints on petition and carried forward investigations of a variety of grievances, such as abuses in the courts of justice and patents and monopolies, they did not examine on oath or, in the 1620s, take final action.[261] The House of Lords could and did examine on oath. It settled cases or referred them to other courts. It had the power to hear cases of error from King's Bench and Exchequer Chamber and assumed power to hear cases from other courts. The two Houses worked together in ridding the king of "evil counsellors" by impeachment. Each House had its own interests to serve. The Commons, as representatives of the realm, brought charges. The Lords, some of whom were playing out their rivalries on the parliamentary stage, passed judgment.[262]

Once the Lords had accepted wider judicial responsibilities, their jurisdiction became attractive. In an age when legal business was rapidly increasing and clogging the courts, litigants, seeking yet another arena for their cases, welcomed the opportunity to present them to the House. There was the hope not only for speedy and cheap remedy (which was frequently disappointed), but also for final settlement. In 1628 a letter writer observed, "My Lady Purbeck hath brought her case into the upper House, and it is thought she will go near to get the sentence of the high commission reversed there, which in case she do, they can never bring her in trouble for the same cause again."[263]

The extension of the Lords' judicial activities was also furthered by the failure of other courts. The Privy Council, which handled some of the investigations undertaken by the Lords in the 1620s, was overburdened.[264] In 1641 its judicial powers were abolished, together with the Courts of Star Chamber and High Commission. The Court of Requests did not meet after 1642.[265] The ecclesiastical courts were in disarray.[266] While other central courts continued to function during the civil wars, the assize courts suffered severely from the breakdown in order in 1642–45. In the years between the wars, people were unwilling to attend the judges sent out by parliament.[267]

There were particular reasons for the growth of some judicial cases. Those protecting privilege multiplied with the increased membership of the House, the generous definition of privilege that the House provided, and the lengthy sessions that characterized the Long Parliament. The expansion in cases of error not only reflected the general litigiousness of the age, but also the decline of the activity of the judges in Exchequer Chamber.[268] By removing obstacles to the process of error, the Lords had made it easier to bring cases to the House. The response was enormous. Sir Matthew Hale noted the difficulties inherent in a procedure that turned complicated legal decisions over to laymen, even if they were guided by the judges; but Sir Roger Twysden believed that the exercise of judicial powers by the Lords gave them a "great opportunity of doing good," that their decisions on writs of error kept "the judges in a straight course in point of judicature."[269]

After the Restoration, the attitude of the Commons toward the extension of the Lords' judicial activities changed. Judicature caused bitter quarrels between the Houses. The Commons and the judges attacked and cut back the jungle of jurisdiction that had developed. By the end of the century, the House of Lords would continue to handle cases in error and to hear cases on appeal from Chancery, but it would cease to function as a court of the first instance in civil cases. In criminal cases it would act only on impeachment from the Commons or to try peers.[270] The period of the uncontrolled growth of its jurisdiction was over.

10

LEGISLATION

Unlike the procedure in judicial matters that developed significantly during the early Stuart period, the Lords' procedure in legislation had been well established and generally accepted by the end of Elizabeth's reign. The basic features of this procedure, already indicated in chapters concerning the clerk and the committees, remained unchanged. However, certain points came under discussion in the Stuart period and the variety of material concerning legislation makes it possible to examine the process in greater detail than in former times.

Bills came to parliament by various routes and from various hands. Neither James nor Charles presented a well-defined program of legislation. James, indeed, tended to play down the importance of the legislative function. In his first parliament, he warned members against making too many laws and was particularly critical of private acts that comprised a substantial portion of the docket of any session. He was concerned not so much for the enactment of new legislation as for the execution of existing laws, "farre more profitable in a Common-wealth."[1] He saw the need also for a review and codification of laws, especially penal laws.[2] The crown's legislative activity was therefore not extensive. James's chief early project was the union of Scotland and England. In 1604 he sent the draft of a bill for union, which he had himself "conceived" and dictated, to the House of Lords.[3] In 1607 the bill for hostile laws, part of the same endeavor, was said to have been drafted by his solicitor general.[4] James followed in some detail other legislation that affected the crown or his own particular interests. He suggested changes in the draft of the preamble to a bill concerning entail.[5] He urged parliament in 1610 to enact legislation for the preservation of woodlands and the protection of game, an interest that continued throughout his life.[6] In 1624 Cranfield planned to introduce into the upper House a bill for protecting wildfowl in Leicestershire, knowing that he would please the king.[7]

Bills affecting the royal family were officially sponsored: bills advancing the interests of the Prince of Wales as duke of Cornwall, a bill for the queen's jointure that came to the upper House with an endorsement indicating the king's pleasure that it should be read, the bill concerning Frederick of the Palatinate, the king's son-in-law.[8] In the preparations for a parliament, the Privy Council sometimes proposed legislation for remedy of known grievances and offered bills of grace to "sweeten" the parliament, especially the lower House, for subsidies. Among these bills were the points of "retribution" offered in 1610 as part of the great contract, and the bills suggested in 1614.[9] During a parliament, legislation or proposals concerning legislation might be put forward for political reasons. In 1624 the suggestion that parliament should appoint treasurers for the subsidy, later incorporated in the subsidy act, came from the crown.[10] Royal initiative, however, was not marked under James and the role of the council in parliamentary affairs declined after Salisbury's death in 1612.[11] Similarly, the death of Archbishop Bancroft in 1610 marked the end of legislation officially sponsored by the church. In the early years of James's reign, Bancroft had brought in a number of bills and in 1607 moved for a committee of lords to study the laws concerning religion and to determine whether more were necessary.[12]

Like his father, Charles turned to parliament primarily for financial grants and showed even less interest in legislation. He was not given to oratory and relied on the lord keeper for the major speech at the opening of a parliament. Williams in 1625 stuck strictly to supply. Although Coventry in 1626 spoke of the king's wish to "consult and advise of provident and good Laws," the main thrust of his oration was the need to support the king's foreign policy with a vote of subsidies. In 1628 he dwelt even more briefly on laws. The king, he said, summoned parliament because "aids" granted there were often "accompanied with wholesome laws and gracious pardons and the like."[13] The king and the council put forward a few proposals to please the subject in 1629.[14] Towards the end of Charles's effective reign in 1641, the lord steward and the great chamberlain brought from the king to the upper House the heads of a bill for triennial parliaments; and in 1642, after inquiring about the proper procedure, two serjeants at law brought in the royal bill concerning the militia and gave it to the clerk.[15] These last efforts represented not royal initiative so much as the attempt of the crown to shape legislation that affected its interests, even if it were initiated elsewhere.

In addition to bills from official sources, a high proportion came into both Houses from corporations and from private persons. When Archbishop Laud was charged in 1641 with opposing eight bills, he replied that most bills were put in by private persons and that every man might have his opinion until the House had voted.[16] Bills also arose from the deliberations of the Houses themselves, particularly the investigations of the House of Commons concerning grievances, which led, among other things, to the bill of monopolies.[17] In 1641 a committee of lords considered the need for a bill concerning the buying of places.[18]

The king's learned counsel drafted certain bills.[19] Private bills were drawn by lawyers engaged for the purpose or regularly retained by lords.[20] Bills also might come from other sources. In 1621 Walter Morrell, "a Gentleman about the Court," offered a group of public bills to the House. They were assigned to the consideration of a special committee and one of the group was introduced.[21] Committee debate often revealed weaknesses in the drafting of a bill, which might be rectified by the committee itself, with the help of its professional attendants.[22] If a bill was beyond redemption, but the substance was approved, a committee might bring in a new bill in place of the old.[23]

There were two major categories of bills, public bills and private bills. The distinction between them was less clear than one might suppose.[24] Hakewill spoke of public bills as those that effected "some publick good": the service of God, the good of the church or the commonwealth (including bills concerning "the person, revenue, or Household of the King, Queen or Prince").[25] Private bills were those designed to benefit single individuals or particular groups. For private bills, one must pay fees to the clerk, his assistant, and the gentleman usher.[26] In the upper House, private bills must be introduced by petition.[27] To a private bill, the royal assent was "Soit fait come il est desire"; to a public, "Le Roy le veult." The text of a private act was not printed or enrolled in the parliament roll, and the act must be specially pleaded in a court of law.[28] It might be transmitted to Chancery or other courts separately by means of a writ of *certiorari*, especially requested and especially paid for.[29]

Not all these distinctions held. Certain acts that might seem to be private acts and to which the royal assent had been "Soit fait" were enrolled on the parliament roll: for example, in 1624 an act for the makers of knives and other cutlery and an act for making the Thames navigable to Oxford, in 1625 an act for the confirmation of copyhold estates in Cheltenham. It is possible that the clerk, under pressure and for a suitable reward, might enroll some "private acts" as public acts, a great advantage to the individual concerned since the act would sometimes be printed when other public acts were printed and would be known to the courts. Some of these enrolled acts that seem to be "private" may have been regarded as quasi-public in nature. It is significant that the customary fees were "forgiven" on the bill for making the Thames navigable.[30] A "particular" bill, the fourth earl of Bedford noted in his commonplace book, is not the same as a private bill,[31] but could be a public bill that affected only a section of the community. The relationship between the form in which a bill had been drawn and the form of the royal assent was not always maintained. By custom, private bills were often drawn as petitions, public bills as acts. Both contained within them enacting clauses. To bills framed as petitions, the appropriate reply was said to be "Soit fait." To bills framed as acts, the king replied "Le Roy le veult."[32] The bill concerning the Thames had been cast as an act, but the king replied "Soit fait." To the bill for York House, which concerned the crown and was also drawn as an act, the royal assent was again "Soit fait." To the bills concerning knives and cutlery in 1624 and to a bill for the tenants of Bromfield in 1628, both framed as petitions, he also replied "Soit fait."[33] On one occasion, the clerk himself or his assistant became understandably confused when he came to present the bills to the king at the end of a session and noted his replies. In a number of instances, he began to write "Le Roy" and then crossed it off and entered "Soit faictz."[34] Finally, acts enrolled and acts printed were not always the same. Two acts in 1625 were not included among the printed sessional acts, but were enrolled.[35] These anomalies may explain the caution of the king's printer. His intention clearly was to print the text of public acts in full and merely list those that were private acts. But he entitled his two categories "Acts Printed" and "Acts not Printed" and did not attempt further classification. The clerk was bolder. In drawing up his enrollment, he ranged the texts of the acts under the heading "Public Acts" and the titles under the heading "Private Acts."[36]

Procedure at this period did not markedly differ for public and private bills. The chief differences occurred when the bill was in committee and at the time of royal assent. It will therefore be convenient to consider the two types of bills together, pointing out distinctions as they occur. A bill began its career in the upper House in the hands of the clerk or one of the lords, who served as sponsor.[37] Those that originated in the upper House were written on paper. Those that came from the lower House had already been engrossed on parchment and carried the superscription "Soit baille aux Seigneurs."[38] When the clerk of the parliaments and the presiding officer of the upper House met together to decide on the agenda for the day, they also determined the schedule for reading bills.[39] In the House the clerk nevertheless went through the ritual of kneeling before the presiding officer and asking whether he should read the bill.[40] After permission was given, the clerk then returned to his table, read the bill aloud, and delivered it with its brief or breviate to the presiding officer.[41] The presiding officer in turn read the brief to the House and announced, "This is the first reading." After the second reading by the clerk, usually on a subsequent day, the presiding officer read only the title of the bill, saying, "This is the second reading," and put the question for committing or engrossing.[42] Although it was customary to commit bills at this stage, if no one spoke against the bill or raised any doubts about it, then the question must be for engrossing or, in the case of a bill from the lower House (already engrossed), for the third reading.[43] In 1614 the archbishop of Canterbury moved that the bill for naturalizing Frederick of the Palatinate, husband of the king's daughter, should not be committed in order to do honor to the bill.[44] Conversely, when the House of Lords disapproved a bill and had no intention of passing it, it sometimes deliberately failed to commit it.[45]

When the House had committed a bill and chosen the committee, the clerk gave the chairman a committee sheet.[46] The committee also had the bill itself and the breviate.[47] It received petitions for and against a bill.[48] Committees on both public and private bills conducted hearings, summoning witnesses and parties concerned and their counsel and calling in such material as they considered necessary for information.[49] Thus, merchants and representatives of companies and the attorney general appeared in 1604 in connection with the bill for free trade;[50] the clerk of the council was to bring in copies of orders and decrees in Star Chamber concerning seditious books for the use of a committee; the plasterers were ordered to appear in connection with a bill presented by the painters; many men of many persuasions were heard on the bill for tanning leather. On private bills, counsel against the bill was heard first.[51]

When a committee finished its business, the chairman or another member reported to the House. If the committee brought in amendments, additions, or provisos to a bill, they were delivered in paper to the clerk, "who goes from his seat, and receives the same from his lordship"; he then read them once and endorsed them "1 vice lecta." He gave the bill with the amendments or other changes to the presiding officer, who read "how the Bill was before, and how if it bee thus amended," explained the effect of any changes, and inquired whether the House was pleased to proceed to a second reading.[52] If so, the clerk read the amendments or other changes again and endorsed them "2 vice lecta."[53] At this stage, the House usually debated a bill.[54] While it was customary for all members of a committee to support the recommendation of the committee, they were nonetheless free to speak in the House as they chose.[55]

To speak to a bill or to any other matter before the House, a lord rose and removed his hat. If several lords rose together, he who rose first spoke first regardless of rank.[56] Occasionally the House made an exception for those unable to stand, in 1621 for Lord Zouche and in 1626 for the archbishop of Canterbury.[57] A lord addressed his speech not to the presiding officer, as was the custom in the lower House, but to the members of the House in general, "as in Council or Star Chamber."[58] He was not to name an individual lord but to refer to him by some circumlocution, such as the lord who spoke last.[59] He was to speak only once to a particular bill or proposition, unless the House gave him leave to explain himself—a rule to which the Lords held their members.[60] Speech was at all times to be decorous.[61] It was usually informal. A lord who spoke from notes in 1614 apologized for doing so.[62] In the same year, Southampton remarked, "I never came with premeditation to speake unto this house and theirfore I hope yor Lopp^s doe not expect from me a sett speeche."[63] It was not fit for a councillor, the earl of Salisbury said, "to shew eloquence which is more proper for a popular assembly."[64] Certain speeches, however, were clearly prepared in advance: the lord chancellor's addresses, Salisbury's oration in 1610 concerning the king's necessities, the earl of Northampton's speeches in James's first parliament, Buckingham's relation in 1624 and his defense in 1626.[65]

When the Lords had finished their debate, the presiding officer put the question for engrossment (in the case of a Lords' bill) or sometimes for recommitment.[66] Engrossment meant making a fair, clerical copy of a bill on parchment. This took time. In 1606 Sir Edward Phelips, then Speaker of the House of Commons, had delayed the reading of a bill on the pretence that it had not yet been wholly engrossed.[67] In 1621 Thomas Crewe observed in the lower House that the bill for the continuance of statutes would require a day's labor for two good scriveners.[68] Provisos were engrossed after they had been twice read.[69] If the bill had begun in the upper House, amendments were incorporated in the engrossed bill.[70] Amendments to a Commons' bill remained in paper and were attached to the bill.[71]

When a bill was ready for its third reading, the clerk notified the presiding officer, and together they found a place for it on the agenda. If the House was willing to proceed on the bill, the clerk read the title and then the bill, which he delivered to the presiding officer, "who demands if it shall bee putt to the Question."[72] This procedure of inquiring whether the Lords were ready to vote on the bill was an informal version of putting the previous question, well known to the House in other contexts and frequently used. In the early part of the century, the presiding officer did not always formally put the question whether the Lords were ready to proceed and call for a vote upon this point. It might be merely agreed on or "not denied." But the procedure became more formalized in the Short and Long Parliaments.[73] If the Lords had agreed to put the question or had voted to do so, the presiding officer then read the title of the bill "and holding it in his hands, saith to this effect. This Bill is now read the third tyme, such of your Lordships as are of opinion, that this Bill is fit to passe, say content, and they which are of a contrary opinion, say not content."[74] On one occasion, a member raised the question of a quorum, but the House voted to proceed with the members present.[75] The Standing Orders that date from 1621 provided that the Lords should vote on bills or any other proposition, one by one, beginning at the "lowest." "Every man in his turn rises uncovered, and only sayes, content, or, not content." The prince voted last.[76] In case there was a question about the outcome of the vote, the House appointed tellers, one for the negative and one for the affirmative.[77] The tellers took a poll by going to each bench in turn, beginning with that of the barons. The lords who had said "content" stood up uncovered and were counted. Next those who had voted "not content" rose and were counted. So the tellers proceeded, bench by bench.[78] Officers of state who sat in the House might vote if they were of the degree of baron or above.[79] The presiding officer, as has been described earlier, stepped down to his place at the head of the earls' bench to do so.[80] In case of a close vote, the House might call for proxies, "whereat the Clerke must shew his Booke, where they are entred, and as the Lords give the Votes of their Proxies, soe they are to bee reckoned."[81] A simple majority carried a measure. If votes were equal, the negative was presumed to prevail and the bill failed.[82]

After a third reading, a bill could not be recommitted, nor, if it had passed the House, could it be "let sleep."[83] In 1624 the Lords discovered defects in a bill after passing it. Since the House could not rescind its vote, nor amend a bill already passed, it forwarded a note with the bill concerning its deficiencies to the House of Commons.[84] The Lords handled the case of the silk-dyers bill in 1610 in another way. They scheduled the reading of a counterpetition after the bill had passed and resolved to delay the decision to send the bill for royal approval until they had heard the opposition at large.[85]

A successful bill that had begun in the lower House and passed the upper remained with the Lords until it was presented for the royal assent. The clerk inscribed it "A ceste Bill les Seigneurs sont assentus" and endorsed the title on the back where he had already made a note of each of the three readings. A bill that had begun in the upper House must move to the Commons. The clerk subscribed it "Soit baille aux Comons" and sent it, usually together with other bills, to the lower House by two or three messengers chosen from the assistants to the House; ordinarily these were the masters in Chancery or, for important bills or bills to be especially honored, the judges or the attorney general.[86] On entering the lower House, the messengers made solemn obeisance and said, "Mr. Speaker, My Lords of the upper House have passed amongst them and do think good there should be enacted by parliament such an Act, and such an Act and so readeth the Title of such an Act or Acts: They pray you to consider them and shew them your advice and so depart."[87] If the House of Commons amended or otherwise altered a bill, the clerk of the lower House subscribed the bill "A ceste [Bille] avecque les Amendments et addicions (or provisions) annexe les Comons sont assentus." At the head of the additions or provisos, he wrote "Soit baille aux Seigneurs."[88] Amendments were returned in paper with the bill to the upper House, additions and provisos were returned engrossed in parchment. The upper House had then to consider the amended bill. If the Lords disliked the amendment and yet wished to "speed the bill," they usually requested a conference but could not of themselves alter the Commons' amendments.[89] If the Commons returned the bill without changes, the clerk of the House of Commons wrote the words "A cest Bill les Comons sont assentu" beneath the Lords' "Soit baille."[90] Members brought the bill from the House of Commons. When they were admitted to the Lords' chamber, the presiding officer came to the middle of the bar, bearing the great seal and sometimes accompanied by other lords. The commoners, making obeisance "with low reverence," delivered their bills and withdrew. The presiding officer returned to his place and informed the Lords what bills had been sent. Bills that originated in the lower House also came to the Lords in this way, inscribed "Soit baille aux Seigneurs."[91]

The pace for bills varied and was normally slow. But bills that the House of Lords chose to honor passed rapidly. Thus, in 1604, it read the bill for recognition of the succession three times in one day to show its "joyful acceptation."[92] As we have seen, the archbishop of Canterbury moved that the bill for naturalizing Frederick of the Palatinate should not be committed.[93] In 1640 the bill for the queen's jointure was read twice in one day.[94] Under pressure, particularly at the end of a session, a bill might be read two or even three times in a single day.[95] Thus, in 1624, the bill of alienations was newly written on Thursday night, read three times in the House on Friday, and sent to the House of Commons, which also read it three times. It went to the king for approval on Saturday.[96]

The final stage in the enactment of bills was the royal assent. The clerk of the parliaments, Clarendon wrote, delivered the bills that had passed both Houses to the clerk of the crown, who in turn brought them to the attorney general. He presented them to the king "sitting in Council," read them, and explained how the bills changed earlier laws, and how they affected the crown. After careful consideration with his council, the king then resolved upon the answers he would give.[97] It would be interesting to know how often this formal procedure was actually carried out. Certainly before the final day of a session, the clerk of the parliaments sent the king a list of bills passed and later waited upon him with the bills in order to understand his pleasure.[98] In 1624 the king gave the clerk a memorial of his interpretation of the earl of Hertford's bill to be entered in the journal and endorsed on the back of the bill. James also bade the clerk ask the judges' opinion concerning the bill of sheriffs' accounts. Satisfied by Elsyng's report, the king gave his assent to the bill.[99]

The ceremonies at the end of a parliament could make a natural and gracious conclusion, a companion piece to the ritual of the opening. The king presided. The lords wore their robes. Members of the Commons stood at the bar with their Speaker. The clerk of the crown, standing on the left of the clerk of the parliaments, read the titles of the bills.[100] The clerk of the parliaments pronounced the king's replies "Le Roy le veult" or "Soit fait come il est desire"; if consent was withheld, "Le Roy s'ad-visera." When the king did not attend parliament on the final day, he empowered a commission under the great seal to perform the necessary functions.[101] The clerk of the crown read the titles of bills and the clerk of the parliaments pronounced the royal replies, as before.[102]

This was the standard procedure for most legislation, public and private. Certain bills required special treatment. The most important were the two subsidy bills and the general pardon. The temporal subsidy traditionally originated in the House of Commons, a custom that came to be regarded by the lower House as a privilege and a right.[103] The Commons strongly resented any direct or indirect suggestion from the Lords concerning a grant and raised a constitutional point of privilege on the matter in the Short Parliament.[104] As Hakewill explained in his treatise on the way statutes are enacted, after its general substance had been voted in the Commons, the body of the bill was usually drawn by some of the king's counsel and the preamble (stating the purpose of the grant) by a select committee of the lower House.[105] As we have seen, the unusual provisions of the bill in 1624 raised some problems for the Lords, which were resolved for them by the judges.[106] In 1628 the Lords complained that the wording of the preamble was faulty so that the grant seemed to come from the Commons alone, rather than from all his Majesty's "humble and loyal Subjects."[107] While the question was still under consideration in the lower House, the Lords nevertheless passed the bill unamended.[108] The subsidy bill proceeded through both Houses in the usual way with three readings in each.[109] In 1621 it was read twice in one day in the upper House, in 1625 three times in a single day.[110] The bill was then returned to the lower House in preparation for the ceremonies at the end of the session,[111] when the Speaker, holding the bill in his hand, presented the subsidy at the bar in a brief speech to the monarch or (if the king was not present) to his commissioners. The Speaker then passed the bill over the bar to one of the lords, "whoe handing it along delivered it to the Clerk of the upper House, whoe layed it before him on the table in the sight of the king."[112] In 1625 there was a difficulty because the bill had been annexed to the commission for the royal assent together with other bills and could not be presented separately by the Speaker; "but it was moved that hee [the Speaker] should intimate that custome in some short speech to the Lords, which . . . was accordingly performed."[113] In 1628 the subsidy was not sent down to be carried up by the Speaker "according to the ancient Custom; to which much Exception was taken."[114]

The royal assent to the temporal subsidy varied slightly: in 1610, "Le Roy le veult"; in 1624, "Le Roy remerciant touts ses loiaux Subjects, accepte leur benevolence et ainsi le veult"; in 1625 and 1628, "Le Roy remerciant ses bones Subiectes, accepte leur benevolence, et ainsi le veult."[115] In 1624 James commented on the subsidy, which he accepted and to which he gave his assent. Since the preamble had been drawn without his advice and might be prejudicial to him "for some reasons of State," he would be forced to alter it "and set his marginal noate upon it."[116] He did not in fact do so, but his comment casts an interesting sidelight on his concept of a statute.[117]

The subsidy of the clergy was brought to the upper House from the convocation of the province of Canterbury by the archbishop or, in his absence, by the senior bishop of that province who was present.[118] The grant was engrossed in parchment and bore the seal of the archbishop. The clerk of the parliaments delivered the grant to the attorney general, who drew a preamble and concluding sections confirming the grant and extending its provisions to the province of York.[119] These were affixed to the original engrossed grant, which then returned to the House for three readings. These customarily occurred after the temporal subsidy had been introduced.[120] At the first reading, all sections were read; at the second and third readings, only the preamble and confirmation.[121] After the bill had passed the upper House, the clerk noted the number of readings on the back of the bill, subscribed it "Soit baille aux Comons," and sent it to the lower House, where it had one reading.[122] The royal assent, later written at the head of the preamble, was "Le Roy remercient ses Prelates, accepte leur Benevolence et ainsi le veult."[123]

The general pardon was an act of grace from the king; it was associated with the closing of a session of parliament[124] and regarded by both king and subjects as a royal gift in remuneration for the subsidy.[125] It was a form of amnesty in which the crown pardoned a variety of offenses and freed subjects from paying certain debts.[126] Its cost to the monarch[127] and its benefit to the subject depended on the terms of the act and were variously estimated.[128] The pardon granted in 1624 was widely hailed as the most generous since the days of Elizabeth.[129] The general pardon was drawn by the attorney general, using earlier grants as a model,[130] on instructions from the king, or the Privy Council, or sometimes from the judges.[131] It came to the upper House engrossed in parchment and signed at the top by the king himself.[132] It was read only once in the House and then forwarded to the House of Commons with the usual subscription, "Soit baille aux Comons."[133] There had been no debate because, as Hakewill explained, "the subject must take it as the King will give it, without any alteration."[134] The lower House failed to respect this principle. Members sometimes complained when the pardon was read, "for that it is not so favourable as in former times."[135]

In 1610 the Commons even suggested exceptions.[136] Their pressure against Sir Stephen Proctor was so strong that the pardon was actually altered by the attorney general in the presence of the king to except Proctor from its provisions.[137] In 1628 and 1641 there was reluctance to pass the pardon for fear it would exonerate the king's ministers then under attack.[138] At the closing of a parliament, when the Speaker of the House of Commons presented the subsidy to the crown, he also expressed the subjects' thanks for the pardon. Later the clerk of the parliaments read the formal phrases of gratitude: "Les Prelats, Seigneurs, & Communs en cest Parliament assembles au nom de toutes vous autres subjects remercient tres humblement vostre Majesty, & prient Dieu vous donner en sante, bone vie, & longe."[139] In writing of the parliaments of Queen Elizabeth, Sir Simonds D'Ewes noted that the queen's assent to the pardon was not necessary "because it is originally her free gift."[140] The royal signature had indicated assent. Nevertheless, both Henry Elsyng and John Browne recorded that the clerk should read the formula of assent, "Le Roy le veult," as he did for other bills. Elsyng entered this phrase on the parliament roll. In 1610 Bowyer had not done so.[141]

In 1606 the clerk, on order of the Lords, entered a note in the journal that persons wishing to offer bills for restitution in blood, that is, bills restoring those who had been attainted, should first petition the king for permission to do so and then present their bills to the upper House. In recent years there had been several errors "by reason of Bills of this Nature begun in the Lower House."[142] The king at the close of the session spoke to the same effect, saying that bills should receive his allowance and signature before being presented.[143] Since they came to the House with the royal imprimatur, they were usually not committed.[144] In addition, after 1606 persons to be restored must come to the House to swear the oaths of allegiance and supremacy required by law and demonstrate that they had taken communion within a month before the first reading of the bill. To meet the terms of this order, Carew Raleigh's bill, first read on 11 February 1625/6, received a second "first reading" on 21 February after he took communion.[145] Persons desiring to be naturalized must also present certificates that they had taken the sacrament within a month of the first reading of their bills. They must swear the oaths of allegiance and supremacy in the House before the second reading and pay the officers' fees.[146]

If we reflect upon the method of enacting bills, we can see several points at which men applied pressure. The first was in the drafting of a bill. Ellesmere, perusing the draft of a bill in 1614, observed that it might raise questions in parliament and proposed to consult with the judges, the king's learned counsel, and the members of the Privy Council about it.[147] Second, it was necessary to keep track of bills as they came into the House. In 1606 the earl of Salisbury took care to notify the earl of Bath of a bill affecting his interests. Bath at once discovered the time and place of the committee meeting on the bill and sent an agent to appear in his behalf.[148] Often it was the clerk or his assistant who relayed or withheld this sort of information. In 1610 Bowyer, then clerk, was to inform Mistress Fisher if a bill came in concerning one Wentworth so that she might warn her father.[149] The assistant clerk made several notes of the same kind in the front of his minute book for 1624.[150]

The next stage was to ensure a bill's place on the agenda of the House, or conversely to block it. Justice Walmsley asked Robert Bowyer to forward a "general" bill on behalf of some friends or clients.[151] In 1621 a peer's private bill was read "though the day was far spent,"[152] when surely another man's would not have been. A bill without a powerful sponsor could easily fall by the wayside and might well never appear.[153] An alert sponsor could influence the selection of a committee since he must have realized that those speaking for a bill or raising doubts about it were normally chosen.[154] The next point of influence was the committee itself. There are numerous examples of the materials submitted at this stage of a bill's progress, petitions and briefs for and against bills as well as evidence of oral testimony from a variety of witnesses. The final stage in influencing the fate of a bill was to sway the vote of members on the floor and then in the lower House, both in committee and in the House. The earl of Pembroke wrote privately to Sir John Eliot in 1629, asking him to prevent the second reading of a private bill; the earl of Northumberland in the same way wrote to Sir John Holles.[155]

We should not take too seriously the statements differentiating the role of the two Houses in handling bills. In 1606 the House of Commons left to the upper House, "who are best acquainted with that Matter," the problem of framing a bill deferring the union until the following session.[156] In 1614 Bacon thought that matters of grace were best handled in the lower House, "such bills of honor and policy as may concern the ornament, safety and strength of the commonwealth" in the upper.[157] In the beginning of the Stuart period, the monarch could and did count on the upper House to kill undesirable legislation, for example, bills concerning purveyance and impositions;[158] but he was less sure of the House as the years went on. Charles and Buckingham were anxiously counting votes in 1626, as the commitment of Arundel (who controlled a block of proxies) and the creation of new peers bear witness.[159] By the end of the session of 1628, the king could no longer rely on the House to carry out his wishes. It defeated the attempt to emasculate the Petition of Right.[160] In 1642 a decisive split occurred. Some peers left to join the king. Others remained at Westminster, engaged in voting ordinances that were far from pleasing to him.

There was a difference of opinion in the early seventeenth century concerning the importance of legislation. The monarchs, especially James, laid less emphasis on new laws than they did on the execution or updating of existing statutes. Their chief interest was in the vote of the subsidy. Bills of grace offered by the crown were part of a program to encourage giving. The king's subjects, on the other hand, particularly those in the House of Commons and the men they represented, regarded the passing of bills as a primary parliamentary obligation.[161] The pressure for bills came from the constituencies. There is little evidence to indicate whether this pressure affected the Lords; but it may be of some significance that, of thirty-three public acts in 1604, twenty-seven originated in the lower House.[162] In 1624 it was said of the upper House: "There was not any one public bill sent to the lower house by them. See what care they have for the commonwealth who were wont to be the chief statesmen, and should be the pillars of the commonwealth."[163] The Lords' role was less to initiate than to debate, revise, consider, and on occasion shunt aside or defeat.

Pressure for bills came also from individuals who sought legislative remedy for private complaints, a pressure felt equally by lords and commoners. In the early days of the fifth session of parliament in 1610, the clerk observed that the earl of Salisbury spoke "to no great purpose" of the general institution of parliaments, which was for "matter moving from the head and for private causes."[164] While matter moving from the head declined, bills for private causes continued to clamor for attention. In writing of the later parliaments of Henry VIII, Professor Lehmberg observed that, of 300 acts, 117 were private.[165] Of 72 bills enacted in 1604, 39 were private; of 73 bills enacted in 1624, 38 were private.[166] If one could conveniently count failed bills, the proportion of private bills would probably loom even larger. Beneficiaries of private bills were usually those who could afford to pay for them in time and money: municipal corporations, chartered companies, members of the upper class, and peers concerned for their titles to land who could send agents to act for them. Of 39 private bills enacted in 1604, 26 originated in the upper House.[167] In 1628 the earls of Arundel and Bristol sent public thanks to the House of Commons after their bills had been passed there. Edward Alford, a keen observer of parliamentary procedure, remarked that it was proper to resume this custom, which had not been observed since the days of Lord Burghley in Elizabeth's reign. Such bills, he said, "are passed of grace and not of duty and this House deserves thanks for neglecting the public to do any particular man a favor."[168]

Although both Houses were necessarily involved in private bills, the judicial activities of the House of Lords greatly increased the proportion of time it devoted to private business. After 1620, when the upper House heard cases on appeal from other courts and cases of the first instance, in addition to cases from King's Bench brought by writs of error, it widely expanded the time directed to alleviating the problems of individuals. It doubtless seemed easier for men and women of lower status and lower income to proceed by way of petition to the upper House than to attempt to launch a private bill that must be drawn by a professional adviser, pass both Houses paying its due fees, and achieve royal assent. Many petitioners plead in forma pauperis.[169] Many complaints were pitifully petty. As floods of petitions poured in and legislative and administrative demands on the House also grew after 1640, justice was often delayed and the hope for cheap and speedy remedy disappointed. Nevertheless, if parliament was, to return to Salisbury's phrase, a place not only for the king's business but also for private causes, the House of Lords was preeminently the House to which individuals increasingly turned for relief in the years 1621–49.

PART THREE

THE END OF A PARLIAMENT

11

CONCLUSION

CLOSING DAYS

Parliament closed with less pageantry than that with which it had opened. Until 1641, when the act providing that the Long Parliament could not be dissolved without its own consent infringed on the royal prerogative, only the king could terminate a parliament or a session of parliament. This was done by prorogation, which ended a session, or by dissolution, which ended the parliament as well.[1] The death of a monarch automatically dissolved a parliament, except in the case of Charles I. With a prorogation, all proceedings ceased and must begin afresh with a new session. Bills must be reintroduced and start their way through both Houses again. The lords must reappoint their proxies.

Just what constituted a session and a parliament was a matter for debate. It was commonly believed that both a session and a parliament meant acts.[2] The commission dissolving "parliament" in 1614 declared it to have been not a parliament, but a convention, because no act had passed. The judges concurred.[3] In 1621, on the other hand, the king's proclamation declared the late convention of parliament to be no session despite the passage of bills that had received his consent.[4] Another problem was whether the royal assent to bills in itself determined a session. Though it was customary for the king to give his answer to bills at the end of a session, this was not always the case. There was a long tradition to the contrary.[5] Nevertheless, a presumption that assent and the end of a session went together was widespread and helps account for the specific provisions in several statutes that royal assent would not terminate the session.[6] It was important to avoid ambiguity. The continuance of many statutes depended on whether a session was a session or a parliament a parliament.[7] Despite difficulties and confusion in the early seventeenth century, the king's prorogation alone determined a session. His command for dissolution concluded a parliament. Assent to bills was coincidental, not the decisive fact.[8]

When the king came to the parliament house on the last day of the session in May 1606, the bells in Westminster rang.[9] The Speaker of the House of Commons, standing at the bar of the Lords' chamber, addressed the king and thanked him for all his gracious benefits and for the general pardon. James spoke briefly and gave his assent to bills. In his name, the lord chancellor then prorogued the parliament until the following November.[10] A fuller account describes how the king came in state in 1624 to dissolve what would be his last parliament. He occupied the royal throne, as before, and wore his parliamentary robes and crown. In his hand he bore the scepter of King Edward the Confessor; heralds stood beside him, as did officers of state bearing the cap of maintenance and the sword. The Speaker spoke for members of the Commons, who crowded behind the bar. He thanked the king for the parliament and for consulting with his subjects. He was particularly grateful that the prince had been permitted "to communicate himselfe in person," and finally he presented the subsidy. The king replied with thanks for the subsidy, but with complaints concerning grievances and advice for the future. He asked the clerk of the crown to read the titles of bills presented for his consideration, but to pause to allow the monarch to comment if he chose.[11]

When royal commissioners performed the final functions, the ceremonies were less impressive. In 1614 the lords wore their robes. The thirty lords commissioners sat on a form set across the House with their backs to the cloth of estate, the archbishop of Canterbury in the middle, the lord chancellor on the right, York on the left. The great officers of state ranged on either side in order of precedence. The clerk of the parliaments read the commission in Latin. The lord chancellor provided an English translation and concluded with "God Save the King." As each commissioner was named, he rose and stood, bareheaded.[12] In 1625, at Oxford when the House was "thin" and the lords did not have their robes with them and in 1626 when the parliament was hastily dissolved, even this ceremonial dropped off. The lords did not wear their formal parliamentary attire and the commissioners occupied their usual seats.[13]

No peal of bells or blast of trumpets marked the final recorded meeting of the House of Lords in 1648/9. On 4 January the lower House voted that the legislative power rested in the Commons, that what the Commons alone "enacted or declared for law . . . hath the force of law," although the king and lords had not consented.[14] The upper House nevertheless continued to sit and transact business. On 1 February it sent a message to the lower House proposing a joint committee to meet the next morning to consider the government of the realm. The messengers were not admitted.[15] On 6 February the Commons voted "that the House of

Peers in Parliament is useless and dangerous, and ought to be abolished."
The lower House directed that this resolution should be incorporated in
an act and charged a committee to investigate and report on the matter of
preserving the Lords' records, of releasing any prisoners committed by
their authority, and of clearing the way for suits against them by revoking
their privileges. On the same day the House of Lords met for the last time.
Six members were present, including the earl of Denbigh as Speaker.[16]

THE HOUSE OF LORDS, 1603-1649

The House that was abolished in 1649 was not the same as the House
that had convened for James's first parliament in 1604. In the intervening
years the composition of the House had markedly changed, expanding
with the creation of new peers and decreasing with the expulsion of the
bishops, the demands of war, and the division of loyalties between king
and parliament. These changes had a variety of effects. The interest in
procedure observable from the meeting of 1621 forward was a natural
by-product of the increased size of the House and of the influx of new
men to the chamber.[17] The shift in the proportion of earls to barons
suggested that the pattern for choosing committees should perhaps be
changed.[18] The House of Lords had never been a unified group; but fac-
tionalism seems to have become more apparent to many observers with
the entry of Buckingham into the House and the proliferation of his supporters. Those who held ancient titles looked down on those with new
ones. Arundel lashed out at Spencer. Digby called Cranfield "an insolent
merchant."[19] Lords uncertain of commanding a majority of the votes in
the House discovered and exploited the usefulness of such forms of procedure as the committee of the whole House and collaboration with
members of the House of Commons.

Beginning in 1641, the changes in the composition of the House also
had their effects. The most significant alteration was the absence of the
king. With the monarch's permanent withdrawal from London, the Lords
joined with the House of Commons in passing legislation without his approval in the form of ordinances and developed processes of joint action
to handle administrative problems. Political divisions in the House were
reflected in the appearance of protests that replaced the earlier desire for
an appearance of consensus or unanimity. The sharp progressive decline
in membership probably affected seating arrangements, the method of
voting, and the way of choosing committees.

There was a change also in the nature of the Lords' business. During
the early Stuart period, the House greatly expanded the quantity and

scope of its judicial activities. The number of cases in error rose from less than ten in the years 1621–29 to hundreds during the Long Parliament. After 1621 the consideration of petitions further enlarged judicial agenda. The committee handled over 270 petitions in the years 1640–41 alone. These brought before the Lords not only cases already depending or decided in other courts, but also cases of the first instance. Later in the century, both the lower House and the judges would raise objections to this immense enlargement of the Lords' judicature, but during the early period it flourished virtually unchallenged save by individual protests.[20] Impeachment, to which both Houses returned in 1621 and the years following, and the trial of peers increased the judicial responsibilities of the House. In the great debate in the lower House on 5 February 1648/9 concerning the fate of the House of Lords, it was proposed that the House might continue as a court of judicature.[21] The suggestion failed, but it bore testimony to the growing importance of judicial business in the agenda of the House and to the growing appreciation by contemporaries of the judicial services that the Lords performed. The upper House participated in the impeachment proceedings that brought offenders against the commonwealth and the king's evil ministers and judges to justice. It offered remedy for large numbers of plaintiffs who brought their cases to the House.

In carrying forward both judicial and legislative business, the House relied on an increasingly sophisticated network of committees. The committee of the whole House, which facilitated debate and fortified the influence of articulate and determined minority groups, developed during this period. The regular use of standing committees dates from 1621. The Committee for Privileges considered matters that ranged widely from questions of individual and institutional privilege to matters of custom and procedure. A subcommittee supervised the preparation of the journal. The Committee for Petitions conducted a series of hearings and investigations, established procedure for doing so, and developed a set of criteria on which to base its determinations. It had its own clerk, who filed its papers, arranged agenda, and kept a record of decisions. Joint committees and frequent conferences facilitated the movement of business from one House to the other. The House worked out methods for selecting committees and laid down guidelines for the relationship between itself and its committees. It also developed the procedure necessary for joint committees, conferences, and the numerous messages between the Houses that these arrangements involved.

In every stage of its work the House was conscious of procedure and insistent that there was a proper way in which things should be done. Even in matters that might well be considered beyond its competence, such as the form of the writ of summons, the Lords corrected error. They also undertook to regulate proxies and in 1626 limited each lord to two. The procedure concerning bills had been developed earlier. In the first half of the seventeenth century, it became more firmly established and after 1642 carried over to legislation by ordinance. In judicial affairs, the procedure concerning writs of error was recalled and confirmed. The committee and the House evolved procedure to deal with petitions as their work went forward. The same was true of impeachment and the trial of peers.

Procedure was recorded in a number of ways. The House established its roll of Standing Orders in 1621; the roll received additions periodically and was read aloud early in each session. Members procured copies for their own use. The clerk recorded procedural decisions in the journals and compiled accounts of procedure and books of precedents. Individual peers, like the earl of Huntingdon and Lord Montagu, took particular note of such matters in their private accounts of the parliaments in which they served.[22] In the years 1603–49, the Lords firmly established a corpus of procedure to which the "other House" under Cromwell would adhere and which would be called back in every detail when Charles II came to the throne.[23] Frequently during the early years of the Restoration, the Committee for Privileges returned to earlier precedents in deciding matters referred to its attention.[24] The Standing Orders begun in 1621 continued to bind the House after 1660. The methods of selecting and using committees, of handling legislative and judicial business, different ways of proceeding with impeachment and with the trial of peers, agreed upon and recorded in the first half of the century, served as the foundation of procedure thereafter.

Perhaps the Lords' most enduring achievement during this period, one certainly the most important to the historian, was the establishment of the archive of parliament. The Lords provided a record office in the Jewel Tower and a conscientious series of clerks carefully endorsed and filed bills and papers. Both the House and the clerks worked to perfect the record of the proceedings of parliament in the parliament rolls and the proceedings of the House in the journal and in a series of books of committees, orders, and precedents. The roll of Standing Orders preserved procedure.

Though the officers of the House were essentially officers of the crown and appointed their own assistants, the Lords undertook to regulate their work. The interest of the House in its records immediately influenced the clerk. A subcommittee supervised the preparation of the journal and the House directed that no orders should be entered without its authorization. The Lords devised an oath of office for clerk and assistant clerk.

They also authorized a schedule of fees for the staff. When the king left London in 1641, the House asserted its right to choose a presiding officer.

All of these activities speak to two points: the vast expansion of the business and responsibilities of the House and the heightened consciousness that the lords had of it as an institution. Though the wide jurisdiction that it exercised during the years 1621–49 would be seriously questioned and cut back after the Restoration, the revolutionary growth of its judicial activities during the earlier period was of signal importance. The establishment of an archive, the careful preparation and supervision of the record, the adoption of standing orders and rules of procedure, and the regulation of officers reflect institutional maturity. The same maturity was revealed in the matter of privilege. Though the lords continued to be preeminently concerned with their rights as individuals, they also came to realize the significance of their privileges as members of the House. They insisted on their right to be summoned and to sit, the right to be free from arrest and other forms of detention during parliament time. They became increasingly aware of threats to their freedom of debate; they were increasingly insistent on managing their own affairs and increasingly competent to do so.

ABBREVIATIONS AND SHORT TITLES

Acts of the Privy Council	*Acts of the Privy Council of England*, 46 vols. (London, 1890–1964).
Adair	E. R. Adair and F. M. Greir Evans, "Writs of Assistance, 1558–1700," *English Historical Review* 36 (1921): 356–72.
AHR	*American Historical Review.*
Baillie, *Letters and Journals*	*The Letters and Journals of Robert Baillie, A.M., Principal of the University of Glasgow. M.DC.XXXVII–M.DC.LXII*, ed. David Laing (Edinburgh, 1841).
Beven, "Appellate Jurisdiction"	Thomas Beven, "Appellate Jurisdiction of the House of Lords," *Law Quarterly Review* 17 (1901): 155–70, 357–71.
BIHR	*Bulletin of the Institute of Historical Research.*
Blackstone, *Commentaries*	*Commentaries on the Laws of England in Four Books by Sir William Blackstone*, ed. William Draper Lewis (Philadelphia, 1897).
Blencowe, *Sydney Papers*	R. W. Blencowe, ed., *Sydney Papers, Consisting of A Journal of the Earl of Leicester and Original Letters of Algernon Sydney* (London, 1825).
Bond, "Clerks of the Parliaments"	Maurice F. Bond, "Clerks of the Parliaments, 1509–1953," *English Historical Review* 73 (1958): 78–85.
Bond, "Formation of the Archives"	Maurice F. Bond, "The Formation of the Archives of Parliament, 1497–1691," *Journal of the Society of Archivists* 1, no. 6 (October 1957): 151–58.
Bond, "Office of the Clerk"	Maurice F. Bond, "The Office of Clerk of the Parliaments," *Parliamentary Affairs* 12 (1959): 297–310.
Bond, unpublished article	Maurice F. Bond, Unpublished Article on the Committee for Petitions in the Short Parliament.
Bond and Beamish	Maurice F. Bond and David Beamish, *The Gentleman Usher of the Black Rod* (London, 1976).

Bowyer	*The Parliamentary Diary of Robert Bowyer, 1606–1607,* ed. David Harris Willson (Minneapolis, 1931).
Burnet	*Burnet's History of My Own Time,* ed. Osmund Airy, pt. 1, *The Reign of Charles II,* 2 vols. (Oxford, 1897–1900).
Cabala	*Cabala Sive Scrinia Sacra, Mysteries of State and Government* (London, 1663).
Calendar of State Papers Venetian	*Calendar of State Papers and Manuscripts, Relating to English Affairs . . . Existing in the Archives and Collections of Venice,* 22 vols. (London, 1864–1919).
Cal. Wynn Papers	*Calendar of Wynn (of Gwydir) Papers (1515–1690) in the National Library of Wales and Elsewhere* (London, 1926).
Chamberlayne, *Angliae Notitia*	[Edward Chamberlayne], *Angliae Notitia; or, The Present State of England* (London, 1669).
CJ	*The Journals of the House of Commons.*
Clarendon, *Life*	*The Life of Edward, Earl of Clarendon . . . in Which is Included, A Continuation of His History of the Grand Rebellion,* 2 vols. (Oxford, 1857).
Clyde	William M. Clyde, "Parliament and the Press, 1643–7," *Transactions Bibliographical Society,* 2d ser., vols. 13 and 14 (1933–34).
Cobb, "Opening of Parliament"	H. S. Cobb, "Descriptions of the State Opening of Parliament, 1485–1601: A Survey," in *Parliamentary History, Libraries and Records: Essays Presented to Maurice Bond,* ed. H. S. Cobb (London, House of Lords Record Office, 1981).
Cobbett, *State Trials*	*Cobbett's Complete Collection of State Trials,* 34 vols. (London, 1809–26).
Cockburn	J. S. Cockburn, *A History of English Assizes, 1558–1714* (Cambridge, 1972).
Coke, *Third Institute*	Sir Edward Coke, *The Third Part of the Institutes of the Laws of England* (London, 1680).
Coke, *Fourth Institute*	Sir Edward Coke, *The Fourth Part of the Institutes of the Laws of England: Concerning the Jurisdiction of Courts* (London, 1681).
Commons Debates 1621	*Commons Debates 1621,* ed. Wallace Notestein, Frances Helen Relf, and Hartley Simpson, 7 vols. (New Haven, 1935).
Commons Debates 1628	*Commons Debates 1628,* ed. Robert C. Johnson, Mary Frear Keeler, Maija Jansson Cole, and William B. Bidwell, 4 vols. (New Haven, 1977–78).
Commons Debates 1629	*Commons Debates for 1629,* ed. Wallace Notestein and Frances Helen Relf (Minneapolis, 1921).

Cope, "The Earl of Bedford's Notes"	Esther S. Cope, "The Earl of Bedford's Notes of the Short Parliament of 1640," *Bulletin of the Institute of Historical Research* 53 (November 1980): 255–58.
Cope, "Lord Montagu and the Short Parliament"	Esther S. Cope, "Lord Montagu and his Journal of the Short Parliament," *Bulletin of the Institute of Historical Research* 46 (November 1973): 209–15.
Cope, *Proceedings of the Short Parliament*	Esther S. Cope, *Proceedings of the Short Parliament of 1640*, Camden Society, 4th ser., vol. 19 (London, 1977).
Court and Times of Charles I	[Thomas Birch], *The Court and Times of Charles the First*, 2 vols. (London, 1848).
Crummett	J. B. Crummett, "The Lay Peers in Parliament, 1640–1644" (Ph.D. thesis, University of Manchester, The John Rylands University Library of Manchester, 1955).
Daly	James Daly, *Cosmic Harmony and Political Thinking in Early Stuart England, Transactions of the American Philosophical Society*, vol. 69, pt. 7 (Philadelphia, 1979).
de Villiers	Lady de Villiers, ed., *The Hastings Journal of the Parliament of 1621, Camden Society Miscellany*, vol. 20, in Camden Society, 3d ser., vol. 83 (London, 1953).
D'Ewes, *Autobiography*	*The Autobiography and Correspondence of Sir Simonds D'Ewes, Bart., during the Reigns of James I and Charles I*, ed. James Orchard Halliwell, 2 vols. (London, 1845).
D'Ewes, *Diary 1622–1624*	*The Diary of Sir Simonds D'Ewes (1622–1624)*, ed. Elisabeth Bourcier (Paris, 1974).
D'Ewes, *Journals of All the Parliaments*	Sir Simonds D'Ewes, *The Journals of All the Parliaments during the Reign of Queen Elizabeth* (London, 1682).
D'Ewes, *Long Parliament*	*The Journal of Sir Simonds D'Ewes from the Beginning of the Long Parliament to the Opening of the Trial of the Earl of Strafford*, ed. Wallace Notestein (New Haven, 1923).
Divisions in the House of Lords	*Divisions in the House of Lords: An Analytical List, 1685 to 1857*, comp. J. C. Sainty and David Dewar, House of Lords Record Office Occasional Publications, no. 2 (London, 1976).
DNB	*Dictionary of National Biography.*
Dugdale	Sir William Dugdale, *A Perfect Copy of All Summons of the Nobility to the Great Councils and Parliaments of This Realm* (London, 1685).
EHR	*English Historical Review.*
Elsyng, *Manner of Holding Parliaments*	Henry Elsynge, *The Manner of Holding Parliaments in England* (London, 1768).
Elsyng, "Method of Passing Bills"	Henry Elsyng, "The Method of Passing Bills in Parliament," *The Harleian Miscellany*, vol. 9 (London, 1810).

Elton, "Lords Journals" — G. R. Elton, "The Early Journals of the House of Lords," *English Historical Review* 89, no. 352 (July 1974): 481–512.

Elton, "Parliament in the Sixteenth Century" — G. R. Elton, "Parliament in the Sixteenth Century: Functions and Fortunes," *The Historical Journal* 22, no. 2 (1979): 255–78.

Elton, "Points of Contact" — G. R. Elton, "Tudor Government: The Points of Contact, I. Parliament," *Transactions of the Royal Historical Society*, 5th ser., vol. 24 (1974).

Elton, "Rolls of Parliament" — G. R. Elton, "The Rolls of Parliament, 1449–1547," *The Historical Journal* 22, no. 1 (1979): 1–29.

Elton, *Tudor Constitution* — G. R. Elton, *The Tudor Constitution* (Cambridge, 1968).

Firth, *House of Lords during the Civil War* — Charles H. Firth, *The House of Lords during the Civil War* (London, 1910).

Flemion, "The Dissolution of Parliament in 1626" — Jess Stoddart Flemion, "The Dissolution of Parliament in 1626: A Revaluation," *English Historical Review* 87, no. 345 (1972): 784–90.

Flemion, "Slow Process, Due Process" — Jess Stoddart Flemion, "Slow Process, Due Process, and the High Court of Parliament," *The Historical Journal* 17 (1974): 3–16.

Flemion, "Struggle for the Petition of Right" — Jess Stoddart Flemion, "The Struggle for the Petition of Right in the House of Lords: The Study of an Opposition Party Victory," *Journal of Modern History* 45 (1973): 193–210.

Foster, "House of Lords and Ordinances" — Elizabeth Read Foster, "The House of Lords and Ordinances, 1641–1649," *The American Journal of Legal History* 21 (1977): 157–73.

Foster, "Journal of the House of Lords" — Elizabeth Read Foster, "The Journal of the House of Lords for the Long Parliament," in *After the Reformation*, ed. Barbara C. Malament (Philadelphia, 1980).

Foster, *Painful Labour of Mr. Elsyng* — Elizabeth Read Foster, *The Painful Labour of Mr. Elsyng*, *Transactions of the American Philosophical Society*, vol. 62, pt. 8 (Philadelphia, 1972).

Foster, "Procedure in the House of Lords" — Elizabeth Read Foster, "Procedure in the House of Lords during the Early Stuart Period," *The Journal of British Studies* 5 (May 1966): 56–73.

Foster, "Procedure of the House of Commons against Patents and Monopolies" — Elizabeth Read Foster, "The Procedure of the House of Commons against Patents and Monopolies, 1621–1624," in *Conflict in Stuart England*, ed. William Appleton Aiken and Basil D. Henning (London, 1960).

Foster, *1610* — Elizabeth Read Foster, ed., *Proceedings in Parliament 1610*, 2 vols. (New Haven, 1966).

Foster, "Staging a Parliament" — Elizabeth Read Foster, "Staging a Parliament in Early Stuart England," in *The English Commonwealth 1547–*

1640, ed. Peter Clark, Alan G. R. Smith, and Nicholas
Tyacke (Leicester, 1979).

Fuller, *Ephemeris*
Parliamentaria

[Thomas Fuller], *Ephemeris Parliamentaria* (London,
1654).

Gardiner, *Oxinden Letters*

Dorothy Gardiner, ed., *The Oxinden Letters, 1607–1642*
(London, 1933).

Gardiner, *Commons*
Debates 1625

Samuel Rawson Gardiner, ed., *Debates in the House of*
Commons in 1625, Camden Society, n.s., vol. 6 (London,
1873).

Gardiner, *Constitutional*
Documents

Samuel Rawson Gardiner, ed., *The Constitutional Docu-*
ments of the Puritan Revolution, 1625–1660 (Oxford,
1899).

Gardiner, *Debates in*
the House of Lords 1621

Samuel Rawson Gardiner, ed., *Notes of the Debates in the*
House of Lords . . . 1621, Camden Society, 1st ser.,
vol. 103 (London, 1870).

Gardiner, *Debates in the*
House of Lords
1624 and 1626

Samuel Rawson Gardiner, ed., *Notes of the Debates in the*
House of Lords . . . 1624 and 1626, Camden Society, n.s.,
vol. 24 (London, 1879).

Glover

Robert Glover, *Nobilitas politicas vel civilis* (London,
1608).

Graves, "Freedom from
Arrest"

Michael A. R. Graves, "Freedom of Peers from Arrest: The
Case of Henry, Second Lord Cromwell, 1571–1572," *The*
American Journal of Legal History 21 (1977): 1–14.

Graves, *House of Lords*
Edward VI and Mary I

Michael A. R. Graves, *The House of Lords in the Parlia-*
ments of Edward VI and Mary I (Cambridge, 1981).

Graves, "Proctorial
Representation"

Michael A. R. Graves, "Proctorial Representation in the
House of Lords during Edward VI's Reign: A Reassessment," *The Journal of British Studies* 10, no. 2 (May
1971): 17–35.

Guide to the Public
Record Office

Guide to the Contents of the Public Record Office, 3 vols.
(London, 1963).

Hacket

John Hacket, *Scrinia Reserata: A Memorial . . . of John*
Williams, D.D., 2 parts in 1 vol. (London, 1692).

Hakewill

William Hakewil, *The Manner How Statutes Are Enacted*
in Parliament by Passing of Bills (London, 1659).

Hargrave, *Jurisdiction*

Francis Hargrave, ed., *The Jurisdiction of the Lords House,*
or Parliament . . . by Lord Chief Justice Hale (London,
1796).

Hargrave, *State Trials*

Francis Hargrave, ed., *A Complete Collection of State*
Trials, The Fourth Edition, 11 vols. in 5 (London, 1776–
79).

Harl. Misc.

The Harleian Miscellany, 12 vols. (London, 1808–11).

Hind

Arthur M. Hind, *Engraving in England in the Sixteenth*

	and Seventeenth Centuries, 2 vols. (Cambridge, 1955).
Hirst	Derek Hirst, "The Privy Council and Problems of Enforcement in the 1620s," *The Journal of British Studies* 18 (1978): 46–66.
HLRO	House of Lords Record Office, London.
HMC, *Buccleuch*	*Historical Manuscripts Commission, Report on the Manuscripts of the Duke of Buccleuch and Queensberry, K.G., K.T., Preserved at Montagu House, Whitehall*, 3 vols. (London, 1899–1926).
HMC, *Cowper*	*Historical Manuscripts Commission, The Manuscripts of the Earl of Cowper, K.G., Preserved at Melbourne Hall, Derbyshire*, 3 vols. (London, 1888–89).
HMC, *De L'Isle*	*Historical Manuscripts Commission, Report on the Manuscripts of Lord De L'Isle & Dudley, Preserved at Penshurst Place, Kent*, 6 vols. (London, 1925–66).
HMC, *Hastings*	*Historical Manuscripts Commission, Report on the Manuscripts of the Late Reginald Rawdon Hastings*, 4 vols. (London, 1928–47).
HMC, *Laing*	*Historical Manuscripts Commission, Report on the Laing Manuscripts Preserved in the University of Edinburgh*, 2 vols. (London, 1914–25).
HMC, *Montagu of Beaulieu*	*Historical Manuscripts Commission, Report on the Manuscripts of Lord Montagu of Beaulieu* (London, 1900).
HMC, *Portland*	*Historical Manuscripts Commission, The Manuscripts of His Grace The Duke of Portland Preserved at Welbeck Abbey*, 10 vols. (London, 1891–1931).
HMC, *Rutland*	*Historical Manuscripts Commission, The Manuscripts of His Grace the Duke of Rutland, G.C.B., Preserved at Belvoir Castle*, 4 vols. (London, 1888–1905).
HMC, *Salisbury*	*Historical Manuscripts Commission, Calendar of the Manuscripts of the Most Hon. The Marquis of Salisbury, K.G., Preserved at Hatfield House, Hertfordshire*, 24 vols. (London, 1883–1976).
Hobbes	Thomas Hobbes, *Behemoth*, ed. Ferdinand Tönnies (New York, 1969).
Holdsworth, *History of English Law*	W. S. Holdsworth, *A History of English Law*, 10 vols. (Boston, 1922).
Holinshed, *Chronicles*	*The Third Volume of Chronicles . . . First Compiled by Raphaell Holinshed* (London, 1587).
Horstman, "Justice and Peers"	Allen Horstman, "Justice and Peers: The Judicial Activities of the Seventeenth-Century House of Lords," (Ph.D. diss., University of California, Berkeley, 1977).

Horstman, "A New Curia Regis"	Allen Horstman, "A New Curia Regis: The Judicature of the House of Lords in the 1620s," The Historical Journal 25, no. 2 (1982): 411–22.
Jones, Chancery	W. J. Jones, The Elizabethan Court of Chancery (Oxford, 1967).
Jones, "Ellesmere and Politics"	W. J. Jones, "Ellesmere and Politics, 1603–1617," in Stuart Studies, ed. Howard Reinmuth (Minneapolis, 1970).
Jones, "Petty Bag"	W. J. Jones, "An Introduction to Petty Bag Proceedings in the Reign of Elizabeth I," California Law Review 51 (1963): 882–905.
Jones, Politics and the Bench	W. J. Jones, Politics and the Bench (London, 1971).
Knafla	Louis A. Knafla, Law and Politics in Jacobean England (Cambridge, 1977).
Lambarde, Eirenarcha	William Lambarde, Eirenarcha, or of the Office of the Iustices of Peace (London, 1607).
Lambarde, Notes	William Lambarde's Notes on the Procedures and Privileges of the House of Commons (1584), ed. Paul L. Ward, House of Commons Library Document no. 10 (London, 1977).
Lambert	Sheila Lambert, "Procedure in the House of Commons in the Early Stuart Period," English Historical Review 95 (October 1980): 753–81.
Larkin and Hughes	James F. Larkin and Paul L. Hughes, eds., Stuart Royal Proclamations (Oxford, 1973–).
Laud, Works	The Works of the Most Reverend Father in God, William Laud, D.D., Sometime Archbishop of Canterbury, 7 vols. in 9 (Oxford, 1854).
Lehmberg, Later Parliaments	Stanford E. Lehmberg, The Later Parliaments of Henry VIII, 1536–1547 (Cambridge, 1977).
Lehmberg, Reformation Parliament	Stanford E. Lehmberg, The Reformation Parliament (Cambridge, 1970).
LJ	Journals of the House of Lords.
Lloyd, State-Worthies	David Lloyd, State-Worthies (London, 1670).
Lowell, "Trial of Peers"	Colin Rhys Lowell, "The Trial of Peers in Great Britain," American Historical Review 55 (October 1949): 69–81.
McClure	Norman Egbert McClure, ed., The Letters of John Chamberlain, 2 vols. (Philadelphia, 1939).
McIlwain	Charles Howard McIlwain, ed., The Political Works of James I (Cambridge, 1918).
Macqueen	John Fraser Macqueen, Appellate Jurisdiction of the House

of Lords and Privy Council (London, 1842).

Macray, *Clarendon's History*	W. Dunn Macray, ed., *The History of the Rebellion and Civil Wars in England . . . by Edward, Earl of Clarendon,* 6 vols. (Oxford, 1958).
Manner of Holding Parliaments (1641)	*The Manner of Holding Parliaments* (London, 1641).
Manuscripts of the House of Lords	*The Manuscripts of the House of Lords,* n.s., 12 vols. (London, 1900–77).
May	*Erskine May's Treatise on the Law, Privileges, Proceedings, and Usage of Parliament,* ed. Sir Barnett Cocks, 17th ed. (London, 1964).
Miklovich, "Royal Sign Manual"	James I. Miklovich, "The Significance of the Royal Sign Manual in Early Tudor Legislative Procedure," *Bulletin of the Institute of Historical Research* 52, no. 12 (May 1979): 23–26.
Milles	Thomas Milles, *The Catalogue of Honor* (London, 1610, large paper edition).
"Moderne Forme of the Parliaments"	" 'The Moderne Forme of the Parliaments of England,' " ed. Catherine Strateman Sims, *American Historical Review* 53, no. 2 (January 1948): 288–305.
Moir	Thomas L. Moir, *The Addled Parliament of 1614* (Oxford, 1958).
Morrill	J. S. Morrill, *The Revolt of the Provinces: Conservatives and Radicals in the English Civil War, 1630–1650* (London, 1976).
Morse, *Elizabethan Pageantry*	H. K. Morse, *Elizabethan Pageantry: A Pictorial Survey of Costume and Its Commentators from c. 1560–1620* (London, 1934).
Neale, "Commons' Privilege of Free Speech in Parliament"	J. E. Neale, "The Commons' Privilege of Free Speech in Parliament," in *Tudor Studies,* ed. R. W. Seton-Watson (London, 1924).
Neale, *Elizabethan House of Commons*	J. E. Neale, *The Elizabethan House of Commons* (New Haven, 1950).
Neale, *1559–1581*	J. E. Neale, *Elizabeth I and Her Parliaments, 1559–1581* (New York, 1953).
Neale, *1584–1601*	J. E. Neale, *Elizabeth I and Her Parliaments, 1584–1601* (London, 1957).
Neale, "Proceedings Relative to Mary Queen of Scots"	J. E. Neale, "Proceedings in Parliament Relative to the Sentence on Mary Queen of Scots," *English Historical Review* 35 (January 1920): 103–13.
Nicholas	[Edward Nicholas], *Proceedings and Debates of the House of Commons in 1620 and 1621,* 2 vols. (Oxford, 1766).

Nichols	John Nichols, *The Progresses, Processions, and Magnificent Festivities of King James the First*, 4 vols. (London, 1828).
Notestein, "Committee of Both Kingdoms"	Wallace Notestein, "The Establishment of the Committee of Both Kingdoms," *American Historical Review* 17, no. 3 (April 1912): 477–95.
Notestein, *House of Commons 1604–1610*	Wallace Notestein, *The House of Commons, 1604–1610* (New Haven, 1971).
Notestein, "Winning of the Initiative"	Wallace Notestein, "The Winning of the Initiative in the House of Commons" (*Proceedings of the British Academy*, London, 1924; reprinted as separate pamphlet, London, 1949).
Of Judicature	John Selden, *Of the Judicature in Parliaments* (London, 1681).
Ogg	David Ogg, *England in the Reign of Charles II*, 2 vols. (Oxford, 1962).
Original Institution	*The Original Institution, Power, and Jurisdiction of Parliaments* (London, 1707).
Palmer	John Palmer, *Practice in the House of Lords on Appeals, Writs of Error, and Claims of Peerage* (London, 1830).
Pearl	Valerie Pearl, *London and the Outbreak of the Puritan Revolution* (Oxford, 1964).
Peck, *Northampton*	Linda Levy Peck, *Northampton: Patronage and Policy at the Court of James I* (London, 1982).
Pettus	Sir John Pettus, *The Constitution of Parliaments in England* (London, 1680).
Pike	Luke Owen Pike, *A Constitutional History of the House of Lords* (London, 1894).
Pollard, "The Clerical Organization of Parliament"	A. F. Pollard, "The Clerical Organization of Parliament," *English Historical Review* 57 (1942): 31–58.
Pollard, *Evolution of Parliament*	A. F. Pollard, *The Evolution of Parliament* (London, 1926).
Pollard, "Receivers of Petitions"	A. F. Pollard, "Receivers of Petitions and Clerks of Parliament," *English Historical Review* 57 (1942): 203–26.
Porritt, *Unreformed House of Commons*	Edward G. Porritt, *The Unreformed House of Commons*, 2 vols. (Cambridge, 1903).
Powell and Wallis, *The House of Lords in the Middle Ages*	J. Enoch Powell and Keith Wallis, *The House of Lords in the Middle Ages* (London, 1968).
Practising Attorney	*The Practising Attorney* (London, 1779).
Priviledges of Parliament	*The Priviledges and Practice of Parliaments in England*

	Collected Out of the Common Lawes of This Land (London, 1640).
Privy Council Registers	*Privy Council Registers Preserved in the Public Record Office* (reported in facsimile, 12 vols. in 6, London, 1967–68).
PRO	Public Record Office, London.
"Red and Green"	"Red and Green," *The Table* 37 (1968): 33–40.
Relf, *Debates in the House of Lords 1621, 1625, 1628*	Frances H. Relf, ed., *Notes of the Debates in the House of Lords . . . 1621, 1625, 1628*, Camden Society, 3d ser., vol. 42 (London, 1929).
Richardson and Sayles	H. G. Richardson and George Sayles, "The Early Statutes," *Law Quarterly Review* 50 (1934): 201–17, 540–70.
Roberts and Duncan, "Parliamentary Undertaking"	Clayton Roberts and Owen Duncan, "The Parliamentary Undertaking of 1614," *English Historical Review* 93 (July 1978): 481–98.
Ruigh	Robert E. Ruigh, *The Parliament of 1624, Politics and Foreign Policy* (Cambridge, Mass., 1971).
Rushworth, *Historical Collections*	John Rushworth, *Historical Collections*, 8 vols. (London, 1721).
Rushworth, *Tryal of Strafford*	John Rushworth, *The Tryal of Thomas, Earl of Strafford*, vol. 8 of *Historical Collections* (London, 1721).
Russell, *Crisis of Parliaments*	Conrad Russell, *The Crisis of Parliaments* (Oxford, 1971).
Russell, "Parliamentary History in Perspective"	Conrad Russell, "Parliamentary History in Perspective, 1604–1629," *History* 61, no. 201 (1976): 1–27.
Russell, *Parliaments and English Politics*	Conrad Russell, *Parliaments and English Politics, 1621–1629* (Oxford, 1979).
Sainty, "Officers of the House of Lords"	J. C. Sainty, "Officers of the House of Lords, 1485 to 1971," House of Lords Record Office Memorandum no. 45 (London, 1971).
Sainty, "Parliament Office"	J. C. Sainty, "The Parliament Office in the Seventeenth and Eighteenth Centuries: Biographical Notes on Clerks in the House of Lords 1600 to 1800" (London, House of Lords Record Office, 1977).
Sainty, "Parliamentary Functions"	J. C. Sainty, "Parliamentary Functions of the Sovereign since 1509," House of Lords Record Office Memorandum no. 64 (London, 1980).
Schoenfeld	Maxwell P. Schoenfeld, *The Restored House of Lords* (The Hague, 1967).
Scobell	Henry Scobell, *Remembrances of Methods, Orders, and Proceedings . . . in the House of Lords* (London, 1689).

Selden, *Priviledges*

John Selden, *The Priviledges of the Baronage of England When They Sit in Parliament* (London, 1689).

Selden, *Table-Talk*

Table-Talk Being the Discourses of John Selden (London, 1941).

Selden, *Titles of Honor*

John Selden, *Titles of Honor* (London, 1672).

Sessional Acts

Anno Regni Iacobi, Regis Angliae, Scotiae, Franciae & Hiberniae xxj. & Scotiae lvij. At the Parliament begun and holden at Westminster, the 19. day of February, in the 21. yeere of the Reigne of our Most Gracious Souereigne Lord, Iames, by the grace of God, of England, France and Ireland King, Defender of the Faith, &c. and of Scotland the 57. . . . To the high pleasure of Almighty God and to the weale publique of the Realme, were enacted as followeth (London, 1624).

Anno Regni Caroli, Regis Angliae, Scotiae, Franciae, & Hiberniae Primo. At the Parliament begun at Westminster the 18. day of Iune, Anno Dom. 1625 in the first yeere of the Reigne of our most gracious Souereigne Lord, Charles, by the grace of God, of England, Scotland, France, and Ireland King, Defender of the Faith, &c. And there continued vntill the 11. day of Iuly following, and then Adiourned vntill the 1. day of August following vnto Oxford. To the high pleasure of Almighty God, and to the weale publike of this Realme, were enacted as followeth (London, 1630).

Anno Regni Caroli, Regis Angliae, Scotiae, Franciae, & Hiberniae Tertio. At the Parliament begun at Westminster the 17. day of March, Anno Dom. 1627. in the third yeere of the Reigne of our most gracious Soueraigne Lord, Charles, by the grace of God, of England, Scotland, France, and Ireland King, Defender of the Faith, &c. And there continued vntill the 26. day of Iune, following, and then Prorogued vnto the 20. day of October now next ensuing. To the high pleasure of Almighty God, and to the weale publike of this Realme, were enacted as followeth (London, 1628).

Sharpe, *Faction and Parliament*

Kevin Sharpe, ed., *Faction and Parliament: Essays on Early Stuart History* (Oxford, 1978).

Sims, "The Speaker of the House of Commons"

Catherine Strateman Sims, "The Speaker of the House of Commons: An Early Seventeenth-Century Tractate," *American Historical Review* 45 (1939): 90–95.

Smith, *De Republica Anglorum*

Sir Thomas Smith, *De Republica Anglorum*, ed. L. Alston (London, 1906).

Snow, "Arundel Case"

Vernon F. Snow, "The Arundel Case, 1626," *The Historian*

26, no. 3 (1964): 323–49.

Snow, *John Hooker*   Vernon F. Snow, ed., *Parliament in Elizabethan England: John Hooker's Order and Usage* (New Haven, 1977).

Spedding, *Letters and Life*   James Spedding, ed., *The Letters and the Life of Francis Bacon*, 7 vols. (London, 1862–74).

Spedding, *Works*   James Spedding et al., eds., *The Works of Francis Bacon*, 7 vols. (London, 1870–76).

Starr   Joseph R. Starr, "The Development of Modes of Communication between the Two Houses of the English Parliament" (Ph.D. diss., University of Minnesota, 1930).

State Tracts   *State Tracts, Being a Collection of Several Treatises Relating to the Government* (London, 1689).

Steele, *Tudor and Stuart Proclamations*   Robert Steele, ed., *Tudor and Stuart Proclamations*, 2 vols. (Oxford, 1910).

Stoddart   Jessie Stoddart, "Constitutional Crisis and the House of Lords, 1621–1629" (Ph.D. diss., University of California, Berkeley, 1966).

Stone, *Crisis of the Aristocracy*   Lawrence Stone, *The Crisis of the Aristocracy, 1558–1641* (Oxford, 1965).

Stone, *Family and Fortune*   Lawrence Stone, *Family and Fortune* (Oxford, 1973).

Tanner   J. R. Tanner, *Tudor Constitutional Documents* (Cambridge, 1922).

Thomas, "James I, Equity, and Williams"   G. W. Thomas, "James I, Equity, and Lord Keeper John Williams," *English Historical Review* 91 (1976): 506–28.

Timberland   *The History and Proceedings of the House of Lords from the Restoration in 1660 to the Present Time* (printed for Ebenezer Timberland, 8 vols., London, 1742–43).

Tite   Colin G. C. Tite, *Impeachment and Parliamentary Judicature in Early Stuart England* (London, 1974).

Turberville, "Protection"   A. S. Turberville, "The 'Protection' of the Servants of Members of Parliament," *English Historical Review* 42, no. 168 (October 1927): 590–600.

Twysden, *Certain Considerations*   *Certain Considerations upon the Government of England by Sir Roger Twysden*, ed. John Mitchell Kemble, Camden Society, 1st ser., vol. 45 (London, 1848).

Twysden, "Journal"   "Sir Roger Twysden's Journal," *Archaeologia Cantiana; Being Transactions of the Kent Archaeological Society* 1 (London, 1858): 184–214; 2 (London, 1859): 174–220; 3 (London, 1860): 145–76; 4 (London, 1861): 131–202.

Usher   Roland G. Usher, *The Reconstruction of the English Church*, 2 vols. (New York, 1910).

Wagner and Sainty   Sir Anthony Wagner and J. C. Sainty, "The Origin of the

Introduction of Peers in the House of Lords," *Archaeologia* 101 (Oxford, 1967): 119–50.

Willson, "James I and   David Harris Willson, "James I and Anglo-Scottish Unity,"
Anglo-Scottish Unity"   in *Conflict in Stuart England*, ed. William Appleton Aiken
                                 and Basil D. Henning (London, 1960).

Willson, *Privy Councillors*   David Harris Willson, *The Privy Councillors in the House
                                 of Commons* (Minneapolis, 1940).

Worden, *The Rump*   Blair Worden, *The Rump Parliament, 1648–1653* (Cam-
Parliament   bridge, 1974).

Yarlott   Ralph Yarlott, "The Long Parliament and the Fear of
                                 Popular Pressure, 1640–1646" (M.A. thesis, University of
                                 Leeds, 1963).

Yonge   *Diary of Walter Yonge, Esq.*, ed. George Roberts, Camden
                                 Society, 1st ser., vol. 41 (London, 1848).

NOTES

INTRODUCTION

1. Stanford E. Lehmberg, *The Reformation Parliament* (Cambridge, 1970) and *The Later Parliaments of Henry VIII, 1536–1547* (Cambridge, 1977); Michael A. R. Graves, *The House of Lords in the Parliaments of Edward VI and Mary I* (Cambridge, 1981); Maxwell P. Schoenfeld, *The Restored House of Lords* (The Hague, 1967).
2. Sir Simonds D'Ewes, *The Journals of All the Parliaments during the Reign of Queen Elizabeth* (London, 1682), pp. 540, 576. Cf. Graves, *House of Lords Edward VI and Mary I*, p. 145.
3. British Library, Additional 36102; HLRO, Braye 93 and Relfe, "Book of Orders 1710."

I. THE MEMBERS OF THE HOUSE AND THEIR CHAMBER

1. The following account is based primarily on the report of a Spanish gentleman who saw the procession in 1614 (PRO, SP15/40/56). I am grateful to Willard F. King for her assistance with the translation of this document. See also *Calendar of State Papers and Manuscripts, Relating to English Affairs . . . Existing in the Archives and Collections of Venice*, 22 vols. (London, 1864–1919), vol. 13, *1613–1615* (London, 1907), p. 115; John Nichols, *The Progresses, Processions, and Magnificent Festivities of King James the First*, 4 vols. (London, 1828), 4:1091–92; Norman Egbert McClure, ed., *The Letters of John Chamberlain*, 2 vols. (Philadelphia, 1939), 1:522; Inner Temple, Petyt 538/44, fols. 284–85v; "The Order of Proceeding to Parliament, 13 April 1640," in *The Manner of Holding Parliaments* (London, 1641); London, Society of Antiquaries, MS 87, fols. 36–38, and PRO, SP14/119/46 (1621); PRO, SP16/20/38 (1626). For the processional roll for November 1640, see HLRO, "Report for 1980," app. 2; and PRO, SP16/471/11. For earlier accounts of the procession and the opening of parliament, see H. S. Cobb, "Descriptions of the State Opening of Parliament, 1485–1601: A Survey," in *Parliamentary History, Libraries, and Records: Essays Presented to Maurice Bond* (London, House of Lords Record Office, 1981).
2. In the reign of Edward VI, all in the procession seem to have been mounted (HLRO, Hist. Coll. 242). In April 1640, only the bishops (with the exception of the great officers of state and the king and prince) rode, "many of them on bob-tailed horses fitter for Mrs. Crayford in my opinion at Bridghill then for an Ecclesiasticall Baron's

gravity and reverence there" (Dorothy Gardiner, ed., *The Oxinden Letters, 1607–1642* [London, 1933], pp. 162–63).

3. Chamberlain spoke of throngs of people in 1621 (McClure, 2:338). In April 1640 the old countess of Westmorland died as she was coming to London to see the king ride to parliament (PRO, SP16/450/88).

4. Nichols, 4:650, 965.

5. *Historical Manuscripts Commission, Report on the Manuscripts of the Duke of Buccleuch and Queensberry, K.G., K.T., Preserved at Montagu House, Whitehall*, vol. 3, *The Montagu Papers*, 6, 2d ser. (London, 1926), p. 387; PRO, SP16/471/11; *Historical Manuscripts Commission, Report on the Manuscripts of the Right Honourable Viscount De L'Isle, V.C., Preserved at Penshurst Place, Kent*, vol. 6, *Sidney Papers, 1626–1698* (London, 1966), p. 339 (3 November 1640). In 1624 the lords were commanded to go meet the king. "Most of the great ones went, but many of the Lords tarried still [in] the house" (*HMC, Buccleuch*, 3:229). In 1625 Lord Keeper Williams, writing to Conway, expressed the hope that the duke would persuade the king to come privately by water to parliament in order to avoid crowds and the dangers of the plague (PRO, SP16/3/62).

6. Elizabeth Read Foster, "Staging a Parliament," in *The English Commonwealth, 1547–1640*, ed. Peter Clark, Alan G. R. Smith, and Nicholas Tyacke (Leicester, 1979), p. 131; PRO, SP16/96/16 and 17. For Laud's prayer for the success of the Long Parliament, see PRO, SP16/471/12. For the prayer for parliament in 1605, see British Library, Additional 38139, fol. 265v.

7. Esther S. Cope, *Proceedings of the Short Parliament of 1640*, Camden Society, 4th ser., vol. 19 (London, 1977), p. 96.

8. McClure, 2:338; HLRO, Hist. Coll. 242; Northumberland MSS, Alnwick Castle MS 468 (1571). "The King put on his crown and his robes in the lobby where the Earls do use to robe themselves" (British Library, Additional 48091, fol. 1 [1625]).

9. *The Third Volume of Chronicles . . . First Compiled by Raphaell Holinshed* (London, 1587), p. 956.

10. The album of Michael van Meer (Edinburgh University Library, Laing MS III. 283) shows aldermen and the sheriff of London as members of the procession; but this information may well be unreliable. (John Nevinson drew this book to my attention and provided useful notes on it.) On this point, see Cobb, "Opening of Parliament," pp. 17, 20. In the impressive "riding of the parliament" in Scotland, all estates were represented (Edward G. Porritt, *The Unreformed House of Commons*, 2 vols. [Cambridge, 1903], 2:111–13).

11. PRO, SP15/40/56.

12. Nichols, 4:650.

13. McClure, 2:546.

14. *HMC, Buccleuch*, 3:387.

15. W. Dunn Macray, ed., *The History of the Rebellion and Civil Wars in England . . . by Edward, Earl of Clarendon*, 6 vols. (Oxford, 1958), 1:220.

16. Clyve Jones, "Seating Problems in the House of Lords in the Early Eighteenth Century: The Evidence of the Manuscript Minutes," *BIHR* 51, no. 124 (November 1978): 132; Foster, "Staging a Parliament," pp. 134–36. The Venetian ambassador stressed gold in the decorations (*Calendar of State Papers Venetian*, 13:115).

17. Foster, "Staging a Parliament," pp. 134–36; *Journals of the House of Lords*, 4:679.

18. I am grateful to Clyve Jones for advice and assistance concerning the windows. See H. M. Colvin, ed., *The History of the King's Works*, vol. 3, pt. 1 (London, 1975), p. 138, and vol. 5 (London, 1976), pl. 52; Oliver Millar, *The Tudor, Stuart, and Early*

Georgian Pictures in the Collection of Her Majesty the Queen, 2 vols. (London, 1963), 1:167, 2: pl. 206; Foster, "Staging a Parliament," p. 131.

19. Jones, "Seating Problems," p. 133; Samuel Rawson Gardiner, ed., *Notes of the Debates in the House of Lords . . . 1621*, Camden Society, 1st ser., vol. 103 (London, 1870), p. 91.

20. *LJ*, 6:554. The tapestries, commissioned by Lord Howard of Effingham, had hung in Arundel House and were sold to James I (PRO, E. 403/2561, fols. 108, 181).

21. Foster, "Staging a Parliament," p. 132. Many pictures of the chamber show a floor marked off in black and white squares (Elizabeth Read Foster, ed., *Proceedings in Parliament 1610*, 2 vols. [New Haven, 1966], 1: front.; J. Enoch Powell and Keith Wallis, *The House of Lords in the Middle Ages* [London, 1968], pls. XX, XXI; Arthur M. Hind, *Engraving in England in the Sixteenth and Seventeenth Centuries*, 2 vols. [Cambridge, 1955], 2: pls. 108, 109).

22. Foster, "Staging a Parliament," p. 132. See Foster, *1610*, 1: front.

23. Foster, "Staging a Parliament," p. 135.

24. Ibid., p. 134.

25. *The Manuscripts of the House of Lords*, n.s., vol. 10, *1712–1714* (London, 1953), pp. 3, 5 (Standing Orders nos. 19 and 31).

26. Richard Hooker described the monarch's place in parliament in the same way (G. R. Elton, *The Tudor Constitution* [Cambridge, 1968], pp. 16–17, 235–36).

27. *Commons Debates 1621*, ed. Wallace Notestein, Frances Helen Relf, and Hartley Simpson, 7 vols. (New Haven, 1935), 2:4.

28. *LJ*, 8:521.

29. *Commons Debates 1621*, 4:292; Holinshed, *Chronicles*, 3:956.

30. Holinshed, *Chronicles*, 3:956. See below, p. 142.

31. PRO, SP14/27/44; SP16/486/75, 20 December 1641. "Though I can take no notice what you say yet beinge a Record I may" (Lady de Villiers, ed., *The Hastings Journal of the Parliament of 1621*, Camden Society Miscellany, vol. 20, in Camden Society, 3d ser., vol. 83 [London, 1953], p. 34).

32. PRO, SP16/486/75.

33. *LJ*, 4:171; British Library, Harleian 6424, fol. 52v (the motion was made by Lord Saye).

34. See below, pp. 205–6.

35. *LJ*, 3:690.

36. de Villiers, p. 29.

37. J. C. Sainty, "Parliamentary Functions of the Sovereign since 1509," House of Lords Record Office Memorandum no. 64 (London, 1980), p. 1; Lehmberg, *Later Parliaments*, p. 251; PRO, SP14/52/41.

38. *HMC, Buccleuch*, 3:233; Samuel Rawson Gardiner, ed., *Notes of the Debates in the House of Lords . . . 1624 and 1626*, Camden Society, n.s., vol. 24 (London, 1879), pp. 35, 56–57; *LJ*, 3:702, 4:78.

39. de Villiers, pp. 25–31.

40. John Rushworth, *The Tryal of Thomas, Earl of Strafford*, vol. 8 of *Historical Collections* (London, 1721), p. 734. In 1641 Charles informed the House of the match between his daughter and the prince of Orange (British Library, Harleian 6424, fols. 16v–17).

41. Cope, *Proceedings of the Short Parliament*, pp. 60–62, 97; *HMC, Buccleuch*, 3:405–7; de Villiers, pp. 8, 11.

42. de Villiers, pp. 8, 11.

43. Ibid.

44. Ibid., p. 8.
45. I do not have any clear evidence concerning the prince's robes. Elstrack's engravings show the prince with a short ermine cape and an ermine-trimmed cap. In 1624 his robes are much like his father's (Hind, vol. 2, pls. 108, 109). The wardrobe accounts give the cost (Foster, "Staging a Parliament," pp. 139–40; see also Nichols, 4:1062, for an order for the prince's robes in 1604). A letter from a later period among the Northumberland MSS discussed the problem of parliament robes for the duke of Cumberland. The writer directed his reader to the wardrobe rather than the heralds for precedents. The robes should differ from those of the Prince of Wales because, though Cumberland was of royal blood, he was not a prince but a duke (Northumberland MSS, Alnwick Castle MS 467). On this point, see also British Library, Additional 6113, fol. 61v; but there may be some confusion here between robes of estate and parliament robes.
46. *LJ*, 3:22–23; [Edward Nicholas], *Proceedings and Debates of the House of Commons in 1620 and 1621*, 2 vols. (Oxford, 1766), vol. 2, app.
47. *LJ*, 3:83; de Villiers, p. 33.
48. For his influence in the House, see PRO, SP14/162/56; Robert E. Ruigh, *The Parliament of 1624, Politics and Foreign Policy* (Cambridge, Mass., 1971), pp. 89–90 and elsewhere; Conrad Russell, *Parliaments and English Politics, 1621–1629* (Oxford, 1979), pp. 145, 191, 237, 274; *Commons Debates 1628*, ed. Robert C. Johnson, Mary Frear Keeler, Maija Jansson Cole, and William B. Bidwell, 4 vols. (New Haven, 1977–78), 2:257.
49. *HMC, Buccleuch*, 3:289.
50. Ibid., p. 291.
51. Foster, "Staging a Parliament," pp. 133–35.
52. Ibid., p. 135; Henry Elsynge, *The Manner of Holding Parliaments* (London, 1768), pp. 108–11.
53. Foster, "Staging a Parliament," pp. 133–35; "'The Moderne Forme of the Parliaments of England,'" ed. Catherine Strateman Sims, *AHR* 53 (January 1948): 296.
54. "Moderne Forme of the Parliaments," p. 296; *LJ*, 4:82; HLRO, Braye 17; Inner Temple, Petyt 537/8, fol. 275v. This is contrary to the engraving used as a frontispiece in D'Ewes, *Journals of All the Parliaments*, which shows the masters in Chancery on the woolsack facing the lord chancellor.
55. "Moderne Forme of the Parliaments," pp. 296–97; Elsyng, *Manner of Holding Parliaments*, p. 112; Foster, "Staging a Parliament," pp. 133–35.
56. Maurice F. Bond and David Beamish, *The Gentleman Usher of the Black Rod* (London, 1976), p. 10.
57. Selden describes the passage of the bill and the way the Lords sat at that time (John Selden, *Titles of Honor* [London, 1672], p. 748). See also Lehmberg, *Later Parliaments*, pp. 58–59; *Manuscripts of the House of Lords*, 10:1 (Standing Order no. 1); Elsyng, *Manner of Holding Parliaments*, pp. 106–12; "Moderne Forme of the Parliaments," pp. 295–97.
58. See below, p. 138.
59. "Moderne Forme of the Parliaments," pp. 295–96. In another account, Elsyng seats only viscounts on the first form below the clerk's woolsack (Elsyng, *Manner of Holding Parliaments*, p. 111). Practice doubtless varied according to the number of peers in these ranks. There is a bit of conflicting evidence concerning the place of the lord chancellor when he was not presiding. "The L. Chauncellor risinge from his seate went to the Barons side, but above the auncient Baron, viz. the Lo. Bergavenny" (Inner Temple, Petyt 537/8, fol. 232v [1610]). However, the statute is quite clear.

60. Elsyng, *Manner of Holding Parliaments*, pp. 108–9.

61. Sir Anthony Wagner and J. C. Sainty, "The Origin of the Introduction of Peers in the House of Lords," *Archaeologia* 101 (Oxford, 1967): 125–28. Pike observed that no definition or explanation of "anciency" was set forth in the statute and that principles only emerged from the settlement of individual cases (Luke Owen Pike, *A Constitutional History of the House of Lords* [London, 1894], p. 119).

62. *LJ*, 3:701–2.

63. Ibid., pp. 705, 708, 715, 732, 734.

64. Ibid., pp. 771, 774.

65. Ibid., pp. 681, 695; 4:39–40. In the case of the earl of Banbury in 1661, the Committee for Privileges overruled the heralds (HLRO, Minute Book no. 1, Committee for Privileges, pp. 60–65). See the tract "Precedency of Peers Determinable in Parliament," signed R. C. (Inner Temple, Petyt 538/14, fols. 232–33); Elizabeth Read Foster, *The Painful Labour of Mr. Elsyng, Transactions of the American Philosophical Society*, vol. 62, pt. 8 (Philadelphia, 1972), pp. 13–14. The original impetus for the appointment of a committee for privileges had been to supervise the clerk's listing of peers. For a discussion of the case of the precedency of Lord Delawarr in 1597 and its importance, see Pike, pp. 119–29. The case was referred by the queen to the House and there decided (*LJ*, 2:195–97).

66. *Divisions in the House of Lords: An Analytical List, 1685 to 1857*, comp. J. C. Sainty and David Dewar, House of Lords Record Office Occasional Publications, no. 2 (London, 1976), pp. 7–8. In 1660 the House charged the Committee for Privileges to consider the need for more seats, "the better to prevent Disorder in the House when they come to voting, for Want of Seats" (*LJ*, 11:211).

67. See below, p. 195.

68. *Burnet's History of My Own Time*, ed. Osmund Airy, pt. 1, *The Reign of Charles II*, 2 vols. (Oxford, 1897–1900), 1:493.

69. *Manuscripts of the House of Lords*, 10:1 (Standing Order no. 1).

70. Ibid., p. 9 (Standing Order no. 50).

71. *HMC, Buccleuch*, 3:398; *LJ*, 4:122.

72. *LJ*, 4:240.

73. Northamptonshire Record Office, Buccleuch MSS, vol. 191, fols. 1/2–1/3.

74. Ibid., fols. 2/1–2/2.

75. Charles H. Firth, *The House of Lords During the Civil War* (London, 1910), p. 112.

76. HLRO, Minute Books nos. 10 and 12.

77. de Villiers, p. 1; Foster, *1610*, 1:3.

78. HLRO, Braye 65, fol. 7; *LJ*, 3:71, 123; *HMC, Buccleuch*, 3:242; Gardiner, *Debates in the House of Lords 1624 and 1626*, pp. 91–92.

79. *HMC, Buccleuch*, 3:252, 303; British Library, Additional 36856, fol. 116; *Historical Manuscripts Commission, The Manuscripts of His Grace the Duke of Portland Preserved at Welbeck Abbey*, vol. 9 (London, 1923), p. 136.

80. HLRO, Braye 65, fol. 2; Foster, *1610*, 1:3.

81. *LJ*, 3:73.

82. *LJ*, 3:698–99.

83. HLRO, Manuscript Lords Journal, vol. 39, 20 October 1646.

84. In June 1625 Lord Keeper Williams wrote to Conway that a decision should be made whether the king would wear his crown when he opened parliament before the coronation and, if not, whether he would wear his robes (PRO, SP16/3/44). He wore both (*LJ*, 3:435).

85. *HMC, Buccleuch*, 3:252; British Library, Additional 36856, fol. 116.

86. HMC, Buccleuch, 3:303; LJ, 3:879; Bodleian Library, Carte 200, fol. 45v.

87. Richard Hakluyt, The Principal Navigations, Voyages, Traffiques, & Discoveries of the English Nation, 12 vols. (Glasgow, 1903–5), 5:232.

88. Wagner and Sainty, pls. XVI, XIX, XX, XXIII, XXIV. See Bodleian Library, Carte 78, fol. 31, which includes a sketch of an earl in his parliamentary robes: "The lace to be like to a parchment lace and to be gold." For a portrait of Thomas Cecil, the second Baron Burghley, in his parliament robes, see H. K. Morse, Elizabethan Pageantry: A Pictorial Survey of Costume and Its Commentators from c. 1560–1620 (London, 1934), p. 89. See also British Library, Additional 6113, fol. 61v.

89. I am grateful to Maurice F. Bond for this information. Thomas Milles says that the bishops were dressed like barons, in hoods lined with miniver (Thomas Milles, The Catalogue of Honor, 2 vols. in 1 [London, 1610], large paper edition, 1:65). Before the Reformation, they may have worn miters (see Wagner and Sainty, pl. XVI). Brinklow in 1543 referred scornfully to "pompos bishops in lordly Parlament robys" as a "cockatryse syght" (quoted in Lehmberg, Later Parliaments, p. 189).

90. Calendar of State Papers Venetian, 13:115.

91. Middlesex County Records, ed. John Cordy Jeaffreson, 4 vols. (Middlesex County Records Society, 1886–92), 2:23. In 1597 the earl of Rutland spent 28s. for "sleeves and labelles" for his parliament robes (Historical Manuscripts Commission, The Manuscripts of His Grace The Duke of Rutland, G.C.B., Preserved at Belvoir Castle, vol. 4 [London, 1905], p. 412).

92. DNB, s.v. "Thomas Vaux."

93. Historical Manuscripts Commission, Calendar of the Manuscripts of the Most Hon. The Marquis of Salisbury, K.G., Preserved at Hatfield House, Hertfordshire, pt. 11 (London, 1906), pp. 456–57.

94. HMC, Rutland, 4:412.

95. Ibid., p. 523.

96. British Library, Additional 46188, fol. 52.

97. Cope, Proceedings of the Short Parliament, p. 104; Historical Manuscripts Commission, Report on the Manuscripts of the Late Reginald Rawdon Hastings, vol. 4 (London, 1947), p. 282; de Villiers, p. 2.

98. The Venetian ambassador observed that when the earls took their places in the parliament chamber for the opening of parliament, they put on small coronets (Calendar of State Papers Venetian, 13:115). "Sir Robert Cecil the first viscount who had a coronet 2 Jaco. before that it was not used" (British Library, Stowe 375, fol. 35). See [Edward Chamberlayne], Angliae Notitia; or, The Present State of England (London, 1669), p. 416; Foster, 1610, 1: front. and other pictures of the opening of parliament. In the reign of Edward VI, the king "commanded the noblemen to sytt and put on there bonnetes" (HLRO, Hist. Coll. 242).

99. See the portrait of the second Baron Burghley by Zuccaro, reproduced in Morse, Elizabethan Pageantry, p. 89. Note also the hats carried by earls in Elstrack's engraving of the opening of parliament, 1604 (above, frontis.).

100. Elsyng, Manner of Holding Parliaments, p. 112. In 1628, when bowling with the king, Buckingham kept his hat on. A soldier who was standing nearby dashed the duke's hat to the ground, saying there were good and loyal men as he who stood bare (PRO, SP16/528/78).

101. Manuscripts of the House of Lords, 10:3 (Standing Order no. 17).

102. Ibid., pp. 1–2 (Standing Orders nos. 5–7).

103. Ibid., pp. 3–5 (Standing Orders nos. 20, 24, 26, 27); Joseph R. Starr, "The Development of Modes of Communication between the Two Houses of the English

Parliament" (Ph.D. diss., University of Minnesota, 1930), pp. 182–85; HLRO, Relfe, "Book of Orders 1710," pp. 147–48.

104. *Manuscripts of the House of Lords*, 10:1–4 (Standing Orders nos. 2, 12, 23, 24); HLRO, Braye 65, fols. 2–3.

105. Samuel Rawson Gardiner, ed., *Debates in the House of Commons in 1625*, Camden Society, n.s., vol. 6 (London, 1873), p. 73.

106. HLRO, Main Papers, H.L., 21 September 1641.

107. PRO, SP16/479/74 and SP16/484/63; HLRO, Braye 2, fols. 117–18; *LJ*, 4:190; Rushworth, *Tryal of Strafford*, p. 40.

108. Elsyng, *Manner of Holding Parliaments*, p. 29. For examples of the warrant, see ibid., pp. 30–32; PRO, SP14/6/34 (1604) and John Hacket, *Scrinia Reserata: A Memorial . . . of John Williams, D.D.*, 2 parts in 1 vol. (London, 1692), 1:173 (1624); British Library, Hargrave 131, fol. 73ff.; Sir John Pettus, *The Constitution of Parliaments in England* (London, 1680), pp. 19–20; W. J. Jones, "An Introduction to Petty Bag Proceedings in the Reign of Elizabeth I," *California Law Review* 51 (1963): 885.

109. PRO, SP14/53/70 and SP15/39/119.

110. Bodleian Library, Bankes MSS, bundle 22, no. 4. For the list of those summoned in the Short Parliament, see Sir William Dugdale, *A Perfect Copy of All Summons of the Nobility to the Great Councils and Parliaments of This Realm* (London, 1685), pp. 559–60; *LJ*, 4:49–50. For Stafford, see *DNB*, s.v. "William Howard"; Lawrence Stone, *The Crisis of the Aristocracy* (Oxford, 1965), p. 117; Pike, p. 271. Cf. Graves, *House of Lords Edward VI and Mary I*, pp. 18–21.

111. *LJ*, 3:10. For the form of writs, see Elsyng, *Manner of Holding Parliaments*, pp. 67–70.

112. de Villiers, p. 8.

113. *Manuscripts of the House of Lords*, 10:5 (Standing Order no. 33).

114. *LJ*, 4:92; HLRO, Main Papers, H.L., 7 December 1640.

115. PRO, C.218, bundle 1. For a printed copy of the pawn for 1661, see Pettus, pp. 23–41, "in which for want of Application to the Heraulds," he says, "the Clerks have Committed many mistakes" (p. 22). Dugdale also mentions clerical errors (Dugdale, preface).

116. E. R. Adair and F. M. Greir Evans, "Writs of Assistance, 1558–1700," *EHR* 36 (1921): 359.

117. Bodleian Library, Bankes MSS, bundle 22, no. 3.

118. Foster, "Staging a Parliament," p. 141. In 1597 the earl of Rutland paid 40s. to the man who brought his writ. In 1679 he paid 4*li*. (*HMC, Rutland*, 4:413, 553). Messengers were paid by those who received proclamations (James F. Larkin and Paul L. Hughes, eds., *Stuart Royal Proclamations* [Oxford, 1973–], 1:11, 14, 15, 16, 19, 46, 49, 51, for example).

119. PRO, SP16/469/92 and SP16/470/49.

120. *LJ*, 3:264; *HMC, Buccleuch*, 3:234.

121. *LJ*, 3:10; Maurice F. Bond, ed., *Guide to the Records of Parliament* (London, 1971), pp. 179–80. See below, p. 48. The assistant clerk in 1625 listed writs received and indicated that some were given back (HLRO, Minute Book no. 4, fol. 2).

122. Cope, *Proceedings of the Short Parliament*, p. 101.

123. *LJ*, 2:362, 3:547, 581. Bowyer wrote, "The writs . . . are remayninge with the clerke of the parliament but not necessarie nor heretofore at any time set downe or entered *ad verbum* in the Journal booke" (Inner Temple, Petyt 537/8, fol. 276).

124. Graves, *House of Lords Edward VI and Mary I*, pp. 29–30; Thomas L. Moir, *The*

Addled Parliament of 1614 (Oxford, 1958), p. 181; Dugdale, pp. 579–80. Firth posited that this was done by Charles to increase royal influence (Firth, *House of Lords during the Civil War*, p. 23).

125. For an example of this writ, see Pettus, p. 313.

126. Adair, pp. 360–70.

127. Ibid., pp. 370–71; Pettus, pp. 376, 382–83.

128. LJ, 2:227. In 1603 the count was fifty-five with thirty-six barons (Stone, *Crisis of the Aristocracy*, p. 99, app. 6 on p. 758).

129. Stone, *Crisis of the Aristocracy*, pp. 99, 103, 104, 117, 119, app. 6 on p. 758. For an analysis of the peers in the upper House in 1614, see Moir, pp. 62–64 and app. 2; Firth, *House of Lords during the Civil War*, pp. 23–24.

130. J. B. Crummett, "The Lay Peers in Parliament 1640–1644" (Ph.D. thesis, University of Manchester, John Rylands University Library, 1955), app. 10, daily attendance, November 1641–March 1642; app. 11, A and B, for an analysis of attendance, November 1640–December 1644.

131. Firth, *House of Lords during the Civil War*, pp. 111–12. The House was sometimes temporarily "thin" at certain times of the year and because of plague and smallpox (PRO, SP16/483/91, August 1641).

132. Firth, *House of Lords during the Civil War*, pp. 115, 131, 136, 153.

133. PRO, 31/3(63), 6 June 1626; [Thomas Birch], *The Court and Times of Charles the First*, 2 vols. (London, 1848), 1:106; Russell, *Parliaments and English Politics*, p. 269.

134. PRO, 31/3(72), 7 March 1640/1.

135. Lehmberg, *Later Parliaments*, p. 51. For the reigns of Edward VI and Mary I, see Graves, *House of Lords Edward VI and Mary I*, p. 31.

136. Russell, *Parliaments and English Politics*, p. 16.

137. PRO, SP16/524/11.

138. In writing of the right of the nobility to be summoned, Elsyng says, "The king at this day inserts into the patent of creation of a baron, that he shall be summoned to Parliament; so that the question doth rest only upon those barons who had not patent of creation; for the earls had charters, and no doubt was ever made of them" (Elsyng, *Manner of Holding Parliaments*, p. 33). See also Dugdale, preface. In 1547 Bishop Gardiner demanded to be released from the Fleet so that he might take his seat in parliament (W. K. Jordan, *Edward VI, the Young King* [Cambridge, Mass., 1968], pp. 211–12).

139. LJ, 3:128–29.

140. Elsyng, *Manner of Holding Parliaments*, p. 58; Gardiner, *Debates in the House of Lords 1624 and 1626*, p. 153.

141. LJ, 3:90, 98, 129, 130.

142. Russell, *Parliaments and English Politics*, pp. 122–23; Nicholas, 2: app.

143. McClure, 2:546. Northumberland and Hertford are listed but absent, Saye is present, and St. Albans not listed (LJ, 3:208–9).

144. PRO, SP16/18/34 and SP16/524/95. Bristol denied that he was in custody.

145. PRO, SP16/524/95; LJ, 3:537.

146. LJ, 3:544. Elsyng was doubtless thinking of this search when he wrote, "Neither can I find, having made diligent search, that any baron hath been omitted, if he were of full age, stood *rectus in curia*, and were within the land" (Elsyng, *Manner of Holding Parliaments*, p. 56). See the arguments and precedents advanced in Inner Temple, Petyt 538/18, fol. 276, that there is no precedent that a lord has been denied his writ on account of the king's displeasure. For the case of Viscount St. Albans, see James Spedding, ed., *The Letters and the Life of Francis Bacon*, 7 vols. (London,

1862–74), 7:454–55, 548–49. It is not clear whether he received his writ in 1626 or not. For Middlesex, see *LJ*, 4:49, 92. He was called, but did not attend. In May 1640 the House voted to admit him (*LJ*, 4:78; Esther S. Cope, "The Earl of Bedford's Notes of the Short Parliament of 1640," *BIHR* 53 [November 1980]: 258).

147. *LJ*, 3:544, 563; HLRO, Braye 1. In 1601 the Privy Council informed Viscount Montagu that he would receive a writ but was not to attend, "so as by the writte your Lordship hath your righte and honor of your place acknowledged without prejudice and by your absence you are to shew your . . . dutie to her pleasure and absolute commandment" (*Acts of the Privy Council*, vol. 32, *1601–4* [London, 1907], p. 221).

148. PRO, SP16/20/43. He had received it by 5 May (*Calendar of Wynn (of Gwydir) Papers, 1515–1690, in the National Library of Wales and Elsewhere* [London, 1926], p. 227, no. 1406; Hacket, 2:68–69). One of the charges against Buckingham in 1626 was said to have been his oppression of Williams by staying his writ, which was his "fee simple" (Bodleian Library, Rawlinson C.674, fols. 22–24v).

149. Hacket, 2:72–73. He attended the House for the first time on 1 April (*LJ*, 3:706). The Venetian ambassador reported that the archbishop of Canterbury, the bishop of Lincoln, and the earl of Bristol had been forbidden to take their seats, but were allowed to do so by the king on request from the House. The rumor was that this act of grace had been deliberately planned to mollify parliament (*Calendar of State Papers Venetian*, vol. 21, *1628–1629* [London, 1916], p. 45).

150. British Library, Sloane MS 1467, fols. 104–104v; Huntingdon Record Office, Manchester MS 32/5/15a (a reference drawn to my attention by Conrad Russell who also suggested the date and the writer); PRO, SP16/453/24. A news writer reported in April 1640 that the Lords Saye and Brooke had received their writs upon telling the king they were sorry he was offended at them (PRO, SP16/450/88).

151. Hacket, 2:137–38; *LJ*, 4:92; *HMC, Buccleuch*, 3:391; *DNB*, s.v. "John Williams, archbishop of York."

152. In 1642 the earl of Portland, sequestered until the Isle of Wight had been secured, wrote to the House praying and demanding "that wch in right and justice I do as humbly conceive belongs to me, wch is my seat and vote in Parliament" (HLRO, Main Papers, H.L., 5 August 1642; *LJ*, 5:261).

153. There are numerous examples of such letters and licenses in the state papers and elsewhere: PRO, SP14/7/27, SP14/16/98, SP14/52/48, SP14/57/88, SP14/57/101, SP14/57/103, SP16/19/67, SP16/523/111, SP16/26/44, SP16/94/62, SP16/95/9, SP16/95/79, SP16/96/42, SP16/98. See PRO, S.O.1/3, fols. 168v, 170, 176v, 177v, 197v, 199v, 208, 242, 250v, 252, 263, 263v, 265–67, 273v, 274, 277, for some examples from the Short and Long Parliaments, a reference that I owe to Esther Cope. See also Huntington Library, Hastings MS L5A9, a letter addressed to James Maxwell as groom of the chamber by the earl of Huntingdon.

154. HLRO, Relfe, "Book of Orders 1710," pp. 517–18; *LJ*, 2:361, 402, 420.

155. *LJ*, 2:402; *Commons Debates 1628*, 2:405.

156. HLRO, Braye 65, fol. 1; *Manuscripts of the House of Lords*, 10:2 (Standing Order no. 14); *LJ*, 4:240, 249; HLRO, Main Papers, H.L., 14 May 1641.

157. *LJ*, 3:465.

158. *LJ*, 2:401; *HMC, Hastings*, 4:248.

159. *Manuscripts of the House of Lords*, 10:2–3 (Standing Order no. 16).

160. Ibid., p. 8 (Standing Order no. 44); *HMC, Buccleuch*, 3:268. For fines levied in the reigns of Henry VIII and Elizabeth, see HLRO, Relfe, "Book of Orders 1710," p. 517.

161. Jessie Stoddart, "Constitutional Crisis and the House of Lords, 1621–1629" (Ph.D.

diss., University of California, Berkeley, 1966), p. 374. Attendance had long been a problem; see Michael A. R. Graves, "Proctorial Representation in the House of Lords during Edward VI's Reign: A Reassessment," *The Journal of British Studies* 10, no. 2 (May 1971): 30–33.

162. *LJ*, 4:506, 658, 712–13, 719.

163. *LJ*, 4:708–9, 5:58–59. For efforts of the House to control attendance in 1642, see Crummett, pp. 234–35.

164. *LJ*, 9:515–16.

165. Elsyng, *Manner of Holding Parliaments*, pp. 132–36; PRO, SP14/16/98 (1605), SP16/26/44 and SP16/523/111 (1626), SP16/479/69 (1641), S.O. 1/3, fols. 168v–277v. In 1640 the king informed the House that Bishop Mainwaring was neither to sit nor to send a proxy (Cope, *Proceedings of the Short Parliament*, p. 102).

166. PRO, SP14/52/48 (1610), SP14/119/5 (1621), SP16/19/19. Elsyng refers to earlier precedents when strangers were appointed to hold proxies (Elsyng, *Manner of Holding Parliaments*, pp. 129–31).

167. Vernon Snow reports a few exceptions (unpublished article, "Proxy Politics in the Early Stuart House of Lords").

168. *Manuscripts of the House of Lords*, 10:8 (Standing Order no. 45).

169. Huntington Library, Ellesmere MS 6942, "a paper of proxies and what Lords are full and who are not 10 Oct. 1640"; Hastings MS 13635 (1672/3), a reference I owe to Caroline Robbins and Henry Horwitz.

170. Hacket, 2:69, 72–73, 138; *HMC, Buccleuch*, 3:391.

171. Gardiner, *Debates in the House of Lords 1624 and 1626*, p. 135.

172. PRO, SP14/27/9. For a discussion of the reasons behind the choice of lords to hold proxies in the 1640s, see Crummett, pp. 243–45.

173. PRO, SP14/159/18 (a reference I owe to Vernon Snow).

174. PRO, SP16/523/111.

175. Yale University Library, The James Marshall and Marie-Louise Osborn Collection, Braye 54/37.

176. D'Ewes, *Journals of All the Parliaments*, p. 4 (for the date, 1630 or after 1646, when this was written, see pp. 7–9). For the standard form of a proxy, see Elsyng, *Manner of Holding Parliaments*, pp. 135–36. For proxies from specific lords, see PRO, SP14/23/64, SP14/23/74; Huntington Library, Ellesmere MS 6943. In 1536 Lord Lisle's agent consulted the clerk of the crown, who charged 11s.3d. for drawing up the proxy and noted that the fee would be 3 angels for anybody else. The cost for registering the proxy in the parliament chamber would be 20s. or more (Lehmberg, *Later Parliaments*, pp. 13, 342).

177. HLRO, Minute Book no. 2, fols. 7, 8, 11; Foster, *Painful Labour of Mr. Elsyng*, p. 14 and n. 59.

178. *LJ*, 2:690, 3:10, 500; *HMC, Hastings*, 4:285.

179. *Manuscripts of the House of Lords*, 10:2 (Standing Order no. 14). "The House was called to see who were present and who absent that it might be seen who had proxies" (de Villiers, p. 11).

180. HLRO, Braye 65, fol. 1; *LJ*, 3:14; Foster, *Painful Labour of Mr. Elsyng*, p. 14 and n. 58. See also D'Ewes, *Journals of All the Parliaments*, p. 18.

181. Huntington Library, Hastings MS 13635.

182. *LJ*, 4:10–11 (1629).

183. *Manuscripts of the House of Lords*, 10:8–9 (Standing Orders nos. 46 and 47).

184. Ibid., p. 8 (Standing Order no. 45).

185. *LJ*, 3:447, 698 (1625 and 1628).

186. Ibid., pp. 486, 698 (1625 and 1628).
187. See below, pp. 56, 58–59, 66; and Lehmberg, *Later Parliaments*, pp. 13, 342.
188. *LJ*, 2:702 (1614), 3:264 (1624).
189. Henry Elsyng, "The Method of Passing Bills in Parliament," *The Harleian Miscellany*, 12 vols. (London, 1808–11), 9:118; "Moderne Forme of the Parliaments," p. 299; HMC, *Buccleuch*, 3:294; Gardiner, *Debates in the House of Lords 1624 and 1626*, p. 203. A manuscript in the Yale University Osborn Collection refers to "the clerkes cheife Clerke who enters the Proxyes upon the Record and into a booke that is used upon all votes in the House" (Braye 52/5).
190. Elsyng, "Method of Passing Bills," p. 118; "Moderne Forme of the Parliaments," p. 299.
191. McClure, 2:630.
192. Macray, *Clarendon's History*, 1:413.
193. *LJ*, 5:163.
194. D'Ewes, *Journals of All the Parliaments*, pp. 5–6; Graves, *House of Lords Edward VI and Mary I*, p. 74; Elsyng, *Manner of Holding Parliaments*, p. 132. Bedford discussed the same point and raised the question whether it should be the first lord named (Bedford Office, Woburn MSS, HMC no. 198, p. 87).
195. *LJ*, 4:191.
196. John Selden, *Of the Judicature in Parliaments* (London, 1681), pp. 143–44.
197. *LJ*, 7:277.
198. Ibid., 8:290, 319; HLRO, Main Papers, H.L., 1 May 1646. D'Ewes said that this move was instigated by members of the House of Commons and that the letter was unique (D'Ewes, *Journals of All the Parliaments*, pp. 7–8).
199. British Library, Harleian 2325, fol. 12; HLRO, Braye 65, fol. 1. For a more detailed description of the two opening days, see below, pp. 28–29.
200. "Moderne Forme of the Parliaments," p. 294; HLRO, Braye 65, fol. 1. Prayers did not precede a morning meeting of a committee of the whole House, but only the meeting of the House itself (*LJ*, 2:646). When the lord chancellor or lord keeper could not serve, a royal commission providing for a presiding officer was read before prayers (*LJ*, 3:51, 104; British Library, Stowe 375, fol. 194v).
201. *LJ*, 3:46, 56.
202. *LJ*, 4:586; HLRO, Main Papers, H.L., 9 January 1643/4.
203. *LJ*, 8:446, 450, 457, 463, 464.
204. HLRO, Braye 65, fol. 1.
205. *Manuscripts of the House of Lords*, 10:2 (Standing Order no. 8); HLRO, Braye 65, fols. 1–2; de Villiers, p. 6; *LJ*, 3:496.
206. In 1621 the Committee for Petitions was appointed later in the sitting. Thereafter, it was chosen in the first days. See below, p. 101.
207. HLRO, Braye 65, fol. 2.
208. "In the parliament of the 25th of H.8 the 3 of Feb. is the first entry of the adjournment of the House by the consent of the Lords" (British Library, Stowe 375, fol. 76).
209. *LJ*, 2:468, 3:63.
210. Ibid., 3:136, 151. In 1621 the king specifically stated that "all Committees, Matters and Business of Parliament shall rest in the State as they now are, until the next Meeting" (*LJ*, 3:159). In 1629 he ordered that committees should be suspended (*LJ*, 4:42).
211. HLRO, Braye 65, fol. 1; "Moderne Forme of the Parliaments," p. 293.
212. *Manuscripts of the House of Lords*, 10:3 (Standing Order no. 20).
213. Ibid. (Standing Order no. 21); *LJ*, 3:151, 466. In 1607 the House was adjourned at

the king's wish (*LJ*, 2:468). Significantly, in 1629, the clerk recorded the Lords' assent (*LJ*, 4:41–42). Attorney General Heath stated that when parliament was adjourned by royal commission, committees were suspended (*LJ*, 3:151); but this was not always the case.

214. Elsyng, *Manner of Holding Parliaments*, pp. 117–18; D'Ewes, *Journals of All the Parliaments*, p. 67.

215. Elsyng, *Manner of Holding Parliaments*, pp. 117–18; *LJ*, 3:82, 678; *HMC, Buccleuch*, 3:238.

216. *HMC, Buccleuch*, 3:268, 282. In 1624, at the request of the prince, it did not sit on the day of the duke of Richmond's funeral (*LJ*, 3:312).

217. Gardiner, *Debates in the House of Lords 1621*, p. 13.

218. *LJ*, 4:61.

219. *LJ*, 3:32–33. Bacon called up this motion to serve his own ends; see below, p. 35.

220. *LJ*, 3:45.

221. Ibid., 4:56.

222. *LJ*, 4:61. For precedents that may have been collected in this connection, see PRO, SP16/451/9; these bear a very close relation to Elsyng's account in his *Manner of Holding Parliaments*, p. 117. Also see HLRO, Main Papers, H.L., [29 April 1640?].

223. *LJ*, 4:350–51; *The Journals of the House of Commons*, 2:246. Starr (p. 159) thinks that this is the first time the House did so, but Elsyng gives some early precedents (Elsyng, *Manner of Holding Parliaments*, pp. 113–14).

224. Montagu observed that "it was late, and one o'clock before this was determined" (*HMC, Buccleuch*, 3:283, 1626).

225. Ibid., p. 409; *LJ*, 3:678, 4:356. The statement that in the summer of 1641, the House did not convene until 11 o'clock is not borne out by the Lords journal (British Library, Harleian 6424, fol. 97).

226. PRO, SP14/121/46; *Commons Debates 1628*, 3:600; *Calendar of State Papers Venetian*, 21:84–85. See also Cope, *Proceedings of the Short Parliament*, p. 240.

227. PRO, SP14/21/15 (1606); *LJ*, 3:82 (Bacon's case, 1621); *HMC, Buccleuch*, 3:239–41 (Cranfield's case, 1624); *HMC, Buccleuch*, 3:273 (defense of the realm, 1626); British Library, Harleian 6424, fol. 88v (king's journey to Scotland); *LJ*, 6:466–69, 481 (the trial of Laud, 1643/4). See also *The Works of the Most Reverend Father in God, William Laud, D.D., Sometime Archbishop of Canterbury*, 7 vols. in 9 (Oxford, 1854), 4:49–50. Sometimes impeachment proceedings left the House with little to do. In 1624 Montagu wrote that "the Lords' committees were so employed in the examination about the Lord Treasurer as little or nothing was done in the House" (*HMC, Buccleuch*, 3:237).

228. PRO, 31/3(73), 6 February 1641/2. For certain lords, with heavy committee responsibilities, this meant a busy schedule. The earl of Essex's man of affairs wrote in 1597, "Every forenoon between seven and eight his Lordship is in the Higher Parliament House; and in the afternoons, upon committees, for the better penning and amendment of matter in bills of importance, both his Lordship, and sometimes myself, are busied" (J. E. Neale, *Elizabeth I and Her Parliaments, 1584–1601* [London, 1957], p. 295). See also "The Jacobean Privy Councillor in Parliament," a study of the committee responsibilities of the earl of Northampton, in Linda Levy Peck, *Northampton: Patronage and Policy at the Court of James I* (London, 1982).

229. Foster, *Painful Labour of Mr. Elsyng*, p. 14.

230. *HMC, Buccleuch*, 3:268, 269, 280, 302, 397, 409; Crummett, p. 241.

231. *HMC, Buccleuch*, 3:333.

232. Ibid., p. 340.

233. *Manuscripts of the House of Lords*, 10:5 (Standing Order no. 31); *LJ*, 4:679.
234. *Manuscripts of the House of Lords*, 10:3 (Standing Order no. 19).
235. Ibid., p. 5 (Standing Order no. 31).
236. Ibid., pp. 2, 5 (Standing Orders nos. 12 and 32); British Library, Additional 36102, fol. 16 (22 March 1620/1).
237. *Manuscripts of the House of Lords*, 10:6 (Standing Order no. 35).
238. Ibid., p. 11 (Standing Order no. 56).
239. *LJ*, 2:336.
240. Huntington Library, Ellesmere MS 6919; de Villiers, pp. 19–20; PRO, SP14/119/106.
241. *DNB*, s.v. "Francis Norris, Earl of Berkshire." *The Diary of Sir Simonds D'Ewes (1622–1624)*, ed. Elisabeth Bourcier (Paris, 1974), pp. 64, 159–60.
242. Southampton and Sheffield interrupted Buckingham "for repeating the same thing over and over again, and that contrary to the received order of Parliament" (Nichols, 4:657). Frances H. Relf, ed., *Notes of the Debates in the House of Lords . . . 1621, 1625, 1628*, Camden Society, 3d ser., vol. 42 (London, 1929), pp. 21–22.
243. Gardiner, *Debates in the House of Lords 1621*, pp. 73, 91; PRO, SP14/121/15, SP14/121/46, SP14/121/54.
244. *LJ*, 3:674, 676; *Manuscripts of the House of Lords*, 10:6 (Standing Order no. 35).
245. *Court and Times of Charles I*, 1:106.
246. Cope, *Proceedings of the Short Parliament*, p. 80.
247. Ibid., p. 236.
248. *HMC, Buccleuch*, 3:398.
249. Northamptonshire Record Office, Buccleuch MS 191, 1/2–1/3.
250. PRO, SP16/480/9 (24 April 1641).
251. Northamptonshire Record Office, Buccleuch MS 191, 2/1–2/2.
252. Gardiner, *Oxinden Letters*, p. 204; British Library, Harleian 6424, fols. 82v–83; PRO, SP16/482/95 and SP16/482/96; HLRO, Braye 2, fols. 177–177v, and Braye 93, fol. 84. Pembroke had offended before (Conrad Russell, *The Crisis of Parliaments* [Oxford, 1971], p. 165).
253. *LJ*, 4:475.
254. *Historical Manuscripts Commission, Report on the Manuscripts of Lord Montagu of Beaulieu* (London, 1900), p. 135.
255. Macray, *Clarendon's History*, 1:544; PRO, SP16/489/4.
256. HLRO, Braye 93, fols. 126–126v, 146v–147v.

2. THE PRESIDING OFFICER

1. Hereafter I have shortened "lord chancellor or lord keeper" to "lord chancellor" when used in this general sense. Sir Thomas Smith, *De Republica Anglorum*, ed. L. Alston (London, 1906), p. 51; *Manuscripts of the House of Lords*, 10:1 (Standing Orders nos. 2–4).
2. *Guide to the Contents of the Public Record Office*, 3 vols. (London, 1963), 1:9; *LJ*, 3:12; Pettus, p. 19. In 1624 Lord Keeper Williams, in a characteristic gesture, is said to have detained the prince's writ so that he could deliver it himself (D'Ewes, *Diary 1622–1624*, p. 176).
3. Pike, pp. 352–54; Adair, p. 372; Pettus, pp. 215–19.
4. Pettus (pp. 211–12) believes this was the usual custom, a position that Adair (p. 372, n. 2) believes is unwarranted.

5. The clerk read the commission for supplying the lord chancellor's place. The man appointed took his place on the woolsack; then the House proceeded to prayers (*LJ*, 3:103–4). Occasionally a substitute presided by royal command, without a formal commission (see HLRO, Relfe, "Book of Orders 1710," p. 330, which cites 5 October, 8 Eliz.). For commissions, see ibid., pp. 39–40, 330; *LJ*, 4:57; PRO, SP14/163/57 (drawn by the attorney general); British Library, Stowe 375, fol. 194v, and Additional 11045, fol. 146. In the reign of Henry VIII, the Lords had sometimes acted by themselves in adjourning the House, when no presiding officer had been present (Lehmberg, *Later Parliaments*, p. 252). The House was still held to be in session if the presiding officer left the chamber. For example, in 1628 Coventry asked leave of the House to withdraw, and was then brought in and introduced as a peer. "By this example, it appears that though the Lord Keeper goes out of the House of Lords, yet are they still a House" (British Library, Stowe 375, fols. 118–19; see also fol. 103v). In 1629 Montagu observed that when the lord keeper left the House to administer an oath in an adjacent chamber, "the House was not adjourned upon it" (*HMC, Buccleuch*, 3:332).

6. *LJ*, 4:357; HLRO, Relfe, "Book of Orders 1710," p. 39; *Manuscripts of the House of Lords*, 10:11. The clerk had been ordered to make the entry in 1641, but he does not seem to have done so.

7. Other writers describe the lord chancellor's robe of state as black damask embroidered with gold lace (Bond and Beamish, pp. 36–37). The purse, which was made of velvet and richly worked with the royal arms, was supplied annually to the lord chancellor, together with a red bag of Spanish leather, lined with taffeta. The cost varied from 22*li*. in 1601 to 25*li*.40s. in 1621 (British Library, Additional 5756, fol. 20; Sir H. C. Maxwell-Lyte, *Historical Notes on the Use of the Great Seal of England* [London, 1926], pp. 318–20). See HLRO, Manuscript Lords Journal, vol. 39 (31 October 1646); *LJ*, 8:553. On one occasion in Elizabeth's reign, the great seal was carried before the lord keeper by a footman (Milles, p. 66). See *CJ*, 9:575, where the seal is described as carried by an attendant in a "bag."

8. Vernon F. Snow, ed., *Parliament in Elizabethan England: John Hooker's Order and Usage* (New Haven, 1977), p. 159; HLRO, Main Papers, H.L., 17 February 1640/1.

9. *Manner of Holding Parliaments* (1641); Society of Antiquaries, MS 87, fol. 37, 1621.

10. In 1628 the lord keeper and lord treasurer were said to *sit* behind the cloth of state "*prout mos est* when the King is here" (Relf, *Debates in the House of Lords 1621, 1625, 1628*, p. 138). See also British Library, Sloane 200, fol. 56, where the presiding officer, if no baron or peer of the realm, "sitteth near to the King behind the cloth of estate."

11. In 1625 prayers were read before members of the Commons were admitted. The king took off his crown and knelt beside the chair of estate (*LJ*, 3:435, 437; British Library, Harleian 2325, fols. 40v–41; "Moderne Forme of the Parliaments," p. 292). In 1624 the clerk could not hear the king's speech because the judges were standing (British Library, Additional 40087, fol. 7).

12. *LJ*, 3:493–94; Folger Shakespeare Library, MS V.b.303, p. 145. The names had been delivered to the clerk the day before by the lord chancellor ("Moderne Forme of the Parliaments," p. 293). The clerk read in French (ibid., p. 292; Inner Temple, Petyt 537/6, p. 311). Lord Montagu observed in 1624 that "exceptions was taken to the Clerk because he read them not in French, but in English" (*HMC, Buccleuch*, 3:229). Judges and masters in Chancery served as receivers of petitions. For petitions for England, Scotland, and Ireland, the lord treasurer, lord president of the council,

lord admiral, and other great officers of state were usually appointed as triers; for the other petitions, "divers Lords" (Henry Scobell, *Remembrances of Methods, Orders, and Proceedings . . . in the House of Lords* [London, 1689], p. 7; Graves, *House of Lords Edward VI and Mary I*, p. 137).

13. Pym noted in his diary in 1621 that Bacon knelt "a prettie while" (*Commons Debates 1621*, 4:8).
14. *LJ*, 3:424–25 (1624).
15. *LJ*, 2:683. In 1621 the prince delivered the king's commission (ibid., 3:200–201).
16. Ibid., 3:492.
17. Laud observed in 1628 that parliament in 1610, 1614, 1621, and 1625 "was dissolved bye Commission upon discontent" (PRO, SP16/96/31).
18. Pettus, p. 220.
19. See above, pp. 28–29.
20. W. J. Jones, "Ellesmere and Politics, 1603–1617," in *Stuart Studies*, ed. Howard Reinmuth (Minneapolis, 1970), p. 14; PRO, LC 5/134, p. 410; Pettus, p. 222.
21. Huntington Library, Ellesmere MS 3042A.
22. British Library, Harleian 6850, fols. 314, 316; Lawrence Stone, *Family and Fortune* (Oxford, 1973), p. 210. Ellesmere petitioned the king for a reward, since his increment as lord keeper did not match his expenses (Jones, "Ellesmere and Politics," p. 19). Clarendon said of the position of lord chancellor after the Restoration, "though in itself and the constant perquisites of it is not sufficient to support the dignity of it, yet was then, upon the king's return; and, after it had been so many years without a lawful officer, would unquestionably bring in money enough to be a foundation to a future fortune, competent to his ambition, and enough to provoke the envy of many" (*The Life of Edward, Earl of Clarendon . . . in Which is Included, A Continuation of His History of the Grand Rebellion*, 2 vols. [Oxford, 1857], 1:310).
23. "The fees due to the Lord Chancellor or Lord Keeper (as Speaker of the House of Peers) are upon every private Bill ten pounds wch is to be paid at the same time with the other officers' fees, and double in like cases wth them." A bill concerning two sets of persons (e.g., landlords and tenants) was a "double bill." In naturalization bills, each person named paid a fee. I think that this was also the case in other private bills (Yale University Library, Osborn Collection, Braye 52/5). Snow, *John Hooker*, p. 159; Huntington Library, Ellesmere MS 34/A/2; HLRO, Main Papers, H.L., 26 June 1610; *LJ*, 22:627–29.
24. HLRO, Main Papers, H.L., 14 April 1645; PRO, A.O. 3/1088(1).
25. Spedding, *Letters and Life*, 7:158. In 1550 he had been richly rewarded (Graves, *House of Lords Edward VI and Mary I*, p. 156).
26. *Manuscripts of the House of Lords*, 10:1 (Standing Orders nos. 2 and 3).
27. *HMC, Hastings*, 4:244.
28. HLRO, Relfe, "Book of Orders 1710," p. 37. Some writers indicate that it was the writ that was presented (Cope, *Proceedings of the Short Parliament*, p. 57; Elsyng, *Manner of Holding Parliaments*, pp. 95, 97–98; Foster, *Painful Labour of Mr. Elsyng*, p. 22). Some indicate that either writ or patent might be presented (HLRO, Braye 65, fol. 1). Today, both writ and patent are brought, a custom that probably began in 1621 (Wagner and Sainty, pp. 119, 134).
29. "Moderne Forme of the Parliaments," p. 298; HLRO, Relfe, "Book of Orders 1710," p. 37. In April 1640 Garter laid Finch's patent on the chair of state. It was removed by Black Rod, who gave it to Finch, who in turn gave it to the clerk (Cope, *Proceedings of the Short Parliament*, p. 58). For another variation, see HLRO, Relfe,

"Book of Orders 1710," p. 473.

30. HLRO, Relfe, "Book of Orders 1710," pp. 355–56. He also swore witnesses; see HLRO, Main Papers, H.L., 25 January 1640/1. Lady Strange, who was pregnant, was sworn in the lord keeper's "withdrawing room" adjacent to the chamber (*HMC, Buccleuch*, 3:331–32).

31. *LJ*, 3:72, 108, 123, 277.

32. See below, pp. 192–95.

33. "Moderne Forme of the Parliaments," p. 298; Elsyng, "Method of Passing Bills," p. 118.

34. HLRO, P.O. 354, Precedents, pp. 73–74; "Moderne Forme of the Parliaments," p. 300. In 1624 Williams, coming to the bar to receive a message, "sate down upon the form and did not stand," Lord Montagu noted, "which I never saw before. And some lords since told me it is against the ancient form" (*HMC, Buccleuch*, 3:231–32). "By a journal 18th of Jaco., fo. 17, it appeareth the Lord Chancellor should not remove from the Bar until the messengers from the Commons house are gon out of the Lords House" (British Library, Stowe 375, fol. 26). On occasion the procedure varied. In May 1610 members of the House of Commons, protesting the way in which a message had been sent to the House, were "called backe to the barre, to whom the L. Chanc. settinge in his seate, delivered that the case is extraordinary, and therefore perhaps hath no president" (Inner Temple, Petyt 537/8, fol. 205v). For questions raised in the Elizabethan period, see D'Ewes, *Journals of All the Parliaments*, p. 540.

35. de Villiers, pp. 16–18.

36. HLRO, Braye 2, fols. 63–64v.

37. HLRO, Relfe, "Book of Orders 1710," pp. 217–20; HLRO, Main Papers, H.L., 21 September 1641, 30 March 1647; *LJ*, 3:681 (15 June 1626), 9:110 (30 March 1647).

38. James Ley, who as chief justice took Bacon's place in March 1620/1 was an exception. Ley was not a member of the Privy Council until 1624, when he was sworn as lord treasurer (*Acts of the Privy Council of England*, vol. 39, 1623–1625 [London, 1933], p. 404).

39. Louis A. Knafla, *Law and Politics in Jacobean England* (Cambridge, 1977), pp. 101, 105, 263–73; Huntington Library, Ellesmere MSS 478, 1225, 1226, 2452, 2613, 2615, 2616, 2617.

40. Huntington Library, Ellesmere MS 2628. See his opinions at the council table in 1614 (Spedding, *Letters and Life*, 5:204–5).

41. Huntington Library, Ellesmere MSS 456, 1217–1219, 2589, 2590, 2613, 2615–2617.

42. Huntington Library, Ellesmere MSS 2589–2590.

43. PRO, SP14/76/31.

44. Huntington Library, Ellesmere MSS 451, 455, 458, 467, 473, 488–489; HLRO, Commonplace book of Francis Drake.

45. Huntington Library, Ellesmere MS 2572.

46. Foster, *1610*, 1:104, 109, 167.

47. Ibid. (in order of citation), pp. 115, 179, 113, 169, 214, 193, 191–92, 180, 186, 197, 204, 205, 207–8, 210–11, 215.

48. Ibid., pp. 129, 214, 237; *HMC, Hastings*, 4:265.

49. *HMC, Hastings*, 4:255, 264; Inner Temple, Petyt 537/8, fol. 285v.

50. *HMC, Hastings*, 4:271.

51. Ibid., pp. 280–82.

52. Knafla, pp. 82–83.
53. *Cabala Sive Scrinia Sacra, Mysteries of State and Government* (London, 1663), p. 29 (Bacon to the king, 12 February 1614/5).
54. Spedding, *Letters and Life*, 4:313, 5:179–80, 182.
55. In 1612, immediately following Salisbury's death, Bacon had asked leave to present the king "with some preparative remembrances touching the future parliament" (ibid., 4:280, 363). He continued to offer advice that has survived in formal letters to James and also in memoranda written by Bacon to himself (ibid., 4:313, 365–73, and 5:1–2, 13–18, 190; *Historical Manuscripts Commission, Report on the Laing Manuscripts Preserved in the University of Edinburgh*, vol. 1 [London, 1914], pp. 141–44). For an estimate of the value of Bacon's advice, see Clayton Roberts and Owen Duncan, "The Parliamentary Undertaking of 1614," *EHR* 93 (July 1978): 489, 492, 495–96. Though ministers may have made suggestions to the monarch about his speech in this period, it was not until after the Restoration that they took major responsibility for it (Burnet, 2:37).
56. Huntington Library, Ellesmere MSS 2610, 2628; Spedding, *Letters and Life*, 5:174–91, 194.
57. He had advised king and council on the aid for the marriage of the Princess Elizabeth, for example (Spedding, *Letters and Life*, 4:304, 319, 337, 339).
58. Ibid., 5:13–18, 33n, 40–41.
59. Ibid., p. 84.
60. Huntington Library, Ellesmere MS 6918.
61. Spedding, *Letters and Life*, 7:167–71.
62. Ibid., pp. 172–73; Nicholas, 1:11–12; de Villiers, pp. 1–2; Huntington Library, Ellesmere MS 6918. When Bacon presented the joint petition against recusants at a meeting of both Houses with the king at Whitehall on 17 February, he used the same kind of simile: "Our petition to your Majesty is like to our petitions to God" (de Villiers, pp. 23–24). On the subject of this "correspondence" between God and king, see James Daly, *Cosmic Harmony and Political Thinking in Early Stuart England, Transactions of the American Philosophical Society*, vol. 69, pt. 7 (Philadelphia, 1979), chap. 2.
63. Spedding, *Letters and Life*, 5:177–79.
64. Relf, *Debates in the House of Lords 1621, 1625, 1628*, pp. 3–4, 5–7, 11, 21.
65. Ibid., pp. 1–2; de Villiers, pp. 11–13; Huntington Library, Hastings MS L5A9.
66. Relf, *Debates in the House of Lords 1621, 1625, 1628*, pp. 4–5; de Villiers, p. 23.
67. McClure, 2:348; Relf, *Debates in the House of Lords 1621, 1625, 1628*, p. 11.
68. He also had a sense of opinion in the lower House. He recommended that Sir Edward Coke receive a caveat from the king and that Buckingham speak at a conference (Spedding, *Letters and Life*, 7:190–92).
69. Ibid., p. 241.
70. *LJ*, 3:51.
71. Knafla, pp. 82–83. Despite Bacon's claim to influence in the House of Commons, there is no evidence that he put it to use in 1621.
72. For the circumstances of Williams's appointment, see G. W. Thomas, "James I, Equity, and Lord Keeper John Williams," *EHR* 91 (1976): 506–28; *Cabala*, pp. 288–89 (Williams to Buckingham, 16 December 1621); Hacket, 1:81.
73. *Cabala*, p. 285 (Williams to Buckingham, 1 August 1621).
74. Hacket, 2:7. He had made the same point in 1621 concerning an annual pension for the earl of Arundel: "This is a very unseasonable time to receive such large pensions from so bountiful a King, and that the Parliament so soon approaching is very like to

take notice." The grant should have been deferred until after parliament (*Cabala*, p. 285, Williams to Buckingham, 1 September 1621).

75. Hacket, 2:20–21.

76. Ibid., pp. 14, 16, 24.

77. Ibid., 1:109.

78. Ibid., 2:17.

79. Ibid., 1:110.

80. Ibid., 1:205–6, 2:80.

81. Ibid., 1:205, 2:83.

82. Ibid., 1:190, 2:17–18.

83. Ibid., 1:186.

84. Ibid., 2:4, 14, 17–18.

85. Ibid., p. 18. He may have been appointed only for a term of years, which had expired (Thomas, "James I, Equity, and Williams," p. 527).

86. *HMC, Buccleuch*, 3:248. See the comment of the earl of Westmorland (*HMC, Rutland*, 1:474).

87. Hacket, 1:53–54, 74.

88. Ibid., 1:76–77; Gardiner, *Debates in the House of Lords 1621*, pp. 123–26.

89. Hacket, 1:77–78.

90. *Cal. Wynn Papers*, p. 155, no. 988.

91. *Commons Debates 1621*, 2:433–35. Chamberlain reported that Williams "was thought to speak more like a divine than a statesman or an orator" (McClure, 2:410).

92. Hacket, 1:76.

93. Ibid., 1:175–76; Huntington Library, Hastings MS L5A9; *LJ*, 3:211–13.

94. *LJ*, 3:493.

95. *HMC, Buccleuch*, 3:266–67.

96. John Rushworth, *Historical Collections*, 8 vols. (London, 1721), 1:221–25. A slightly different version is among the Hastings papers at the Huntington Library (Hastings MS L5A9). Also see *LJ*, 3:519, 526, 542, 553, 566, 567, 571, 576, 579, 581, 588, 651–55, 670, 682.

97. Foster, *Painful Labour of Mr. Elsyng*, pp. 14–16.

98. Gardiner, *Debates in the House of Lords 1624 and 1626*, pp. 117, 138, 162, 166, 171, 184, 185; *LJ*, 3:553, 580, 590, 654.

99. *LJ*, 3:500; *HMC, Buccleuch*, 3:268.

100. "Moderne Forme of the Parliaments," p. 295; *LJ*, 3:672. This had been originally suggested by Lord Hunsdon and ordered by the House in 1621 (*LJ*, 3:78).

101. *LJ*, 3:91, 134, 147, 631–32, 669, 681.

102. *Commons Debates 1628*, 2:3–10, 13–14, 19–24.

103. He was introduced on 14 April and spoke in debate on 16 April (*LJ*, 3:738; Relf, *Debates in the House of Lords 1621, 1625, 1628*, p. 112n).

104. Clarendon, who called him "that great and good lord" (Clarendon, *Life*, 1:46), noted that he "perplexed" the "counsels and designs" of those opposed to the king "with inconvenient objections in law" (Macray, *Clarendon's History*, 1:68).

105. Relf, *Debates in the House of Lords 1621, 1625, 1628*, pp. 138–39.

106. Ibid., pp. 153–55, 175, 182, 205.

107. Ibid., pp. 77, 98, 152.

108. Ibid., pp. 112, 114, 116, 157–58, 161, 173–74, 177–78, 182–84, 197–98.

109. Ibid., pp. 116, 157, 161, 183–84, 218.

110. Ibid., pp. 118–19, 210, 220n.

111. Ibid., pp. 134, 159, 160, 162, 164, 167, 204.

112. Ibid., pp. 121–23, 128–30, 144, 145, 147, 208–9, 212; Macray, *Clarendon's History*, 1:58.

113. Macray, *Clarendon's History*, 1:58. "Hee was of a very fyne and grave Elocution in a kind of gracefull lisping, soe that where Nature might seeme to cast something of Imperfeccon on his speech, on due examinacon shee added a grace to the perfeccon of his delivery. For his words rather flowed from him in a kind of Native pleasingnes, then by any artificiall helpe or Assistance" (Inner Temple, Petyt 538/17, fols. 364–364v).

114. Relf, *Debates in the House of Lords 1621, 1625, 1628*, p. 167. "All those Councels which did disserve his Majesty, he was an earnest disswader, and did much disaffect those sticklers who laboured to make the Prerogative rather tall than great" (David Lloyd, *State-Worthies* [London, 1670], p. 980).

115. *DNB*, s.v. "Sir Thomas Coventry"; *Calendar of State Papers Venetian*, 21:580 (a reference I owe to Conrad Russell); Hacket, 2:137.

116. *DNB*, s.v. "Sir John Finch," says he became a member of the Privy Council in March 1638/9. According to the Privy Council Register, he was sworn as lord keeper and privy councillor in January 1639/40 (*Privy Council Registers Preserved in the Public Record Office* [reproduced in facsimile, 12 vols. in 6, London, 1967–68], 8:3, 248).

117. *LJ*, 4:55.

118. "The lord keeper keeps such a clatter in his new place that they are more weary of him in the Chancery than they were before in the Common Pleas" (Cave to Rose, cited in *DNB*, s.v. "Sir John Finch").

119. *LJ*, 4:46–48; Cope, *Proceedings of the Short Parliament*, pp. 293–94; Rushworth, *Historical Collections*, 4:12–16.

120. Among the state papers, there is a note in Secretary Windebank's hand, endorsed by him as the lord keeper's speech on 3 November. Short and bristling with classical allusions, it may have been, as the calendar suggests, one of the many squibs concerning Finch circulating at the time. The speeches that have come down to us, however, do not justify any such parody. They are considerably less elaborate than those of Ellesmere, Bacon, or Williams (PRO, SP16/539/31; cf. Huntington Library, Ellesmere MS 2621).

121. *LJ*, 4:62–63, 75–77.

122. Cope, *Proceedings of the Short Parliament*, pp. 83–84, 103, 294, 315; *LJ*, 4:72–73, 75–77.

123. Cope, *Proceedings of the Short Parliament*, pp. 265, 304, 310; *LJ*, 4:68, 71, 78.

124. Cope, *Proceedings of the Short Parliament*, p. 86.

125. *LJ*, 4:64; Cope, *Proceedings of the Short Parliament*, pp. 60, 67, 80, 98, 107, 219–20, 234.

126. Macray, *Clarendon's History*, 1:279.

127. *DNB*, s.v. "Sir Edward Littleton"; *Privy Council Registers*, 9:322.

128. *LJ*, 4:114, 168; *DNB*, s.v. "Sir Edward Littleton."

129. *LJ*, 4:136, 173.

130. Macray, *Clarendon's History*, 2:108–9.

131. It was reported that his was the decisive vote (Gardiner, *Oxinden Letters*, p. 301, May 1642).

132. Macray, *Clarendon's History*, 2:109.

133. *LJ*, 4:357.

134. Smith, *De Republica Anglorum*, p. 51.

135. Spedding, *Letters and Life*, 7:150.

136. *LJ*, 2:326, 361, 3:812.
137. PRO, SP14/8/29; Hatfield House, Cecil Papers, 128/134; HLRO, Main Papers, H.L., 1641 (Odling to the earl of Manchester and Duckett's petition), 29 July 1648, 31 August 1648, 16 October 1648. For a significant debate about the order of business, see Relf, *Debates in the House of Lords 1621, 1625, 1628*, pp. 151–55; *Calendar of State Papers Venetian*, 21:104.
138. See *HMC, Buccleuch*, 3:232. In 1624 Williams moved to read bills. Others wished to wait for the king's answer to a message. The matter was finally resolved by vote in favor of Williams.
139. Relfe noted that he stepped a little aside from the middle of the cross woolsack (HLRO, Relfe, "Book of Orders 1710," p. 39), but this reflected later practice. On these occasions, he put on his hat until he spoke. As Speaker of the House, he was uncovered (de Villiers, p. 9; *Manuscripts of the House of Lords*, 10:1, Standing Order no. 2).
140. *LJ*, 2:280, 307; HLRO, Braye 93, fols. 7v–8; British Library, Stowe 375, fol. 196.
141. See pp. 34–35 above.
142. 16 *Car*. I, c. 1.
143. *LJ*, 4:164.
144. "*Sic transit*," wrote John Browne, clerk of the parliaments (HLRO, Minute Book no. 9, 7 April 1643). *LJ*, 5:698; 6:315 (28 November 1643); 8:544, 552–53 (31 October 1646); and 9:370 (3 August 1647), 433 (14 September 1647); HLRO, Main Papers, H.L., 23 March 1645/6, October 1646.
145. Bond and Beamish, p. 8; Burnet, pt. 1, 1:493; "A Letter from a Person of Quality," in *State Tracts, Being a Collection of Several Treatises Relating to the Government* (London, 1689), p. 192.

3. THE CLERK

1. On the clerk's gown, adopted in the late sixteenth century, see HLRO, Memorandum no. 32 (1965); "Moderne Forme of the Parliaments," pp. 296–97. For other references to a table in the chamber, see Elsyng, "Method of Passing Bills," p. 112; PRO, SP14/165/61; HLRO, Braye 65, fol. 11; Foster, *Painful Labour of Mr. Elsyng*, p. 11. Accounts refer to the clerk's table, which was one of his perquisites. It was "a wainscot table with a cupboard to it, and boarded about the sides, being 5 feet long and 3 feet broad" (Foster, "Staging a Parliament," pp. 133, 141). This may have been the same table at which he worked in the House. Montagu in 1640 referred to the clerk's table as a "cupboard" (*HMC, Buccleuch*, 3:396, 405, 408). This arrangement is more sensible than the usual picture of the clerk kneeling behind a woolsack, a posture that would have made it impossible for him to perform his many duties in the House (see, for example, Foster, *1610*, vol. 1, front.). After the Restoration, the clerk's woolsack was often occupied by lords. The House recommended that it be reduced in size to discourage this practice (*LJ*, 13:508, 15:122).
2. The terms "clerk of the parliament" and "clerk of the parliaments" were both used in the seventeenth century (Maurice F. Bond, "Clerks of the Parliaments, 1509–1953," *EHR* 73 [1958]: 81).
3. Maurice F. Bond, "The Formation of the Archives of Parliament, 1497–1691," *Journal of the Society of Archivists* 1, no. 6 (October 1957): 152; British Library, Cotton MSS, Tib. D.1, fol. 3.
4. J. C. Sainty, "The Parliament Office in the Seventeenth and Eighteenth Centuries:

Biographical Notes on Clerks in the House of Lords, 1600 to 1800" (London, House of Lords Record Office, 1977), p. 22; Bond, "Formation of the Archives," p. 153. As an inexperienced clerk, Smith made some errors in sending bills and amendments to the lower House, whose clerk attempted to help him (D'Ewes, *Journals of All the Parliaments*, pp. 576–77).

5. Bond, "Formation of the Archives," p. 153. D'Ewes's comments are quoted by A. F. Pollard, "The Clerical Organization of Parliament," *EHR* 57 (1942): 52; Foster, *1610*, 1:xxvii.

6. Bond, "Formation of the Archives," p. 153.

7. Sainty, "Parliament Office," p. 12.

8. Foster, *1610*, 1:xxii–xxix.

9. Sainty, "Parliament Office," pp. 15, 26; Foster, *Painful Labour of Mr. Elsyng*, pp. 5–6, 21–35; Elsyng, *Manner of Holding Parliaments*, p. 97; Bond, "Formation of the Archives," p. 156. Even Bowyer had disposed of some parliamentary papers in his will.

10. Sainty, "Parliament Office," pp. 11, 12, 18, 26, 28; Foster, *Painful Labour of Mr. Elsyng*, p. 6; Bond, "Formation of the Archives," p. 156; HLRO, Memorandum no. 61 (1979), p. 14.

11. HLRO, Memorandum no. 61, pp. 13–14; Bond, "Formation of the Archives," p. 156.

12. Bond, "Formation of the Archives," pp. 156–57.

13. *LJ*, 3:59–60. The same oath is recorded in John Browne's commonplace book (Yale University Library, Osborn Collection, Braye 96, p. 264).

14. On Bowyer, see British Library, Cotton MSS, Tib. D.1, fol. 2; on Elsyng, see Foster, *Painful Labour of Mr. Elsyng*, pp. 9–10; and *LJ*, 3:59–60.

15. Foster, *Painful Labour of Mr. Elsyng*, pp. 14–16. For similar practice in modern times, see Maurice F. Bond, "The Office of Clerk of the Parliaments," *Parliamentary Affairs*, 12 (1959): 299. For some of Browne's agenda sheets, see HLRO, Braye 95; Braye 10, vol. 3, fols. 103–13; HLRO, Main Papers, H.L., 6 June 1645, fols. 21–21v.

16. de Villiers, p. 6.

17. On a few occasions, Elsyng was busy elsewhere and an assistant took notes in the House for him. Browne was excused by the House for a short time. Foster, *Painful Labour of Mr. Elsyng*, p. 22; HLRO, Main Papers, H.L., 2 June 1647; HLRO, Memorandum no. 61, p. 14.

18. Foster, *Painful Labour of Mr. Elsyng*, p. 16; *The Parliamentary Diary of Robert Bowyer, 1606–1607*, ed. David Harris Willson (Minneapolis, 1931), p. ix.

19. Inner Temple, Petyt 537/6, p. 311; "Moderne Forme of the Parliaments," pp. 292–93.

20. "Moderne Forme of the Parliaments," p. 294. On occasion, Bowyer and Elsyng mistakenly began with the prince (Foster, *Painful Labour of Mr. Elsyng*, pp. 13–14).

21. "Moderne Forme of the Parliaments," p. 294.

22. See below, pp. 88, 92, 93, 192, 193.

23. Foster, *Painful Labour of Mr. Elsyng*, p. 18. The House retained this power to itself until 1640/1 when it granted a commission to Browne, empowering him to swear witnesses himself. A phrase enabling his deputy also to do so was deleted (HLRO, Main Papers, H.L., 5 February 1640/1).

24. HLRO, Main Papers, H.L., 25 January 1640/1.

25. Scobell, p. 35.

26. Foster, *Painful Labour of Mr. Elsyng*, p. 16; HMC, *Buccleuch*, 3:410. See, for

example, *LJ*, 3:327-28, 352-58, 373-74. The attorney general did some reading when committees reported on which he served as an assistant (see below, p. 84).

27. See the suggestion in Sainty, "Parliament Office," p. 4; "Moderne Forme of the Parliaments," pp. 292, 294-95, 297-98; Foster, *Painful Labour of Mr. Elsyng*, p. 14, n. 58; Relf, *Debates in the House of Lords 1621, 1625, 1628*, p. 91; HLRO, Braye 18 (14 May 1641), Braye 19 (18 June 1641); see also HLRO, Main Papers, H.L., 14 May 1641.

28. Foster, "Staging a Parliament," pp. 137-39.

29. Foster, *Painful Labour of Mr. Elsyng*, pp. 13-14; Wagner and Sainty, pp. 133-34.

30. Foster, *Painful Labour of Mr. Elsyng*, p. 14. The assistant clerk received a fee for doing this in 1640 (Yale University Library, Osborn Collection, Braye 52/5, fol. 262). A proxy expired when a lord returned to parliament (*Manuscripts of the House of Lords*, 10:8, Standing Order no. 46).

31. Foster, *Painful Labour of Mr. Elsyng*, pp. 15, 17. For Elizabethan lists of the same kind, see J. E. Neale, *The Elizabethan House of Commons* (New Haven, 1950), p. 381.

32. See Bowyer's efforts to recall bills from committee chairmen and Elsyng's notes indicating to whom he had given them (Foster, *1610*, 1:xxvii-xxviii; HLRO, Committee Books, Appointments, 1624, fol. 8v). For committee sheets, see below, p. 93.

33. Foster, *Painful Labour of Mr. Elsyng*, p. 30. For sending bills to the printer, see HLRO, Manuscript Lords Journal, vol. 6, p. 292; Foster, *Painful Labour of Mr. Elsyng*, pp. 17-18, 30; HLRO, Minute Book no. 7, where a receipt for a bill is entered in the back. For the form of the printer's receipt, see *LJ*, 2:448. "And so for everie Act delivered to the Kings Printer and when such Acte is brought backe the Title is to be wrighten in the last side of the Journall Booke and in the margent to be wrighten thus, viz. Returned" (Inner Temple, Petyt 537/8, fol. 106). Cf. Graves, *House of Lords Edward VI and Mary I*, p. 122.

34. Foster, *Painful Labour of Mr. Elsyng*, p. 18.

35. Ibid., pp. 20-21. In 1641 Henry Morris copied orders for the clerk (HLRO, Main Papers, H.L., 1641).

36. HLRO, Main Papers, H.L., 9 December 1640.

37. HLRO, Main Papers, H.L., 10 August 1641, 17 April 1645. See below, pp. 56, 61.

38. Foster, *Painful Labour of Mr. Elsyng*, pp. 18-20; Bond, "Formation of the Archives," p. 155. For a case of error, see HLRO, Main Papers, H.L., 16 November 1646.

39. HLRO, Main Papers, H.L., 23 December 1640-6 August 1641, the cause of John Godfrey dated 10 July 1641; 19 July 1641; 25 June 1644; 13 April 1645; 8 January 1646/7. See also the case of the Muscovy Company (Foster, *Painful Labour of Mr. Elsyng*, p. 19).

40. Foster, *Painful Labour of Mr. Elsyng*, pp. 8, 9.

41. HLRO, Main Papers, H.L., 17 April 1645; Foster, *Painful Labour of Mr. Elsyng*, p. 9; Yale University Library, Osborn Collection, Braye 94; HMC, *Buccleuch*, 3:244.

42. Bond, "Formation of the Archives," p. 156. In 1657/8, Henry Scobell asked for repayment for £250 he had spent on the Jewel Tower and on the clerk's house (PRO, SP18/79/36).

43. *The Autobiography and Correspondence of Sir Simonds D'Ewes, Bart., during the Reigns of James I and Charles I*, ed. James Orchard Halliwell, 2 vols. (London, 1845), 1:411-13.

44. Foster, *Painful Labour of Mr. Elsyng*, pp. 18-19.

45. Cope, *Proceedings of the Short Parliament*, p. 178.

46. *LJ*, 2:314, 328.
47. Inner Temple, Petyt 537/8, fols. 32, 39v.
48. See G. R. Elton, "The Early Journals of the House of Lords," *EHR* 89, no. 352 (July 1974): 491. Lawrence Stone provides an interesting description of the persistence of older forms in another context, that of estate accounts (Stone, *Family and Fortune*, p. 185).
49. Inner Temple, Petyt 537/8, fol. 12.
50. HLRO, Manuscript Lords Journal, vol. 7, pp. 187–88, 215–16, 251–52, 253–54, 269–70, 287–88, 309–10.
51. See HLRO, Manuscript Lords Journal, vol. 6, where there is a difference in the hands in some of the entries. The appearance of the original manuscript journal makes it unlikely that these sheets were prepared before the House sat (see Elton, "Lords Journals," pp. 502, 504, 511). In one case, a subcommittee has been renumbered in order of precedence (Manuscript Lords Journal, vol. 7, 9 March 1606/7).
52. Inner Temple, Petyt 537/8, fol. 60.
53. "The Journals, Minutes, and Committee Books of the House of Lords," HLRO, Memorandum no. 13 (London, 1957), pp. 18–19.
54. HLRO, Manuscript Lords Journal, vol. 7, p. 170.
55. *LJ*, 2:195; Foster, *Painful Labour of Mr. Elsyng*, p. 23, n. 38.
56. *LJ*, 2:307, 345–48. Smith's draft of the order was read in the House and considered by a committee.
57. J. E. Neale, "Proceedings in Parliament Relative to the Sentence on Mary Queen of Scots," *EHR* 35 (January 1920): 104; G. R. Elton, "The Rolls of Parliament, 1449–1547," *The Historical Journal* 22, no. 1 (1979): 24. The rolls of 14 and 28 Eliz. were exceptions that did not affect what Smith did. The enrollment of private acts continued until 1593 and in some circumstances even later (Elton, "Rolls of Parliament," p. 28). See below, p. 191.
58. Quoted in Neale, "Proceedings Relative to Mary Queen of Scots," p. 104, n. 4.
59. Bond, "Formation of the Archives," p. 154.
60. Foster, *1610*, 1:xxii, xxvii–xxix, 247. For some pages of Bowyer's draft journal, see HLRO, Main Papers, H.L., Addenda, 23 May 1610; Supplementary, 16 June 1610.
61. Foster, *1610*, 1:xxv–xxvi. For the early Tudor period, see Graves, *House of Lords Edward VI and Mary I*, p. 166.
62. Foster, *1610*, 1:xxvi–xxvii.
63. Foster, *Painful Labour of Mr. Elsyng*, p. 30.
64. Ibid. Elton observes that the custom of omitting subsidy acts and the general pardon dates from 1553 (Elton, "Rolls of Parliament," p. 27).
65. Foster, *Painful Labour of Mr. Elsyng*, pp. 23–24. Later, the lords' work is less evident.
66. Ibid., pp. 25, 27, 28; for certain interesting omissions, see p. 29.
67. In 1621 the subsidy acts were not enrolled, although the temporal subsidy was printed (PRO, SP46/65, fols. 122–40). In 1624 Elsyng included the subsidies with the narrative account of the negotiations with Spain, registered other acts in a separate roll, and prepared a third for the proceedings concerning Cranfield (PRO, C65/186, pt. 1; C65/187, pt. 2; C65/188, pt. 3). In 1625 and 1628 the subsidies were enrolled (PRO, C65/189 and C65/190). For the general pardon in 1624, see PRO, C65/187, pt. 2. For the pattern of earlier rolls, see Elton, "Rolls of Parliament," pp. 1–29.
68. Foster, *Painful Labour of Mr. Elsyng*, pp. 29–35, 46.
69. Neale, "Proceedings Relative to Mary Queen of Scots," pp. 106–13. In 14 Eliz. there

had been entries at the end of the parliament roll in addition to the acts (ibid., p. 104, n. 3).

70. Ibid., pp. 103–5.

71. Cope, *Proceedings of the Short Parliament*, pp. 19–22, 63–95; HLRO, Manuscript Minutes no. 6; Elizabeth Read Foster, "The Journal of the House of Lords for the Long Parliament," in *After the Reformation*, ed. Barbara C. Malament (Philadelphia, 1980), pp. 130–31, 142, n. 10.

72. HLRO, Manuscript Lords Journal, vol. 14. Dr. Cope suggests that this final version may not have been completed until after the Restoration (Cope, *Proceedings of the Short Parliament*, p. 21).

73. Browne's notes are scattered throughout the Main Papers. See, for example, HLRO, Main Papers, H.L., 26 May, 10 June, 8 and 12 September, 2, 6, 7, 19, 24, and 27 October, 7, 13, and 22 November, and 4 December 1643. His notes for 29 April–15 June 1642 are bound in the front of the Manuscript Lords Journal, vol. 21. They are not an "incorrect Duplicate" (*LJ*, 5:56).

74. Foster, "Journal of the House of Lords," pp. 131–34; HLRO, Committee for Privileges, Minute Book no. 2, p. 31.

75. PRO, C65/194, 195, 196; HLRO, Parchment Collection, 3 March 1650/1.

76. Letters were addressed to both Bowyer and his assistant Reynolds at their houses in Westminster, although Bowyer also had a house at Tower Hill (HLRO, Main Papers, H.L., 15 March 1609/10, 20 May 1610, [May 1611]). In 1614 the king granted Bowyer land in Westminster near the river for a rental of 20s. per annum. The property was later acquired by Sir Robert Cotton ("The House, Library, and Garden of Sir John Cotton," *The Wren Society* 11 [1934]: 57). For Reynolds, see Sainty, "Parliament Office," p. 21. For Elsyng, see Foster, *Painful Labour of Mr. Elsyng*, p. 10 and n. 10. In 1641 the Lords ordered one Cundall to cease building a house upon a new foundation "in the Olde Palace of Westminster upon a parcel of ground belonging to a house of his Majesty, wch is now in possession of the clerk of the parliaments, by letters patents for life" (HLRO, Main Papers, H.L., 6 September 1641; *LJ*, 4:389). See n. 42 above.

77. PRO, SP14/10/63.

78. British Library, Additional 5756, fol. 4; Yale University Library, Osborn Collection, Braye 54/34, 54/40, 54/41, 55/90; Foster, "Staging a Parliament," pp. 133, 138.

79. Gardiner, *Debates in the House of Lords 1624 and 1626*, pp. 231, 233; Relf, *Debates in the House of Lords 1621, 1625, 1628*, p. 194; *LJ*, 3:682. For Elsyng's account of those who had not paid and a summary of what he had received, see Yale University Library, Osborn Collection, Braye 94. An accurate figure is difficult because one must reckon the number of lords present without knowing on what day the count was to be taken. Probably the clerk counted as present all those who had presented writs of summons. Lords who held proxies were to pay the fees of those they represented. For efforts to collect what was due, see HLRO, Minute Book no. 1, fol. 1; Minute Book no. 2, fols. 54v–55; Minute Book no. 5, fol. 3.

80. Huntington Library, Ellesmere MS 34/A/2, pp. 1–2. In 1725/6 this provision was modified (*LJ*, 22:627–29). The discussion of the fees of the clerk and other officers is based on several sources. Fees for 1597 are listed in the Lords journal (*LJ*, 2:225). There are schedules of fees among the Braye manuscripts. One (Yale University Library, Osborn Collection, Braye 55/86) is endorsed: "This Copie was writ out of a note that Mr. Bowyer had writ with his own hand"; it therefore relates to the years between 1610 and March 1620/1. In addition, it also includes fees paid in 1621 and 1624. Another schedule of fees (Yale University Library, Osborn Collection,

Braye 52/5) is undated but probably was prepared for the subcommittee of the Committee for Privileges, which studied fees in 1640 (see also HLRO, Main Papers, H.L., 29 April 1640). The chairman of the committee, the earl of Warwick, reported a schedule of fees to the House on 29 April 1640, and it was confirmed and voted by the House on 1 May (Huntington Library, Ellesmere MS 34/A/2). It is interesting that this report and schedule were not entered in the journal. A similar omission had occurred in 1628 (Foster, *Painful Labour of Mr. Elsyng*, p. 29). A committee of lords examining fees in March 1725/6 suggested why this may have been so. It noted that a report had been made on 29 April 1640, which was read and approved on 1 May. It observed that the schedule had not on either occasion been entered in the journal. All that remained for the record was a roll signed by the earl of Warwick and this, it remarked, had erasures and later entries increasing the amounts (*LJ*, 22:627–29). Clearly, clerks had thought it to their advantage to keep the schedule flexible and thus omitted to enter it in the journal. However, the survival of a copy of Warwick's original report among the Ellesmere papers, taken together with notations in "scribbled books," minute books, and the Main Papers of the House indicating what was actually charged and paid, suggests that changes in the roll were not made in the early Stuart period but later. The original roll drawn up in 1640 fairly reflected practice at the time. See also HLRO, Main Papers, H.L., 15 July 1641; Relf, *Debates in the House of Lords 1621, 1625, 1628*, p. 67. For some fees that seem higher, see p. 253, n. 32.

81. Huntington Library, Ellesmere MS 34/A/2; Yale University Library, Osborn Collection, Braye 52/5.
82. *LJ*, 2:225; Yale University Library, Osborn Collection, Braye 55/86 and 52/5; Huntington Library, Ellesmere MS 34/A/2.
83. Yale University Library, Osborn Collection, Braye 52/5 and 55/86; Huntington Library, Ellesmere MS 34/A/2. It is not entirely clear when the fee for a private bill was to be paid. "For a private bill upon the first reading" is the stipulation in Braye 52/5 and in Ellesmere MS 34/A/2 (1640). In 1641 the deputy clerk, Throckmorton, indicated that fees must be paid before a bill was read (HLRO, Main Papers, H.L., 15 July 1641). In 1725/6 the fee on a private bill was to be paid before the second reading. At that time, the clerk's assistant received the fee for a committee sheet (*LJ*, 22:626–28).
84. Huntington Library, Ellesmere MS 34/A/2; Yale University Library, Osborn Collection, Braye 55/91, "Fees received by R. B. for certificates." Bowyer was charging £3 6s8d. for the first sheet, or sometimes "five marks."
85. Huntington Library, Ellesmere MS 34/A/2; Yale University Library, Osborn Collection, Braye 52/5.
86. Yale University Library, Osborn Collection, Braye 55/86; Huntington Library, Ellesmere MS 34/A/2. According to Braye 52/5 (Osborn Collection), the fee was 14s.6d.
87. Yale University Library, Osborn Collection, Braye 52/5; Huntington Library, Ellesmere MS 34/A/2.
88. HLRO, Main Papers, H.L., 14 June 1610.
89. HLRO, Main Papers, H.L., 29 June 1610.
90. PRO, SP16/479/38.
91. *HMC, De L'Isle*, 6:253, a reference I owe to Conrad Russell.
92. HLRO, Main Papers, H.L., 4 October 1644.
93. HLRO, Main Papers, H.L., 3 March 1647/8.
94. PRO, SP14/15/46. Allicock, who had served Anthony Mason (who was clerk,

1574–97), may have supplemented his income by disposing of acts of parliament. Bowyer wrote that an act passed in 13 Eliz. was not in the parliament office, nor in the calendar of acts. "Allicock . . . did among some other Acts (for reward or other speciall ende) embecell and convey this Act out of the said office in the lyfe of Mr. Mason" and did not return it. He did bring back to Sir Thomas Smith other acts that he had "conveied or carried forth" in Mason's time (Inner Temple, Petyt 537/6, pp. 149–50; Bond, "Clerks of the Parliaments," p. 83).

95. Yale University Library, Osborn Collection, Braye 54/37; Foster, *Painful Labour of Mr. Elsyng*, p. 11; Sainty, "Parliament Office," p. 21.

96. Foster, *Painful Labour of Mr. Elsyng*, p. 11.

97. Ibid., pp. 6, 9; Sainty, "Parliament Office," p. 15.

98. Foster, *Painful Labour of Mr. Elsyng*, pp. 9, 11–12.

99. Sainty, "Parliament Office," pp. 22–23.

100. He was said to be a "fat man" (HLRO, Main Papers, H.L., 21 September 1647). Whether this description was accurate or whether it was cited to indicate that the witness was incompetent is impossible to say.

101. HLRO, Main Papers, H.L., 4 March 1640/1, 26 July 1645, 24 January 1645/6, 15 April 1647. In March 1641/2 Rushworth, who was assisting the clerk in the House of Commons, wrote a note to Throckmorton on a draft order forwarded from the lower House, asking, for Pym's information, what had been done on it in the upper House (HLRO, Main Papers, H.L., 21 March 1641/2).

102. HLRO, Main Papers, H.L., 2 June 1647. In 1644 he was assessed for property in St. Martin's-in-the-Fields (HLRO, Main Papers, H.L., 19 June 1644). In January 1645/6 he had a house in St. James Street, Westminster (HLRO, Main Papers, H.L., 24 January 1645/6). In 1641, when Sir Richard Wiseman accused him of corruption, Throckmorton replied that "neither his purse nor any others should work with him." When Wiseman threatened to have him turned out of his place, Throckmorton "answered he scorned to have it thought he deserved that and that he spake unworthy and that excepting his knighthood he had as good blood run in his veins as he" (HLRO, Main Papers, H.L., 5 August 1641). Throckmorton was sufficiently important to share the criticism cast upon the clerk's office (see below, p. 62).

103. Yale University Library, Osborn Collection, Braye 54/37.

104. Yale University Library, Osborn Collection, Braye 55/86.

105. Huntington Library, Ellesmere MS 34/A/2.

106. *LJ*, 4:77.

107. Gardiner, *Debates in the House of Lords 1624 and 1626*, p. 233; Relf, *Debates in the House of Lords 1621, 1625, 1628*, p. 194; *LJ*, 3:682.

108. For some examples, see de Villiers, p. 35; HLRO, Braye 17, 18, 19; HLRO, Main Papers, H.L., 6 and 15 March 1609/10, 20 May and 29 June 1610; HLRO, Minute Book no. 1, fol. 1, and Minute Book no. 2, fols. 59v–60v.

109. *LJ*, 7:286; HLRO, Main Papers, H.L., 25 March 1644/5. Henry Morris, one of the clerical assistants, petitioned for a salaried place in 1645 and was granted one in the wine office in July 1648; see HLRO, Main Papers, H.L., 24 April 1645, 29 July 1648; *LJ*, 7:334. See below, p. 60.

110. There is a list of proxies, some of which are marked "paid," in the minute book kept by Browne's assistant (HLRO, Minute Book no. 7).

111. Foster, *Painful Labour of Mr. Elsyng*, pp. 11–12.

112. "Moderne Forme of the Parliaments," pp. 296–97.

113. Foster, *Painful Labour of Mr. Elsyng*, pp. 24–25. Bowyer noted that in the journal for 8 Eliz. "p." had not been entered opposite the names of lords present on 19 De-

cember, "which seemeth to have been the error of the Clerks man" (Inner Temple, Petyt 537/6, p. 128). Thus he held the assistant responsible for preparing the "presents" list in the journal itself. HLRO, Minute Book no. 5 (1628), fol. 70: "I was constrained to be in ye office when I should have taken the presence."

114. This is abundantly clear in the HLRO, Minute Book no. 7.

115. See above, p. 48.

116. HLRO, Minute Book no. 1, fol. 1; Minute Book no. 2, fols. 54v–55; Minute Book no. 5, fol. 3; Minute Book no. 7, inside back cover; and Minute Book no. 8, inside back cover.

117. For Elsyng's assistants, see Foster, *Painful Labour of Mr. Elsyng*, p. 12. In 1628 a memorandum was addressed to Thomas Knyvett as "clerk of the parliaments" (PRO, SP16/529/50). Philip Perceval worked for Browne in 1640, and Robert Brooke in 1641 (Yale University Library, Osborn Collection, Braye 2, fols. 108–9, 183). John Walker assisted in 1646 (HLRO, Main Papers, H.L., 16 December 1646). For his later career as reading clerk, see Sainty, "Parliament Office," p. 23. "Mr. Phipps" was helping draft the *remittitur* on writs of error in 1646 (HLRO, Main Papers, H.L., 16 December 1646). For Thomas Ken, see Sainty, "Parliament Office," pp. 5, 17; HLRO, Main Papers, 17 October 1650.

118. For Harrison, see Foster, *Painful Labour of Mr. Elsyng*, p. 12. For Smith, see HLRO, Main Papers, H.L., 25 May, July (no date), and 20 August 1641.

119. HLRO, Main Papers, H.L., 1641.

120. *CJ*, 4:425, a reference I owe to Sheila Lambert; *LJ*, 7:334, 8:139.

121. HLRO, Main Papers, H.L., 5 August 1641.

122. HLRO, Main Papers, 17 October 1650 (affidavit of Thomas Elslyott).

123. *LJ*, 4:836; Bedford Office, Woburn MSS, HMC no. 22, fol. 8v.

124. *HMC, De L'Isle*, 6:346.

125. Ibid., pp. 253, 340. For Rossingham, see Cope, *Proceedings of the Short Parliament*, pp. 35–37.

126. HLRO, Main Papers, H.L., 4 and 6 September 1644.

127. HLRO, Main Papers, H.L., 11 February 1644/5.

128. On the Mimms Commons incident, see *LJ*, 10:552. On the Browne and Poyntz affair, see HLRO, Main Papers, H.L., 25 May 1647; *LJ*, 9:441.

129. HLRO, Main Papers, H.L., 23 June 1647; *LJ*, 9:441.

130. *LJ*, 10:460; HLRO, Main Papers, H.L., 21 September, 7 October, and 2 November 1647; 9 February 1647/8; 26 August, 26 October, 2 November, and 25 November 1648; 19 March 1648/9; 3 January 1649/50; 17 October and November (no date) 1650; 10 March 1655/6; *Cobbett's Complete Collection of State Trials*, 34 vols. (London, 1809–26), 4:951–58.

4. OTHER OFFICERS OF THE HOUSE

1. I am grateful to Maurice F. Bond for information concerning the lord great chamberlain. A small beginning may be seen in 1641 when the lord great chamberlain was to provide security for Strafford's trial and execute previous orders for keeping people from the doors of the chamber and from coming into the "little" chamber and the lobby (*LJ*, 4:190, 396–97; Foster, "Staging a Parliament," p. 129).

2. Foster, "Staging a Parliament," pp. 134–35; PRO, LC 5/134, p. 445; PRO, LC 5/132, p. 71; PRO, LC 5/38; PRO, A.O. 3/1115; Northumberland MSS, Alnwick Castle MS 468.

3. Foster, "Staging a Parliament," pp. 137–39.

4. PRO, LC 5/132, pp. 130–31; Foster, "Staging a Parliament," pp. 136–37. In 1629 the Privy Council authorized the payment of 13*li*.13s. to Richard Crane, yeoman usher, for his services in parliament at Oxford (1625) and 62*li*.10s. for his services and to cover his disbursements in 1625 and 1628–29 (*Acts of the Privy Council*, vol. 43, *1627–1628* [London, 1940], no. 1155; vol. 45, *1629–1630* [London, 1960], no. 461).

5. PRO, LC 5/132, p. 52.

6. HLRO, Main Papers, H.L., 22 July 1646; *LJ*, 8:439.

7. PRO, LC 5/134, p. 422 (1640).

8. HLRO, Main Papers, H.L., 22 June 1643.

9. Pettus, p. 387; *LJ*, 4:447, 7:506; PRO, LC 5/132, pp. 51, 131. Waiters: "We wait here on your honours with the leave and permission of the Gentleman Usher, but receive neither wages, nor anything else from him for our attendance here on your honours" (HLRO, Main Papers, H.L., 24 July 1645). Messengers: HLRO, Main Papers, H.L., 31 July 1643. Concerning the appointment of the yeoman usher, see Bond and Beamish, p. 5.

10. Bond and Beamish, p. 9.

11. *HMC, Hastings*, 4:289–90. The yeoman usher was to take the same oath.

12. *LJ*, 2:402, 9:515–16.

13. *LJ*, 4:319, 396, 491, and 9:531.

14. Wagner and Sainty, p. 119; Cope, *Proceedings of the Short Parliament*, p. 57; Pettus, p. 386.

15. HLRO, P.O. 354, Precedents, p. 73; Starr, pp. 12–13.

16. HLRO, P.O. 354, Precedents, p. 76.

17. The Commons protested in 1641 (Starr, p. 32; *CJ*, 2:141). See HLRO, Main Papers, H.L., 12 September 1643, for a detailed description of the ceremony when the Commons came to hear the charge against Justice Berkeley.

18. British Library, Harleian 163, fol. 122.

19. Bond and Beamish, pp. 12–14; *Commons Debates for 1629*, ed. Wallace Notestein and Frances Helen Relf (Minneapolis, 1921), p. 106.

20. *LJ*, 4:166. See below, p. 68.

21. *Of Judicature*, p. 185; HLRO, Main Papers, H.L., 15 April 1647.

22. *HMC, Buccleuch*, 3:283.

23. *LJ*, 4:533; HLRO, Main Papers, H.L., 5 April 1642; William M. Clyde, "Parliament and the Press, 1643–7," *Transactions Bibliographical Society*, 2d ser., vols. 13 and 14 (1933–34), p. 401.

24. *LJ*, 8:122.

25. Maxwell had leave to go to Scotland in May 1643 (*LJ*, 6:54).

26. HLRO, Relfe, "Book of Orders 1710," pp. 355–56, 443.

27. HLRO, Main Papers, H.L., 22 May 1647.

28. *The Manuscripts of the House of Lords*, n.s., vol. 4, *1699–1702* (London, 1908), pp. 508, 526.

29. See the warrants of the Privy Council, 13 March 1628/9, to pay Black Rod 82*li*. for his services at parliament in Oxford (1625), and 27 September 1629 to pay him 98*li*.15s. for 1625, 1626, 1627, and 1628 (*Acts of the Privy Council*, vol. 43, no. 1155; vol. 45, no. 460). Northumberland MSS, Alnwick Castle MS 468; PRO, LC 5/132, pp. 51, 130, 131; PRO, E. 351/3237, E. 351/3239, E. 351/3261.

30. HLRO, Main Papers, H.L., 27 June 1646; *LJ*, 8:397.

31. PRO, SP14/58; PRO, E. 403/2561, fol. 301; PRO, A.O. 3/1276 (pt. 2).

32. Huntington Library, Ellesmere MS 34/A/2; HLRO, Main Papers, H.L., 15 July 1641; PRO, SP16/479/38. After 1662 the item of £2 for the entertainment of committees was assigned as salary to the reading clerk; see below, p. 94. For actual fees collected in 1640–42 on behalf of Black Rod and the yeoman usher by the assistant clerk, see HLRO, Minute Books nos. 7 and 8. These fees seem to be higher than those approved by the House.

33. HLRO, Main Papers, H.L., 31 July 1643, 7 August 1645, 11 February 1645/6, 12 May 1648. For a bill in 1642 for various services, see LJ, 5:287–88.

34. Foster, "Staging a Parliament," pp. 134, 137–38, 141.

35. PRO, E. 351/3240, E. 351/3242. For his annuity, see PRO, E. 403/1717, E. 403/1718 (66li.13s.4d. semiannually in 1614), and E. 403/1736 (500li. annually in 1625).

36. PRO, LC 5/132, p. 73.

37. 1625: PRO, LC 5/117; 1640: PRO, LC 5/134, p. 386.

38. HLRO, Main Papers, H.L., 19 June 1644, Maxwell. Thayne lived in the same parish and was assessed at £7 6s. on land and 3s.4d. on goods.

39. HLRO, Main Papers, H.L., 21 March 1643/4, 2 October 1644, 25 July 1645; LJ, 6:490, 7:509. See below, p. 142.

40. John Hooker's description "of the Sergeants or Porters of the higher house" is singularly inaccurate (Snow, John Hooker, pp. 162–63). He has confused the duties of two officers of the House of Lords: the gentleman usher or Black Rod and the sergeant-at-arms and possibly also the duties of the sergeant-at-arms in the upper House with those of the sergeant-at-arms in the lower. The sergeant (in the upper House) did not have "the charge of keeping of the doors," nor were the doorkeepers "at his assignment." He was not in charge of admitting persons to the House or of denying admission to those who did not belong there. He had no housekeeping responsibilities. He did not "see the house be cleene and kept sweet." He did take charge of prisoners and also brought to the House "such as he shalbe commaunded to fetch." He had an allowance for each prisoner. He had "a standing allowance for every day of the Parlement"; but there is no record that he received 40s. for "every private Bil which is enacted" or that "he hath of every Baron or Lord of that house, a certain rewarde."

41. Pettus, pp. 388–89.

42. Gardiner, Debates in the House of Lords 1624 and 1626, pp. 91–92; HMC, Buccleuch, 3:252.

43. Of Judicature, p. 186; LJ, 3:199; HLRO, Main Papers, H.L., 17 February 1640/1.

44. D'Ewes, Journals of All the Parliaments, pp. 603, 607. For Elsyng's account, see Inner Temple, Petyt 538/12, fols. 179–179v.

45. J. C. Sainty, "Officers of the House of Lords, 1485 to 1971," HLRO, Memorandum no. 45 (London, 1971), pp. 9–10.

46. LJ, 3:199.

47. LJ, 4:166; HLRO, Main Papers, H.L., 17 February 1640/1; Bond and Beamish, pp. 4–5.

48. HLRO, Relfe, "Book of Orders 1710," p. 351. A note relating to July 1660 indicates that the gentleman usher and sergeant had come to a private agreement: "Upon this diverse Orders for sending for Delinquents were read with Blanks to whom to be directed as the House should please to appoint 'till about a month after the house was informed that the Gentleman Usher and Serjeants were privately agreed that all Delinquents should be fetch't by the Serjeant, and afterwards delivered to the Gentleman Usher, which method the Lords afterwards observed accordingly" (British

Library, Additional 36102, fol. 96v).

49. Bond and Beamish, p. 9.

50. For messengers' fees paid to deputies of the gentleman usher, see HLRO, Main Papers, H.L., 31 July 1643, 3 June 1647. For fees paid to the sergeant-at-arms or his men, see *LJ*, 3:199 (1621), 514 (1626); HLRO, Relfe, "Book of Orders 1710," p. 87.

51. Huntington Library, Ellesmere MS 6919; *HMC, Buccleuch*, 3:280–81. Possibly the House considered it more honorable for the earl to be brought by the gentleman usher rather than by the sergeant. Bristol's exact status, whether delinquent or not, was uncertain (see below, pp. 163–64, 167).

52. *HMC, Buccleuch*, 3:280–81. This is the distinction that May also stresses (*Erskine May's Treatise on the Law, Privileges, Proceedings, and Usage of Parliament*, ed. Sir Barnett Cocks, 17th ed. [London, 1964], p. 245).

53. *Of Judicature*, p. 185.

54. Pettus, p. 389.

55. For similar disputes in the Irish parliament, see Snow, *John Hooker*, p. 82.

56. Huntington Library, Ellesmere MS 34/A/2.

57. He was paid from the Hanaper (see PRO, C66/1696, the letters patent of 4 Jac. I appointing John Tyler as sergeant). See also Society of Antiquaries, MS 40.

58. Bond and Beamish, p. 4; *LJ*, 5:287–88. For the usual practice of payment of fees by those served with orders, see HLRO, Main Papers, H.L., 31 July 1643, 7 August 1645, 3 June 1647. In 1677 the House voted that the gentleman usher might receive the same fees for conveying lords committed by the House to the Tower as were charged by the sergeants-at-arms who conveyed noblemen to the Tower on order of the king or council. Twysden gives an interesting list of these sergeants' fees for the year 1417 ("Sir Roger Twysden's Journal," *Archaeologia Cantiana; Being Transactions of the Kent Archaeological Society* 4 [London, 1861]: 158–59).

5. THE ASSISTANTS

1. Pike, p. 247; Adair, p. 360, n. 4. Pike notes that the term "assistant" was used in 1660. However, there are numerous occasions when it was used earlier. See British Library, Cotton MSS, Titus F IV, fol. 285v (1614); *HMC, Hastings*, 4:254 (1614); *LJ*, 3:408 (1624).

2. For the writ, see Pettus, p. 313.

3. Adair, p. 360. "It is plain by the writ directed to the judges which summoneth them to the parliament that they are to treat with the King but not with the Lords so as they may not speak but when the Lords require them whereas the Lords are to treat with the King and with one another about business of parliament which is the main if not the only difference between the Lords' writs of summons and that of the judges" (British Library, Harleian 2243, fol. 28, Lord Robartes's notes). The judges ruled in 1624 that they had no inherent right of being called as assistants (*LJ*, 3:408).

4. Smith, *De Republica Anglorum*, p. 51; HLRO, Braye 17 (3 November 1640); Elsyng, *Manner of Holding Parliaments*, p. 111.

5. Milles, p. 64; *HMC, Hastings*, 4:280. See also the colored plate in Robert Glover, *Nobilitas politica vel civilis* (London, 1608), at the Folger Shakespeare Library; and Foster, *1610*, 1:96.

6. *Manuscripts of the House of Lords*, 10:1–2 (Standing Order no. 5) and 3–4

(Standing Order no. 23); HLRO, Relfe, "Book of Orders 1710," p. 80.

7. Cope, *Proceedings of the Short Parliament*, p. 100.

8. HLRO, Relfe, "Book of Orders 1710," p. 80.

9. Adair, p. 360, writes that judges had "no lot or share in the privileges" of the upper House. This is incorrect. In 1625 a judge complained that, contrary to privilege, his horse had been seized to ride post. The Lords ordered punishment of the offender (HLRO, Relfe, "Book of Orders 1710," p. 80). See also HLRO, Main Papers, H.L., 5 June 1641, and *LJ*, 4:266, concerning the petition of Philip Holman, who said that he could not proceed against Judge Heath because he was a justice. By action of the House, however, Heath was required to respond. On 14 August 1643 it was voted by the House that judges and other assistants should have protection for their houses, chambers, and goods (*LJ*, 6:179). When he was accused of high treason and imprisoned in the Tower in 1644, Sir John Glanville's goods and estates were protected until he should be convicted (*LJ*, 6:647). On the question of privilege for masters in Chancery who served as assistants in the House, see *LJ*, 4:565; and John Fraser Macqueen, *Appellate Jurisdiction in the House of Lords and Privy Council* (London, 1842), pp. 67–68.

10. Nicholas, 2:110.

11. McClure, 2:558.

12. *HMC, Hastings*, 4:251. In 1621 all the judges were ordered to attend the House "in their robes" on the day appointed for the sentencing of Francis Bacon, "save 1 in each Courte" (Gardiner, *Debates in the House of Lords 1621*, p. 61). The judges were unable to attend the House at the afternoon session on 10 May 1626 because they were meeting in Exchequer Chamber on a case of error out of King's Bench (Gardiner, *Debates in the House of Lords 1624 and 1626*, p. 191).

13. HLRO, Relfe, "Book of Orders 1710," p. 80.

14. *LJ*, 4:213, 270. In 1648 one judge of each bench was ordered to attend every day (*LJ*, 10:613).

15. Adair, pp. 362–63; HLRO, Relfe, "Book of Orders 1710," p. 81.

16. Foster, *1610*, 1:250.

17. See *LJ*, 3:7, 208, and 4:48; HLRO, Relfe, "Book of Orders 1710," p. 45; A. F. Pollard, "Receivers of Petitions and Clerks of Parliament," *EHR* 57 (1942): 224.

18. Starr, p. 20; Adair, p. 362; *Manuscripts of the House of Lords*, 10:4 (Standing Order no. 25); William Hakewil, *The Manner How Statutes Are Enacted in Parliament by Passing of Bills* (London, 1659), pp. 177–78; HLRO, Braye 65, fol. 4; HLRO, Relfe, "Book of Orders 1710," p. 196.

19. HLRO, Relfe, "Book of Orders 1710," p. 197; *LJ*, 2:269.

20. Adair, p. 362; Starr, p. 20.

21. H. G. Richardson and George Sayles, "The Early Statutes," *Law Quarterly Review* 50 (1934): 544–45; C. H. McIlwain, *The High Court of Parliament and Its Supremacy* (New Haven, 1910), p. 325.

22. A. F. Pollard, *The Evolution of Parliament* (London, 1926), p. 252.

23. Graves, *House of Lords Edward VI and Mary I*, pp. 132, 140.

24. See Ellesmere to Lake, 23 February 1613/4 (PRO, SP14/76/31); and Tey's letter to the Speaker (*CJ*, 1:175).

25. Scobell, p. 14.

26. Lehmberg, *Later Parliaments*, p. 259; Graves, *House of Lords Edward VI and Mary I*, p. 133.

27. Bowyer, writing about the parliament of 5 Eliz., noted that "judges were sometimes committees. Whereas since the reign of King James and in latter years before . . . by

the custom of the upper House no judge nor other whosoever, but only lords spiritual or temporal can be committees. And the judges, masters of the Chancery etc., are named and appointed only to attend the Lords Committees" (Inner Temple, Petyt 537/6, fol. 84; see also fol. 134 for similar comments on 13 Eliz.). In the parliament of 8 and 9 Eliz., judges served on committees, "a thing unusual at this day" (Bodleian Library, Carte 78, fol. 402). Bedford Office, Woburn MSS, HMC no. 198, p. 83; Adair, pp. 360–61.

28. HLRO, Braye 62; HLRO, H.L., Committee Books, Appointments, 1620/1, 1623/4, 1625/6, and 1627/8.
29. HLRO, Relfe, "Book of Orders 1710," p. 80; Scobell, p. 14.
30. *LJ*, 2:290, 392; HLRO, Relfe, "Book of Orders 1710," p. 129.
31. Gardiner, *Debates in the House of Lords 1621*, pp. 102–5. Montagu MSS at Boughton, vol. 29, 1 December 1621 (I am grateful to Esther S. Cope for drawing this passage to my attention).
32. *LJ*, 2:407, 461, 551, 561.
33. Ibid., 3:175–76.
34. Ibid., pp. 406–8.
35. Ibid., p. 336.
36. Ibid., pp. 253–55.
37. *Commons Debates 1621*, 4:253–54; Nicholas, 1:312–13; Starr, pp. 186–87.
38. Nicholas, 2:35–36.
39. *Commons Debates 1621*, 4:377.
40. *Commons Debates 1628*, 2:483.
41. HLRO, Main Papers, H.L., 23 December 1640–6 August 1641, pp. 49, 65.
42. *LJ*, 3:408, 414.
43. For a discussion of the House of Lords' judicature in error, see below, pp. 179–83. The greatest increase came during the Long Parliament. Cobbett, *State Trials*, 2:667 (6 James I); British Library, Additional 36856, fols. 17–17v.
44. HLRO, Main Papers, H.L., 4 January 1646/7.
45. Francis Hargrave, ed., *The Jurisdiction of the Lords House, or Parliament . . . by Lord Chief Justice Hale* (London, 1796), pp. 155, 158–59.
46. *LJ*, 2:82, 94, 96–97, and 10:646.
47. *LJ*, 8:407, 551.
48. See below, pp. 104–6; Relf, *Debates in the House of Lords 1621, 1625, 1628*, p. xxx; Jess Stoddart Flemion, "Slow Process, Due Process, and the High Court of Parliament," *The Historical Journal* 17 (1974): 3, 14.
49. Some petitions went to the committee for abuses in imprisonment and courts of justice and some to committees especially appointed. For the Committee for Petitions in 1621, see *LJ*, 3:141.
50. Ibid., pp. 157, 179.
51. Ibid., pp. 253, 505, 694; Gardiner, *Debates in the House of Lords 1624 and 1626*, p. 113.
52. *LJ*, 4:56, 84.
53. HLRO, Main Papers, H.L., 9 February 1640/1.
54. HLRO, Main Papers, H.L., 31 August 1641. See the cases of Andrews, Bland, *Baker* v. *Walsingham*, Beare, Claxton, and Coghill in HLRO, Main Papers, H.L., 23 December 1640–6 August 1641, pp. 2, 8, 11, 13, 20, 21, 22; *Lincoln* v. *Lindsey* in HLRO, Main Papers, H.L., 15 December 1640; and *Lane* v. *Baud* in HLRO, Braye 2, fols. 166v–167v, and in Main Papers, H.L., 18 February 1641/2.
55. See Chamberleyne's case in HLRO, Main Papers, H.L., 23 December 1640–6 August 1641, p. 24.

56. See *Walsingham* v. *Baker* in HLRO, Main Papers, H.L., 27 April 1644; *LJ*, 6:530.
57. See Ward's case in HLRO, Main Papers, H.L., 23 December 1640–6 August 1641, p. 48.
58. For Lady Purbeck's case, see ibid., pp. 61–62.
59. See the cases of the almsmen of Eastham and of John Farmer in HLRO, Main Papers, H.L., 23 December 1640–6 August 1641, pp. 31, 35–36.
60. British Library, Additional 36856, fol. 59v.
61. PRO, SP14/7/38, 48, 74, and 85; *LJ*, 2:287–88; David Harris Willson, "James I and Anglo-Scottish Unity," in *Conflict in Stuart England*, ed. William Appleton Aiken and Basil D. Henning (London, 1960), pp. 49–50; British Library, Harleian 6850, fol. 63.
62. In preparing for further conference with the Commons, the Lords decided "to signify unto them, that the Judges having delivered their Opinions, that the Name cannot be altered now without Prejudice to the State . . . therefore that Point was at an End" (*LJ*, 2:287–88).
63. Ibid., pp. 476, 478; British Library, Additional 48101, fols. 126–31.
64. "It was said by some that the Lords had already delivered their opinions by the judges, but that was contradicted by others alleging that ought not to be taken so" (Wilson to Salisbury, 4 March 1606/7, in PRO, SP14/26/70). On 2 March 1606/7 the House of Lords had sent a message to the Commons to the effect that "the Lords, conceiving the greatest Portion to be yet undebated, namely the Point of Naturalization, saving that one Branch of it hath been spoken of, wherein the Lords have no ways expressed their Opinions" (*LJ*, 2:481). This point was reiterated on 4 March and again on 27 March (*LJ*, 2:483, 495).
65. Bowyer, pp. 218–19. The earl of Bedford raised the same point in his commonplace book (Bedford Office, Woburn MSS, HMC no. 11, p. 2258).
66. Bowyer, p. 240, n. 1; PRO, SP14/26/91 (15 March 1606/7).
67. Cobbett, *State Trials*, 2:666–67.
68. McClure, 1:273.
69. *LJ*, 2:383; Wallace Notestein, *The House of Commons, 1604–1610* (New Haven, 1971), p. 204.
70. *CJ*, 1:297.
71. Bowyer, p. 121.
72. PRO, SP14/20/36 (17 April 1606).
73. PRO, SP14/24/23 (Carleton to Chamberlain, 18 December 1606). See also the notes by Coke and others on wardships and tenures, PRO, SP14/24/61, 62, 63, and 65).
74. Foster, *1610*, 1:197.
75. Ibid., pp. 55–60, 199–204, 211–15.
76. Ibid., p. 70.
77. Ibid., 2:83, 221.
78. Inner Temple, Petyt 537/8, fol. 285v.
79. *HMC, Hastings*, 4:254.
80. Ibid., pp. 256–57.
81. *Commons Debates 1621*, 7:632; Moir, pp. 121–22; *HMC, Hastings*, 4:262–63; Jones, "Ellesmere and Politics," pp. 47–48.
82. Montagu MSS at Boughton, vol. 29 (1 December 1621).
83. Relf, *Debates in the House of Lords 1621, 1625, 1628*, pp. 98–104; [Thomas Fuller], *Ephemeris Parliamentaria* (London, 1654), pp. 146–50, where it is noted that no entry of the judges' accounts was to be made in the journal.
84. Relf, *Debates in the House of Lords 1621, 1625, 1628*, p. 114.
85. Ibid., pp. 180, 185, 188, 197, 203. The earl of Bridgewater's notes concerning the

debate on the king's right to imprison without cause shown are endorsed "Advise with judges and counsell what shall be a leeggall cause" (Huntington Library, Ellesmere MS 7717).

86. *LJ*, 4:212; PRO, SP16/479/22; HLRO, Main Papers, H.L., 19 March 1640/1.

87. PRO, SP16/480/20. "Some of the Judges, in Lord Strafford's case being asked some Questions, did, with the like Caution, deliver their Opinions, and did speak with Reservations, (as the Case is put) though they, upon Hearing, did know the Case misput; which, after, troubled the Conscience of one of them" (*The History and Proceedings of the House of Lords from the Restoration in 1660 to the Present Time* [printed for Ebenezer Timberland, 8 vols., London, 1742–43], 1:65).

88. HLRO, Braye 93, fol. 171. Cf. the judges' opinion in the case of Bristol's charges against Clarendon in 1663 (below, pp. 166–67).

89. Gardiner, *Debates in the House of Lords 1624 and 1626*, pp. 186–87, 191; *HMC, Buccleuch*, 3:287, 289, 291; HLRO, Braye 93, fols. 65v–67v; Bedford Office, Woburn MSS, HMC no. 22, fol. 1. See the marginal note in a manuscript entitled "Of Judicature" (Huntington Library, Ellesmere MS 8392, fol. 75v): "K. Charles should have had his testimony used against the Earl of Bristol for treason when he was prince." The bishop of Mende wrote to Richelieu that it was Buckingham who had persuaded the king to forbid the judges to reply (PRO, 31/3[63]).

90. Quoted by Pike, p. 248, from the rolls of parliament.

91. Sir Edward Coke, *The Fourth Part of the Institutes of the Laws of England: Concerning the Jurisdiction of Courts* (London, 1681), p. 15.

92. *The Original Institution, Power, and Jurisdiction of Parliaments* (London, 1707), p. 11.

93. *CJ*, 1:166, 168. For the judges' opinion, see British Library, Additional 48101, fols. 176–178v.

94. *LJ*, 3:155, 157; Inner Temple, Petyt 538/12, fol. 176v.

95. Gardiner, *Debates in the House of Lords 1624 and 1626*, p. 162.

96. *LJ*, 3:578.

97. Relf, *Debates in the House of Lords 1621, 1625, 1628*, pp. 70n, 81; *LJ*, 3:705, 714.

98. See, for example, the case of Lord Grey (HLRO, Main Papers, H.L., 1 February 1640/1); Hargrave, *Jurisdiction*, p. 60; the title of Lord Hastings and Ruthin (HLRO, Relfe, "Book of Orders 1710," p. 764, 1640/1); the case of the earldom of Oxford in 1626 (*HMC, Buccleuch*, 3:273, 276–78; *LJ*, 3:542–43; HLRO, P.O. Paper 384).

99. HLRO, Braye 93, fols. 55–55v; de Villiers, pp. 21–22; *LJ*, 3:21.

100. Relf, *Debates in the House of Lords, 1621, 1625, 1628*, p. 17n. For later developments on this point, see W. J. Jones, *Politics and the Bench* (London, 1971), pp. 59–60.

101. Relf, *Debates in the House of Lords 1621, 1625, 1628*, p. 98.

102. PRO, SP14/76/26, 31.

103. Spedding, *Letters and Life*, 7:114.

104. Jones, *Politics and the Bench*, pp. 51, 52, 164–65; PRO, SP16/136/39.

105. Jones, *Politics and the Bench*, p. 63.

106. Foster, *1610*, 1:68 (n. 2), 2:82–83, and elsewhere.

107. Jones, *Politics and the Bench*, p. 215.

108. *LJ*, 2:551, 3:422–23.

109. Spedding, *Letters and Life*, 4:367.

110. Adair, p. 360. Masters in Chancery attended the House, but were not called to do so by writs of assistance.

111. See above, p. 13.

112. Spedding, *Letters and Life*, 4:52, 92.

113. Hakewill, p. 132; PRO, SP14/18/76.

114. *LJ*, 3:50; HLRO, Braye 65, fol. 6; Bowyer, p. 179, n. 1.

115. HLRO, Main Papers, H.L., 5 March 1609/10; PRO, SP14/8/29.

116. *LJ*, 2:404, 407. He also explained the bill of attainder in the lower House, being expressly permitted to do so because he was not then a member of that House. Others who were members and who served as counsel for the king were explicitly excluded from speaking (*CJ*, 1:296).

117. *LJ*, 2:269; Adair, p. 364.

118. Bowyer, pp. 188–89; David Harris Willson, *The Privy Councillors in the House of Commons* (Minneapolis, 1940), p. 215.

119. Adair, p. 365; Willson, *Privy Councillors*, pp. 216–17.

120. Starr, pp. 186–87; *Commons Debates 1621*, 3:72; Nicholas, 1:312–13; *LJ*, 3:746; *Commons Debates 1628*, 2:525.

121. *LJ*, 3:75, 79, 258–59, 265, 273, 283, 287, 289, 291, 317, 408.

122. *HMC, Buccleuch*, 3:403; British Library, Harleian 2325, fol. 13; *LJ*, 2:392.

123. *LJ*, 3:43, 74, 79, 85, 105, 114–15, 144, 146, 301, 318, 373, 380–81.

124. Gardiner, *Debates in the House of Lords 1624 and 1626*, p. 69.

125. *HMC, Hastings*, 4:256, 258, 262–64.

126. *LJ*, 2:336; Foster, *1610*, 2:65, 198–201, 249–50.

127. *LJ*, 3:551.

128. Ibid., pp. 735–37; Relf, *Debates in the House of Lords 1621, 1625, 1628*, pp. 87–91, 92–95.

129. *LJ*, 4:135, 481.

130. Russell, *Parliaments and English Politics*, p. 118n; Foster, *Painful Labour of Mr. Elsyng*, p. 31; *LJ*, 3:576; Gardiner, *Debates in the House of Lords 1624 and 1626*, p. 172.

131. See below, pp. 158–60; *LJ*, 3:300–301.

132. HLRO, Braye 65, fols. 6–7; *HMC, Buccleuch*, 3:285; *LJ*, 4:500–501; PRO, SP16/488/8 and 21. Also see below, p. 173.

133. Willson, *Privy Councillors*, pp. 213–17.

134. See above, p. 84.

135. *LJ*, 3:513, 4:423, 494.

6. COMMITTEES

1. George O. Sayles, *The King's Parliament of England* (New York, 1977), p. 112.

2. William Huse Dunham, *The Fane Fragment of the 1461 Lords' Journal* (New Haven, 1935), pp. 19, 74.

3. Lehmberg, *Later Parliaments*, pp. 69, 258–60. For Edward VI, see HLRO, Relfe, "Book of Orders 1710," p. 109; Graves, *House of Lords Edward VI and Mary I*, pp. 133–35, 160–63.

4. *Manuscripts of the House of Lords*, 10:3 (Standing Order no. 22).

5. Scobell, p. 19.

6. *LJ*, 1:105.

7. Snow, *John Hooker*, pp. 15–17, 34–35, 157. Cf. Graves, *House of Lords Ed-*

ward VI and Mary I, p. 162.

8. Folger Shakespeare Library, MS V.b. 303, p. 146.

9. D'Ewes, *Journals of All the Parliaments*, p. 18; Elsyng, "Method of Passing Bills," pp. 114–15. Cf. "Moderne Forme of the Parliaments," p. 298.

10. Elsyng, "Method of Passing Bills," p. 114; *LJ*, 1:683, 684, and 2:200, 201, 295.

11. Foster, *1610*, 1:xxv; HLRO, Braye 61, fols. 112, 118v, 131v, 134v. His notes for the early months of 1621 and Elsyng's notes for this parliament and others indicate that the number to be chosen from each bench was predetermined (Inner Temple, Petyt 538/7, fols. 23, 24v, 25, 30v, 35v, 200v, 203, 205v, 212, 214v, 215; British Library, Additional 40085, fols. 7, 80v, 150; Additional 40086, fols. 27, 29, 47v, 50; Additional 40087, fols. 20, 22, 39v, 46, 56, 62v; Additional 40088, fols. 7v, 10; Additional 40089, fol. 57; and Additional 40090, fols. 5v, 87).

12.   Committees: 1610 to 15 February 1641/2

	Two Benches Equal	First Two Benches Equal with Double the Number of Barons
1610	43/66	22/66
1614	4/8	2/8
1621	51/71	46/71
1624	91/103	82/103
1625	20/25	13/25
1626	26/52	19/52
1628/9	50/74	2/74
1640	2/9	0/9
1640–42	72/207	0/207

In computing these figures, viscounts have been counted with the earls, as was the practice of the clerk of the parliaments (HLRO, Manuscript Lords Journal, vol. 15, p. 79, 1640). The viscounts sat "on the first form of the clerks woolsacks" (Elsyng, *Manner of Holding Parliaments*, p. 111). Reporters chosen for conferences and additions to committees have not been included in the count of committees. After the bishops left the House in 1642, the Lords continued to balance the two remaining benches on a number of committees. Of 146 committees appointed between 16 February 1641/2 and 25 March 1643, the benches were equal in 31.

13. HLRO, Braye 20, 24 August 1641.

14. For deletions, see Inner Temple, Petyt 538/7, fol. 215v, 1621; HLRO, Braye 16, 23 April 1640, and Braye 17, 10 December 1640. For excuses of lords who declined to serve, see Inner Temple, Petyt 538/7, fols. 205 and 231, 1621.

15. In the Manuscript Lords Journal for 26 November 1640, Browne, the clerk of the parliaments, has listed the names of a committee in three columns and has totaled the number in each (HLRO, Manuscript Lords Journal, vol. 15, p. 79). In December 1640 the committee to take preliminary examinations in Strafford's case provides an interesting example of nomination by benches: "After the Earls were nominated, they named Bishops, but that was cried out against" (*HMC, Buccleuch* 3:396).

16. Bodleian Library, Rawlinson A 106, 29 May 1628; HLRO, Minute Books nos. 10 and 12; HLRO, Braye 16, 17, 19, 20, 22; HLRO, Manuscript Lords Journal, vols. 23 and 44.

17. HLRO, Braye 93, fols. 7v–8.

18. Inner Temple, Petyt 538/7, fols. 203, 205, 210, 223v.

19. Ibid., fols. 121, 201v; HLRO, Minute Book no. 5, 23 April 1628.

20. *HMC, Buccleuch*, 3:222, 230.

21. Elsyng, "Method of Passing Bills," p. 114.

22. Ibid.

23. HLRO, Committee for Privileges, Minute Book no. 2, November 1664–November 1668, p. 160.

24. See table in n. 12 above.

25. Stoddart, pp. 49–50. Elsyng did some research for a committee to examine precedents concerning the election of committees (HLRO, Main Papers, H.L., [1628]). The same question was raised in 1679/80 because the earls and barons had greatly increased while the number of bishops remained the same. It was recommended that the House choose double the number of earls and barons as bishops (*LJ*, 13:582).

26. See table in n. 12 above.

27. *LJ*, 4:546.

28. See below, p. 169.

29. *LJ*, 4:168, 173, 182, 198.

30. Ibid., p. 235.

31. British Library, Harleian 6424, fol. 62v; *LJ*, 4:245, 250, 287, 306, 311, 314, 321, 355, 419.

32. *LJ*, 4:258, 355, 365, 371, 399, 437.

33. Ibid., pp. 450, 451, 456.

34. Ibid., pp. 416, 456.

35. Ibid., pp. 321, 329, 331, 333, 334, 337, 463, 482.

36. Ibid., pp. 311, 312, 313, 322, 329, 336, 343, 355, 366, 377, 379, 460, 515, 518.

37. Ibid., pp. 314, 351, 388, 411.

38. Ibid., pp. 306, 309, 315, 406, 417, 474, 535.

39. HLRO, Minute Books nos. 10 and 12 passim.

40. *LJ*, 2:371, 409.

41. Ibid., p. 611.

42. de Villiers, pp. 16–17.

43. Relf, *Debates in the House of Lords 1621, 1625, 1628*, pp. 60, 169, 228; Gardiner, *Debates in the House of Lords 1624 and 1626*, p. 101; *LJ*, 3:165, 172, 174, 185, 630.

44. *LJ*, 4:84.

45. HLRO, Main Papers, H.L., 5 March 1643/4; see also 10 December 1640.

46. *LJ*, 2:323; Elsyng, "Method of Passing Bills," p. 115. The order was reiterated a number of times: HLRO, Relfe, "Book of Orders 1710," pp. 111–13; HLRO, Braye 93, fol. 56. In 1649 there is a special note in the margin of the Lords journal: "Memorand. that the Earls of Sarum and Nottingham, and the L. Mountagu, were named of this Committee, though they were absent" (*LJ*, 10:649). "Those that are absent are to be left out of the committee till they come" (HLRO, Minute Book no. 2, 23 February 1623/4, fol. 9v).

47. HLRO, Main Papers, H.L., 12 May 1607.

48. Stoddart, pp. 108–10, 136–38, 279–80.

49. Crummett, pp. 263–64, 267.

50. Ibid., p. 267.

51. Ibid., pp. 267–73. Bishop Nicolson in 1705 regarded it as an honor to be named early; see his diary for 15 December (through the courtesy of Geoffrey Holmes and Clyve Jones, I have used their transcript).

52. Elsyng, "Method of Passing Bills," p. 115. See HLRO, Braye 93, fol. 84v, 29 June 1641, which indicates that a lord who spoke against the body of a bill at the second

reading should not be of the committee.

53. Elsyng, "Method of Passing Bills," p. 115.

54. "Moderne Forme of the Parliaments," p. 295; *LJ*, 2:372, 399, 400.

55. Elsyng, "Method of Passing Bills," p. 115.

56. D'Ewes, *Journals of All the Parliaments*, pp. 607, 610; but see Neale, *1584–1601*, p. 333.

57. *LJ*, 2:269.

58. Ibid., pp. 389, 461, 480.

59. Huntington Library, Ellesmere MS 34/A/2; Yale University Library, Osborn Collection, Braye 52/5, 1640. The fifth earl of Bedford paid the same sum to the clerk of the lower House for a committee sheet in 1641 (Bedford Office, Papers of the fifth Earl of Bedford, Account Book 1641–42, ex Bedford County Record Office 756).

60. HLRO, Main Papers, H.L., Addenda 1556–1621, 7 April 1607; HLRO, Main Papers, H.L., Supplementary 1604–10, 4 June 1604, 12 February 1605/6, 26 February 1605/6, 26 May 1606 (several drafts of a proviso and a drawing), 14 February 1606/7, 21 March 1606/7, 1 June 1607, 22 March 1609/10, 19 May 1610; HLRO, Main Papers, H.L., 30 May, 21 June, 18 October, and 10 November 1610; 23 April, 14 November, and 10 December 1640; 6 February and 4 March 1640/1; 22 April, 5 August, and 26 August 1641; HLRO, Braye 10; Foster, *Painful Labour of Mr. Elsyng*, pp. 16–17 and nn. 78, 79; PRO, SP14/55/35 (several sheets copied for Salisbury), SP14/160/9 (1624), and SP16/472/27.

61. Foster, *Painful Labour of Mr. Elsyng*, p. 17; HLRO, Main Papers, H.L., Supplementary 1604–10, 22 March 1609/10; Yale University Library, Osborn Collection, Braye 95; HLRO, Braye 62; HLRO, Committee Books, Appointments, 1621–28.

62. *LJ*, 3:78, 106, 262, 264, 295, 549, 672, 771.

63. D'Ewes spoke of the "first or chief" of the committee (D'Ewes, *Journals of All the Parliaments*, p. 607). For the use of the term "first committee" in Elizabethan and Stuart times, see *LJ*, 2:210, 385, and 3:15, 114; Foster, *1610*, 1:177; HLRO, Braye 65, fol. 3. In the same way, the senior alderman of the Court of Aldermen in London was its leader or chairman (Frank Freeman Foster, *The Politics of Stability, A Portrait of the Rulers in Elizabethan London* [London, 1977], p. 79). For the terms "second" and "third" as applied to other members of committees, see *LJ*, 2:392; D'Ewes, *Journals of All the Parliaments*, p. 610.

64. *LJ*, 2:385, 392. In 1611 the lord chancellor wrote to the late Archbishop Bancroft's nephew, asking for the return of bills that the archbishop had had as "the first of the committees to whome the Bills weare referred." Ellesmere observed that Bancroft did not, "according to the accustomed and usuall order of the higher House of Parliament in like case, returne the said Bills into the House," nor give them to the clerk (HLRO, Main Papers, H.L., 9 October 1611).

65. *LJ*, 3:74.

66. HLRO, Committee for Privileges, Minute Book no. 1.

67. Gardiner, *Debates in the House of Lords 1621*, p. 53. In the margin is the word "Ordered"; but there is no entry in the Lords journal.

68. Elsyng, "Method of Passing Bills," p. 115; *LJ*, 3:176.

69. *LJ*, 3:455, 499.

70. Ibid., pp. 691, 694, 696, and 4:103, 107, 109, 115 and elsewhere; HLRO, Main Papers, H.L., 10 December 1640, 4 January 1646/7; HLRO, Manuscript Lords Journal, vol. 39 (18 November 1646). Under the Protectorate, all committees were to have a quorum of five unless otherwise provided (*Manuscripts of the House of Lords*, 4:529).

71. PRO, SP14/58/13; HLRO, Main Papers, H.L., Supplementary 1604–10, 12 February 1605/6; HLRO, Main Papers, H.L., 29 February 1643/4, 30 March 1644; *HMC, Buccleuch*, 3:237. For references to the "outward chamber," see British Library, Harleian 767 (26 March, 19 April, and 28 April 1604). In January 1640/1 the cloth of estate in the committee chamber was taken down and the table set lengthwise (*HMC, Buccleuch*, 3:404).

72. HLRO, Relfe, "Book of Orders 1710," p. 80. The accounts of the quarrel between Maltravers and Pembroke mention a table (see above, p. 26). In 1640 the House ordered "that the Order of the House may be kept, that none but Earls and the Lords Committees do sit at the Table in the Painted Chamber at a Conference" (*LJ*, 4:111). For furniture in rooms used by the lords, see Foster, "Staging a Parliament," pp. 132–33.

73. *LJ*, 2:413; *Manuscripts of the House of Lords*, 10:5 (Standing Order no. 28).

74. *Manuscripts of the House of Lords*, 10:3–4 (Standing Order no. 23). For evidence of the relaxation of these rules in case of infirmity and during the Short Parliament, see above, p. 71.

75. See above, p. 66. Among the costs for a bill for Westminster in 1585 had been 32s. for one "perisse" and wafers (Neale, *Elizabethan House of Commons*, p. 390).

76. Foster, *1610*, 1:146; Scobell, p. 19.

77. Foster, *1610*, 1:149.

78. *Manuscripts of the House of Lords*, 10:3 (Standing Order no. 23); Scobell, p. 19. See also the remark in 1610 that a committee was a mean between dealing suddenly and letting a bill slip (Foster, *1610*, 1:152).

79. Elsyng, "Method of Passing Bills," p. 116.

80. Foster, *Painful Labour of Mr. Elsyng*, p. 17, n. 79.

81. The Committee for Petitions in 1626, the committee for abuses in imprisonment and courts of justice in 1640 and 1641 (Foster, *Painful Labour of Mr. Elsyng*, p. 19; HLRO, Main Papers, H.L., 3 June 1641).

82. *LJ*, 3:47, 286; Gardiner, *Debates in the House of Lords 1624 and 1626*, p. 50. On the question of a committee examining on oath, note the reference in British Library, Stowe 375, fol. 14, to referees appointed by the House on 19 December 1585, to whom it gave the power to examine on oath. Whether they actually administered the oath is not entirely clear (*LJ*, 2:76).

83. Elsyng, "Method of Passing Bills," p. 116; *LJ*, 3:270.

84. "Committees may adjourn themselves *de die in die* as they please, but if they meet not at the time to which they are adjourned they are then *sine die*, and cannot meet again till the House appoint the time," 19 March 1623/4 (HLRO, Relfe, "Book of Orders 1710," p. 113). *LJ*, 2:400.

85. HLRO, Main Papers, H.L., 31 March 1628, 8 June 1641; *LJ*, 3:674.

86. *LJ*, 3:676; see above, p. 26.

87. Elsyng, "Method of Passing Bills," p. 116; HLRO, Braye 65, fol. 3; de Villiers, p. 11. "The first Person named to be of a Committee, made Reports from that Committee" (Scobell, p. 21).

88. *LJ*, 2:462, 637, 650, 653, and 3:15, 29, 36, 38, 708, 732, 782, 845, 868.

89. Ibid., 2:598, 632, 642, 645.

90. Ibid., 3:21, 41, 449, 502, 536, 553, 558, 564.

91. Ibid., pp. 408, 414.

92. Ibid., 3:521, 525, and 7:34.

93. Elsyng, "Method of Passing Bills," p. 116; *HMC, Buccleuch*, 3:222.

94. HLRO, Braye 93, fol. 14. On the 1624 case, see Gardiner, *Debates in the House of Lords 1624 and 1626*, pp. 93–94.

95. HLRO, Braye 93, fols. 49v–50.

96. Ibid., fol. 6v; *LJ*, 3:151.

97. *LJ*, 3:66, 282; *CJ*, 1:750.

98. HLRO, Main Papers, H.L., 21 September, 5 October 1641; *LJ*, 4:397.

99. *LJ*, 3:151; HLRO, Braye 93, fols. 6v–7.

100. *LJ*, 3:422, 878. In 1626 the subcommittee for the journal was not permitted to continue its work after the dissolution (Gardiner, *Debates in the House of Lords 1624 and 1626*, p. 233).

101. Maurice F. Bond, unpublished article on the Committee for Petitions in the Short Parliament.

102. *Manuscripts of the House of Lords*, 10:2 (Standing Order no. 9). In July 1641 the House used the term "standing committee" in an unusual way to refer to a committee "to consider of some fit and due Maintenance to be settled upon the Puny Judges" (*LJ*, 4:322). This seems to be a departure from its usual terminology.

103. "Moderne Forme of the Parliaments," p. 294; HLRO, Braye 65, p. 1.

104. *LJ*, 3:10, 13.

105. *Manuscripts of the House of Lords*, 10:2 (Standing Order no. 9).

106. *LJ*, 3:10, 165, 215, 442, 499, 691, and 4:6, 55, 83. See HLRO, Braye 65, pp. 1–2; Cope, *Proceedings of the Short Parliament*, pp. 97–98.

107. *LJ*, 3:552; HLRO, Main Papers, H.L., 31 December 1640, 1 July 1644. It is interesting that this term was used in the upper House for a large select committee, usually to differentiate it from a subcommittee, but at the same time in the lower House it was becoming synonymous with the term "committee of the whole." In the minute book for 23 February 1623/24, the assistant clerk refers to the "grand committee for privileges" and to the lords subcommittees (HLRO, Minute Book no. 2, fol. 9v).

108. Cope, *Proceedings of the Short Parliament*, p. 99. For an analysis of the membership of the Committee for Privileges, see Stoddart, pp. 46–48.

109. *LJ*, 3:17. The list in the printed journal (*LJ*, 3:17) differs from that in the committee book, which includes bishops (HLRO, Committee Books, Appointments, 1620/1, fol. 21).

110. *LJ*, 3:73.

111. Inner Temple, Petyt 538/7, fol. 201v; *LJ*, 3:73; HLRO, Committee Books, Appointments, 1620/1, fol. 20.

112. British Library, Additional 40087, fol. 17v; HLRO, Minute Book no. 2, fol. 9v. For the necessary alterations in the 1621 lists for both committee and subcommittee and for the final list, see HLRO, Committee Books, Appointments, 1620/1, fols. 20, 21; ibid., Appointments, 23 February 1623/4–22 March 1623/4, fols. 1–1v.

113. HLRO, Minute Book no. 4, 17 May–12 August 1625, fols. 16, 18v.

114. British Library, Additional 40089, fol. 19; HLRO, Committee Books, Appointments, 11 February 1625/6–24 May 1626, pp. 4, 5.

115. HLRO, Minute Book no. 5, 17 March 1627/8–20 October 1628, fols. 6–8; Inner Temple, Petyt 538/7, fols. 13v, 16v.

116. Cope, *Proceedings of the Short Parliament*, p. 59; HLRO, Braye 16, fols. 9–9v, and Braye 17, fols. 7v–8.

117. In 1625 for the subcommittee, in 1626 for the grand committee (*LJ*, 3:445, 499).

118. HLRO, Committee Books, Appointments, 1620/1, 1623/4, and 1625/6; HLRO, Minute Book no. 5, fol. 8; Inner Temple, Petyt 538/7, fol. 16v; *LJ*, 4:55–56, 84.

119. *LJ*, 3:17 and 4:71.
120. HLRO, Main Papers, H.L., 31 December 1640.
121. See below, chapter 8.
122. *LJ*, 3:10; see also HLRO, Main Papers, H.L., 7 December 1640, when the matter was again under discussion.
123. *LJ*, 3:174; HLRO, Main Papers, H.L., 27 May and 9 June 1641.
124. *LJ*, 3:782; *Manuscripts of the House of Lords*, 10:10 (Standing Order no. 54).
125. HLRO, Main Papers, H.L., 10 June 1648; *LJ*, 10:317.
126. *LJ*, 3:526–27, 537.
127. Ibid., pp. 701–2, 774.
128. HLRO, Main Papers, H.L., 30 July 1641; *LJ*, 4:353.
129. HLRO, Braye 2, fols. 177–178v, 181v–182; *LJ*, 3:443, 446, 862, and 4:253.
130. *Manuscripts of the House of Lords*, 10:1–11 (Standing Orders passim).
131. *LJ*, 3:114, 184, 189; HLRO, Braye 65, fols. 10–11.
132. *Manuscripts of the House of Lords*, 10:1–2 (Standing Orders nos. 4, 5, 6).
133. HLRO, Main Papers, H.L., 18 November 1645.
134. *LJ*, 4:73, 77, and 7:319. For the fee list, 29 April 1640, see below, p. 248, n. 80.
135. *LJ*, 3:443.
136. Bodleian Library, Carte 78, fols. 450–451v, 499–500. See the precedents for "privileges for noblemen's servants in time of a parliament as well as for themselves" (ibid., fol. 497).
137. Foster, *Painful Labour of Mr. Elsyng*, pp. 9 and n. 19, 35–46; Foster, *1610*, 1:xxii. See Elsyng's treatises: "Moderne Forme of the Parliaments" and "The Method of Passing Bills in Parliament." John Browne or one of his assistants made a subject index for the Book of Orders and Ordinances so that the House might know what had been done and, "as occasion serves, make use of such or such a precedent, wch comes nearest their purpose, wch this way doth best produce" (HLRO, Book of Orders and Ordinances, 6 November 1642–3 November 1643); *HMC, Buccleuch*, 3:244.
138. *LJ*, 3:782. The question recurred in several parliaments. See Relf, *Debates in the House of Lords 1621, 1625, 1628*, pp. 16–17; HLRO, Main Papers, H.L., 16 November, 30 November, and 7 December 1640; *LJ*, 3:41–42 and 4:120; PRO, SP16/10/35. For the comments of the fourth earl of Bedford, see Bedford Office, Woburn MSS, HMC no. 22, Commonplace Book, fol. 40 (upside down from the back).
139. HLRO, Main Papers, H.L., 4 May, 16 November, 30 November, and 7 December 1640.
140. Among the papers of the committee was a certificate from the records of the prerogative court of Canterbury, as early as 1512, concerning peers and their wives and widows, who wished to act as executors and took an oath; see HLRO, Main Papers, H.L., 7 December 1640; *Manuscripts of the House of Lords*, 10:10 (Standing Order no. 53); *LJ*, 4:120.
141. HLRO, Main Papers, H.L., 5 May 1628.
142. HLRO, Committee for Privileges, Minute Book no. 1, p. 36.
143. Ibid., p. 66.
144. Ibid., p. 59.
145. Ibid., pp. 21–22. For 1667 there is an illustration of a proposed plan for committee seating in the Painted Chamber with a "bar" at each end of the table (ibid., Minute Book no. 2, between pp. 31 and 32).
146. Ibid., Minute Book no. 1, p. 71.

147. Ibid., p. 70.
148. Ibid., pp. 56, 82.
149. See above, p. 94; HLRO, Committee for Privileges, Minute Book no. 2, pp. 32, 81; ibid., Minute Book no. 3, p. 26.
150. Ibid., Minute Book no. 1, pp. 76–79.
151. Ibid., pp. 15, 57–58. The committee relied on the authority of the House to summon witnesses.
152. Ibid., Minute Book no. 2, p. 32.
153. HLRO, Committee Books, Appointments, 1620/1, fol. 31; LJ, 3:141.
154. British Library, Additional 40087, fol. 65. For changes required to bring the 1621 list up to date, see HLRO, Committee Books, Appointments, 1620/1, fol. 31; LJ, 3:253. The lists in the committee books vary from those in the journal. Frances Relf concluded that the committee was "not yet a regular standing committee" because it was not selected in the early days of the parliament, a questionable distinction for this period (Relf, *Debates in the House of Lords 1621, 1625, 1628*, pp. xxiii–xxv).
155. Elsyng lists only fifteen members in his scribbled book, but twenty-four in the journal. Other names were added during the session. See British Library, Additional 40089, fol. 20; HLRO, Committee Books, Appointments, 11 February 1625/6–24 May 1626, p. 3; LJ, 3:500, 540, 630.
156. HLRO, Minute Book no. 5, fol. 8; HLRO, Committee Books, Appointments, 20 March 1627/8–23 June 1628, fol. 2v; Inner Temple, Petyt 538/7, fol. 16v; LJ, 3:694; Relf, *Debates in the House of Lords 1621, 1625, 1628*, p. xxvii.
157. LJ, 4:56; Cope, *Proceedings of the Short Parliament*, pp. 59–60; Bond, unpublished article. For the original committee sheet, see HLRO, Main Papers, H.L., 16 April 1640. The bishops and Lord Clifford have all been crossed off.
158. LJ, 4:84. For later additions, see pp. 138, 272. For committee sheets, see PRO, SP16/471/27 and SP16/539/26, one of which is annotated and dated 25 November 1640. In his notes on procedure, John Browne indicated that the Committee for Petitions was appointed on the "third day of Parliament" (HLRO, Braye 65, fol. 2). During the Protectorate, January 1657/8, the Committee for Petitions was chosen on the third day. "These Lords or any five or more of them to have the same powers that formerly Committees for Petitions had" (*Manuscripts of the House of Lords*, 4:509, 527).
159. LJ, 3:141, 174, 296, 505, 540, and 4:56; Cope, *Proceedings of the Short Parliament*, pp. 59–60.
160. LJ, 4:176, 326. Bishop Warner, reporting this order in March 1640/1, added "that nothing be concluded at the Committee but what is materially included in the Petition" (British Library, Harleian 6424, fols. 43v–44).
161. 10 February 1640/1. The order in May 1641 referred to the "great Concourse of Petitioners daily resorting hither" and provided that only public petitions or those concerning privileges of the House or privileges of peers should be received. In June 1641 a subcommittee was to meet daily at 7:00 A.M., and petitions of most public concern were to be heard first (LJ, 4:158, 260, 266, 271, 302, 325, 455, 524, 649, 724; 5:45; and 6:492, 700). By December 1644, the House assigned two of the judges to sort petitions (ibid., 7:92).
162. It was composed of fourteen from the earls' bench, fourteen from the barons' bench, and four bishops (LJ, 4:98) and included many of the members of the Committee for Petitions. The committee for abuses in imprisonment and courts of justice had its own clerk, "Mr. Smyth," and the two committees proceeded in the same way (HLRO, Main Papers, H.L., 3 June 1641, 8 February 1640/1). For reports from the

committee for courts of justice, see *LJ*, 4:100-101, 106, 113-14, 117, 119, 136-37, 139, 152, 156-57, 170-71, 180. Sometimes the consideration of a petition moved from one committee to the other. See Walker's petition, which was initially before the Committee for Petitions, but was reported from the committee for courts of justice (HLRO, Main Papers, H.L., 23 December 1640-6 August 1641, p. 50; *LJ*, 4:183).

163. *LJ*, 4:188. Thereafter Mr. Smith worked for the Committee for Petitions (HLRO, Main Papers, H.L., [1641], Morris account).

164. *LJ*, 3:179, 500; Gardiner, *Debates in the House of Lords 1624 and 1626*, p. 113.

165. Cope, *Proceedings of the Short Parliament*, p. 60; *LJ*, 4:84.

166. *LJ*, 3:253, 270, 296, 500, 630, 694, and 4:56, 84.

167. Foster, *Painful Labour of Mr. Elsyng*, pp. 18-20; Huntington Library, Ellesmere MS 7950.

168. Foster, *Painful Labour of Mr. Elsyng*, p. 19; HLRO, Main Papers, H.L., 17 March 1627/8.

169. Bond, unpublished article; HLRO, Braye 2, fols. 160-167v. For the numbers and letters on petitions for filing purposes, see the petitions themselves: HLRO, Main Papers, H.L., April, November, and December 1640; May, June, and July 1641 passim. Several petitions are endorsed "out of the Redd Bagg" (HLRO, Main Papers, H.L., 6 July 1641 and 9 September 1641, both of which are related to Strafford's trial). For minute books of the committee, see HLRO, Main Papers, H.L., 17 March 1627/8-23 June 1628, 23 December 1640-6 August 1641.

170. For an example of an endorsement, see HLRO, Main Papers, H.L., 21 December 1640; HLRO, Books of Orders and Judgment, B 9-B 17 (volumes B 10 and B 12 are fair copies, the rest are rough drafts). Henry Morris in 1641 submitted a bill to Mr. Smith for copying orders, noting "md. there is no allowance to him for the aforesaid writings" (HLRO, Main Papers, H.L., [1641]).

171. *LJ*, 3:783-84, 811, 837, and 4:131, 132, 139, 140, 141, 144, 247. In 1621 a petition was referred to the committee without being read in the House, because it was too long (ibid., 3:151).

172. Brookes's petition was dismissed in 1641 by the Committee for Petitions because it was pending in the House of Commons (HLRO, Main Papers, H.L., 23 December 1640-6 August 1641, p. 11). Petitions were drawn by scriveners (HLRO, Main Papers, H.L., 24 January 1642/3).

173. HLRO, Main Papers, H.L., 23 December 1640-6 August 1641, Roth's petition, pp. 59, 61.

174. HLRO, Main Papers, H.L., 21 January 1640/1, William Hull to the House and also to Lord Saye and Sele to ask the clerk of the parliaments to read his petition in the House. For other sponsors, see HLRO, Main Papers, H.L., 19 May, 3 June, 17 June, 18 June, and 6 August 1641; *LJ*, 4:165. On 20 August 1641, Samuel Hopkins sent a second petition to the earl of Essex stating that, "having spent much time to his great charges, and harvest now being at hand, he doth earnestly with all humility intreat and beg that his petition in Mr. Smith's custody now at last may be read" (HLRO, Main Papers, H.L., 20 August 1641).

175. *LJ*, 4:277.

176. Ibid., p. 208.

177. Ibid., 3:837.

178. HLRO, Main Papers, H.L., 6 March 1640/1, Roger Calcott.

179. Foster, *Painful Labour of Mr. Elsyng*, p. 19. HLRO, Main Papers, H.L., 25 May 1641: "Good Mr. Smith remember to present the petition of Magdalen Weale . . .

and I will be thankful to you." This note is on the back of a list of witnesses for Atkins. The petition in question was read in the committee on 21 June 1641 (HLRO, Main Papers, H.L., 21 June 1641).

180. *LJ*, 3:539, 540, 675. Counsel was assigned for those who pleaded *in forma pauperis* (HLRO, Main Papers, H.L., 5 February 1628/9).

181. Cope, *Proceedings of the Short Parliament*, p. 83; HLRO, Main Papers, H.L., 23 December 1640–6 August 1641, pp. 55, 67–68.

182. HLRO, Main Papers, H.L., 23 December 1640–6 August 1641, p. 35.

183. *LJ*, 3:509, 4:187; HLRO, Main Papers, H.L., 24 December 1640; HLRO, Braye 93, fol. 138v.

184. *LJ*, 3:509, 518, 539, 673, and elsewhere. In 1641 the House ordered that masters in Chancery should assist the clerk, but revoked this order the following day (ibid., 4:152–53).

185. British Library, Stowe 375, fol. 73, 14 December 1621; *LJ*, 3:195, 4:342.

186. HLRO, Main Papers, H.L., 16 April 1641.

187. HLRO, Main Papers, H.L., 22 June 1641; *LJ*, 4:262.

188. British Library, Harleian 2325, fol. 24. Andrews was to have *habeas corpus* without fee for his witnesses (HLRO, Main Papers, H.L., 23 December 1640–6 August 1641, pp. 2–3).

189. *LJ*, 4:266; Huntington Library, Ellesmere MSS 7937 and 7938; Foster, *Painful Labour of Mr. Elsyng*, p. 19; HLRO, Main Papers, H.L., 24 December 1640.

190. *LJ*, 4:670; HLRO, Main Papers, H.L., 23 December 1640–6 August 1641, pp. 2, 7, 9. See also HLRO, Main Papers, H.L., 6 March 1640/1 and 16 July 1641, *Lindsey v. Norton*, for depositions in Star Chamber. Macqueen points out that there was only gradual adoption of the principle that the evidence presented in an appeal should be the same as that on which the case had been decided earlier. In the 1640s use of the same evidence was allowed chiefly as a favor because the plaintiff was poor or the like (Macqueen, pp. 171–74).

191. *LJ*, 3:296; HLRO, Main Papers, H.L., 8 June 1641.

192. HLRO, Main Papers, H.L., 17 March 1627/8–23 June 1628, 23 December 1640–6 August 1641.

193. In 1672 and 1678 the House confirmed that proceedings on petitions of appeal and writs of error continued from parliament to parliament (Macqueen, pp. 32–33; *LJ*, 13:457, 463, 466).

194. *LJ*, 3:157–58; Relf, *Debates in the House of Lords 1621, 1625, 1628*, p. xxi; Allen Horstman, "A New *Curia Regis*, The Judicature of the House of Lords in the 1620s," *The Historical Journal* 25, no. 2 (1982): 413.

195. *LJ*, 3:151.

196. Huntington Library, Ellesmere MS 6473; *LJ*, 3:157; Hargrave, *Jurisdiction*, p. xxix.

197. Hargrave, *Jurisdiction*, p. xxvii; Relf, *Debates in the House of Lords 1621, 1625, 1628*, p. xxii; *LJ*, 3:189, 192.

198. Matthew's case (Hargrave, *Jurisdiction*, pp. xxxviii–xl; *LJ*, 3:417, 420–21). On 10 March 1625 it was reported that the king had refused to issue a commission (Macqueen, pp. 74–76).

199. Relf, *Debates in the House of Lords 1621, 1625, 1628*, pp. xxv–xxx; Hargrave, *Jurisdiction*, p. liii.

200. The committee considered eighteen petitions (Bond, unpublished article).

201. Hargrave, *Jurisdiction*, p. 194.

202. HLRO, Main Papers, H.L., 1640.

203. HLRO, Main Papers, H.L., 23 December 1640–6 August 1641, p. 69; HLRO, Main

Papers, H.L., [1641], Sir Arthur Ingram.

204. HLRO, Main Papers, H.L., 20 September 1642, 27 May 1643.

205. HLRO, Main Papers, H.L., 12 December 1640.

206. J. S. Cockburn, A History of English Assizes, 1558–1714 (Cambridge, 1972), pp. 136–37, 150, 241–45.

207. HLRO, Main Papers, H.L., 23 December 1640–6 August 1641, pp. 19, 46.

208. See Hargrave, Jurisdiction, pp. 189–90.

209. The petitions of Lord Brooke (HLRO, Main Papers, H.L., 8 December 1640) and of Elizabeth Bosse (ibid., 15 December 1640).

210. The petition of Christopher Browne (HLRO, Main Papers, H.L., 23 December 1640–6 August 1641, p. 7).

211. The petitions of John Godfrey (HLRO, Main Papers, H.L., 23 December 1640–6 August 1641, p. 76); and of Sir Thomas Westropp and William Pargiter (HLRO, Main Papers, H.L., 21 and 24 December 1640).

212. The petitions of Gerard Wright (HLRO, Main Papers, H.L., 21 December 1640); and of Nicholas Bloxam (ibid., 10 March 1640/1; LJ, 4:181–82).

213. The petition of Charles and Mary Stanford (HLRO, Main Papers, H.L., 23 December 1640–6 August 1641, pp. 55–56).

214. The petitions of Thomas Crompton on behalf of Dame Mary Powell (HLRO, Main Papers, H.L., 10 July 1641); of Henry Lyne and Robert Partridge (ibid., 2 and 7 July 1641); and of Abraham Chamberleyne (ibid., 23 December 1640–6 August 1641, p. 24).

215. The petitions of Thomas Boughton and Edward Clarke (HLRO, Main Papers, H.L., 23 December 1640–6 August 1641, p. 12); and of Archibald Mackeller (HLRO, Braye 2, fol. 166).

216. The petition of Robert Cooke and others (HLRO, Main Papers, H.L., 9 February 1640/1; LJ, 4:156, 217, 272, 300).

217. The petition of Theophilus, earl of Lincoln (HLRO, Main Papers, H.L., 19 November 1640).

218. The petition of Mathewe Cooper (ibid., [1640]).

219. The petitions of Freeman, Yelverton, and Brooke (ibid., 1 December 1640; LJ, 4:101); of Richard Gittaway (HLRO, Main Papers, H.L., 19 December 1640); and of the inhabitants of Lincolnshire and the earl of Lindsey against Sir Walter Norton, late sheriff of the county (LJ, 4:224, 275, 297; HLRO, Main Papers, H.L., 18 June and 16 July 1641).

220. HLRO, Main Papers, H.L., 24 November 1640 and elsewhere.

221. The petition of Anthony Danvers (HLRO, Main Papers, H.L., 24 December 1640; LJ, 4:140, 307).

222. Foster, Painful Labour of Mr. Elsyng, p. 19.

223. LJ, 4:155.

224. HLRO, Braye 2, fols. 162v, 163v, 166, 166v, 167–167v (there are two folios numbered 167).

225. HLRO, Braye 2, fol. 160, 162, 163, 164, 164v, 166.

226. HLRO, Main Papers, H.L., 23 December 1640–6 August 1641, pp. 6–7, 13.

227. Ibid., pp. 15–17; HLRO, Main Papers, H.L., 8 February 1640/1.

228. HLRO, Main Papers, H.L., 23 December 1640–6 August 1641, pp. 34, 37–39, 54, 55, 59, 61–62, 66.

229. HLRO, Main Papers, H.L., 23 December 1640–6 August 1641, pp. 81–82.

230. Ibid., pp. 55–56, 75. On the question of the admiralty, see George F. Steckley, "Merchants and the Admiralty Courts during the English Revolution," American Journal

of Legal History 22 (1978): 137–75.

231. LJ, 3:303; Relf, Debates in the House of Lords 1621, 1625, 1628, p. xxiv.

232. LJ, 4:208.

233. HLRO, Main Papers, H.L., 23 December 1640–6 August 1641, pp. 1, 29, 30, 47–48, 58, 80–81.

234. HLRO, Braye 2, fols. 163v–165.

235. LJ, 3:296, 303, 413, 415, 511, 532, 541, 546, 680.

236. Ibid., p. 532.

237. Ibid., pp. 700, 736, 812, 831, 862, 863, 864. On the question of reporters, see above, p. 95.

238. LJ, 4:78. Meetings of the committee can be deduced from endorsements on the original petitions (Bond, unpublished article).

239. LJ, 4:110, 135, 140, 175, 178, 181–82.

240. Ibid., 3:862.

241. Ibid., p. 680.

242. For example, the committee for abuses in imprisonment and courts of justice, the Committee for Privileges, and the Committee for Trade (ibid., 4:127).

243. Ibid., 7:92.

244. Ibid., 6:42, 223. The House heard counsel on both sides in the case of Walsingham v. Baker. Walsingham's complaint was that a decree in Exchequer concerning the manor of Hunton deprived him of his remedy to try his title to the manor at law. The House perceived that the case involved the overthrow of a decree in which the king was concerned, "and that it is depending in this House but by Petition." The House ordered that if the plaintiff "will sue to have this House take Cognizance of the said Decree, that the Proceedings be by Way of Bill and Answer, as is usually done in inferior Courts of Justice in Cases of this Nature, that so the Counsel of the King may be heard in this Business, if it be desired, in Behalf of the King" (LJ, 6:581).

245. Relf, Debates in the House of Lords 1621, 1625, 1628, p. xxix; HLRO, Main Papers, H.L., 23 March 1647/8.

246. LJ, 3:812, 871, and 4:78; HLRO, Main Papers, H.L., 19 November 1640.

247. HLRO, Main Papers, H.L., 17 July 1641. John Milton gives a brief but telling vignette in the "Second Defense of the English People": "No man has ever seen me . . . clinging, with suppliant expression to the doors of Parliament, or loitering in the hallways of the lower Assemblies" (Complete Prose Works of John Milton, vol. 4 [New Haven, 1966], pt. 1, p. 627).

248. HLRO, Main Papers, H.L., 7 July 1641.

249. Elsyng, Manner of Holding Parliaments, p. 270. Hale observed that the appointment of the triers was "a piece of formality" and that their business was "now for the most part transacted in the lords house, or by committees of petitions, and other committees of their own nomination" (Hargrave, Jurisdiction, p. 79). Frances Relf thought it of some significance that in 1628 members of the Committee for Petitions were also on the list of triers of petitions appointed at the opening of parliament, and that this meant the committee "was being recognized as performing the function which was once performed by the tryers" (Relf, Debates in the House of Lords 1621, 1625, 1628, p. xxvii). Since the triers were selected by the lord chancellor and the committee by the House, I am not convinced that this is so. However, it is interesting that in 1660, members of the Committee for Petitions were called "Receivers and Triers of Petitions" (LJ, 11:184).

250. Elizabeth Read Foster, "The Procedure of the House of Commons against Patents

and Monopolies, 1621–1624," in *Conflict in Stuart England*, ed. William Appleton Aiken and Basil D. Henning (London, 1960), pp. 62, 80 (n. 24).

251. The great number of petitions forced both Houses to decline at certain times to receive private complaints at all. A draft ordinance (never passed) in 1648 against arbitrary government forbade the consideration of individual petitions by either House (with certain exceptions) and the Rump Parliament was said to have ignored ten thousand petitions brought before it until forced to accede to Cromwell's and Harrison's demand in 1652 for a committee to investigate the backlog (HLRO, Main Papers, H.L., 14 April 1648; *LJ*, 10:193; Blair Worden, *The Rump Parliament 1648–1653* [Cambridge, 1974], pp. 89–90, 312).

252. Hargrave, *Jurisdiction*, p. 194.

253. I.e., select committee.

254. *LJ*, 2:456–57.

255. Sheila Lambert, "Procedure in the House of Commons in the Early Stuart Period," *EHR* 95 (October 1980): 765; *CJ*, 1:371; Graves, *House of Lords Edward VI and Mary I*, pp. 56, 144.

256. Lambert, pp. 760–68; Neale, *Elizabethan House of Commons*, pp. 377–79; Wallace Notestein, "The Winning of the Initiative in the House of Commons" (*Proceedings of the British Academy*, London, 1924; reprinted as separate pamphlet, London, 1949), pp. 36–37.

257. *LJ*, 2:555.

258. HMC, *Buccleuch*, 3:274, 279; Gardiner, *Debates in the House of Lords 1621*, pp. 56–58; Relf, *Debates in the House of Lords 1621, 1625, 1628*, p. 95.

259. *Manuscripts of the House of Lords*, 10:9 (Standing Order no. 51). HLRO, Braye 93, fol. 9v, refers to what may have been an order to this effect on 18 April 1626. Relf, *Debates in the House of Lords 1621, 1625, 1628*, p. 95, refers to a similar order made on 9 May 1626; but neither can be found in the journal for these dates.

260. *LJ*, 2:456–57.

261. Ibid., pp. 647–49, 651.

262. Ibid., p. 457.

263. Ibid., p. 646. In 1621 the committee met after prayers (ibid., 3:111).

264. Foster, *1610*, 1:147–52; Gardiner, *Debates in the House of Lords 1624 and 1626*, pp. 195–200.

265. *LJ*, 3:47, 55, 63, 289, 507.

266. *LJ*, 4:74; Cope, *Proceedings of the Short Parliament*, p. 90.

267. G. F. Trevallyn Jones, "The Peers' Right of Protest," *BIHR* 31 (1958): 215. Speaking in 1679 concerning the committee of the whole House, Lord Robartes said "that till 1642 there was no chairman of any Committee, and that the olde Earle of Manchester (who was Lord Privy Seale) was the first chairman of a Committee" (HLRO, Minute Books, 26 May 1679 P.M., a reference I owe to Richard W. Davis). Laud mentions that during the Long Parliament, at a committee of the whole House in 1644, the earl of Northumberland was "on the woolsack" (Laud, *Works*, 4:415–17). Since Laud was in the Tower in 1644 and was not present in the House on the day mentioned, his information, though interesting, may well have been garbled. Chairmen were appointed after the Restoration (Timberland, 1:339).

268. Elizabeth Read Foster, "The Procedure of the House of Lords in the Early Stuart Period," *The Journal of British Studies* 5 (May 1966): 68; Foster, *1610*, 1:177, 199–205, 229; *LJ*, 2:646.

269. Foster, *Painful Labour of Mr. Elsyng*, p. 22.

270. See Cope, *Proceedings of the Short Parliament*, pp. 71–79, for example.

271. *LJ*, 2:555, 575.

272. Ibid., p. 573 (1610). See also Foster, *1610*, 1:198; *LJ*, 3:590, and 4:179; HLRO, Braye 93, fol. 65v; Gardiner, *Debates in the House of Lords 1624 and 1626*, p. 185.

273. Timberland, 1:165–66; Foster, *1610*, 1:75, 230. The order was that a lord speaking in the House should not name another lord, but refer to him indirectly (*Manuscripts of the House of Lords*, 10:2 [Standing Order no. 12]).

274. Foster, *1610*, 1:198, 231.

275. Ibid., p. 231. The order for "every Lord to sit during a committee, that the House be not disturbed," was an order against wandering about the House (Gardiner, *Debates in the House of Lords 1624 and 1626*, p. 185; see *LJ*, 3:590).

276. HMC, *Hastings*, 4:251; *LJ*, 2:706–7.

277. Gardiner, *Debates in the House of Lords 1624 and 1626*, pp. 118–19; Cope, *Proceedings of the Short Parliament*, p. 90; HLRO, Relfe, "Book of Orders 1710," p. 683. For a record of a vote in a select committee, see HLRO, Main Papers, H.L., 8 June 1641.

278. Foster, *1610*, 1:235–36.

279. Ellesmere's summary to the House on 2 May 1614 was questioned by some of the lords (*HMC, Hastings*, 4:251–52; *LJ*, 2:706–7).

280. *LJ*, 2:707. If the committee of the whole House did vote (a point that is uncertain), a vote in committee did not bind the House (HLRO, Relfe, "Book of Orders 1710," p. 683).

281. *LJ*, 2:555, 573, 706.

282. Gardiner, *Debates in the House of Lords 1621*, p. 129; Relf, *Debates in the House of Lords 1621, 1625, 1628*, p. 33; HMC, *Buccleuch*, 3:274; *LJ*, 3:590.

283. *LJ*, 2:456–57, 706.

284. HMC, *Buccleuch*, 3:335; Relf, *Debates in the House of Lords 1621, 1625, 1628*, p. 121. An excellent example of debate and rebuttal is the debate on the Petition of Right, 24 May 1628 (Relf, *Debates in the House of Lords 1621, 1625, 1628*, pp. 200–203).

285. *LJ*, 3:46, 55, 77, 85, 87, 95, 104, 105, 108.

286. Ibid., pp. 110, 113, 190, 581, 627, 669.

287. Ibid., 2:584; Foster, *1610*, 1:75–79.

288. Foster, *1610*, 1:146n, 147–52.

289. *LJ*, 2:706, and 3:563–64; HMC, *Buccleuch*, 3:279.

290. *LJ*, 3:236, 239.

291. Ibid., pp. 379, 382.

292. Ibid., pp. 289, 397, 453.

293. Ibid., pp. 507, 526, 651, 653, 782.

294. Ibid., pp. 796, 797, 807, 822.

295. See, for example, HLRO, Main Papers, H.L., 1 July 1641; *LJ*, 4:298. For the use of the committee of the whole House for ordinances, see HLRO, Main Papers, H.L., 8 June 1644, 4 November 1644, 25 November 1644, 3 March 1644/5, 28 March 1644/5, 3 April 1645, 12 June 1645, 9 September 1645, 20 October 1645, 13 January 1645/6, 2 October 1646, 21 October 1646, 11 February 1646/7, 24 December 1647, 11 February 1647/8, 10 July 1648; *LJ*, 8:508, 541–42, 635.

296. HLRO, Main Papers, H.L., 8 June 1644; *LJ*, 6:581–82.

297. HLRO, P.O. 354, Precedents, p. 75.

298. Starr, pp. 191–94, 229.

299. For examples, see Gardiner, *Debates in the House of Lords 1621*, pp. 71–74; Relf, *Debates in the House of Lords 1621, 1625, 1628*, pp. 74–78.

300. It is not clear that this was always the case in the lower House, a suggestion that I owe to Marylynn Salmon.

301. Neale, *Elizabethan House of Commons*, pp. 377–79. Salisbury had been a member of the House of Commons in 1584, 1586, 1589, and 1601, and Ellesmere in 1584–86.

302. See the opinion of the French ambassador (PRO, 31/3/41, 19 March 1606/7); see also Kevin Sharpe, ed., *Faction and Parliament: Essays on Early Stuart History* [Oxford, 1978], p. 71).

303. *LJ*, 2:555.

304. See below, pp. 127–28.

305. Starr, pp. 89–109; Bowyer, pp. 230, 239–40, 243, 249, 321–22.

306. Gardiner, *Debates in the House of Lords 1621*, pp. 56–57.

307. Relf, *Debates in the House of Lords 1621, 1625, 1628*, p. 95. In 1626, when his power had been threatened by the proposal to limit to two the number of proxies a single lord might hold, the duke had moved that the House go into committee. Doubtless he hoped that he and his supporters could speak more than once in opposition and win the day. But he had made a tactical error. He was defeated in committee and on the floor (Gardiner, *Debates in the House of Lords 1624 and 1626*, pp. 113–15).

308. Huntingdon Record Office, Manchester MS 32/5/15a. See also *Court and Times of Charles I*, 1:349. A list of questions concerning activities that had taken place in parliament in 1621 may also refer to a similar use of the committee of the whole House. One asked whether there was "a combination of some of the Lords" at the beginning of parliament? "Whether have those Lords succenturiated one another in their Parliamental speeches protracting the time to the hindrance of the public service?" (Lambeth Palace MS 251, fol. 208).

309. Clarendon, *Life*, 2:333.

310. *LJ*, 12:29.

311. Starr, pp. 214–17. Throughout this section and the chapter that follows, I have relied heavily on Starr's dissertation and, with some exceptions, have followed his general argument.

312. Lehmberg, *Later Parliaments*, p. 261; Graves, *House of Lords Edward VI and Mary I*, p. 171; *LJ*, 1:213, 243; Starr, pp. 218–19; J. E. Neale, *Elizabeth I and Her Parliaments, 1559–1581* (New York, 1953), pp. 235–36, 247, 262, 287, 290, 387, 405, 412–13.

313. Starr, pp. 220, 222–23, 225; Gardiner, *Debates in the House of Lords 1621*, pp. 70–71; *LJ*, 3:113, 116.

314. *Commons Debates 1621*, 3:297, and 4:374–77; Starr, pp. 224, 225–28, 229–32; *Commons Debates 1628*, 3:590, 594–607.

315. Starr, pp. 233–39; Firth, *House of Lords during the Civil War*, p. 138.

316. Wallace Notestein, "The Establishment of the Committee of Both Kingdoms," *AHR* 17, no. 3 (April 1912): 477–78; Starr, pp. 239–41.

317. Notestein, "Committee of Both Kingdoms," pp. 481–82; Starr, p. 240.

318. For the records of some of these committees, see PRO, State Papers Domestic, Interregnum: SP19/6, SP22/1, and SP22/3.

319. *LJ*, 7:306.

320. See HLRO, Main Papers, H.L., 4 March 1643/4, where joint control is insisted upon; *LJ*, 6:474–76, and HLRO, Main Papers, H.L., 19 March 1643/4, where the same regulations appear, signed by members of the committee from both Houses.

321. *LJ*, 7:5, 105, 107, 422.

322. Ibid., p. 680; HLRO, Main Papers, H.L., 7 November 1645.
323. *LJ*, 9:499.
324. Starr, p. 254.
325. Lehmberg, *Later Parliaments*, p. 261; *LJ*, 1:243.
326. Neale, *1559–1581*, p. 247. HLRO, Braye 93, fol. 4, indicates that there were twenty-two lords and forty-four commoners.
327. HLRO, Main Papers, H.L., 19 July 1644, 26 March 1647; *LJ*, 4:517, and 5:615. The custom was finally abandoned in 1864 (Starr, p. 258). The same proportion was observed at conferences (*CJ*, 1:154; Starr, p. 59).
328. HLRO, Main Papers, H.L., 23 November and 27 December 1647.
329. HLRO, Braye 93, fols. 170v–71; *LJ*, 6:675.
330. See the instructions sent by the Lords to the Commons on this point, 26 February 1606/7 (*LJ*, 2:478; *CJ*, 1:342). For the similar practice concerning conferences, see Starr, pp. 59, 180.
331. Starr, p. 183; Cope, *Proceedings of the Short Parliament*, p. 201.
332. *LJ*, 11:355; Starr, p. 246.
333. *CJ*, 8:342. See also *Debates of the House of Commons from the Year 1667 to the Year 1694: Collected by the Honble Anchitell Grey, Esq.*, 10 vols. (London, 1763), 4:32.
334. HLRO, Main Papers, H.L., 21 September 1641.
335. Rushworth, *Tryal of Strafford*, pp. 37, 39–40, 41. At a meeting of both Houses, members should be covered and the Speaker should go, but this would not pertain if the meeting were between committees of both Houses (Gardiner, *Commons Debates 1625*, pp. 92–93). PRO, SP16/479/74. For the dispute concerning procedure at Strafford's trial, see also PRO, SP16/484/63. *LJ*, 7:102.
336. Macray, *Clarendon's History*, 3:462–63.
337. HLRO, Main Papers, H.L., 13 November 1644; *LJ*, 7:63.
338. See above, p. 71.
339. At the Common Council of London, early in the century, it had been the custom for members to stand while the aldermen sat. During the civil war, members sat with their hats on (Ralph Yarlott, "The Long Parliament and the Fear of Popular Pressure, 1640–1646" [M.A. thesis, University of Leeds, 1963], p. 135, where he cites M. James, *Social Problems and Policy during the Puritan Revolution, 1640–1660* [London, 1930], p. 235).
340. Starr, p. 255.
341. PRO, SP21/7, Day Book, February 1643/4; HLRO, Main Papers, 15 August 1649. See *Guide to the Contents of the Public Record Office*, 2:5.
342. Starr, p. 226 and n. 54.
343. *CJ*, 1:729. Starr follows the first interpretation and concludes that the lords and commoners always voted together. I am inclined to follow the second interpretation. Other accounts of the report fail to clarify the point. I do not think that Starr's general conclusion that the committee always voted as a whole is justified.
344. *LJ*, 9:86. Among the Main Papers of the House there is a committee sheet for the fourteen lords appointed to meet with a proportional number from the House of Commons to advise on an answer to the king. "C" and "n" have been marked after the peers' names, presumably indicating whether they voted "content" or "not content" on the resolution written at the bottom of the sheet (HLRO, Main Papers, H.L., 19 December 1644).
345. *LJ*, 6:528; HLRO, Main Papers, H.L., 28 July 1645, 16 June 1648; Starr, p. 220, n. 22.

346. Notestein, "Committee of Both Kingdoms," pp. 483–88.

347. *LJ*, 6:405, 564–65.

348. Notestein, "Committee of Both Kingdoms," pp. 482, 490.

349. *CJ*, 3:391.

350. Ibid., pp. 391–92; Notestein, "Committee of Both Kingdoms," pp. 491–92.

351. *LJ*, 6:426–27; Notestein, "Committee of Both Kingdoms," pp. 492–94.

352. *LJ*, 6:429–30. Compare the version of the ordinance in *CJ*, 3:392. See also Notestein, "Committee of Both Kingdoms," pp. 494–95, nn. 70, 71.

353. On 23 May 1644. *CJ*, 3:504; *LJ*, 6:564–65; Firth, *House of Lords during the Civil War*, pp. 140–41.

354. Notestein, "Committee of Both Kingdoms," p. 490.

355. *CJ*, 3:391. For 1604, see ibid., 1:199.

356. They reiterated this point on 13 April, when they finally gave up their idea of a separate committee (*LJ*, 6:477, 502).

357. *LJ*, 6:542, 554, 557.

358. There was also debate concerning the matter of the quorum. Vane's and St. John's original version of the ordinance for the Committee of Both Kingdoms provided that one member of each House should be of the quorum, thus altering the usual proportion of one lord to two members of the House of Commons. The amended ordinance voted by the House of Commons on 7 February provided for a quorum of six, of whom one should be a lord and two commoners. The Lords suggested a larger quorum of nine rather than six. The Commons stuck to the smaller number, advancing precedents from the Committee of Safety and other joint committees recently established. On this point, they carried the day (*LJ*, 6:418, 422, 429–30, 564–65; *CJ*, 3:391–92).

359. *LJ*, 6:435–36.

360. *LJ*, 6:440. For the suggested oath, see HLRO, Main Papers, H.L., 20 February 1643/4, and compare with *LJ*, 6:641, which is the same, though the oath was said to have been altered in March (*LJ*, 6:477–79).

361. *LJ*, 6:497, 641.

362. Ibid., pp. 472, 477, 483.

363. Ibid., pp. 501–2.

364. Ibid., pp. 514, 519.

365. *CJ*, 6:109–10; R. W. Blencowe, ed., *Sydney Papers, Consisting of A Journal of the Earl of Leicester and Original Letters of Algernon Sydney* (London, 1825), pp. 48–49.

7. CONFERENCES

1. Starr, pp. 50–52.

2. Ibid., p. 56, and app. table 3, which analyzes the subjects addressed in conferences.

3. Ibid., pp. 60–63.

4. See above, p. 115.

5. Foster, *1610*, 2:24, 77.

6. Ibid., pp. 122, 138; see also 1:127, and 2:132. The Commons used the term "meeting" somewhat differently (ibid., 2:326).

7. Ibid., 2:301.

8. Ibid., pp. 77, 122–23.

9. Ibid., 1:81.

10. Ibid., 2:78, 122.

11. Ibid., 1:11–13, 228, and 2:33, 76, 77.

12. Ibid., 2:77.

13. Ibid., 1:248.

14. *HMC, Hastings*, 4:233. Bacon's note concerning preparations for the parliament is interesting in this connection: "To consider whether it will be fit to steer the K's business as it was last time by conferences with the upper house, which will be hard to do now the Treasurer is gone, who had a kind of party in both houses" (Spedding, *Letters and Life*, 4:368). Bacon incorporated these ideas in a memorandum to James (*HMC, Laing*, 1:142–43).

15. *LJ*, 2:705.

16. Huntington Library, Hastings MS L5A9, Sir Edwin Sandys's report, 12 May 1614.

17. *HMC, Hastings*, 4:249.

18. Ibid., pp. 249–51, 257.

19. Ibid., pp. 251–55, 261, 263.

20. Ibid., pp. 263–64.

21. See the interesting statement of "Reasons why the Lords have done well not to meet with the Commons upon the conference in point of Impositions . . . out of a copy in my lord Canc. hand" (British Library, Cotton MSS, Titus F.IV, fols. 257–58).

22. Starr, p. 122; Gardiner, *Debates in the House of Lords 1621*, p. 75; *LJ*, 3:116.

23. *LJ*, 3:116. See the reference to proceedings in this case as a precedent (*Commons Debates 1628*, 3:597).

24. *CJ*, 1:629; *LJ*, 3:138–39.

25. At the conference, one of the lords indicated that the House would answer the Commons later (Starr, pp. 122–23; Nicholas, 2:118–19).

26. Starr, p. 122; *LJ*, 3:148–50.

27. Relf, *Debates in the House of Lords 1621, 1625, 1628*, p. 11.

28. *Commons Debates 1628*, 3:562; see also pp. 371–72, 452, 457. Sir Edward Coke termed a conference at which only the lords spoke a "half conference" (ibid., p. 369).

29. Cope, *Proceedings of the Short Parliament*, pp. 78–79.

30. *LJ*, 4:99; Starr, p. 129.

31. Starr, pp. 129–30.

32. *LJ*, 4:99–102, 296; *The Journal of Sir Simonds D'Ewes from the Beginning of the Long Parliament to the Opening of the Trial of the Earl of Strafford*, ed. Wallace Notestein (New Haven, 1923), pp. 85–86.

33. Starr, pp. 108–9.

34. Starr believed that the practice developed after the Restoration (p. 145); but see *LJ*, 6:425–26, 483, 563, and 7:159–61 and elsewhere.

35. See above, p. 124.

36. *LJ*, 6:477–79, 7:159–60.

37. Ibid., 6:501–2, 514.

38. Starr, pp. 148–51.

39. HLRO, Braye 93, fol. 84v (1641); Starr, pp. 58, 209–10.

40. In 1625 a member of the lower House remembered precedents in many kings' reigns, as late as the time of Henry VIII, when the Lords did not have the appointment of time and place but came to the House of Commons (Gardiner, *Commons Debates 1625*, p. 157).

41. Starr, p. 59.

42. See above, pp. 88–92.

43. See above, p. 114.

44. *LJ*, 2:367–78; *HMC, Buccleuch*, 3:231; HLRO, Braye 2, fols. 65–66v. Starr makes the point that the Commons' preparations were usually more extensive (p, 87).

45. Cope, *Proceedings of the Short Parliament*, p. 201. For a suggested rearrangement after the Restoration, see below, p. 265, n. 145.

46. "Because if anything fell out which might occasion the committee to resort to the Lords" (*HMC, Buccleuch*, 3:233, 1624).

47. Starr, p. 198. They might adjourn or resolve themselves into a committee of the whole House (*LJ*, 3:451, 454).

48. Cope, *Proceedings of the Short Parliament*, p. 201.

49. *Manuscripts of the House of Lords*, 10:4–5 (Standing Orders nos. 26 and 27); HLRO, P.O. 354, Precedents, pp. 77–78; Starr, p. 183. They doffed their hats in the eighteenth century, but I have no direct evidence for the seventeenth.

50. *HMC, Buccleuch*, 3:250, 287–88. In 1640 the usual procedure was carried out (Cope, *Proceedings of the Short Parliament*, p. 201).

51. Foster, *1610*, 2:134.

52. *Manuscripts of the House of Lords*, 10:5 (Standing Orders nos. 28 and 29).

53. Relf, *Debates in the House of Lords 1621, 1625, 1628*, pp. 18–20.

54. PRO, SP16/102/57.

55. Crummett, p. 275.

56. British Library, Harleian 2325, fol. 61; *LJ*, 3:306, 307.

57. Gardiner, *Debates in the House of Lords 1624 and 1626*, pp. 189–90; *LJ*, 3:589, 593, 594–95, 715.

58. Gardiner, *Debates in the House of Lords 1624 and 1626*, pp. 183, 190; Starr, pp. 202–5; *LJ*, 3:589.

59. *Manuscripts of the House of Lords*, 10:5 (Standing Order no. 29); Elsyng, "Method of Passing Bills," p. 116.

60. Bowyer, pp. 232–33; PRO, SP14/26/84. Salisbury's speech in 1610 at a conference took two hours (Foster, *1610*, 2:28). A conference in 1626 lasted all afternoon and the following morning (Starr, p. 181).

61. Bowyer, pp. 233–35.

62. Starr, pp. 97–101.

63. Ibid., pp. 134–42, 151.

64. HLRO, Relfe, "Book of Orders 1710," pp. 154, 179. Similarly, Starr regards the Lords' insistence in 1628 on going to a conference before taking a vote as a "mistaken" view of the free conference (Starr, p. 128). It was not mistaken, but reflected the Lords' concept of a free conference in 1628.

8. PRIVILEGE

1. *LJ*, 3:10.

2. de Villiers, p. 7.

3. *LJ*, 3:12–13, 439, 496; *Manuscripts of the House of Lords*, 10:xxxix–xliv, 1–11; de Villiers, p. 8.

4. de Villiers, pp. vi–vii. For the document that Selden presented to the House, see HLRO, Main Papers, H.L., 15 December 1621. Printed versions have garbled parts of the text, so it is useful to refer to the original manuscript.

5. See above, p. 97.

6. *LJ*, 3:10.

7. Ibid., p. 150.

8. *LJ*, 3:196–98, 781–82, 785–86, 805, 834; PRO, SP16/103/35.

9. *LJ*, 3:198.

10. May, p. 42; *LJ*, 3:386, 4:297; John Selden, *The Priviledges of the Baronage of England When They Sit in Parliament* (London, 1689), p. 15.

11. *Manuscripts of the House of Lords*, 10:1–11; de Villiers, pp. 8–10.

12. HLRO, Main Papers, H.L., 15 December 1621, fol. 1.

13. Pike, pp. 162–65; Foster, *1610*, 1:136–37; de Villiers, pp. 9–10; Selden, *Priviledges*, pp. 152–55; *Manuscripts of the House of Lords*, 10:5 (Standing Order no. 34). A question was raised on this point in 1625 (*LJ*, 3:439). In 1640 Bishop Williams referred to himself as a "peer of parliament" (PRO, SP16/452/42).

14. HLRO, Main Papers, H.L., 15 December 1621, fol. 1.

15. Ibid., fols. 2v, 10; Selden, *Priviledges*, pp. 7–141.

16. Selden, *Priviledges*, pp. 142–76; Pike, pp. 254–67; 1 E.VI, c. 12, secs. 13 and 14. The original statute of *scandalum magnatum* (3 E. I, c. 34) had been reenacted in 1379 (2 R. II, st. 1, c. 5) when the classes of persons reckoned as magnates were defined. A further enactment in 1389 (12 R. II, c. 11) provided that disseminators of scandalous tales could be punished if the originators could not be found (Giles Jacob, *A New Law-Dictionary*, [London, 1744], s.v. *"scandalum magnatum"*).

17. *Manuscripts of the House of Lords*, 10:5–6 (Standing Order no. 34).

18. PRO, SP14/8/55; *LJ*, 3:406, 408.

19. *LJ*, 3:269–70, 272, 275–77, 417, 676.

20. Ibid., pp. 741–43.

21. Ibid., pp. 822, 825, 827, 830, 831, 836, 838, 842, 845, 849.

22. *LJ*, 5:22–25. For other cases concerning *scandalum magnatum*, see ibid., 4:118, 131, 418, 425.

23. *LJ*, 6:24.

24. *LJ*, 8:578.

25. Ibid., pp. 426–27, 429–30, 432–33.

26. Pike indicates that the privilege belonged to both temporal and spiritual lords (Pike, pp. 259–60). Also see May, pp. 67–68, 74; Chamberlayne, *Angliae Notitia*, p. 417; David Ogg, *England in the Reign of Charles II*, 2 vols. (Oxford, 1962), 2:460.

27. For some examples, see HLRO, Relfe, "Book of Orders 1710," p. 644; *LJ*, 2:597, 599, 633; 3:25; and 7:180, 314, 638.

28. *LJ*, 3:195; Selden, *Priviledges*, pp. 12–13. A lord on occasion might waive this privilege (*LJ*, 3:553, 7:380). In 1645 the earl of Carlisle insisted that this privilege could be waived only by the House, not by a committee, for while parliament sat, "there is a Public Interest in every Peer in the Realm" (*LJ*, 7:380).

29. Selden, *Priviledges*, pp. 13, 165–66; HLRO, Braye 93, fol. 11v; W. J. Jones, *The Elizabethan Court of Chancery* (Oxford, 1967), pp. 321–22; *LJ*, 1:727; Michael A. R. Graves, "Freedom of Peers from Arrest: The Case of Henry, Second Lord Cromwell, 1571–1572," *The American Journal of Legal History* 21 (1977): 1–14.

30. *LJ*, 4:27; Graves, "Freedom from Arrest," p. 14. In July 1629 the judges resolved that a *capias* did lie against a peer of the realm for contempt (British Library, Hargrave 132, fol. 73v; Jones, *Politics and the Bench*, pp. 173–75).

31. *Manuscripts of the House of Lords*, 10:7, 9, 10 (Standing Orders nos. 41, 48, 49, 54). Viscountess Purbeck was not permitted privilege against her husband (*LJ*, 3:774). HLRO, Main Papers, H.L., 28 April 1642, 8 February 1644/5, 15 October 1645.

32. *LJ*, 3:120, 6:428.

33. "This House declared, 'That, he being disabled by Judgment of Parliament from sitting in Parliament, the Privilege is taken away, it being allowed in regard of his sitting in Parliament, that so he should not be distracted from that Duty'" (*LJ*, 6:428). British Library, Harleian 2224, fols. 17v–18. Freedom from arrest, in effect, meant freedom from outlawry in civil actions (Pike, p. 260).

34. *LJ*, 5:222–23, 8:638–39, 673–74; HLRO, Main Papers, H.L., 31 December 1646.

35. *LJ*, 3:447, 4:110; *HMC, Buccleuch*, 3:399.

36. *LJ*, 5:469.

37. *LJ*, 6:642; HLRO, Main Papers, H.L., 18 November 1647.

38. HLRO, Main Papers, H.L., 11 August 1646, December 1648.

39. *Manuscripts of the House of Lords*, 10:7–8 (Standing Orders nos. 41 and 42). The proclamation for parliament in 1604 had warned against the practice (Robert Steele, ed., *Tudor and Stuart Proclamations*, 2 vols. [Oxford, 1910], 1:112–13, no. 979). For earlier precedents, see Bodleian Library, Carte 78, fol. 497; Inner Temple, Petyt 538/12, fols. 175–79 (the folios are out of order in the bound volume).

40. *LJ*, 2:702. This privilege was confirmed in 1624 (*LJ*, 3:264).

41. Inner Temple, Petyt 538/12, fol. 177.

42. A. S. Turberville, "The 'Protection' of the Servants of Members of Parliament," *EHR* 42, no. 168 (October 1927): 592–93, 599–600. For the form of a protection, see *The Priviledges and Practice of Parliaments in England Collected Out of the Common Lawes of This Land* (London, 1640), pp. 20–21; HLRO, Braye 5, p. 18. For an unsigned protection for a servant of Viscount Conway in 1641, see PRO, SP16/479/10.

43. Selden said, "What a scorn it is to a person of Honour, to put his Hand to two Lies at once, that such a man is my Servant and employed by me, when haply he never saw the man in his Life, nor before never heard of him" (*Table-Talk, Being the Discourses of John Selden* [London, 1941], no. 83, p. 77). Also see Inner Temple, Petyt 538/12, fol. 176v; Clarendon, *Life*, 2:349.

44. McClure, 2:409; HLRO, Relfe, "Book of Orders 1710," p. 594; *LJ*, 3:537, 539, 676; 4:64–65, 158, 164, 168, 175; and 7:476; HLRO, Main Papers, H.L., 25 June 1642.

45. *Priviledges of Parliament*, p. 18; *LJ*, 7:87, 605–6; 8:685; and 10:439; HLRO, Main Papers, H.L., 3 December 1644, 11 February 1644/5, 2 June 1646.

46. See below, p. 255, n. 9.

47. *LJ*, 5:620, 7:15, HLRO, Main Papers, H.L., 29 September 1645, 21 November 1646, 22 March 1647/8.

48. *LJ*, 6:147–48; 7:230; and 10:134; HLRO, Main Papers, H.L., 22 March 1647/8.

49. *LJ*, 7:16, 30, 34; HLRO, Main Papers, H.L., 22 February 1644/5.

50. *LJ*, 3:120.

51. Lehmberg, *Later Parliaments*, pp. 165–71. For the question in Elizabeth's reign, see Inner Temple, Petyt 538/12, fol. 175v; *LJ*, 2:230–31. For the reign of James I, see *LJ*, 3:156, 256, 425. In 1604 in the case of Nicholas Reading, one of the yeomen of the king's chamber who had been arrested at the suit of Sir Edward Hales, the Lords arranged a settlement of the debt at issue; but there was never any question concerning Reading's privilege (*LJ*, 2:308, 312–13, 317–18). The clerk was to search precedents (Bedford Office, Woburn MSS, HMC no. 198, pp. 110, 112). The memorandum entitled "Cases of Priviledges of the Kings servants during the time of Parliament" may be his report (Inner Temple, Petyt 538/17, fols. 70–75).

52. "Hee thought he might have had the privilege of a Parliament man for his servants,

as a member of the Howse may for his; Mountague was his servant in ordinarie, and the Howse had proceeded against him without taking notice of it" (British Library, Additional 48091, fol. 20v). See the debate on the issue in 1693 and the protests against the resolution not to receive petitions for protection of royal servants (Timberland, 1:420–21).

53. *LJ*, 4:318, 718, 722, and 5:25, 30, 263, 381, 596; PRO, SP16/485/109. The House declined (*LJ*, 6:642).

54. *LJ*, 4:187; 5:381; and 9:546.

55. HLRO, Main Papers, H.L., 24 June 1645.

56. HLRO, Main Papers, H.L., 21 November 1646; *LJ*, 9:77, 547, and 10:536.

57. For those who had causes pending before the House and their counsel see *LJ*, 4:144, 262; HLRO, Main Papers, H.L., 22 June 1641, 23 April 1645. For witnesses in cases before the House, see HLRO, Main Papers, H.L., 11 August 1643, 3 April 1645; *LJ*, 6:184.

58. HLRO, Main Papers, H.L., 24 November 1642, 7 June 1645.

59. See above, pp. 109–10.

60. Stone, *Crisis of the Aristocracy*, pp. 98–99. Sir Roger Twysden, writing sometime between 1650 and 1660, remarked that short parliaments were not burdensome in this respect, "Which of late hath been so great, as for my part I have been of opinion, that during their sitting, the justice of England did in great measure sleep" (*Certain Considerations upon the Government of England by Sir Roger Twysden*, ed. John Mitchell Kemble, Camden Society, 1st ser. 45 [London, 1848], p. 140; see also p. 168). The same point was made by Lord Shaftesbury concerning parliament in 1675: "The very Privilege of the Members, and of those they protect in a Parliament of so long Duration, is a Pressure that the Nation cannot well support itself under: So many thousand Suits of Law stopped, so vast a Sum of Money withheld from the right Owners, so great a Quantity of Land unjustly possessed, and in many Cases the Length of Time securing the Possession, and creating a Title" (Timberland, 1:180).

61. This last section has been crossed off in the manuscript. "Enough of this," Elsyng wrote, "if not too much, leave it out" (Inner Temple, Petyt 538/12, fols. 176v–177). For discussions in the House about the abuse of protections in 1621, see Gardiner, *Debates in the House of Lords 1621*, pp. 94, 111, 118, 126.

62. HLRO, Main Papers, H.L., 29 June 1641, 7 December 1642; *LJ*, 5:481.

63. Clarendon, *Life*, 2:349; Twysden, "Journal," 4:149.

64. See, for example, HLRO, Main Papers, H.L., 5 August and 21 September 1642.

65. Macray, *Clarendon's History*, 2:369–70.

66. HLRO, Main Papers, H.L., 27 May and 27 October 1641; Valerie Pearl, *London and the Outbreak of the Puritan Revolution* (Oxford, 1964), p. 117.

67. HLRO, Main Papers, H.L., [1641], petition of Robert Stevens, tallow chandler of London.

68. HLRO, Main Papers, H.L., 24 November 1646.

69. HLRO, Main Papers, H.L., 27 May 1641; Turberville, "Protections," p. 597.

70. PRO, SP16/485/109.

71. Parliament is sensible of the matter of protections, it read, "that therein they intended to give them whatsoever ease may stand with honour and justice, and are in a way of passing a bill to give them satisfaction" (Samuel Rawson Gardiner, ed., *The Constitutional Documents of the Puritan Revolution, 1625–1660* [Oxford, 1899], pp. 276–77).

72. In 1642 the Common Council of London complained that protections had not been suppressed (*LJ*, 4:538). See also the petition in 1646 (HLRO, Main Papers, H.L.,

19 December 1646).

73. Horses: *LJ*, 5:469, 504, and 6:111; garrisons: *LJ*, 7:588; military service: see n. 49, above; billeting: *LJ*, 7:87, 443; military assessments: *LJ*, 10:439.

74. *LJ*, 5:381.

75. HLRO, Main Papers, H.L., 27 June 1643.

76. HLRO, Main Papers, H.L., 18 August 1646.

77. HLRO, Main Papers, H.L., 24 September 1647.

78. See, for example, the remarks made by Richard Pim in 1645 that "he would keep William Jackson [servant of the earl of Warwick] in prison in spite of my Lord of Warwicke his power, and for any order that should come from the House of Lords, he did not weigh it neither should it be obeyed; and further said that he was as good a man as any Lord of them all" (HLRO, Main Papers, H.L., 2 August 1645).

79. *LJ*, 3:552-53; *Manuscripts of the House of Lords*, 10:9 (Standing Orders nos. 48 and 49); Vernon F. Snow, "The Arundel Case, 1626," *The Historian* 26, no. 3 (1964): 325.

80. *LJ*, 3:526, 528.

81. Ibid., pp. 558-62; PRO, SP16/524/25; HLRO, Braye 93, fols. 61v-62v, 69v-70v; Inner Temple, Petyt 538/18, fols. 275-278v.

82. *LJ*, 3:552-53, 558-62, 564, 566, 581, 591-92, 594, 650-55; PRO, SP16/524/25.

83. *LJ*, 4:92; HLRO, Braye 93, fols. 80v-81.

84. *LJ*, 4:500-501, 504-5, 507, 510-11, 514, 517, 528, 530, 554, 564, 566, 592, and 5:11.

85. "A privilege as often in all parliaments insisted upon by the Commons as rarely prayed and descried by the Lords and Peers" (Folger Shakespeare Library, MS V.b. 189, p. 46).

86. *HMC, Hastings*, 4:271. The earl of Bedford commented that the House of Commons had erred in questioning Neile, "for the King was willing to give way to them the better to make an example against them in the House" (Bedford Office, Woburn MSS, HMC no. 11, Commonplace Book, p. 2258, Tit. Parl.).

87. Nicholas, 2: app.; Hacket, 1:68-69.

88. *Cabala*, p. 285 (Williams to Buckingham, August 1621).

89. *LJ*, 4:86-87, 89; HLRO, Relfe, "Book of Orders 1710," p. 319; PRO, SP16/539/27; *HMC, Buccleuch*, 3:389-90.

90. HLRO, Main Papers, H.L., 21 September 1641; *LJ*, 4:397, and 6:233, 255.

91. *LJ*, 4:476; Macray, *Clarendon's History*, 1:440-41; Thomas Hobbes, *Behemoth*, ed. Ferdinand Tönnies (New York, 1969), pp. 80-81. See above, p. 6.

92. Firth, *House of Lords during the Civil War*, pp. 86-88, 103-6. In 1642 the earl of Bath requested the king's license to be absent from parliament because he could no longer freely debate or vote with safety or indemnity (PRO, SP16/489/8).

93. See above, pp. 17-18.

94. See above, pp. 9-10.

95. See above, p. 19.

96. See below, pp. 185-86.

97. In 1648 the Lords objected to a resolution of the House of Commons banishing Lord Goring, the earl of Holland, and Lord Capel, and brought in their own ordinance to that effect (*LJ*, 10:586).

98. Firth, *House of Lords during the Civil War*, p. 85.

99. British Library, Harleian 2243, fols. 32v-35; HLRO, Relfe, "Book of Orders 1710," p. 245.

100. *LJ*, 3:386.

101. *LJ*, 4:297; 6:71; 7:337, 357, 568; 8:447, 452; and 10:400–401; HLRO, Main Papers, H.L., 16 September 1644, 4 March 1645/6.
102. *LJ*, 3:813.
103. *LJ*, 6:405, 409.
104. See above, p. 25–26, 95.
105. For a discussion of this privilege, see Pike, pp. 252–54; May, p. 87.
106. HLRO, Main Papers, H.L., 27 May and 27 October 1641. These complaints applied to the privileges of both Houses.
107. Cited in Gerald Aylmer, *The Levellers* (London, 1975), p. 85; and in Christopher Hill, *The World Turned Upside Down* (London, 1972), p. 221.
108. Worden, *The Rump Parliament*, p. 107.
109. *LJ*, 4:86–87, 89.

9. JUDICATURE

1. *Of Judicature*, pp. 1–10. For the attribution of this treatise to Henry Elsyng, see Foster, *Painful Labour of Mr. Elsyng*, pp. 42–45; Bodleian Library, Carte 103, fols. 421–421v.
2. Russell, *Parliaments and English Politics*, pp. 36, 191n.
3. See above, p. 106; Horstman, "A New *Curia Regis*," pp. 412–13.
4. Elsyng drafted a section on how servants of peers had been delivered from arrest and assembled a number of precedents, beginning with Mary's reign (Inner Temple, Petyt 538/12, fols. 175–79). *Manuscripts of the House of Lords*, 10:7–8 (Standing Orders nos. 41 and 42). Those who were able to claim and establish privilege before arrest were to be released at once. Those who were already under arrest before privilege was established could only be delivered at the bar of the House (*LJ*, 3:565). A peer's solicitor who petitioned the House for privilege in a case at the assizes was told that he should have had an order from the House, and his petition was rejected (*LJ*, 3:547).
5. May, p. 73; *LJ*, 3:776–77, 10:611. "The plea of a peer in parliament to an action is in this manner, *Quod unus est magnatum et parium huius regni habens locum et vocem in quolibet parliamento eiusdem regni*. Plow. fol. 117a" (HLRO, Braye 93, fol. 10v).
6. *LJ*, 3:30–31, 97, 777. For a writ of privilege, see ibid., 2:278.
7. HLRO, Braye 93, fols. 139v–140. This punishment is reminiscent of that meted out to Floyd in 1621.
8. *LJ*, 4:65, 3:172. See also Thomas Beven, "Appellate Jurisdiction of the House of Lords," *Law Quarterly Review* 17 (1901): 165.
9. According to the statute 8 H. VI, c. 1, members of convocation enjoyed the same privileges as lords and members of the House of Commons. *LJ*, 3:805, 809, 870; PRO, SP46/166, no. 224.4d.
10. *LJ*, 3:463.
11. Ibid., 4:118, 123–24, 127, 131.
12. See above, p 140. "Reputation" in the original; "reparation" has been inserted by the editors (*LJ*, 5:22).
13. *LJ*, 5:22–25.
14. Ibid., 7:707 (where the locality is "Wisbich").
15. Ibid., 3:511, 800. For a list of petitions concerning peerage claims and claims to office, see HLRO, Relfe, "Book of Orders 1710," p. 437.

16. *LJ*, 2:274. For the earlier history of this case, see William Huse Dunham, Jr., "William Camden's Commonplace Book," *The Yale University Library Gazette* 43 (January 1969): 145–55.

17. *LJ*, 2:276 (where the serjeant is called *Altome*), 283, 285. See PRO, SP14/7/21 and 22 for material connected with this case, with Lord Cecil's memoranda.

18. Certain problems concerning this case were not settled until 1610. *LJ*, 2:293, 297, 300, 302–3, 306–7, 343, 625–28. See also HLRO, Main Papers, H.L., Supplementary 1604–10, 9 June 1604.

19. *LJ*, 3:510–11.

20. *HMC, Buccleuch*, 3:271–72; Gardiner, *Debates in the House of Lords 1624 and 1626*, p. 121.

21. *LJ*, 3:535.

22. Ibid., pp. 513, 524, 535. Elsyng's assistant included part of the argument in his fair copy of the proceedings of 6 March in the Lords journal (ibid., p. 517).

23. Ibid., pp. 535, 537, 545–48, 551–52. For material concerning this case, see British Library, Harleian 6846, fols. 285–87; PRO, SP16/24/48.

24. *Commons Debates 1621*, 2:174–76, 179–98.

25. *Of Judicature*, p. 30; Colin G. C. Tite, *Impeachment and Parliamentary Judicature in Early Stuart England* (London, 1974), p. 23.

26. Tite, pp. 23, 109–10.

27. *Of Judicature*, pp. 6–7; "Moderne Forme of the Parliaments," pp. 301–3.

28. Tite, pp. 109–10.

29. Ibid., pp. 104–6.

30. Relf, *Debates in the House of Lords 1621, 1625, 1628*, p. 45; Tite, p. 107.

31. *LJ*, 3:72.

32. Tite, p. 108; Foster, *Painful Labour of Mr. Elsyng*, pp. 30, 32; *LJ*, 3:135.

33. Tite, p. 117.

34. *Commons Debates 1621*, 2:242, 4:168.

35. *LJ*, 3:53–54. See *Of Judicature*, p. 31.

36. *LJ*, 3:55, 57, 61–62, 75.

37. Ibid., pp. 58, 67; Russell, *Parliaments and English Politics*, p. 113.

38. de Villiers, p. 32; *LJ*, 3:75.

39. *LJ*, 3:78–80, 84–85; Gardiner, *Debates in the House of Lords 1621*, p. 16.

40. *LJ*, 3:104.

41. Ibid., pp. 105–6.

42. Foster, *Painful Labour of Mr. Elsyng*, pp. 30, 32. For Selden's opinion that the judgment against Bacon was of no force because there was no record, see ibid., p. 33, and Spedding, *Letters and Life*, 7:332–33.

43. Tite, p. 135; *Of Judicature*, p. 31.

44. *LJ*, 3:87–88, 130–31, 144–48.

45. Ibid., p. 148.

46. Tite, p. 135.

47. Tite, pp. 150–58.

48. *LJ*, 3:307–10.

49. *Of Judicature*, pp. 64–65.

50. *LJ*, 3:311, 319.

51. *LJ*, 3:323–25, 327–35, 337–39.

52. Ibid., p. 341. For the great number of witnesses, see Tite, p. 162, n. 29.

53. *LJ*, 3:344, 345–58, 358–61.

54. Ibid., pp. 364–77.

55. Ibid., pp. 378–81; Gardiner, *Debates in the House of Lords 1624 and 1626,* pp. 74–91; Tite, pp. 166–67.

56. *CJ,* 1:789; *LJ,* 3:383.

57. Gardiner, *Debates in the House of Lords 1624 and 1626,* p. 92.

58. *LJ,* 3:383. Possibly the error was the clerk's, not the lord keeper's.

59. Foster, *Painful Labour of Mr. Elsyng,* p. 31.

60. *LJ,* 3:344.

61. Ibid., pp. 323, 351, 377.

62. Ibid., pp. 337–39.

63. Ibid., p. 344.

64. See ibid., pp. 374, 377 (the attorney is referred to as an "attendant" in the House).

65. *Of Judicature,* pp. 31–32, 64–65.

66. Tite, pp. 168–69. They had also instructed the Speaker to repeat the heads of the charges and to demand judgment on each, which he did not do.

67. *Manuscripts of the House of Lords,* 10:7 (Standing Orders nos. 38, 39, 40); *LJ,* 3:418.

68. British Library, Harleian 159, fols. 129v–130. I have used Hartley Simpson's transcript at the Yale Center for Parliamentary History. Also see PRO, SP14/165/61.

69. *LJ,* 3:287–88; *Manuscripts of the House of Lords,* 10:6 (Standing Order no. 37). For the procedure for certifying fines into Chancery, see *LJ,* 3:135, 142.

70. *LJ,* 3:143.

71. Ibid., p. 135.

72. Russell, *Parliaments and English Politics,* p. 104. In capital cases, "no judgment for death" could be given until he agreed (see below, n. 80).

73. Colin Rhys Lowell, "The Trial of Peers in Great Britain," *AHR* 55 (October 1949): 69, 75–77; W. S. Holdsworth, *A History of English Law,* 10 vols. (Boston, 1922), 1:388–90. See p. 288, n. 154 below, which also mentions the white staff that symbolized the lord high steward's authority and was broken at the end of the trial. For this procedure, used in later trials, see HLRO, P.O. 354, Precedents, pp. 98–102.

74. *Of Judicature,* pp. 3, 176–77.

75. Ibid., p. 3.

76. Ibid., pp. 7, 11–88.

77. Ibid., pp. 97, 102, 120, 176.

78. Ibid., pp. 133, 147.

79. Ibid., p. 167. The decision was undoubtedly reached by majority vote, as indicated by later writers (see Holdsworth, *History of English Law,* 1:389), though I find no contemporary documentation for this statement.

80. *Of Judicature,* p. 136; HLRO, Braye 65, fol. 8, a description of proceedings in the upper House in John Browne's hand.

81. *Of Judicature,* pp. 158, 164.

82. "Moderne Forme of the Parliaments," p. 303.

83. See below, pp. 172–75.

84. See below, pp. 175–76.

85. See Tite, pp. 219–20.

86. *LJ,* 3:567–68.

87. Ibid., pp. 537, 563–64.

88. *LJ,* 3:567–68, 574; Gardiner, *Debates in the House of Lords 1624 and 1626,* pp. 150–53; *HMC, Buccleuch,* 3:282. A contemporary memorandum reflects this stage of the proceedings. Though not in Elsyng's hand, it reads so much like his work, particularly in the analysis of medieval precedents and the inferences drawn

from them, that it can, I think, be safely attributed to him. The heading reads: "The Question is what hath beene usually done when any Peere hath beene sent for to be brought before the Lords in the upper House of Parliament." On 25 April a subcommittee of the Committee for Privileges had been charged to search precedents. Elsyng rehearsed the medieval precedents, noting that none concerned a peer who had had a writ and was later sent for to answer as a delinquent. Turning to modern times, he observed that Bacon absented himself from the House in 1621; the bishop of Norwich (1624) answered in his place; Cranfield (1624) forbore to attend when his case was under debate. "Touching this of the Earle of Bristoll though the Committee reported (21 Aprill) that they found him charged by a letter read here and by a message from the king yet *reverâ* . . . the letter was only read and the Earle had his writt of sommons after it was read. By the Message the king sayes he will charge him, that is *in futuro*. The king sayes farther that he would have him sent for as a delinquent to answere offences but that is against the priviledge of parlement (unless they be offences of treason) before tryall. And therefore the house did well (in my opinion) to order that he should be brought before their Lordships in generall wordes and when he comes if he clayme *locum et vocem* before the charge come in against him, I see not how it can be denied him. And if the charge be not capitall he ought to answer in his place." The problem remained, Elsyng went on, of how to reconcile the king's demand to have the earl brought before the Lords as a delinquent with the privilege of peers. Among points to be considered was the question "whether his accusation be for matter Capitall (for then he must be committed) or matter not Capitall for then such Lords have answered in their place" (Inner Temple, Petyt 538/18, fols. 291–296v).

89. *LJ*, 3:576; HMC, *Buccleuch*, 3:283.
90. *LJ*, 3:578.
91. Ibid., p. 580.
92. Elsyng remarked that no information had been exhibited against Northumberland, but that king's counsel must have opened his offenses to the Lords (*Of Judicature*, pp. 54–57).
93. Gardiner, *Debates in the House of Lords 1624 and 1626*, p. 166; HMC, *Buccleuch*, 3:285. Elsyng noted: "Having perused all the Judgments I do not find any one Peer indicted in Parliament . . . no Peer can be indicted in Parliament, for it is contradictory to the use of Parliament . . . a Lord of Parliament may be indicted out of Parliament" (*Of Judicature*, pp. 39–40).
94. Montagu believed that the House had resolved on 2 May to go by way of indictment, a decision abandoned on 4 May when it was resolved that "all the cause [was] to be heard and determined among ourselves" (HMC, *Buccleuch*, 3:285). But see Gardiner, *Debates in the House of Lords 1624 and 1626*, pp. 166–67.
95. *Manuscripts of the House of Lords*, 10:7 (Standing Orders nos. 38 and 39); Gardiner, *Debates in the House of Lords 1624 and 1626*, pp. 166–71. For the case against proceeding on indictment in King's Bench, see Bodleian Library, Carte 77, fols. 270–270v. A somewhat garbled version appears in Rushworth, *Historical Collections*, 1:267–68.
96. Gardiner, *Debates in the House of Lords 1624 and 1626*, p. 171; *LJ*, 3:581; HMC, *Buccleuch*, 3:285.
97. *LJ*, 3:582; Gardiner, *Debates in the House of Lords 1624 and 1626*, p. 172. Since the charges against Bristol involved his activities overseas, some question was raised concerning the statute 35 H. VIII, c. 2, which provided for the trial of such cases. "The question is, how the Earl of Bristol being accused for treason committed be-

yond the seas, shall be tried before his peers in parliament. The statute of 35 H. 8 appoints the enquiry of such trials to be by commissioners and an order of the upper House cannot avoid a statute. Therefore this enquiry and trial must be by an act done by the King, Lords, and Commons, which may be in this manner. The Court of Requests to be prepared for both Houses to sit in, as it was 7° *Jacobi*, when Prince Henry was created Prince of Wales and as must be presumed it was A° 5 Henr. 4° at the trial of the Earl of Northumberland. And then the E. of Bristol may be brought to the Bar, before the King, Lords and Commons, and there be charged by the L. Keeper with the said treasons committed beyond the seas, and so tried, and judged by his peers only. And this manner of trial is an act of parliament" (British Library, Harleian 6850, fol. 246). Elsyng debated the matter and decided that the statute was not applicable to Bristol's case (*Of Judicature*, pp. 50—53).

98. *LJ*, 3:418; Gardiner, *Debates in the House of Lords 1624 and 1626*, p. 169; *HMC, Buccleuch*, 3:293; *Manuscripts of the House of Lords*, 10:7 (Standing Orders nos. 38 and 39).

99. Gardiner, *Debates in the House of Lords 1624 and 1626*, pp. 173, 176; *LJ*, 3:585, 587.

100. Gardiner, *Debates in the House of Lords 1624 and 1626*, p. 178; *LJ*, 3:588. The bishop of Mende, writing to Richelieu, said that it was Buckingham who tried to prevent Bristol from having counsel (PRO, 31/3(63), 25 May 1626).

101. Gardiner, *Debates in the House of Lords 1624 and 1626*, p. 182. Elsyng observed that the Lords thought Bristol guilty merely of misdemeanors "when they allowed him Counsel in Parliament" (*Of Judicature*, p. 105).

102. *LJ*, 3:627; Gardiner, *Debates in the House of Lords 1624 and 1626*, pp. 200–201; *HMC, Buccleuch*, 3:293. For the king's reply, see British Library, Harleian 2325, fol. 31v; *LJ*, 3:629–30; *HMC, Buccleuch*, 3:294.

103. *LJ*, 3:585; *HMC, Buccleuch*, 3:287.

104. Gardiner, *Debates in the House of Lords 1624 and 1626*, pp. 185–87; *LJ*, 3:590–91.

105. Gardiner, *Debates in the House of Lords 1624 and 1626*, p. 191; *LJ*, 3:594; *HMC, Buccleuch*, 3:289, 291.

106. *LJ*, 3:632, 648–49, 668–69.

107. Gardiner, *Debates in the House of Lords 1624 and 1626*, pp. 219–20; *LJ*, 3:669.

108. *LJ*, 3:672–74, 676, 678, 680. For the interrogatories on behalf of the king against the earl of Bristol, see PRO, SP16/29/50–53.

109. It is interesting to note that while the attorney and the lord keeper pressed for an indictment in King's Bench, Buckingham was in favor of keeping the case within the House (Gardiner, *Debates in the House of Lords 1624 and 1626*, p. 170). Perhaps he thought he could control the event better there.

110. *LJ*, 3:632.

111. Gardiner, *Debates in the House of Lords 1624 and 1626*, p. 170.

112. Ibid., p. 182. Conrad Russell has emphasized the reluctance of the House to proceed in the case and its hope that the parties would compromise (Russell, *Parliaments and English Politics*, p. 311).

113. *LJ*, 3:563, 576–77.

114. *Of Judicature*, p. 11; Pike, p. 209.

115. Tite, pp. 188–89, n. 19.

116. Cobbett, *State Trials*, 6:315, 317; *LJ*, 11:559; Timberland, 1:59–60, 64–65.

117. *LJ*, 3:578, 669; *HMC, Buccleuch*, 3:283.

118. *LJ*, 3:578, 585.

119. Gardiner, *Debates in the House of Lords 1624 and 1626*, p. 173.

120. *LJ*, 3:585, 668–69.

121. This was finally done by Bristol's own counsel with advice from the counsel for the king (ibid., pp. 671–72, 674–75; Gardiner, *Debates in the House of Lords 1624 and 1626*, pp. 221, 223, 225).

122. *LJ*, 3:594–608, 610–24.

123. Ibid., p. 649; Gardiner, *Debates in the House of Lords 1624 and 1626*, p. 210. The French ambassador reported that the king had commanded his officers to plead the duke's cause, but that parliament had been opposed (PRO, 31/3(63), 6 June 1626). There is an undated copy of a warrant among the state papers authorizing the attorney general to assist Buckingham in framing answers to the "observations" against him in parliament and freeing the attorney of any scruple as the king's servant (PRO, SP16/523/110).

124. *HMC, Buccleuch*, 3:298; Gardiner, *Debates in the House of Lords 1624 and 1626*, p. 211.

125. *LJ*, 3:652; Gardiner, *Debates in the House of Lords 1624 and 1626*, p. 211.

126. *LJ*, 3:655–67.

127. There is a difference of opinion as to whether Strafford spoke at this time. Clarendon said that he was barely allowed "to answer in his place which could not be denied him" (Macray, *Clarendon's History*, 1:227). The clerk of the parliaments indicated that he had not been permitted to speak (*LJ*, 4:88–89). Robert Baillie, the Scottish commissioner, made the same point (*The Letters and Journals of Robert Baillie, A.M., Principal of the University of Glasgow, M.DC.XXXVII–M.DC.LXII.*, ed. David Laing, 2 vols. [Edinburgh, 1841], 1:272).

128. *LJ*, 4:95, 96–97.

129. *HMC, Buccleuch*, 3:394; *LJ*, 4:99–100, 102.

130. D'Ewes, *Long Parliament*, p. 92; *LJ*, 4:101, 103–4.

131. *LJ*, 4:95, 103, 118, 133, 148; D'Ewes, *Long Parliament*, pp. 85, 303–4; *HMC, Buccleuch*, 3:403.

132. British Library, Harleian 6424, fol. 26.

133. *LJ*, 4:171.

134. *LJ*, 4:171, 177.

135. See below, p. 260, n. 15; British Library, Harleian 6424, fols. 13–13v; Hacket 2:153–60; *LJ*, 4:103, 150, 171; *The Manuscripts of the House of Lords*, n.s., vol. 11, *Addenda 1514–1714* (London, 1962), pp. 235–36; Macray, *Clarendon's History*, 1:287–88; HLRO, Relfe, "Book of Orders 1710," p. 77.

136. *LJ*, 4:178, 184–85.

137. Rushworth, *Tryal of Strafford*, p. 40; *LJ*, 4:190; *CJ*, 2:109. Baillie noted that at the trial the lords were covered, all others uncovered "when the lords came, not else"; but he also observed that on 10 April 1641, when the commoners angrily prepared to withdraw from the hall, they "on with their hatts, cocked their beavers in the King's sight" (Baillie, *Letters and Journals*, 1:316, 346).

138. *LJ*, 4:184.

139. Ibid., pp. 178, 181, 184. See Baillie's summary of the advantages won by the Commons in Strafford's trial (Baillie, *Letters and Journals*, 1:309).

140. HLRO, Main Papers, H.L., 11 March 1640/1: "Mr. Whitelocke explained their meaning concerning the word *voting* given at the Conference, that the House of Commons had no intention thereby to partake or intrench upon the judicature of this House, but for their better Satisfaction against they come up to demand judgment."

141. *LJ*, 4:169, 171, 178, 179.
142. Ibid., p. 184. Several days later, Strafford reported that his counsel were "discouraged for giving him any Assistance, even in Matter of Law," and prayed they might be instructed how to proceed. They were referred to the order of the House permitting counsel (ibid., p. 186).
143. *Manuscripts of the House of Lords*, 11:236–38; *LJ*, 4:190.
144. There is no reference to a royal commission. Possibly the Lords considered it unnecessary. In August 1641 they would arrogate to themselves the right to select their own presiding officer; and in Danby's case later in the century they would declare that the House could proceed to trial even if no lord high steward was named (*LJ*, 4:190; British Library, Harleian 6424, fol. 52v; Holdsworth, *History of English Law*, 1:383, 389). Arundel was said to be "a person notoriously disaffected to the earl of Strafford" (Macray, *Clarendon's History*, 1:287–88). This selection was an exception to the general practice of choosing the presiding officer of the House of Lords (Lowell, "Trial of Peers," p. 77).
145. For an estimate of the lord steward's role, see British Library, Lansdowne 515, fol. 243: "The Lord High Steward is no more then the president or prolocutor for order sake."
146. *LJ*, 4:181, 184–85.
147. PRO, LC5/134, p. 445; *LJ*, 4:194; HLRO, Braye 8, p. 1. For the usual arrangements for parliament, see Foster, "Staging a Parliament," pp. 134–35. Baillie says that the forms for the earls and lords were covered with "green freese" and that the bar was also covered in green (Baillie, *Letters and Journals*, 1:315). For the use of red and green in state trials later in the century, see "Red and Green," *The Table* 37 (1968): 39.
148. Rushworth, *Tryal of Strafford*, p. 41; HLRO, Braye 8, p. 1; Baillie, *Letters and Journals*, 1:316.
149. *LJ*, 4:190.
150. Baillie, *Letters and Journals*, 1:315; Rushworth, *Tryal of Strafford*, p. 41; HLRO, Minute Book no. 7, 22 March 1640/1. Strafford several times protested that the witnesses should be separated from the managers (Rushworth, *Tryal of Strafford*, pp. 143, 156).
151. British Library, Harleian 164, fol. 142; Rushworth, *Tryal of Strafford*, p. 41; HLRO, Braye 8, p. 1. Baillie said there were *eleven* stages or ranks of forms (Baillie, *Letters and Journals*, 1:315). Hollar's picture shows ten (C. V. Wedgwood, *Thomas Wentworth, First Earl of Strafford, 1593–1641: A Revaluation* [London, 1961], plate at p. 352). Later, the gentleman usher vainly tried to claim the timber as a perquisite of office (see above, p. 60).
152. *LJ*, 4:190. Baillie indicated that he kept order with difficulty. The gentleman usher and several assistants were also on hand (Baillie, *Letters and Journals*, 1:315–16). On the lord great chamberlain, see above, p. 64.
153. For the arrangements made by the lower House for attendance of their members, see D'Ewes, *Long Parliament*, pp. 514–15. MPs were to proceed from their lodgings directly to Westminster Hall by 8:00 A.M. and present tickets for admission. Baillie said that one must be at the hall shortly after 5:00 A.M. and that it was full by 7. The king was in the hall by 7:30, Strafford by 8 (Baillie, *Letters and Journals*, 1:316).
154. For a rather garbled account of a procession that may have been planned for a trial of Bristol or Buckingham, see PRO, LC5/200, p. 7: "Upon the day of Tryall my Lord Coventry Ld Keeper of the Greate Seale being for that tyme Lord High Steward of England came to the Court attended by seaven serjeant at Armes then followed

the King of Herralds, then He that bore the Purse And then Mr. Maxwell as his Gentleman Usher with a White Rodd in his hand and then came the Lord Steward who was placed in a chayre of State by the Gentleman Usher and then the Gentleman Usher delivered the White Rodd into his hand and received it againe and satt at his feete holding the Rodd Serjeant Lee one of the serjeants at Armes stood upon the Table haveing a Cusheon whereon to lye or sitt downe on that syde of the Court which was on the left hand of the Lord High Steward Mr.Willis then clerke of the Crowne in Chauncery rose from his place and made them conjees and then delivered the Commission to my Lord Steward and returned to his place makeing them more Then Sir Thomas Fanshaw Clerke of the Crowne in the Kings Bench made them Conjees [here the account breaks off]." The lords wore hats; see Hollar's picture of the trial and Baillie's note that when Strafford entered the hall "some few of the Lords lifted their hats to him" (Baillie, *Letters and Journals*, 1:316).

155. The porter of the hall asked the gentleman usher whether the axe should be carried before Strafford. Maxwell replied that the king had expressly forbidden it, "nor was it the Custom of England to use that Ceremony, but only when the Party accused was to be put upon his Jury" (Rushworth, *Tryal of Strafford*, p. 41). The charges and the answer were read by John Browne, clerk of the parliaments, and two assistants (British Library, Harleian 164, fol. 142).

156. *LJ*, 4:190.

157. Baillie, *Letters and Journals*, 1:329.

158. On the legal background of this point, see Cobbett, *State Trials*, 6:777–78n; Rushworth, *Tryal of Strafford*, pp. 145, 163.

159. Rushworth, *Tryal of Strafford*, pp. 128, 154; Baillie, *Letters and Journals*, 1:318.

160. *LJ*, 4:212–13. "It kythed Strafford's friends were strongest in the Higher House" (Baillie, *Letters and Journals*, 1:345–46). See also Francis Hargrave, ed., *A Complete Collection of State Trials, The Fourth Edition*, 11 vols. in 5 (London, 1776–79), 1:754.

161. Rushworth, *Tryal of Strafford*, p. 734; Hargrave, *State Trials*, 1:761; British Library, Harleian 163, fol. 113; HLRO, Braye 8, p. 39.

162. *LJ*, 4:115, 136. The articles were presented at a conference on 15 January, but were not reported to the House until 20 January. The clerk has not entered them in the Lords journal. See Cobbett, *State Trials*, 4:11–18.

163. Cobbett, *State Trials*, 4:10; *LJ*, 4:143, 150.

164. Cobbett, *State Trials*, 4:138–39, 142, 173–76.

165. *LJ*, 4:501.

166. Ibid. In 1624 a question had been raised concerning a charge drawn by king's counsel against a member of the House (see above, p. 84).

167. *LJ*, 4:501, 503. For the committee sheet that gives the committee the same charge as that of the committee of the whole House, see PRO, SP16/488/8.

168. *LJ*, 4:507.

169. Ibid., p. 511; Cobbett, *State Trials*, 4:129; *LJ*, 3:564.

170. *LJ*, 4:517.

171. Ibid., pp. 510, 528, 530, 649, 669; Cobbett, *State Trials*, 4:109.

172. See a contemporary letter describing the reaction of the two Houses (PRO, SP16/488/21).

173. Hargrave, *Jurisdiction*, p. 94.

174. Cobbett, *State Trials*, 4:983–86.

175. *LJ*, 9:575, 667, 672.

176. Ibid., 9:667.

177. Ibid., 10:11–12. The charges are not entered, though the clerk intended that they should be.

178. Ibid., pp. 15, 18, 33–34, 308.

179. Ibid., 4:148.

180. HLRO, Main Papers, H.L., 12 February 1640/1; *LJ*, 4:160.

181. *LJ*, 4:152, 162, 167, 169–70.

182. Ibid., pp. 272, 277, 280.

183. Ibid., pp. 282, 290, 304.

184. Ibid., pp. 295, 322, 327.

185. Ibid., pp. 335, 338, 340, 356.

186. Ibid., p. 358.

187. Ibid., pp. 548, 565, and 5:33, 64.

188. Cobbett, *State Trials*, 6:1310, 1313–14, 1350.

189. *Manuscripts of the House of Lords*, 11:236–38.

190. Baillie, *Letters and Journals*, pp. 315–16, 330.

191. HLRO, Main Papers, H.L., 28 June 1641; *LJ*, 4:292; British Library, Harleian 2224, fol. 5v.

192. Clarendon, *Life*, 2:473–74. Laud had made the same point earlier concerning members of the House (British Library, Additional 11045, fol. 137v). See the Lords' doubts on this point in connection with the impeachment of Lord Kimbolton and the seven peers, above, pp. 173, 174–75.

193. Cobbett, *State Trials*, 6:364–65. Actually, the eradication had not yet been done, and nothing was done until the following March. Later the Lords determined that it had been a mistake to obliterate the record of the impeachment proceedings and that the statute had provided only for the obliteration of the record of attainder (Foster, "Journal of the House of Lords," p. 136).

194. HLRO, Committee for Privileges, Minute Book no. 2, pp. 143–44; *LJ*, 13:193. Among the papers in Lord Delamere's case, there are several pages of notes concerning Strafford's trial (British Library, Lansdowne 515, fols. 246–246v).

195. *LJ*, 13:584, 689–90.

196. Rushworth, *Tryal of Strafford*, p. 156. See also PRO, SP16/524/10.

197. On judicature on accusation from the Commons, see Tite, table 2, pp. 224–27.

198. Allen Horstman, "Justice and Peers: The Judicial Activities of the Seventeenth-Century House of Lords" (Ph.D. diss., University of California, Berkeley, 1977), p. 125.

199. J. R. Tanner, *Tudor Constitutional Documents* (Cambridge, 1922), p. 343; Holdsworth, *History of English Law*, 1:244–45. I use the term Exchequer Chamber as defined by this statute. It was also applied to two other institutions.

200. For a discussion of this point, see Hargrave, *Jurisdiction*, pp. 127, 132, 138–43. In his transcript of the Elizabethan journals of the House of Lords, Robert Bowyer noted a petition in 8 Eliz. that asked the chief justice to bring the record of a case to parliament in order that the Lords and Commons might advise on the reformation of errors. Bowyer observed that this petition indicated that members of the Commons "are called and equally judges with the Lords in writs of error, whereof experience and longe practise proveth the contrary." He thought that the Commons lost this right in 1 H. IV, but that the ancient form of the petition suing for a writ of error had continued. A later hand, possibly that of William Petyt, has added, "They were never judges but as one Courte, when both Houses sate together" (Inner Temple, Petyt 537/6, fol. 112).

201. Tanner, p. 343.

202. Horstman, "Justice and Peers," p. 125.
203. Coke said he knew of more than twenty-five writs of error brought into the House (Horstman, "Justice and Peers," p. 130). He mentions Sir Christopher Heydon's case in 1614 (Coke, *Fourth Institute*, pp. 22–23).
204. Horstman, "Justice and Peers," pp. 129–30; Hargrave, *Jurisdiction*, pp. viii–ix.
205. See above, pp. 79–80.
206. Horstman, "Justice and Peers," p. 131; Hargrave, *Jurisdiction*, pp. xxvii–xxviii.
207. Hargrave, *Jurisdiction*, pp. vii, 135–36; Holdsworth, *History of English Law*, 1:370–71. See the letter from Sir Robert Heath to Mr. Read, 5 November 1640, asking him to move Mr. Secretary for the king's warrant for a writ of error in parliament to reverse a judgment against a poor widow. "It is drawn accordinge to the usuall forme in the like cases, and is an act of Justice for his Majesty to grant, and without his Majesty's warrant cannot be had." He asks for the king's signature "with this only direction *Fiat Justitia* which is the forme used in other presidents" (Inner Temple, Petyt 538/17, fol. 476).
208. Hargrave, *Jurisdiction*, p. 136; *LJ*, 2:94.
209. Hargrave, *Jurisdiction*, p. 145; *LJ*, 2:92, 94, 165.
210. Horstman, "Justice and Peers," p. 53; Holdsworth, *History of English Law*, 1:215–16; John Palmer, *Practice in the House of Lords on Appeals, Writs of Error, and Claims of Peerage* (London, 1830), pp. 144–45.
211. Coke, *Fourth Institute*, pp. 21–22; Hargrave, *Jurisdiction*, pp. 150–51; *LJ*, 2:94, 165.
212. Hargrave, *Jurisdiction*, p. 153; Palmer, pp. 128–29; *The Practising Attorney* (London, 1779), p. 303; Coke, *Fourth Institute*, p. 22 (John Beauchamp), and the references there cited; [Sir James Dyer], *Cy ensuont ascun novel Cases, Collectes per les iades tresreverend Judge, Mounsieur Jasques Dyer, chiefe Justice del Common Banke* (London, 1601), p. 375.
213. Hargrave, *Jurisdiction*, p. 151; Macqueen, p. 408.
214. Palmer, pp. 163–64; *LJ*, 4:192; Relfe, "Book of Orders 1710," pp. 290–91.
215. Palmer, p. 165; Holdsworth, *History of English Law*, 1:371; *LJ*, 8:551, and 10:555–56, 646. For instructions concerning the drawing of a *remittitur*, the order to return a case to the court from which it came, see HLRO, Main Papers, H.L., 16 November and 16 December 1646. It was to be engrossed and annexed to the record, with a copy annexed to the book "which is to remain in the Parliament Office. The Record being sent back into K's Bench"; "Mr. Phipps can direct if there be need of his help."
216. HLRO, Braye 65, fols. 10–11; Hargrave, *Jurisdiction*, p. 149.
217. *LJ*, 3:132.
218. HLRO, Main Papers, H.L., 6 April 1641, 25 February 1641/2, 20 September 1642; Horstman, "Justice and Peers," pp. 296–97; Macqueen, pp. 359–60.
219. *LJ*, 4:270. See ibid., p. 569 for a slightly different order in February 1641/2.
220. Ibid., 8:324, 335.
221. Ibid., 7:140; HLRO, Main Papers, H.L., 16 January 1644/5.
222. Hargrave, *Jurisdiction*, p. 145.
223. *CJ*, 4:422; Horstman, "Justice and Peers," p. 299. The House of Lords refused to pass the order to this effect prepared by the Commons; it preferred to issue its own order, which was read once (HLRO, Main Papers, H.L., 30 January 1645/6; *LJ*, 8:134).
224. *LJ*, 6:554–55.
225. Macqueen, pp. 359–60. For Standing Order no. 54, see *Manuscripts of the House*

of Lords, n.s., vol. 12, *1714–1718* (London, 1977), p. 12.

226. *LJ*, 8:336–37.

227. HLRO, Main Papers, H.L., 12 April 1647, petition of Ann Loftus; *Of Judicature*, p. 8. See also Bodleian Library, Carte MS 78, fols. 563–563v: a collection of precedents showing that parliaments may err and that erroneous judgments in parliament in civil matters should not be perpetually binding, but should be reversed by the same parliament or another; *Matthew v. Matthew* (28 May 1624) is cited.

228. Horstman, "Justice and Peers," p. 298. I differ slightly from Horstman in my count for the early period.

229. Ibid., p. 299.

230. Holdsworth, *History of English Law*, 1:245.

231. Hargrave, *Jurisdiction*, p. 125.

232. See below, p. 187.

233. See above, p. 102.

234. In his treatise on the privileges of the barons of England, Selden observed that the statute 14 E. III, st. 1, c. 5 was the basis of the power of the House of Lords to appoint judges out of themselves to examine judgments and delays in other courts (Selden, *Priviledges*, p. 138).

235. See above, pp. 106–8.

236. Pike, p. 283; *LJ*, 4:162.

237. Pike, p. 283; *LJ*, 4:175.

238. J. S. Morrill, *The Revolt of the Provinces: Conservatives and Radicals in the English Civil War, 1630–1650* (London, 1976), p. 34. In July 1641 the House had issued a general order to secure possessions and enclosures against riots and tumults (*LJ*, 4:312). For Lincoln's case, see *LJ*, 4:281, 289, 304. For Sussex, see ibid., p. 699; 5:32, 43, 66, 83; 6:625; and 7:32, 417, 429; HLRO, Main Papers, H.L., 10 July 1644.

239. HLRO, Main Papers, H.L., 3 December 1641; *LJ*, 4:481.

240. HLRO, Main Papers, H.L., 30 August 1646.

241. PRO, SP14/132/77.

242. *LJ*, 3:412–13, 569–70, 865.

243. HLRO, Main Papers, H.L., 8 July 1641; *LJ*, 4:281, 289, 304.

244. HLRO, Main Papers, H.L., 2 July and 25 August 1641; *LJ*, 4:208, 297, 375–76.

245. HLRO, Main Papers, H.L., 8 September 1641; *LJ*, 4:390; British Library, Sloane 1467, fol. 38v.

246. HLRO, Main Papers, H.L., 24 May 1645; *LJ*, 7:389.

247. *LJ*, 6:247.

248. HLRO, Main Papers, H.L., 10 July 1646.

249. HLRO, Main Papers, H.L., 22 and 23 April 1648.

250. *LJ*, 9:441–42; HLRO, Main Papers, H.L., 26 August 1648, fol. 97.

251. Tite, pp. 120–22. "That as he was put into their hands by your Majestie, soe you would not take him out of their hands which they conceive breaks the liberty and priviledges of their House" (de Villiers, p. 33).

252. Tite, pp. 122–29. In 1610 the House had been concerned whether a bill would affect its right to try peers, but was reassured by the king's promise to maintain its privileges (Foster, *1610*, 1:247).

253. See above, p. 73; PRO, SP14/8/55; Gardiner, *Debates in the House of Lords 1624 and 1626*, pp. 104–5. They raised a similar point concerning ordinances of sequestration (*LJ*, 6:12).

254. Cope, *Proceedings of the Short Parliament*, p. 88.

255. Lincoln's Inn, Hale MS 12, fol. 481v. In Bacon's case, the Lords had ruled that "none be urged to accuse himself" (*LJ*, 3:68).

256. *LJ*, 3:398; PRO, SP14/165/34; *HMC, Buccleuch*, 3:244. This was also a convenient way to gain time in an awkward political situation. A number of peers were listed among the recusants (*CJ*, 1:776).

257. *Manuscripts of the House of Lords*, 10:7 (Standing Orders nos. 38 and 39).

258. See above, p. 168; HLRO, Braye 93, fol. 82v; Main Papers, H.L., 9 February 1640/1.

259. Relf, *Debates in the House of Lords 1621, 1625, 1628*, pp. xx–xxx; Tite, pp. 84–85. Possibly the king also encouraged it (Horstman, "Justice and Peers," pp. 139–41). For Lord Sheffield's role in pressing Bourchier to forward a petition for a review of a decree in Chancery, see Hacket, 1:75.

260. Tite, pp. 122–45.

261. Foster, "Procedure of the House of Commons against Patents and Monopolies," pp. 69, 75–76; Horstman, "A New *Curia Regis*," p. 413.

262. Russell, *Parliaments and English Politics*, p. 15.

263. Cockburn, pp. 136–37; Horstman, "Justice and Peers," p. 144; *Court and Times of Charles I*, 1:346.

264. Derek Hirst, "The Privy Council and Problems of Enforcement in the 1620s," *The Journal of British Studies* 18 (1978): 66; Horstman, "A New *Curia Regis*," p. 414.

265. Holdsworth, *History of English Law*, 1:415–16; HLRO, Main Papers, H.L., December 1646, the petition of Isabell Meeringe; ibid., [1641], petition of Sir Arthur Ingram.

266. See the petition of Anne Rigby: she "is informed that the power and jurisdiction of the ecclesiastical courts being not yet settled, she cannot expect redress in that or any other ordinary way" (HLRO, Main Papers, H.L., 17 June 1645).

267. Cockburn, pp. 241–45.

268. *LJ*, 6:554–55, 9:672; Horstman, "Justice and Peers," p. 299.

269. Hargrave, *Jurisdiction*, pp. 200–201; Twysden, *Certain Considerations*, p. 165.

270. Pike, pp. 231–34, 295–98. For earlier attempts to limit jurisdiction, see the proposed ordinance in HLRO, Main Papers, H.L., 14 April 1648; and the Humble Petition and Advice (1657) (Gardiner, *Constitutional Documents*, pp. 447–59).

10. LEGISLATION

1. McIlwain, pp. 277, 288.

2. Ibid., p. 312; British Library, Additional 11402, fols. 160–160v, a reference I owe to Conrad Russell; Yale University Library, Osborn Collection, Braye 52/1.

3. *LJ*, 2:284. See also PRO, SP14/10/40, for his views on the nature of the proposed act.

4. Spedding, *Letters and Life*, 3:343.

5. PRO, SP14/8/60. The additional clause suggested by the king gave as a reason for the act the possibility that the importunity of great subjects and well-deserving persons might so diminish the revenue of the crown that the king would be compelled to get money from his subjects. Cf. PRO, SP14/9/39.

6. McIlwain, pp. 323–24.

7. PRO, SP14/162/5, 6.

8. Russell, *Parliaments and English Politics*, p. 48; PRO, SP14/8/29; *LJ*, 2:689.

9. Foster, *1610*, 1:15–16, 2:35–56. Russell notes that six of these points were finally

embodied in legislation in 1624 (*Parliaments and English Politics*, p. 110n). Also see Roberts and Duncan, "Parliamentary Undertaking," p. 490.

10. Conrad Russell, "Parliamentary History in Perspective, 1604–1629," *History* 61, no. 201 (1976): 8.

11. Russell, *Parliament and English Politics*, pp. 45–47.

12. Foster, *1610*, 1:221–22; Roland G. Usher, *The Reconstruction of the English Church*, 2 vols. (New York, 1910), 1:351–53, and 2:119, 127, 259. In 1606 Bancroft informed the House that the king desired a bill to limit the use of excommunication (*LJ*, 2:405).

13. For legislation proposed in 1625, see PRO, SP16/521/34. *LJ*, 3:493; *Commons Debates 1628*, 2:6. Russell interprets Coventry's remarks in 1626 as an invitation to members to bring forward bills (*Parliaments and English Politics*, p. 274).

14. PRO, SP16/124/10. Some bills in 1626 may have been officially sponsored (Russell, *Parliaments and English Politics*, p. 274).

15. *HMC, Buccleuch*, 3:411; HLRO, Main Papers, H.L., 28 January 1640/1; HLRO, Braye 93, fols. 124–124v.

16. Laud, *Works*, 4:359.

17. Foster, "Procedure of the House of Commons against Patents and Monopolies," pp. 76–77. The bill for purveyance in 1624 is said to have originated in a petition from the Buckingham grand jury (Russell, *Parliaments and English Politics*, p. 183n). It also owed something to bills of purveyance in earlier parliaments.

18. HLRO, Braye 93, fols. 81v–82.

19. See above, pp. 72, 83; *HMC, Buccleuch*, 3:243, 403; British Library, Harleian 2325, fol. 13. In 1610 the attorney general drafted the bill for the restitution of the children of George Brooke (HLRO, Main Papers, H.L., 5 March 1609/10).

20. On this point, see Hakewill, pp. 131–33.

21. *LJ*, 3:25, 79. For Morrell, see *Commons Debates 1621*, 2:294 (n. 1), a reference I owe to Cordelia Stone.

22. Elsyng, "Method of Passing Bills," p. 117; *LJ*, 2:368–69. For amendments by the judges, see HLRO, Main Papers, H.L., 16 June 1610. For problems with the bill of monopolies, see Russell, *Parliaments and English Politics*, pp. 190–91.

23. *LJ*, 2:435, and 3:178–79, 524; British Library, Stowe 375, fol. 88; Russell, *Parliaments and English Politics*, p. 275.

24. Holdsworth, *History of English Law*, 11:292–301. For Conrad Russell's observations on this point, see *Parliaments and English Politics*, p. 48n.

25. Hakewill, pp. 131–32, 134.

26. See above, pp. 56, 59, 66.

27. "No Lord is to introduce any private business without a Petition exhibited to this house It being a Court of Record 8 Dec. 1641" (British Library, Additional 36102, fol. 19). For an example of such a petition, see HLRO, Main Papers, H.L., 20 January 1640/1.

28. Though they were public acts, subsidy acts and the general pardon were not always enrolled (see above, p. 52). See Holdsworth, 11:294–98.

29. For the form of certifying private acts, see Inner Temple, Petyt 537/8, fol. 106; *LJ*, 3:225; British Library, Cotton MSS, Titus B.V., fol. 281. For this and for the fees received by Bowyer for the certification of private acts, see Yale University Library, Osborn Collection, Braye 55/91; Foster, *Painful Labour of Mr. Elsyng*, pp. 10, 17 (n. 88), 18, 33–34.

30. PRO, C65/187 (pt. 2), C65/189; Sessional Acts for 1624: *Anno Regni Iacobi, Regis Angliae, Scotiae, Franciae, & Hiberniae, viz. Angliae, Franciae & Hiberniae, xxj. &*

Scotiae lvij. At the Parliament begun and holden at Westminster, the 19. day of February, in the 21. yeere of the Reigne of our most gracious Souereigne Lord, Iames by the grace of God, of England, France and Ireland King, Defender of the Faith, &c. and of Scotland the 57 . . . To the high pleasure of Almighty God and to the weale publique of this Realme, were enacted as followeth (London, 1624); British Library, Additional 40087, fol. 91.

31. Bedford Office, Woburn MSS, HMC no. 11, Commonplace Book, p. 2258. Conversely, a modern hybrid bill is a public bill that in certain respects affects private rights (May, p. 296).

32. Elton, "Rolls of Parliament," pp. 16–17.

33. PRO, C65/187 (pt. 2), C65/190. For similar problems in the reign of Henry VIII, see James I. Miklovich, "The Significance of the Royal Sign Manual in Early Tudor Legislative Procedure," *BIHR* 52, no. 12 (May 1979): 30.

34. HLRO, Parchment Collection, Box 178A.

35. PRO, C65/189; Sessional Acts for 1625: *Anno Regni Caroli, Regis Angliae, Scotiae, Franciae, & Hiberniae Primo. At the Parliament begun at Westminster the 18. day of Iune, Anno Dom. 1625. in the first yeere of the Reigne of our most gracious Souereigne Lord, Charles . . . To the high pleasure of Almighty God, and to the weale publike of this Realme, were enacted as followeth* (London, 1630).

36. Sessional Acts for 1624, 1625, and 1628: *Anno Regni Caroli, Regis Angliae, Scotiae, Franciae, & Hiberniae Tertio. At the Parliament begun at Westminster the 17. day of March, Anno Dom. 1627. in the third yeere of the Reigne of our most gracious Soueraigne Lord, Charles . . . To the high pleasure of Almighty God, and to the weale publike of this Realme, were enacted as followeth* (London, 1628); PRO, C65/181, C65/182, C65/183, C65/184, C65/187 (pt. 2), C65/189, C65/190, C65/194, C65/195, C65/196.

37. "Moderne Forme of the Parliaments," p. 297.

38. Ibid., p. 301; Hakewill, p. 154.

39. See above, p. 47; Foster, *Painful Labour of Mr. Elsyng*, pp. 14–16.

40. "Moderne Forme of the Parliaments," p. 297.

41. The clerk's man received 10s. "upon the enteringe of every private bill as for breviating it" (Yale University Library, Osborn Collection, Braye 55/86). For a brief, see below, n. 47.

42. "Moderne Forme of the Parliaments," p. 297; Elsyng, "Method of Passing Bills," pp. 113–14.

43. *HMC, Hastings*, 4:265 (1614); HLRO, Braye 93, fol. 20 (2 April 1606); Elsyng, "Method of Passing Bills," p. 114.

44. *HMC, Hastings*, 4:238.

45. Macray, *Clarendon's History*, 1:313.

46. Foster, *Painful Labour of Mr. Elsyng*, pp. 16–17; Elsyng, "Method of Passing Bills," p. 115; HLRO, Main Papers, H.L., 30 May, 21 June, 18 October, and 10 November 1610.

47. See PRO, SP14/162/47, for a printed breviate of a bill on which is written the date of the committee meeting. Also see HLRO, Main Papers, H.L., 23 April 1640, 27 July 1641.

48. See, for example, the petitions of the tinners against the bill for the stannaries, the barber surgeons against the physicians' bill, and the vintners of London against the bill of deceitful wines in HLRO, Main Papers, H.L., 5 June, 16 July, and 26 August 1641. The vintners offered a counterbill. There is a good deal of material of this sort in the state papers and in the Main Papers of the House of Lords. See PRO, SP14/

26/82 (objections to the curriers' bill); SP14/21/30, 33 (papers relating to the act against recusants); and SP14/19/19 (reasons on behalf of the bill to import wines, 1606). For other material against bills, see PRO, SP14/19/21, 35, 97; SP14/55/37; and SP14/77/28; and supporting bills, see PRO, SP14/19/84; SP14/19/20; and SP14/20/9.

49. Elsyng, "Method of Passing Bills," p. 116.

50. *LJ*, 2:334, 336.

51. *LJ*, 2:290, 295, 320; Elsyng, "Method of Passing Bills," p. 116.

52. Elsyng, "Method of Passing Bills," pp. 116–17. Bacon had introduced this procedure in 1621 (de Villiers, p. 11). "Moderne Forme of the Parliaments," p. 298.

53. Elsyng, "Method of Passing Bills," p. 117; HLRO, Braye 65, fol. 3; Gardiner, *Debates in the House of Lords 1621*, p. 76.

54. *Manuscripts of the House of Lords*, 10:2 (Standing Orders nos. 11 and 12). Curiously, Salisbury in 1606 reserved a speech on the bill for Welsh cottons until the third reading (*LJ*, 2:412).

55. Elsyng, "Method of Passing Bills," p. 117. See above, p. 95.

56. Foster, *1610*, 1:231; Cope, *Proceedings of the Short Parliament*, p. 80.

57. *LJ*, 3:25; Gardiner, *Debates in the House of Lords 1624 and 1626*, pp. 148, 167.

58. These words in the original draft of the Standing Orders for 1621 were omitted in 1624; see *Manuscripts of the House of Lords*, 10:5, n. 5 (Standing Order no. 32).

59. Ibid., p. 2 (Standing Orders nos. 11 and 12).

60. HLRO, Braye 93, fols. 5v, 54–54v; Inner Temple, Petyt 537/8, fol. 285v; Relf, *Debates in the House of Lords 1621, 1625, 1628*, p. 33; *LJ*, 3:590; Gardiner, *Debates in the House of Lords 1624 and 1626*, pp. 184–85.

61. See above, p. 25.

62. *HMC, Hastings*, 4:257.

63. Ibid., p. 260.

64. Foster, *1610*, 1:4.

65. For Ellesmere, see Huntington Library, Ellesmere MSS 443, 451, 455, 458, 459, 467, 468, 473, 488, 489, 2608, 2621. For Northampton's speeches, see British Library, Cotton MSS, Titus C.VI. For Salisbury, see Foster, *1610*, 1:3–8. In 1626 Buckingham spoke from notes (*HMC, Buccleuch*, 3:291). For a speech prepared for him, see PRO, SP16/26/80.

66. Elsyng, "Method of Passing Bills," pp. 117–18; "Moderne Forme of the Parliaments," p. 298.

67. Bodleian Library, Ashmole 824, fol. 126; PRO, SP14/19/51.

68. Nicholas, 2:353.

69. Gardiner, *Debates in the House of Lords 1621*, p. 76.

70. *LJ*, 2:394.

71. Elsyng, "Method of Passing Bills," p. 121; Hakewill, pp. 163–65.

72. "Moderne Forme of the Parliaments," p. 298; Elsyng, "Method of Passing Bills," p. 118. See also Smith, *De Republica Anglorum*, p. 53.

73. Gardiner, *Debates in the House of Lords 1624 and 1626*, p. 115; Cope, *Proceedings of the Short Parliament*, pp. 79, 89; *LJ*, 7:359–60, 8:551, 9:96. There was an interesting instance in 1628 when the lords disagreed about the order of business. The lord keeper said, "When my Lord Westmerland moved to have the Bill read, there was question made of it and greate contradiction, and I stopped the Clerke twice or thrice from reading the Bill and asked your lordships whether you would goe on with my Lord of Abergavennys byll [or] whether you would goe forward in the Buysynes of the daye" (Relf, *Debates in the House of Lords 1621, 1625, 1628*,

p. 153n; cf. p. 151). The implication in this debate was that any decision on the matter must be unanimous (ibid., pp. 153–54), but I have no other evidence to indicate that this must be the case.

74. "Moderne Forme of the Parliaments," p. 298. In 1641/2 all lords who had not been present when a matter was debated withdrew at the time of a vote (HLRO, Braye 24, 16 March 1641/2).

75. *LJ*, 3:117.

76. *Manuscripts of the House of Lords*, 10:2 (Standing Order no. 13). Exceptionally in the Bergavenny-Le Despenser case, the lords indicated their vote by saying "Neville" or "Fane" (*LJ*, 2:345–46; British Library, Stowe 375, fol. 87v). Also see Elsyng, "Method of Passing Bills," p. 118.

77. Inner Temple, Petyt 537/8, fol. 285v (23 May 1614); HMC, *Hastings*, 4:289; Relf, *Debates in the House of Lords 1621, 1625, 1628*, p. 2.

78. Elsyng, "Method of Passing Bills," p. 118. Bowyer in 1614 noted "*Content* stand up bare. *Not content* set still covered. Hereupon one Lord of each side did count them" (Inner Temple, Petyt 537/8, fol. 285v). See HMC, *Buccleuch*, 3:232: "So that the house was divided, the contents standing up bareheaded, and the not-contents sitting still." Possibly this describes a shortcut by which the lords voted without going through the time-consuming process of voting individually and later proceeding to a poll. There is some inconclusive, undated evidence that the lords may have abbreviated the voting procedure by raising their hands. "When Question is made in the upper House the tryall is made by holding up of hands and if they be doubtfull then by telling the Poles without dividing the house" (Bodleian Library, Tanner 391, fol. 162; British Library, Additional 36856, fol. 44v; PRO, CRES 40/18, p. 89, a version of Hakewill's chapter, "The Manner How Statutes Are Enacted in Parliament by Passing of Bills," drawn to my attention by Conrad Russell). Professor Beatty has misread the evidence he presents in "Committee Appointments in the House of Lords," *Huntington Library Quarterly* 29, no. 2 (February 1966): 121–22. As J. C. Sainty has pointed out, the system of voting by individual voices given one after the other was probably closely linked with sitting in order of precedence (*Divisions in the House of Lords*, p. 8).

79. 31 H. VIII, c. 10.

80. "Moderne Forme of the Parliaments," p. 299; Elsyng, "Method of Passing Bills," p. 118; see above, p. 31.

81. "Moderne Forme of the Parliaments," p. 299; Elsyng, "Method of Passing Bills," p. 118; HMC, *Buccleuch*, 3:340; see above, p. 21.

82. British Library, Additional 36102, fols. 39–39v; HLRO, Braye 93, fols. 11v, 14–14v; *LJ*, 9:88.

83. Elsyng, "Method of Passing Bills," p. 121; *LJ*, 3:172, 177; Gardiner, *Debates in the House of Lords 1621*, p. 104; British Library, Additional 36102, fol. 41v.

84. *LJ*, 3:218–19, 253–55. See also the case of a private bill in 1606 (Elsyng, "Method of Passing Bills," pp. 121–22; *LJ*, 2:402).

85. *LJ*, 2:653, 655.

86. "Moderne Forme of the Parliaments," p. 299–301. See above, pp. 71–72, 83.

87. "Moderne Forme of the Parliaments," p. 299; British Library, Additional 36856, fol. 27v.

88. Hakewill, p. 164; "Moderne Forme of the Parliaments," p. 299.

89. "Moderne Forme of the Parliaments," pp. 299–300.

90. Ibid. The spelling varies: "sont assentus," "ont assentus"; "Communs," "Comons."

91. Ibid.; HLRO, Braye 65, fol. 5.

92. *LJ*, 2:270.

93. *HMC, Hastings*, 4:238.

94. Cope, *Proceedings of the Short Parliament*, p. 63.

95. *LJ*, 3:110, 540; *HMC, Buccleuch*, 3:243, 245.

96. The Lords had offered a proviso at the last moment that displeased the lower House. When the upper House reconsidered its position and withdrew its proviso, there was no need to debate the bill further and it went through rapidly (PRO, SP14/165/61; Elsyng, "Method of Passing Bills," p. 122).

97. Macray, *Clarendon's History*, 1:262.

98. *LJ*, 3:422, 463; "Moderne Forme of the Parliaments," p. 304; British Library, Harleian 2325, fol. 49.

99. *LJ*, 3:422–23.

100. "It is to be noted that all the time of Parliament he [the clerk of the crown] sitteth on the right hand of the Clerk of Parliament, and when he readeth the Acts, he standeth on his left hand, which is the higher place, being on the King's right hand" (quoted "from an ancient manuscript" by Macqueen, pp. 65–66).

101. For an account of a commission in the reign of Edward VI, see W. K. Jordan, ed., *The Chronicle and Political Papers of King Edward* (Ithaca, 1966), pp. 118–19.

102. *LJ*, 4:580.

103. "Moderne Forme of the Parliaments," p. 301; HLRO, Braye 65, fol. 6; Cope, *Proceedings of the Short Parliament*, p. 269. Conrad Russell has pointed out that it was a custom as frequently honored in the breach as in the observance (Russell, *Parliaments and English Politics*, p. 180).

104. *Commons Debates 1625*, pp. 112–13; Cope, *Proceedings of the Short Parliament*, pp. 183–84.

105. Hakewill, pp. 132–33. See also Paul L. Ward, ed., *William Lambarde's Notes on the Procedures and Privileges of the House of Commons (1584)*, House of Commons Library Document no. 10 (London, 1977), p. 79. In 1606 Chief Justice Popham and the lord chief baron of the Exchequer advised Salisbury concerning amendments to the subsidy bill (PRO, SP14/24/28).

106. See above, p. 73.

107. *LJ*, 3:858, 860; Relf, *Debates in the House of Lords 1621, 1625, 1628*, p. 225. The Commons had suggested that the Lords return the bill so that it could be amended in the lower House. This the upper House indignantly declined to do (*Court and Times of Charles I*, 1:367).

108. *LJ*, 3:862; PRO, SP16/107/70. In 1641 there was a rumor that Vane and others proposed to change the wording of the subsidy bill in order to embroil the Houses with each other (PRO, 31/3(72)).

109. Nicholas is in error in thinking that the Lords read the bill only once (Nicholas, 1:192). Elsyng observed that the subsidy bill used to be read only once, but that in his time every bill except the pardon was read three times (Elsyng, "Method of Passing Bills," pp. 113, 115). See below, n. 121.

110. *LJ*, 3:51–52, 461.

111. Lambarde, *Notes*, p. 79.

112. PRO, SP14/165/61.

113. Gardiner, *Commons Debates 1625*, p. 67; *LJ*, 3:465; British Library, Additional 48091, fol. 23v. The same situation had occurred in March 1620/1 (*LJ*, 3:64).

114. *CJ*, 1:919.

115. PRO, C65/184, 186, 189, 190.

116. PRO, SP14/165/61.

117. Perhaps he was influenced by his experience in Scotland (McIlwain, p. 302). In En-

gland, by the time of Elizabeth, the older practice that the monarch might amend a bill or enter provisions when giving his assent had disappeared, and it was generally held that no alteration could be made without the assent of Lords and Commons (J. E. Neale, "The Commons' Privilege of Free Speech in Parliament," in *Tudor Studies*, ed. R. W. Seton-Watson [London, 1924], p. 276). See also the king's action on the earl of Hertford's bill in 1624 and the judges' resolution concerning the bill of sheriffs' accounts (*LJ*, 3:422–23).

118. *LJ*, 3:50, 462.

119. See above, p. 83.

120. *HMC, Buccleuch*, 3:244.

121. *LJ*, 3:52. For evidence that these parts were read three times in the upper House, see *LJ*, 3:52, 403, 406, 490, 847. In 1628 all three readings took place on the same day (ibid., p. 847). John Browne, who became clerk in 1638, observed that the bill was read only once; but he was in error or may have been referring to the original grant, not to the other sections (HLRO, Braye 65, fol. 6). There had been no confirmed grant in the Short Parliament, only a "benevolence" direct from the convocation of Canterbury (for this, see HLRO, Main Papers, H.L., 13 August 1641; and Laud's diary in *Works*, 3:285–86), so Browne had no firsthand experience from which to speak. Hakewill also indicated that the clerical subsidy was read once in each House (Hakewill, p. 138). This was correct for the lower House (Nicholas, 1:205–6), but not for the upper. See also the Nicholas diary for 1624 (PRO, SP14/166, fol. 230). In 1621 Elsyng wrote to Sir Robert Cotton, "I have this day read the Subsidy of the Temporalty and the Subsidy of the Clergy twice, which makes me faint and weary" (British Library, Cotton MSS, Julius C.III, fol. 170).

122. In 1601, "The subsidy of the Clergy was sent in a Roll according to the usual Acts, to which Sir Edward Hobbie took Exceptions, because it was not sent in a long Skin of Parchment under the Queens Hand and Seal. So it was sent back again, and then the other sent" (D'Ewes, *Journals of All the Parliaments*, p. 688).

123. HLRO, Original Act, 1 *Car.* I, no. 5; *LJ*, 3:52. See also HLRO, Braye 62, fol. 190.

124. *Commons Debates 1621*, 2:163, 4:383, 7:609; *Commons Debates 1625*, p. 55; *LJ*, 3:69.

125. See Bacon's remark concerning the general pardon in his life of Henry VII (James Spedding et al., eds., *The Works of Francis Bacon*, 7 vols. [London, 1870–76], 6:39); the Commons' petition of 1606 (Inner Temple, Petyt 537/8, fol. 235); the letter from the judges to Buckingham in 1620 (Spedding, *Letters and Life*, 7:148); and James's speech in parliament in 1621 (*LJ*, 3:69).

126. Russell, *Parliaments and English Politics*, p. 52.

127. PRO, SP14/158/59, SP14/124/27; Rushworth, *Historical Collections*, 1:51.

128. *Commons Debates 1621*, 2:163, 5:100; Rushworth, *Historical Collections*, 1:42–43; Bodleian Library, Carte 121, fols. 13–13v. Blackstone believed that one need not plead a legislative pardon; but Lambarde and Coke stated that it was necessary to do so in the case of a legislative pardon drawn with exceptions like the general pardons of the seventeenth century (*Commentaries on the Laws of England in Four Books by Sir William Blackstone*, ed. William Draper Lewis [Philadelphia, 1897], bk. 4, p. 402; William Lambarde, *Eirenarcha, or of the Office of the Iustices of Peace* [London, 1607], pp. 551–52; Sir Edward Coke, *The Third Part of the Institutes of the Laws of England* [London, 1680], cap. 105). The pardon did not apply to actions already begun, hence the hasty introduction of bills in Star chamber when a pardon was rumored in 1623 (*Commons Debates 1621*, 7:626–27; *Cal. Wynn Papers*, no. 1157).

129. Coke, *Third Institute*, cap. 105.

130. PRO, SP14/21/29; Pym's diary for 1624, Finch-Hatton MS 50, fol. 71 (I have used the transcript at the Yale Center for Parliamentary History); British Library, Harleian 6424, fol. 88v.

131. PRO, SP14/124/32, 49; *Commons Debates 1621*, 7:626–27.

132. PRO, SP14/21/29. For examples, see the pardons for 1628 and 1641; neither was passed and both were signed by the king (HLRO, Parchment Collection, Box 178A, 178B). In the reign of Henry VIII, a number of bills affecting the royal prerogative came to parliament with the royal sign manual (Miklovich, "Royal Sign Manual," pp. 23–24).

133. "Modern Forme of the Parliaments," p. 301; HLRO, Braye 65, fol. 6; Elsyng, "Method of Passing Bills," p. 115; HLRO, Parchment Collection, Box 178A.

134. Hakewill, p. 138. The procedure followed for the general pardon of 1540 differed greatly from the Stuart period (Lehmberg, *Later Parliaments*, pp. 118–19). Elsyng recorded a precedent from 3 E. VI that a proviso to the general pardon must be read three times (Elsyng, "Method of Passing Bills," p. 113).

135. Hakewill, p. 138.

136. For exceptions, see *LJ*, 2:657. In 1621 Mompesson was excepted from all future pardons (*LJ*, 3:72). In 1628 the Commons vainly tried to discover from the attorney general the terms of the pardon before it was brought to the House (*Commons Debates 1628*, 4:291, 295, 298, 331, 333, 336, 345, the debates on 13, 16, and 17 June; *CJ*, 1:912, 914).

137. *LJ*, 2:657–58.

138. PRO, SP16/108/52. "The Lords think not fit to tender his Majesty's general pardon until they shall find by some of their friends in both Houses that it will be accepted; for that it will not be for his Majesty's honour to have it rejected" (PRO, SP16/483/41, 13 August 1641); *Court and Times of Charles I*, 1:370.

139. Hakewill, p. 182.

140. D'Ewes, *Journals of All the Parliaments*, p. 274.

141. "Moderne Forme of the Parliaments," p. 305; HLRO, Braye 65, fol. 9; PRO, C65/187, C65/184.

142. *LJ*, 2:439. *Manuscripts of the House of Lords*, 10:12–13 (Standing Order no. 60).

143. *LJ*, 2:445. In the reigns of Henry VIII and Elizabeth, such bills came to parliament with the royal sign manual (Miklovich, "Royal Sign Manual," pp. 24–25; D'Ewes, *Journals of All the Parliaments*, pp. 20, 147).

144. HLRO, Braye 93, fols. 47–47v. Blackstone observed that only parliament could purify blood once attainted (*Commentaries*, bk. 4, p. 402).

145. *LJ*, 3:503–4; British Library, Harleian 2325, fol. 14. See Graves, *House of Lords Edward VI and Mary I*, p. 149.

146. HLRO, Relfe, "Book of Orders 1710," p. 626. The Commons' Committee for Privileges in 1624 considered that a person naturalized by letters patent was unfit to sit as a member of parliament. Presumably naturalization by act of parliament was more desirable (*Reports of Certain Cases, Determined and Adjudged by the Commons in Parliament, in the Twenty-first and Twenty-second Years of the Reign of King James the First: Collected by John Glanville, Esq., Serjeant at Law, then Chairman of the Committee of Privileges and Elections* [London, 1775], p. 122). Naturalization bills usually proceeded smoothly. However, in 1628 a bill for naturalizing Gerbier came close to being cast out because of the antagonism to the duke of Buckingham (PRO, SP16/108/52).

147. PRO, SP14/76/31.

148. The earl continued to follow the bill in 1610 (HLRO, Main Papers, H.L., 29 June

1610). See also PRO, SP14/19/75, 76, 77.

149. HLRO, Main Papers, H.L., Supplementary 1604–10, 16 April 1610.

150. HLRO, Minute Book no. 2. See also Foster, *Painful Labour of Mr. Elsyng*, p. 16. In 1641 John Sharpe wrote that he had been to Job Throckmorton, deputy clerk, concerning a bill, and Throckmorton promised that "Sir A. J." should not have sight or copy of it until it had been read in the House (HLRO, Main Papers, H.L., 15 July 1641).

151. HLRO, Main Papers, H.L., 14 June 1610. The clerk of the lower House similarly could advance or block a bill. In 1610 Carleton wrote Edmondes that his naturalization bill "hath been smothered in the clerk's pocket." When Carleton found the clerk at fault in another matter, Edmondes's bill emerged (Foster, *1610*, 2:148n).

152. *LJ*, 3:325.

153. Similarly, the influence of sponsors was important in the passage of ordinances during the Long Parliament (Elizabeth Read Foster, "The House of Lords and Ordinances, 1641–1649," *The American Journal of Legal History* 21 [1977]: 167). Cf. Lehmberg, *Later Parliaments*, pp. 255–56.

154. See above, p. 92.

155. Harold Hulme, *The Life of Sir John Eliot* (London, 1957), p. 305; *HMC, Portland*, 9:156.

156. *LJ*, 2:414.

157. *HMC, Laing*, 1:142–43.

158. Bowyer, p. 63; Notestein, *The House of Commons 1604–1610*, p. 186; PRO, SP46/127/64. Elsyng still assigned this role to the upper House in 1630 (Foster, *Painful Labour of Mr. Elsyng*, pp. 50, 63). On the role of the upper House in the Elizabethan period, see G. R. Elton, "Parliament in the Sixteenth Century: Functions and Fortunes," *The Historical Journal* 22, no. 2 (1979): 275–77. For the early Stuart period, see Russell, *Parliaments and English Politics*, pp. 42–45.

159. Jess Stoddart Flemion, "The Dissolution of Parliament in 1626: A Revaluation," *EHR* 87, no. 345 (1972): 787–88.

160. Jess Stoddart Flemion, "The Struggle for the Petition of Right in the House of Lords: The Study of an Opposition Party Victory," *Journal of Modern History* 45 (1973): 206–10.

161. Russell, *Parliaments and English Politics*, pp. 181, 190, 233–34. The parliament of 1625 was an exception.

162. HLRO, Original Acts. Graves's analysis for the earlier period is interesting in this regard (Graves, *House of Lords Edward VI and Mary I*, pp. 175–76).

163. *Diary of Walter Yonge, Esq.*, ed. George Roberts, Camden Society, 1st ser., vol. 41 (London, 1848), p. 76.

164. Foster, *1610*, 1:252.

165. Lehmberg, *Later Parliaments*, pp. 117, 182–83, 197, 256.

166. HLRO, Original Acts; PRO, C65/187 (pts. 1 and 2). I have followed the clerk's classification of public acts for 1624. In 1604 seven of the private acts were acts of restitution. There were no acts of restitution in 1624. See G. R. Elton, "Tudor Government: The Points of Contact, "*Transactions of the Royal Historical Society*, 5th ser., vol. 24 (1974), pp. 194–96.

167. HLRO, Original Acts. Cf. Lehmberg, *Later Parliaments*, p. 255.

168. *Historical Manuscripts Commission, Twelfth Report*, app., pt. 1, *The Manuscripts of the Earl of Cowper, K.G., Preserved at Melbourne Hall, Derbyshire*, vol. 1 (London, 1888), pp. 352–53; *Commons Debates 1628*, 4:368–69. In this last account, Alford seems to refer not to Burghley, but to Robert Cecil.

169. In 1621 the clerk, Henry Elsyng, recommended a petition to the attention of the chairman of the Committee on Petitions. He thought the case should be reviewed in Chancery, "but," he added, "it will do the poor man little good, for that he is not able to wage law, unless the petition be especially commended by your lordship to the master of the rolls" (Foster, *Painful Labour of Mr. Elsyng*, p. 20).

11. CONCLUSION

1. In the seventeenth century, there was confusion concerning the terms "prorogue" and "adjourn." As Attorney General Coventry explained in 1621, "prorogue" was often used in place of "adjourn," but never vice versa (*LJ*, 3:151). Sometimes the two terms were used together. For example, when the king postponed the opening of parliament in 1621, he did "prorogue and adjourn" it, first by proclamation, then by writ. When a distinction was made between the two terms, prorogation applied to the termination of a session (as it does in modern parlance). Relfe believed that proclamations were used in case of long postponements, writs for shorter ones (HLRO, "Book of Orders 1710," p. 27).

2. Twysden, *Certain Considerations*, p. 141.

3. *LJ*, 2:717; HMC, *Portland*, 9:138; HMC, *Hastings*, 4:283; Foster, *Painful Labour of Mr. Elsyng*, p. 30, n. 7 (Hobart's Reports). John Chamberlain believed that the bill naturalizing Frederick of the Palatinate had passed, but he may have been mistaken (McClure, 1:546). There are no original acts at the House of Lords Record Office for 1614, and no engrossed bill for the naturalization of Frederick. The paper bill, among the Main Papers, has been endorsed with the usual formulas for transmission to the Commons and for the Commons' assent; but there is no indication on it of royal assent. I am grateful to H. S. Cobb, clerk of the records, for this information.

4. Steele, *Tudor and Stuart Proclamations*, 1: no.1323. The clerical and lay subsidy bills had been enacted.

5. Lehmberg, *Later Parliaments*, pp. 146, 171, 234–35; Hakewill, pp. 179–80; *LJ*, 2:284, 286.

6. *LJ*, 3:204, 490; PRO, SP46/65. See the suggestion in 1640 (*LJ*, 4:47). For John Selden's opinion in 1621, see Spedding, *Letters and Life*, 7:332.

7. See Jones, *Politics and the Bench*, pp. 157–58 (Hutton's Reports).

8. Coke, *Fourth Institute*, pp. 27–28.

9. The bell ringers were paid 2s.4d. (Nichols, 2:49).

10. *LJ*, 2:445.

11. PRO, SP14/165/61. For other accounts of the closing ceremonies, see PRO, SP14/165/70, SP14/167/10; "Moderne Forme of the Parliaments," p. 304. For ceremonies at the end of a session in the reign of Henry VIII, see Lehmberg, *Reformation Parliament*, pp. 104, 158, 199, 248. For the Elizabethan period, see Neale, *Elizabethan House of Commons*, pp. 420–32.

12. HMC, *Portland*, 9:138; HMC, *Hastings*, 4:282–83. Sir George Coppin, clerk of the crown, received 13s.4d. for drawing a commission for prorogation in the reign of James I (British Library, Additional 5746, fol. 54).

13. HLRO, Relfe, "Book of Orders 1710," p. 335; HMC, *Buccleuch*, 3:303.

14. *CJ*, 6:111.

15. *LJ*, 10:649.

16. *CJ*, 6:132; *LJ*, 10:650. For the story of the final days, see Firth, *House of Lords during the Civil War*, pp. 206–13.

17. See Stone, *Crisis of the Aristocracy*, p. 121. fig. 7.
18. See above, p. 90.
19. Stone, *Crisis of the Aristocracy*, p. 123.
20. Pike, pp. 231–34.
21. Firth, *House of Lords during the Civil War*, p. 212.
22. Foster, *1610*, 1:xxxii; Esther S. Cope, "Lord Montagu and His Journal of the Short Parliament," *BIHR* 46 (November 1973): 212–13; *HMC, Buccleuch*, 3:222–23, 228–45, 330–42, 386–413.
23. See the Journal of the Protectorate (*Manuscripts of the House of Lords*, 4:508–62); Schoenfeld, chap. 8.
24. For references to precedents, see HLRO, Committee for Privileges, Minute Book no. 1, pp. 84, 90. On one occasion, the committee had difficulty resolving a question concerning fees because no lord was present who had been in the House in 1640 (ibid., 4 May 1663, p. 90).

INDEX

The date following a title indicates the year in which a peer assumed that rank; *above* and *below* in cross-references indicate that the reference is to another subheading under the same heading, not to a separate heading.

Abbey, Westminster, 3, 4, 5
Abbot, George, archbishop of Canterbury
  (1611–33), 95, 193, 196
  allowed to sit while speaking, 193
  as royal commissioner, 206
  attendance at parliament (1628), 233
    (n. 149)
  requests House not sit on convocation
    days, 23–24, 35
Abergavenny. *See* Bergavenny
Acts
  allegedly forged, 61, 62
  calendar of, 48, 58
  continuance of, 205
  enrollment of, 192
  fees for copies, 51, 61
  printing of, 48, 52, 192
  private, 191–92
  public: House of origin, 201
  record of. *See* Roll, parliament; Roll,
    statute
  storage of, 44, 49
  See also Bills; Legislation
Acunas, Don Diego Sarmiento de, Condé
  de Gondomar, Spanish ambassador, 5
Adjournment, 23, 302 (n. 1)
  by House, 23, 41, 95, 235 (n. 208)
  by king, 7, 23, 29; Lords' consent to, 38,
    235 (n. 213)
  Committee for Privileges considers pro-
    cedure, 138
  committees' status during, 23, 95–96,
    235 (n. 213)
  in presiding officer's absence, 238 (n. 5)
  writ for, 23
Admiral, lord high
  as trier of petitions, 238 (n. 12)

See also Howard, Charles, Baron How-
  ard of Effingham (1585–1619); Vil-
  liers, George (1619–28); Percy,
  Algernon (1636–42); Rich, Robert,
  2nd earl of Warwick (1643–45)
Admiralty, Committee for, 119
Admiralty, Court of, 105, 108
Agenda. *See under* House of Lords
Alford, Edward, MP, 73, 74, 202
Alienations, bill of, 196
Allen, Edward, 184
Allicock (clerk's assistant), 249 (n. 94)
Altham, James, serjeant at law, 152
Ambassadors
  French. *See* Ferté-Imbaut, Marquis de la;
    Fontaine, M. de la; Mende, bishop of
  Spanish, 5
  Venetian, 11, 233 (n. 149)
Andrews, Euseby: case of, 256 (n. 54), 268
  (n. 188)
Andrews, Lancelot, bishop of Winchester
  (1619–26), 18
Anne of Denmark, queen of England: bill
  concerning, 83, 190
Appeal, cases of
  continue from parliament to parliament,
    268 (n. 193)
  Lords' jurisdiction in, 149, 187, 188
  use of evidence in, 268 (n. 190)
  See also Error, cases of
Appeal of treason or felony, 162–63
  Bristol's charges against Buckingham as,
    166–67
Army Plot, 90
Arundel, earls of. *See* Howard, Thomas
  (2nd earl, 1604); Howard, Henry
  Frederick (3rd earl, 1646)